A Short Course in Intermediate Microeconomics with Calculus

This book provides a concise treatment of the core concepts of microeconomic theory at the intermediate level with calculus integrated into the text. The authors, Roberto Serrano and Allan M. Feldman, start with consumer theory and then discuss preferences and utility, budget constraints, the consumer's optimal choice, demand, and the consumer's choices about labor and savings. They next turn to welfare economics: When is one policy better for society than another? Following are chapters presenting the theory of the firm and profit maximization in several alternative models. Next they discuss partial equilibrium models of competitive markets, monopoly markets, and duopoly markets. The authors then provide general equilibrium models of exchange and production, and they analyze market failures created by externalities, public goods, and asymmetric information. They also offer introductory treatments of decision theory under uncertainty and of game theory. Graphic analysis is presented when necessary, but distractions are avoided.

Roberto Serrano is Harrison S. Kravis University Professor at Brown University, Rhode Island. He has contributed to different areas in microeconomic theory and game theory, and his research has been published in top journals, including *Econometrica*, the *Journal of Political Economy*, the *Review of Economic Studies*, the *Journal of Economic Theory, Games and Economic Behavior, SIAM Review*, and *Mathematics of Operations Research*. He has received prestigious fellowships and prizes, including the Alfred P. Sloan Foundation Fellowship in 1988 and the Fundación Banco Herrero Prize in 2004, awarded to the best Spanish economist under 40, as well as teaching prizes at Brown. He is managing editor of *Economics Letters* and the associate editor of the *International Journal of Game Theory and Mathematical Social Sciences*. He was director of graduate studies in economics at Brown from 2006 to 2010 and has served as Economics Department chair since 2010.

Allan M. Feldman is Professor Emeritus of Economics at Brown University. His research has appeared in the *Review of Economic Studies, Econometrica, American Economic Review, Public Choice*, the *Journal of Economic Theory, American Law and Economics Review*, and other journals. He is coauthor (with Roberto Serrano) of *Welfare Economics and Social Choice Theory*. Professor Feldman taught economics at Brown University for thirty-eight years, including the Intermediate Microeconomics course. He was director of undergraduate studies in the Economics Department at Brown for many years.

A Short Course in Intermediate Microeconomics with Calculus

ROBERTO SERRANO
Brown University

ALLAN M. FELDMAN
Brown University, Emeritus

CAMBRIDGE
UNIVERSITY PRESS

CAMBRIDGE
UNIVERSITY PRESS

University Printing House, Cambridge CB2 8BS, United Kingdom

One Liberty Plaza, 20th Floor, New York, NY 10006, USA

477 Williamstown Road, Port Melbourne, VIC 3207, Australia

4843/24, 2nd Floor, Ansari Road, Daryaganj, Delhi – 110002, India

79 Anson Road, #06–04/06, Singapore 079906

Cambridge University Press is part of the University of Cambridge.

It furthers the University's mission by disseminating knowledge in the pursuit of education, learning and research at the highest international levels of excellence.

www.cambridge.org
Information on this title: www.cambridge.org/9781107623767

© Roberto Serrano and Allan M. Feldman 2013

First published 2013
3rd printing 2017

Printed in the United States of America by Sheridan Books, Inc.

A catalog record for this publication is available from the British Library.

Library of Congress Cataloging in Publication data
Serrano, Roberto.
A short course in intermediate microeconomics with calculus / Roberto Serrano, Allan M. Feldman.
p. cm.
Includes bibliographical references and index.
ISBN 978-1-107-01734-4 (hardback) – ISBN 978-1-107-62376-7 (pbk.)
1. Microeconomics – Mathematical methods. I. Feldman, Allan, 1943– II. Title.
HB172.S465 2012
338.5–dc23   2012024937
ISBN 978-1-107-01734-4 Hardback
ISBN 978-1-107-62376-7 Paperback

Contents

Preface

Welcome to this intermediate microeconomics course. At this point, you should already have taken an introductory economics class that exposed you to the method and main ideas of the two parts of economic theory, microeconomics and macroeconomics. In addition, you should have taken a calculus course. The reason is simple: calculus is basic to microeconomics, much of which is about *maximizing* something (for instance, utility, or profit), or about *minimizing* something else (for instance, costs). Calculus is the area of mathematics most suited to maximization and minimization problems; using it makes microeconomic theory straightforward, transparent, and precise.

Microeconomics begins with the study of how economic agents in the private sector (*consumers* and *firms*) make their decisions. We start this course with a brief introduction, in Chapter 1. Then we turn to the main events: Part I of our course (Chapters 2 through 7) is about the theory of the consumer, and Part II (Chapters 8 through 10) is about the theory of the producer – that is, the firm. Part I provides a foundation for the demand curves that you saw in your principles course, and Part II provides a foundation for the supply curves that you saw.

Most economic decisions are made in the private sector, but governments also make many important economic decisions. We touch on these throughout the course, particularly when we discuss taxes, monopolies, externalities, and public goods. Our main focus, though, is the private sector, because in market economies the private sector is, and should be, the main protagonist.

Next, Part III (Chapters 11 through 13) combines theories of the consumer and the producer into the study of individual markets. Here, our focus is on different types of market structure, depending on the market power of the firms producing the goods. Market power is related to the number of firms in the market. We begin, in Chapter 11, with the case of *perfect competition*, in which each firm is powerless to affect the price of the good it sells; this is usually a consequence of there being many firms selling the same good. In Chapter 12, we analyze the polar opposite case, called *monopoly*, in which only one firm provides the good. We also consider intermediate cases between these extremes: in Chapter 13 we analyze *duopoly*, in which two firms compete in the market. One important point that we emphasize is the strong connection between competition and the welfare of a society. This is the connection that was first discussed by Adam Smith, who wrote in 1776 that the invisible hand of market competition leads self-interested buyers and sellers to an outcome that is beneficial to society as a whole.

Our analysis in Part III is called *partial equilibrium* analysis because it focuses on *one* market in isolation. In Part IV (Chapters 15 and 16), we develop models that look at *all* markets simultaneously; this is called *general equilibrium* analysis. The general equilibrium approach is useful to understand the implications of interactions among the different markets. These interactions are, of course, essential in the economy. A main theme in Part IV is the generalization of the invisible hand idea that market competition leads to the social good. We shall see that under certain conditions there are strong connections between competition in markets and the efficient allocation of resources. These connections, or *fundamental theorems of welfare economics*, as economists call them, are important both to people interested in economic ideas and to people simply interested in what kind of economic world they want to inhabit.

Finally, Part V (Chapters 17, 18, and 20) focuses on the circumstances under which even competitive markets, left by themselves, fail to allocate resources efficiently. This is a very important area of study, because these market failures are common; when they occur, governments, policy makers, and informed citizens must consider what policy interventions would best improve the performance of the unregulated market.

Our course includes two chapters that are not really part of the building-blocks flow from consumer theory through market failure. Chapter 14 is a basic introduction to game theory. The use of game theory is so prevalent in economics today that we think it is important to provide a treatment here, even if the theories of the consumer, the firm, competitive markets, and market failure could get along without it. A similar comment applies to Chapter 19, on uncertainty and expected utility. Although most of this course describes decision problems and markets under complete information, the presence of uncertainty is crucial in much of economic life, and much modern microeconomic analysis centers around it. Some instructors may choose to ignore these chapters in their intermediate microeconomics courses, but others may want to cover them. To free up some time to do that, we offer some suggestions:

We include two alternative treatments of the theory of the firm in this book. The first is contained in Chapter 8, the single-input model of the firm, which abstracts from the cost minimization problem. The second is contained in Chapters 9 and 10, the multiple-input model of the firm, which includes the cost minimization problem. Chapter 8 can be viewed as a quick route, a "highway" to the supply curve. An instructor looking for time to teach some of the newer topics covered in Chapter 14 or Chapter 19 might cover Chapter 8 and omit Chapters 9 and 10. Another shortcut in the theory of firm section would be to omit Chapter 10, on the short-run, multiple-input model. Furthermore, our chapters on market failure generally contain basic theory in their first sections and applications in later sections. Instructors might choose to include or omit some of the theory or some of the applications, depending on time and interests.

This book has grown out of the lecture notes that Roberto Serrano developed to teach the Intermediate Microeconomics course at Brown University. The notes were shared with other instructors at Brown over the years. One of these instructors, Amy Serrano (Roberto's wife), first had the idea of turning them into a book: "This looks like a good skeleton of something; perhaps flesh can be put around these bones." Following this suggestion, Roberto and Allan began work on the book project.

We are grateful to all our Intermediate Microeconomics students who helped us develop and present this material. Martin Besfamille, Dror Brenner, Pedro Dal Bó, EeCheng Ong, and Amy Serrano were kind enough to try out preliminary versions of the manuscript in their sections of the course at Brown. We thank them and their students for all the helpful comments that they provided. Amy also provided numerous comments that improved the exposition throughout, and her input was especially important in Chapter 7. EeCheng provided superb assistance completing the exercises and their solutions, as well as doing a comprehensive proofreading and editing. Elise Fishelson gave us detailed comments on each chapter at a preliminary stage; Omer Ozak helped with some graphs and TEX issues; and Rachel Bell helped with some graphs. Barbara Feldman (Allan's wife) was patient and encouraging. We thank the anonymous reviewers selected by Cambridge University Press for their helpful feedback, Scott Parris and Chris Harrison, our editors at Cambridge, for their encouragement and support of the project, and Deborah Wenger, our copy editor.

Chapter 1

Introduction

Economists have always studied the *economic problem*. The nature of the economic problem, however, has changed over time. For the *classical school* of economists (including Adam Smith (1723–1790), David Ricardo (1772–1823), Karl Marx (1818–1883), and John Stuart Mill (1806–1873)), the economic problem was to discover the laws that governed the production of goods and the distribution of goods among the different social classes: land owners, capitalists, workers. These laws were thought to be like natural laws or physical laws, similar to Newton's law of gravitational attraction. Forces of history, and phenomena such as the Industrial Revolution, produce "universal constants" that govern the production of goods and the distribution of wealth.

Toward the end of the nineteenth century, however, there was a major shift in the orientation of economics, brought about by the *neoclassical school* of economists. This group includes William Stanley Jevons (1835–1882), Leon Walras (1834–1910), Francis Ysidro Edgeworth (1845–1926), Vilfredo Pareto (1848–1923), and Alfred Marshall (1842–1924). The neoclassical revolution was a shift in the emphasis of the discipline, away from a search for natural laws of production and distribution, and toward a new version of the economic problem, the analysis of decision making by individuals and firms.

In this book we will describe *modern microeconomics*, which mostly follows the neoclassical path. For us, and for the majority of contemporary microeconomists, the economic problem is the problem of the "economic agent," who lives in a world of scarcity. Economists focus on the fact that resources are limited or *constrained*. These constraints apply to men, women, households, firms, governments, and even humanity. On the other hand, our wants and needs are unlimited. We want more and better material things, for ourselves, our families, our children, our friends. Even if we are not personally greedy, we want better education for our children, better culture, better health for people in our country, and longer lives for everyone. Economics is about how decision makers choose among all the things that they want, given that they cannot have everything. The economic world is the world of limited resources and unlimited needs, and the economic problem is how to best meet those needs given those limited resources.

The key assumption in microeconomics, which could be taken as our credo, is this: economic agents are rational. This means that they will choose the best alternatives, given what is available, given the constraints. Of course we know that (to paraphrase Abraham Lincoln) some of the people behave irrationally all the time, and all of the people behave irrationally some of the time. But we will take rationality as our basic assumption, especially when important goods and services, and money, are at stake.

Economics applies the scientific method to the investigation and understanding of the economic problem. As with the natural sciences, such as biology, chemistry, or physics, economics has theory, and it has empirical analysis. Modern economic theory usually involves the construction of abstract, often mathematical models, which are intended to help us understand some aspect of the economic world. A useful model makes simplifying assumptions about the world. (A completely realistic economic model would usually be too complicated to be useful.) The assumptions incorporated in a useful model should be plausible or reasonable, and not absurd on their face. For instance, it is reasonable to assume that firms want to maximize profits, even though some firms may not be concerned with profits in some circumstances. It is reasonable to assume that a typical consumer wants to eat some food, wear some clothing, and live in a house or an apartment. It would be unreasonable to assume that a typical consumer wants to spend all his or her income on housing, and eat no food. Once a model has assumptions, the economic analyst applies deductive reasoning and logic to it to derive conclusions. This is where the use of mathematics is important.

Correct logical and mathematical arguments clarify the structure of a model and help us avoid mistaken conclusions. The aim is to have a model that sheds some light on the economic world. For example, we might have a logical result such as this: if we assume A, B, and C, then D holds, where D = "when the price of ice cream rises, the consumer will eat less of it." If A, B, and C are very reasonable assumptions, then we feel confident that D will be true. On the other hand, if we do some empirical work and see that D is in fact false, then we are led to the conclusion that either A, B, or C must also be false. Either way, the logical proposition "A, B, and C together imply D" gives us insight into the way the economic world works.

Economics is divided between *microeconomics* and *macroeconomics*. Macroeconomics studies the economy from above, as if seen from space. It studies aggregate magnitudes, the big things such as booms and busts, gross domestic product, rates of employment and unemployment, money supply, and inflation. In contrast, microeconomics takes the close-up approach to understand the workings of the economy. It begins by looking at how individuals, households, and firms make decisions, and how those decisions interact in markets. The individual decisions result in market variables, quantities demanded by buyers and supplied by sellers, and market prices.

When people, households, firms, and other economic agents make economic decisions, they alter the allocation of resources. For example, if many people suddenly want to buy some goods in large quantities, they may drive up the prices of those goods, employment and wages of the workers who make those goods, and the profits of the firms that sell them, and they may drive down the wages of people making other goods and the profits of firms that supply the competing goods. When a microeconomist analyzes a market in isolation, assuming that no effects are taking place in other markets, he or she is doing what is called *partial equilibrium analysis*. Partial equilibrium analysis focuses on the market for one good, and assumes that prices and quantities of other goods are fixed. *General equilibrium analysis* assumes that what goes on in one market does affect prices and quantities in other markets. All markets in the economy interact, and all prices and quantities are determined more or less simultaneously. Obviously, general equilibrium analysis is more difficult and complex than partial equilibrium analysis. Both types of analysis, however, are part of microeconomics, and we will do both in this book. Doing general equilibrium analysis allows the people who do microeconomics to connect to the aggregates of the economy, to see the "big picture." This creates a link between microeconomics and macroeconomics.

We now move on to begin our study, and we do so by considering how individual households make consumption decisions. This is called the *theory of the consumer*.

Part I

Theory of the Consumer

Chapter 2

Preferences and Utility

2.1 Introduction

Life is like a shopping center. A consumer enters it and sees lots of goods, in various quantities, that she might buy. A *consumption bundle*, or a *bundle* for short, is a combination of quantities of the various goods (and services) that are available. For instance, a consumption bundle might be 2 apples, 1 banana, 0 cookies, and 5 diet sodas. We would write this as $(2, 1, 0, 5)$. Of course the consumer prefers some consumption bundles to others; that is, she has tastes or *preferences* regarding those bundles.

In this chapter we discuss the *economic theory of preferences* in some detail. We make various assumptions about a consumer's feelings about alternative consumption bundles. We assume that when given a choice between two alternative bundles, the consumer can make a comparison. (This assumption is called *completeness*.) We assume that when looking at three alternatives, the consumer is rational in the sense that, if she says she likes the first better than the second and the second better than the third, she will also say that she likes the first better than the third. (This is part of what is called *transitivity*.) We examine other basic assumptions that economists usually make about a consumer's preferences: one says that the consumer prefers more of each good to less (called *monotonicity*), and another says that a consumer's *indifference curves* (or sets of equally desirable consumption bundles) have a certain plausible curvature (called *convexity*). We describe and discuss the consumer's rate of tradeoff of one good against another (called the *marginal rate of substitution*).

After discussing the consumer's preferences, we turn to the *utility function*. A utility function is a numerical representation of how a consumer feels about alternative consumption bundles: if she likes the first bundle better than the second, then the utility function assigns a higher number to the first than to the second, and if she likes them equally well, then the utility function assigns the same number

7

to both. We analyze utility functions and describe *marginal utility*, which, loosely speaking, is the extra utility provided by one additional unit of a good. We derive the relationship between the marginal utilities of two goods and the marginal rate of substitution of one of the goods for the other. We provide various algebraic examples of utility functions; in the appendix, we briefly review the calculus of derivatives and partial derivatives.

In this chapter and others to follow, we often assume that there are only two goods available, with x_1 and x_2 representing quantities of goods 1 and 2, respectively. Why only two goods? For two reasons: first, for simplicity (two goods gives a much simpler model than three goods or five thousand, often with no loss of generality); and second, because we are often interested in one particular good, and we can easily focus on that good and call the second good "all other goods," "everything else," or "other stuff." When there are two goods, any consumption bundle can easily be shown in a standard two-dimensional graph, with the quantity of the first good on the horizontal axis and the quantity of the second good on the vertical axis. All the figures in this chapter are drawn this way.

In this chapter we focus on the consumer's preferences about bundles of goods, or how she feels about various things that she might consume. In the shopping center of life, though, some bundles are *feasible* or *affordable* for the consumer; these are the ones that her budget will allow. Other bundles are *nonfeasible* or *unaffordable*; these are the ones her budget will not allow. We will focus on the consumer's budget in Chapter 3.

2.2 The Consumer's Preference Relation

The consumer has preferences over consumption bundles. We represent consumption bundles with symbols such as X and Y. If there are two goods, X is a vector (x_1, x_2), where x_1 is the quantity of good 1 and x_2 is the quantity of good 2. The consumer can compare any pair of bundles and decide which one is better, or decide they are equally good. If she decides one is better than the other, we represent her feelings with what is called a *preference relation*; we use the symbol $\succ$ to represent the preference relation. That is, $X \succ Y$ means the consumer prefers bundle X over bundle Y. Presented with the choice between X and Y, she would choose X. We assume that if $X \succ Y$, then $Y \succ X$ cannot be true; if the consumer likes X better than Y, then she had better not like Y better than X! Obviously, a consumer's preferences might change over time, and might change as she learns more about the consumption bundles. (The $\succ$ relation is sometimes called the *strict preference relation* rather than the *preference relation*, because $X \succ Y$ means the consumer definitely, unambiguously, prefers X to Y, or *strictly prefers X to Y*.)

If the consumer likes X and Y equally well, we say she is *indifferent* between them. We write $X \sim Y$ in this case, and $\sim$ is called the *indifference relation*. Sometimes we will say that X and Y are indifferent bundles for the consumer. In this case, if presented with the choice between them, the consumer might choose X, might choose Y, might flip a coin, or might even ask us to choose for her. We assume that if $X \sim Y$, then $Y \sim X$ must be true; if the consumer likes X exactly as well as Y, then she had better like Y exactly as well as X!

The reader might notice that the symbols for preference and for indifference are a little like the mathematical symbols $>$ and $=$, for *greater than* and *equal to*, respectively. This is no accident. Furthermore, just as there is a mathematical relation that combines these two, $\geq$ for *greater than or equal to*, there is also a preference relation symbol $\succeq$, for *preferred or indifferent to*. That is, we write $X \succeq Y$ to represent the consumer's either preferring X to Y, or being indifferent between the two. (The $\succeq$ relation is sometimes called the *weak preference relation*.)

Assumptions on Preferences

At this point, we make some basic assumptions about the consumer's preference and indifference relations. Our intention is to model the behavior of what we would consider a rational consumer. In this section we assume that the two goods are desirable to the consumer; we touch on other possibilities (such as neutral goods or bads) in the Exercises.

Assumption 1: *Completeness*. For all consumption bundles X and Y, either $X \succ Y$, or $Y \succ X$, or $X \sim Y$. That is, the consumer must like one better than the other, or like them equally well. This may seem obvious, but sometimes it is not. For example, what if the consumer must choose what is behind the screen on the left, or the screen on the right, and she has no idea what might be hidden behind the screens? That is, what if she does not know what X and Y are? We force her to make a choice, or at least to say she is indifferent. Having a *complete ordering* of bundles is very important for our analysis throughout this book. (In Chapters 19 and 20 we analyze consumer behavior under uncertainty, or incomplete information.)

Assumption 2: *Transitivity*. This assumption has four parts:

- First, transitivity of preference: if $X \succ Y$ and $Y \succ Z$, then $X \succ Z$.
- Second, transitivity of indifference: if $X \sim Y$ and $Y \sim Z$, then $X \sim Z$.
- Third, if $X \succ Y$ and $Y \sim Z$, then $X \succ Z$.
- Fourth and finally, if $X \sim Y$ and $Y \succ Z$, then $X \succ Z$.

The transitivity of preference assumption is meant to rule out irrational preference cycles. You would probably think your friend needs psychiatric help if she says she prefers Econ. 1 (the basic economics course) to Soc. 1 (the basic sociology course), and she prefers Soc. 1 to Psych. 1 (the basic psychology course), *and* she prefers Psych. 1 to Econ. 1. Cycles in preferences seem irrational. However, do not be too dogmatic about this assumption; there are interesting exceptions in the real world. We will provide one later on in the Exercises.

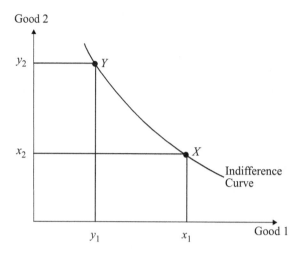

Fig. 2.1. At bundle X, the consumer is consuming x_1 units of good 1 and x_2 units of good 2. Similarly, at bundle Y, she is consuming y_1 units of good 1 and y_2 units of good 2. Because X and Y are on one indifference curve, the consumer is indifferent between them.

The transitivity of indifference assumption (that is, if $X \sim Y$ and $Y \sim Z$, then $X \sim Z$) makes *indifference curves* possible.

An *indifference curve* is a set of consumption bundles (or, when there are two goods, points in a two-dimensional graph) that the consumer thinks are all equally good; she is indifferent among them. We use indifference curves frequently throughout this book, starting in Figure 2.1. The figure shows two consumption bundles, X and Y, and an indifference curve. The two bundles are on the same indifference curve, and therefore, the consumer likes them equally well.

Assumption 3: *Monotonicity*. We normally assume that goods are *desirable*, which means the consumer prefers consuming more of a good to consuming less. That is, suppose X and Y are two bundles of goods such that (1) X has more of one good (or both) than Y does and (2) X has at least as much of both goods as Y has. Then $X \succ Y$. Of course there are times when this assumption is inappropriate. For instance, suppose a bundle of goods is a quantity of cake and a quantity of ice cream, which you will eat this evening. After three slices of cake and six scoops of ice cream, more cake and more ice cream may not be welcome. But if the goods are more generally defined (e.g., education, housing), monotonicity is a very reasonable assumption.

Some important consequences of monotonicity are the following: indifference curves representing preferences over two desirable goods cannot be thick or upward sloping, nor can they be vertical or horizontal. This should be apparent from Figure 2.2, which shows an upward-sloping indifference curve and a thick indifference curve. On any indifference curve, the consumer is indifferent between any pair of consumption bundles. A brief examination of the figure should convince the

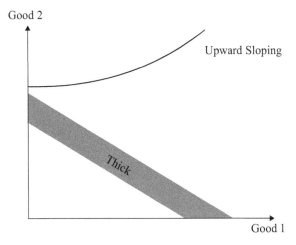

Fig. 2.2. Each indifference curve shown is a set of equally desirable consumption bundles – for example, for any pair of bundles X and Y on the upward-sloping curve, $X \sim Y$. Can you see why the monotonicity assumption makes the upward-sloping indifference curve impossible? How about the thick indifference curve?

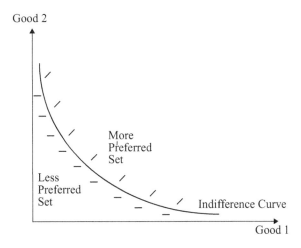

Fig. 2.3. The only graph compatible with monotonic preferences is a downward-sloping thin indifference curve.

reader that the monotonicity assumption rules out both types of indifference curves shown, and similar arguments rule out vertical and horizontal indifference curves.

In Figure 2.3, we show a downward-sloping thin indifference curve, which is what the monotonicity assumption requires. The figure also shows the set of bundles that, by the monotonicity assumption, must be preferred to all the bundles on the indifference curve (the *more preferred set*), and the set of bundles that, by the monotonicity assumption, must be liked less than all the bundles on the indifference curve (the *less preferred set*).

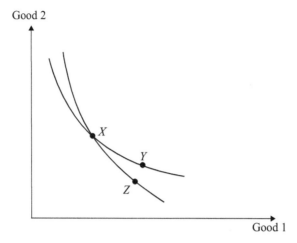

Fig. 2.4. Two distinct indifference curves cannot cross. Here is why. Suppose the curves did cross at the point X. Because Y and X are on the same indifference curve, $Y \sim X$. Because X and Z are on the same indifference curve, $X \sim Z$. Then by transitivity of indifference, $Y \sim Z$. But by monotonicity, $Y \succ Z$. Therefore, having the indifference curves cross leads to a contradiction.

Another implication of the assumptions of transitivity (of indifference) and monotonicity is that two distinct indifference curves cannot cross. This is shown in Figure 2.4.

Assumption 4: *Convexity for indifference curves.* This assumption means that averages of consumption bundles are preferred to extremes. Consider two distinct points on one indifference curve. The (arithmetic) average of the two points would be found by connecting them with a straight line segment, and then taking the midpoint of that segment. This is the standard average, which gives equal weight to the two extreme points. A *weighted average* gives possibly unequal weights to the two points; geometrically, a weighted average would be any point on the line segment connecting the two original points, not just the midpoint. The assumption of convexity for indifference curves means this: for any two distinct points on the same indifference curve, the line segment connecting them (excepting its end points) lies above the indifference curve. In other words, if we take a weighted average of two distinct points, between which the consumer is indifferent, she prefers the weighted average to the original points. We show this in Figure 2.5.

We call preferences *well behaved* when indifference curves are downward sloping and convex.

In reality, of course, indifference curves are sometimes concave. We can think of many examples in which a consumer might like two goods, but not in combination. You may like sushi and chocolate ice cream, but not together in the same dish; you may like classical music and hip-hop, but not in the same evening; you may like pink clothing and orange clothing, but not in the same outfit. Again, if the

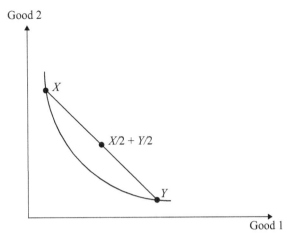

Fig. 2.5. Convexity of preferences means that indifference curves are convex, as in the figure, rather than concave. This means that the consumer prefers averaged bundles over extreme bundles. For example, the bundle made up of $1/2$ times X plus $1/2$ times Y – that is, $X/2 + Y/2$ – is preferred to either X or Y. This is what we normally assume to be the case.

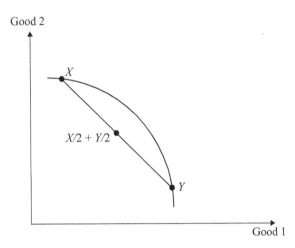

Fig. 2.6. A concave indifference curve. This consumer prefers the extreme points X and Y to the average $X/2 + Y/2$.

goods are defined generally enough, such as classical music consumption per year, hip-hop consumption per year, or pink and orange clothing worn this year, the assumption of convexity of indifference becomes very reasonable. We show a concave indifference curve in Figure 2.6.

2.3 The Marginal Rate of Substitution

The *marginal rate of substitution* is an important and useful concept because it describes the consumer's willingness to trade consumption of one good for consumption of the other. Consider this thought experiment: The consumer gives up a unit of good 1 in exchange for getting some amount of good 2. How much of good 2 does she need to get to end up on the same indifference curve? This is the quantity of good 2 that she needs to replace one unit of good 1.

Consider a slightly different thought experiment. The consumer gets a unit of good 1 in exchange for giving up some amount of good 2. How much of good 2 can she give up and end up on the same indifference curve? This is the quantity of good 2 that she is willing to give up in exchange for a unit of good 1.

The answer to either of these questions is a measure of the consumer's *valuation of a unit of good 1, in terms of units of good 2*. This is the intuitive idea of the marginal rate of substitution of good 2 for good 1. It is the consumer's rate of tradeoff between the two goods, the rate at which she can substitute good 2 for good 1 and remain as well off as she was before the substitution.

Let Δx_1 represent a change in her consumption of good 1 and Δx_2 represent a change in her consumption of good 2, and suppose the two changes move her from a point on an indifference curve to another point on the same indifference curve. Remember that for well-behaved preferences, indifference curves are downward sloping; therefore, one of the Δs will be positive and the other negative. If $\Delta x_i > 0$, the consumer is getting some good i; if $\Delta x_i < 0$, she is giving up some good i. In the first thought experiment, we let $\Delta x_1 = -1$; in the second, we let $\Delta x_1 = +1$. In both, we were really interested in the magnitude of the resulting Δx_2, the amount of good 2 needed to replace a unit of good 1, or the amount of good 2 that the consumer would be willing to give up to get another unit of good 1.

At this point, rather than thinking about the consumer swapping a unit of good 1 in exchange for some amount of good 2, we consider the ratio $\Delta x_2 / \Delta x_1$. This ratio is the rate at which the consumer has to get good 2 in exchange for giving up good 1 (if $\Delta x_1 < 0$ and $\Delta x_2 > 0$), or the rate at which she has to give up good 2 in exchange for getting good 1 (if $\Delta x_1 > 0$ and $\Delta x_2 < 0$). Also, we assume that the Δs are very small, or infinitesimal. More formally, we take the limit as Δx_1 and Δx_2 approach 0.

Because we are assuming that Δx_1 and Δx_2 are small moves from a point on an indifference curve that leave the consumer on the same indifference curve, the *ratio* $\Delta x_2 / \Delta x_1$ represents the *slope* of that indifference curve at that point. Because the indifference curves are downward sloping,

$$\Delta x_2 / \Delta x_1 = \text{Indifference curve slope} < 0.$$

The definition of the *marginal rate of substitution of good 2 for good 1*, which we will write MRS_{x_1, x_2}, or just MRS for short, is

$$MRS_{x_1, x_2} = MRS = -\Delta x_2 / \Delta x_1 = -\text{Indifference curve slope}.$$

More formally,

$$MRS = \lim_{\Delta x_1, \Delta x_2 \to 0} -\Delta x_2 / \Delta x_1 = -\text{Indifference curve slope}.$$

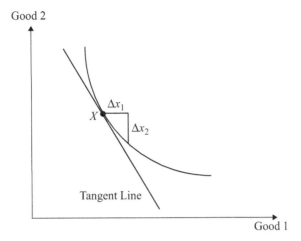

Fig. 2.7. Intuitively, the marginal rate of substitution is an answer to one of these questions: "If I take away Δx_1 units of good 1, how much good 2 do I need to give you for you to remain indifferent?" or "If I give you Δx_1 of units of good 1, how much good 2 can I take away from you and have you remain indifferent?" The second question is illustrated here.

In Figure 2.7, we show a downward-sloping indifference curve and a tangent line at a point X on the indifference curve. We show two increments from X, Δx_1 and Δx_2, that get the consumer back to the same indifference curve. Note that $\Delta x_1 > 0$ and $\Delta x_2 < 0$ in the figure. If the consumer gets Δx_1 units of good 1, she is willing to give up $-\Delta x_2$ units of good 2. Her marginal rate of substitution is the limit of $-\Delta x_2/\Delta x_1$, as Δx_1 and Δx_2 approach zero. That is, her marginal rate of substitution is -1 times the slope of the indifference curve at X, or -1 times the slope of the tangent line at X.

For well-behaved preferences, the MRS decreases as you move down and to the right along an indifference curve. This makes good sense. It means that if a consumer consumes more and more of a good while staying on the same indifference curve, she values an additional unit of that good less and less. To convince yourself that this is plausible, consider the following story.

A well-off woman (Ms. Well-Off) is lost in the middle of a desert. She is almost dying of thirst. She has no water (good 1), but she does have $100 (good 2) in her pocket. A profit-seeking local trader (Mr. Rip-Off), carrying water, offers her a drink, and asks her: "What's the most you would pay me for your first glass of water?" (That is, "What is your MRS of money for water when you have no water, but $100?") Honest to a fault, she answers $25. Mr. Rip-Off immediately proposes this trade, and the first glass of water is sold for $25. At this point, Mr. Rip-Off asks again: "You are probably still thirsty, aren't you? How much are you willing to pay for a second glass of water?" (That is, "What is your MRS of money for water when you already have had a glass of water, and you have $75 left?") She now answers: "Yes, I am still thirsty. I would pay you $10 for a second glass."

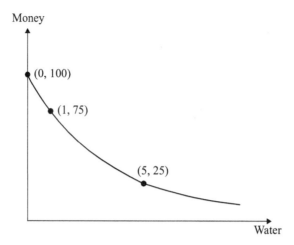

Fig. 2.8. The *MRS* is decreasing because the consumer gets satiated with water as she consumes more of it. She is willing to pay less and less for the incremental drink.

They make this trade also. Her valuation of the second glass of water, her *MRS* of money for water, has dropped by more than half. This process continues for a while. By the time Ms. Well-Off has had nine or ten glasses of water, her *MRS* has dropped to zero, because at this point her need for water is much less pressing than her need for a bathroom (Figure 2.8).

2.4 The Consumer's Utility Function

Mathematically, it is much easier to work with functions than with relations, such as the preference relation and the indifference relation. Our goal now is to construct a function that will represent the preferences of a consumer. Such a function is called a *utility function*.

Imagine that we assign a number to each bundle. For example, we assign the number $u(X) = u(x_1, x_2) = 5$ to the bundle $X = (x_1, x_2)$; we assign the number $u(Y) = u(y_1, y_2) = 4$ to $Y = (y_1, y_2)$; and so on.

We say that such an assignment of numbers to bundles is a *consumer's utility function* if:

- First, $u(X) > u(Y)$ whenever $X \succ Y$
- Second, $u(X) = u(Y)$ whenever $X \sim Y$

Note how this assignment of numbers to bundles is a faithful translation of the consumer's preferences. It gives a higher utility number to the preferred bundle, and it gives the same number to two bundles that the consumer likes equally well. This is the sense in which this function accurately represents the preferences of the consumer.

Our consumer's utility function is said to be an "ordinal" utility function rather than a "cardinal" utility function.

An *ordinal* statement gives information only about relative magnitudes; for instance, "I like Tiffany more than Jennifer." A *cardinal* statement provides information about magnitudes that can be added, subtracted, and so on. For instance, "Billy weighs 160 pounds and Johnny weighs 120 pounds." We can conclude from the latter statement that Billy weighs 40 pounds more than Johnny, that the ratio of their weights is exactly 4/3, and that the sum of their weights is 280 pounds. Is utility an ordinal or a cardinal concept? The utilitarians, led by the English philosopher Jeremy Bentham (1748–1832), believed that utility is a cardinal magnitude, perhaps as measurable as length, weight, and so on. For them, statements such as these would make sense: "I get three times as much utility from my consumption bundle as you get from your consumption bundle" or "I like a vacation cruise in the West Indies twice as much as you do." Today, for the most part, we treat utility simply as an ordinal magnitude. All we care about is whether an individual's utility number from one consumption bundle is larger than, equal to, or smaller than the same individual's utility number from another bundle. For one individual, differences or ratios of utility numbers from different bundles generally do not matter, and comparisons of utilities across different individuals have no meaning.

Under the ordinal interpretation of utility numbers, if we start with any utility function representing my preferences, and we transform it by adding a constant, it still represents my preferences perfectly well; if we multiply it by a positive number, it still works perfectly well; or, assuming all my utility numbers are positive, if we square all of them, or raise them all to a positive power, we are left with a modified utility function that still represents my preferences perfectly well. In short, if we start with a utility function representing my preferences, and modify it with what is called an *order-preserving transformation*, then it still represents my preferences. All this is summed up in the following statement:

If $u(X) = u(x_1, x_2)$ is a utility function that represents the preferences of a consumer, and f is any order-preserving transformation of u, the transformed function $f(u(X)) = f(u(x_1, x_2))$ is another utility function that also represents those preferences.

What is the connection between indifference curves and utility functions? The answer is that we use indifference curves to represent constant levels of utility. Remember that we are assuming that the consumer's utility level depends on her consumption of two goods, measured as variables x_1 and x_2. We need one axis to represent the amount of x_1, and a second axis to represent the amount of x_2. If we were to show utility in the same picture as quantities of the two goods, we would need a third axis to represent the utility level u that corresponds to the consumption bundle (x_1, x_2). A utility function in such a three-dimensional picture looks like a hillside. However, three-dimensional pictures are hard to draw. It is much easier to draw two-dimensional graphs with level curves.

A *level curve* for a function is a set of points in the function's domain, over which the function takes a constant value. If you have hiked or climbed mountains with the help of a topographical map, you have used a picture with level curves; an elevation contour on the map is a level curve. Similarly, a weather map has level curves; the isobar lines represent sets of points with the same barometric pressure. (*Isobar* means the *same barometric pressure.*)

An indifference curve is a set of points in the consumption bundle picture, among which the consumer is indifferent. Because she is indifferent among these points, they all give her the same utility. Hence, the indifference curve is a level curve for her utility. Therefore, to represent a consumer's utility function, we will simply draw its level curves, its indifference curves, in the (x_1, x_2) quadrant. Figure 2.9 shows a three-dimensional utility function picture, and the corresponding level curves, or indifference curves.

2.5 Utility Functions and the Marginal Rate of Substitution

Next we explain the connection between the marginal rate of substitution and the utility function that represents the consumer's preferences. Figure 2.10 is similar to Figure 2.7. The marginal rate of substitution of good 2 for good 1, at the point X, is $-\Delta x_1/\Delta x_2$, roughly speaking. (And, precisely speaking, in the limit.) How does this relate to a utility function for this consumer?

The *marginal utility* of good 1 is the rate at which the consumer's utility increases as good 1 increases, while we hold the quantity of good 2 constant. Loosely speaking, it is the *extra utility from an extra unit of good 1*. More formally, let Δx_1 represent an increment of good 1. The marginal utility of good 1, which we write MU_1, is defined as:

$$MU_1 = \lim_{\Delta x_1 \to 0} \frac{u(x_1 + \Delta x_1, x_2) - u(x_1, x_2)}{\Delta x_1}.$$

If it were not for the presence of the variable x_2, students would recognize this as the derivative of the function $u(x_1)$. This is almost exactly what it is, except the function $u(x_1, x_2)$ is really a function of two variables, the second of which, x_2, is being held constant. The derivative of a function of two variables, with respect to x_1 while x_2 is being held constant, is called the *partial derivative* of the function $u(x_1, x_2)$ with respect to x_1. A derivative is commonly shown with a d symbol, as in $df(x)/dx$. A partial derivative is commonly shown with a ∂ symbol instead of a d, so the marginal utility of good 1 can be written as

$$MU_1 = \frac{\partial u(x_1, x_2)}{\partial x_1} = \frac{\partial u}{\partial x_1}.$$

The marginal utility of good 2, which we write MU_2, is defined as:

$$MU_2 = \lim_{\Delta x_2 \to 0} \frac{u(x_1, x_2 + \Delta x_2) - u(x_1, x_2)}{\Delta x_2} = \frac{\partial u}{\partial x_2}.$$

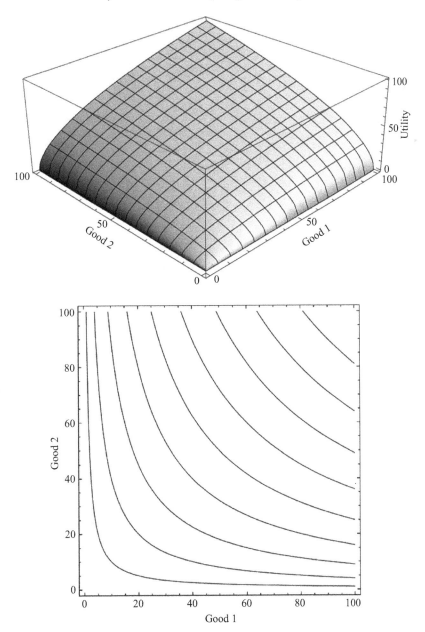

Fig. 2.9. The indifference curves (bottom) are the level curves of the utility function (top).

Because marginal utility is derived from the utility function, which is ordinal, it should not be interpreted as a cardinal measure. That is, we do not attach any meaning to a statement such as "My marginal utility from an additional apple is 3." We do attach meaning to a statement such as "My marginal utility from an additional apple is 3, and my marginal utility from an additional banana is 2." This simply means "I prefer an additional apple."

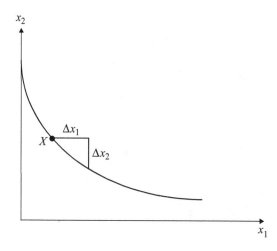

Fig. 2.10. Marginal utility and the marginal rate of substitution.

Our main use of the marginal utility concept at this point is to calculate the consumer's MRS. Consider Figure 2.10 again. From the bundle $X = (x_1, x_2)$, we increase good 1 by Δx_1 and simultaneously decrease good 2 by Δx_2 to get back to the original indifference curve. If we evaluate the change in utility along the way (keeping in mind that we are really thinking of very small moves), we have the following: utility increases because of the increase in good 1, by an amount equal to the marginal utility of good 1 times Δx_1. At the same time, utility decreases because of the decrease in good 2, by an amount equal to the marginal utility of good 2 times Δx_2. The sum of the increase and the decrease is zero, because the consumer ends up on the original indifference curve. This gives the following equation (note that Δx_1 is positive and Δx_2 is negative):

$$MU_1 \Delta x_1 + MU_2 \Delta x_2 = 0.$$

From this, we easily get

$$-\frac{\Delta x_2}{\Delta x_1} = \frac{MU_1}{MU_2}.$$

But $MRS = -\Delta x_2 / \Delta x_1$. We conclude that

$$MRS = \frac{MU_1}{MU_2}.$$

This gives us a convenient tool for calculating the consumer's marginal rate of substitution, either as a function of (x_1, x_2), or as a numerical value at a given point.

2.6 A Solved Problem

The Problem

For each of the following utility functions, find the marginal rate of substitution function, or MRS.

(a) $u(x_1, x_2) = x_1 x_2$

(b) $u(x_1, x_2) = 2x_2$

(c) $u(x_1, x_2) = x_1 + x_2$

(d) $u(x_1, x_2) = \min\{x_1, 2x_2\}$

(e) $u(x_1, x_2) = x_2 - x_1^2$

The Solution

We use the fact that the MRS equals the ratio of the marginal utilities, or $MRS = \frac{MU_1}{MU_2}$. In each case, we first calculate the marginal utilities, and then we find their ratio.

(a) Assume $u(x_1, x_2) = x_1 x_2$.

$$MU_1 = \frac{\partial(x_1 x_2)}{\partial x_1} = x_2 \quad \text{and} \quad MU_2 = \frac{\partial(x_1 x_2)}{\partial x_2} = x_1.$$

Therefore,

$$MRS = \frac{MU_1}{MU_2} = \frac{x_2}{x_1}.$$

(b) Assume $u(x_1, x_2) = 2x_2$.

$$MU_1 = \frac{\partial(2x_2)}{\partial x_1} = 0 \quad \text{and} \quad MU_2 = \frac{\partial(2x_2)}{\partial x_2} = 2.$$

Therefore,

$$MRS = \frac{MU_1}{MU_2} = \frac{0}{2} = 0.$$

(c) Assume $u(x_1, x_2) = x_1 + x_2$.

$$MU_1 = \frac{\partial(x_1 + x_2)}{\partial x_1} = 1 \quad \text{and} \quad MU_2 = \frac{\partial(x_1 + x_2)}{\partial x_2} = 1.$$

Therefore,

$$MRS = \frac{MU_1}{MU_2} = \frac{1}{1} = 1.$$

(d) Assume $u(x_1, x_2) = \min\{x_1, 2x_2\}$. The marginal utilities depend on whether $x_1 < 2x_2$, or $x_1 > 2x_2$.

If $x_1 < 2x_2$, then

$$MU_1 = \frac{\partial(\min\{x_1, 2x_2\})}{\partial x_1} = 1 \quad \text{and} \quad MU_2 = \frac{\partial(\min\{x_1, 2x_2\})}{\partial x_2} = 0.$$

Therefore,

$$MRS = \frac{MU_1}{MU_2} = \frac{1}{0} = \infty.$$

If $x_1 > 2x_2$, then

$$MU_1 = \frac{\partial(\min\{x_1, 2x_2\})}{\partial x_1} = 0 \quad \text{and} \quad MU_2 = \frac{\partial(\min\{x_1, 2x_2\})}{\partial x_2} = 2.$$

Therefore,

$$MRS = \frac{MU_1}{MU_2} = \frac{0}{2} = 0.$$

Finally, if $x_1 = 2x_2$, then MRS is undefined.

(e) Assume $u(x_1, x_2) = x_2 - x_1^2$.

$$MU_1 = \frac{\partial(x_2 - x_1^2)}{\partial x_1} = -2x_1 \text{ and } MU_2 = \frac{\partial(x_2 - x_1^2)}{\partial x_2} = 1.$$

Therefore,

$$MRS = \frac{MU_1}{MU_2} = \frac{-2x_1}{1} = -2x_1.$$

Exercises

1. We assumed at the beginning of the chapter that a consumer's preferences must be transitive, but we hinted that there might be interesting exceptions. Here are two:

   (a) A consumer likes sugar in her coffee, but she simply cannot taste the difference between a cup of coffee with n grams of sugar in it and a cup of coffee with $n + 1$ grams. Suppose a teaspoon of sugar is 6 grams, and suppose she takes her coffee with one teaspoon of sugar. Why does this violate transitivity?

   (b) Let's call a committee of three people a "consumer." (Groups of people often act together as "consumers.") Our committee makes decisions using majority voting. When the committee members compare two alternatives, x and y, they simply take a vote, and the winner is said to be "preferred" by the committee to the loser. Suppose that the preferences of the individuals are as follows: Person 1 likes x best, y second best, and z third best. We write this in the following way: Person 1 : x, y, z. Assume the preferences of the other two people are: Person 2 : y, z, x; and Person 3 : z, x, y. Show that in this example the committee preferences produced by majority voting violate transitivity. (This is the famous "voting paradox" first described by the French philosopher and mathematician Marquis de Condorcet (1743–1794).)

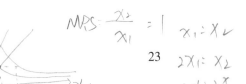

2. Consider the utility function $u(x_1, x_2) = x_1 x_2$.
   (a) Graph the indifference curves for utility levels 1 and 2. (They are symmetric hyperbolas asymptotic to both axes.)
   (b) Graph the locus of points for which the MRS of good 2 for good 1 is equal to 1, and the locus of points for which the MRS is equal to 2.

3. Different students at World's Greatest University (WGU) have different preferences about economics. Draw the indifference curves associated with each of the following statements. Measure "economics books" along the horizontal axis and "books about other subjects" along the vertical axis. Draw arrows indicating the direction in which utility is increasing.
   (a) "I care only about the total amount of knowledge I acquire. It is the same whether that is economics knowledge or knowledge of any other kind. That is, all books on all subjects are perfect substitutes for me."
   (b) "I hate the Serrano/Feldman textbook and all other economics books. On the other hand, I love everything else in the WGU curriculum."
   (c) "I really like books about economics because I want to understand the economic world. Books about other subjects make no difference to me."
   (d) "I like all my courses and the liberal education that WGU offers. That is, I prefer to read books on a variety of different subjects, rather than to read lots on one subject and little on the others."

4. Sketch indifference curves for utility levels 1 and 2 for each of the following utility functions. Describe in a sentence or two the consumer's preferences for the two goods.
   (a) $u(x_1, x_2) = 2x_2$
   (b) $u(x_1, x_2) = x_1 + x_2$
   (c) $u(x_1, x_2) = \min\{x_1, 2x_2\}$
   (d) $u(x_1, x_2) = x_2 - x_1^2$

5. Donald likes fishing (x_1) and hanging out in his hammock (x_2). His utility function for these two activities is $u(x_1, x_2) = 3x_1^2 x_2^4$.
   (a) Calculate MU_1, the marginal utility of fishing.
   (b) Calculate MU_2, the marginal utility of hanging out in his hammock.
   (c) Calculate MRS, the rate at which he is willing to substitute hanging out in his hammock for fishing.
   (d) Last week, Donald fished 2 hours a day, and hung out in his hammock 4 hours a day. Using your formula for MRS from (c) find his MRS last week.
   (e) This week, Donald is fishing 8 hours a day, and hanging out in his hammock 2 hours a day. Calculate his MRS this week. Has his MRS increased or decreased? Explain why.
   (f) Is Donald happier or sadder this week compared with last week? Explain.

6. Suppose you are choosing between hours of work (a bad measured on the horizontal axis) and money (a good measured on the vertical axis).
   (a) Explain the meaning of MRS in words.
   (b) Should your MRS be positive or negative in this case?
   (c) Is your MRS increasing, constant or decreasing as you increase the hours of work along an indifference curve? Explain and draw some indifference curves for this example.

Appendix. Differentiation of Functions

This short appendix is not meant to be a substitute for a calculus course. However, it may serve as a helpful review. Let us begin with functions of one variable. Consider a function $y = f(x)$. Its derivative, y', is

$$y' = f'(x) = \frac{dy}{dx} = \lim_{\Delta x \to 0} \frac{f(x + \Delta x) - f(x)}{\Delta x}.$$

The derivative of the function f is the rate at which f increases as we increase x, the infinitesimal increment in f divided by the infinitesimal increment in x.

Some examples of differentiation of functions of one variable are:

- $y = 4x$, $y' = 4$.
- $y = 7x^2$, $y' = 14x$.
- $y = \ln x$; $y' = 1/x$.

What about functions of several variables? Consider a function $u(x_1, x_2)$, like our utility function. We define two partial derivatives of u, with respect to x_1 and with respect to x_2:

$$\frac{\partial u}{\partial x_1} = \lim_{\Delta x_1 \to 0} \frac{u(x_1 + \Delta x_1, x_2) - u(x_1, x_2)}{\Delta x_1}$$

and

$$\frac{\partial u}{\partial x_2} = \lim_{\Delta x_2 \to 0} \frac{u(x_1, x_2 + \Delta x_2) - u(x_1, x_2)}{\Delta x_2}.$$

The first is the rate at which u increases as we increase x_1, while holding x_2 constant. The second is the rate at which u increases as we increase x_2, while holding x_1 constant.

How do we partially differentiate a function of several variables? Almost exactly the same way we differentiate a function of one variable, except that we must remember that if we are diffentiating with respect to variable x_i, we treat any other variable x_j as a constant.

Some examples are:

- $u(x_1, x_2) = x_1 x_2$; $\partial u / \partial x_1 = x_2$, $\partial u / \partial x_2 = x_1$.
- $u(x_1, x_2) = x_1^2 x_2^3$, $\partial u / \partial x_1 = 2 x_1 x_2^3$, $\partial u / \partial x_2 = 3 x_1^2 x_2^2$.
- $u(x_1, x_2) = \ln x_1 + 2 \ln x_2$, $\partial u / \partial x_1 = 1/x_1$, $\partial u / \partial x_2 = 2/x_2$.

Chapter 3

The Budget Constraint and the Consumer's Optimal Choice

3.1 Introduction

In Chapter 2 we described the consumer's preferences and utility function. Now we turn to what constrains him, and what he should do to achieve the best outcome given his constraint. The consumer prefers some bundles to other bundles. He wants to get to the most-preferred bundle, or the highest possible utility level, but he cannot afford everything. He has a *budget constraint*. The consumer wants to make the best choice possible, the *optimal choice*, or the *utility-maximizing choice*, subject to his budget constraint.

In this chapter, we describe the consumer's standard budget constraint. We give some examples of special budget constraints created by nonmarket rationing devices, such as coupon rationing. We also analyze budget constraints involving consumption over time.

After describing various budget constraints, we turn to the consumer's basic economic problem: how to find the best consumption bundle, or how to maximize his utility, subject to the budget constraint. We do this graphically using indifference curves, and we do it analytically with utility functions. In the appendix to this chapter, we describe the Lagrange function method for maximizing a function subject to a constraint.

3.2 The Standard Budget Constraint, the Budget Set, and the Budget Line

A consumer cannot spend more money than he has. (We know about credit and will discuss it in a later section of this chapter.) We call what he has his *income*, written M, for "money." He wants to spend it on goods 1 and 2. Each has a price, represented by p_1 and p_2, respectively. The consumer's *standard budget constraint*, or *budget constraint* for short, says that the amount he spends (the sum

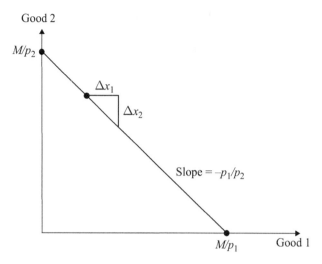

Fig. 3.1. The budget line is a downward-sloping straight line. The intercepts are M/p_1 and M/p_2, and the slope is $-p_1/p_2$.

of price times quantity for each of the two goods) must be less than or equal to the money he has. This gives:

$$p_1 x_1 + p_2 x_2 \leq M.$$

The *budget set* is the set of all bundles that satisfy the budget constraint – that is, all the bundles the consumer can afford. Of course, there will generally be many bundles available in the budget set.

The *budget line* is the set of bundles for which the consumer is spending exactly what he has. That is, it is the set of bundles (x_1, x_2) satisfying the equation

$$p_1 x_1 + p_2 x_2 = M.$$

Figure 3.1 shows the consumer's budget line.

The horizontal intercept of the budget line is the amount of good 1 the consumer would have if he spent all his money on that good; that is, if he consumed $x_2 = 0$. This is $x_1 = M/p_1$ units of good 1. Similarly, he would have M/p_2 units of good 2 if he spent all his money on that good. Because the price per unit of each good is a constant, the budget line is a straight line connecting these two intercepts.

The slope of the budget line is obviously negative. The absolute value of the slope, p_1/p_2, is sometimes called the *relative price* of good 1. This is the amount Δx_2 of good 2 that the consumer must give up if he wants to consume an additional amount Δx_1 of good 1. (Compare this with the MRS of good 2 for good 1 – the amount Δx_2 of good 2 that the consumer is just willing to give up to consume an additional amount Δx_1 of good 1.)

The budget line defines a tradeoff for the consumer who wants to increase his consumption of good 1 and simultaneously decrease his consumption of good 2. In

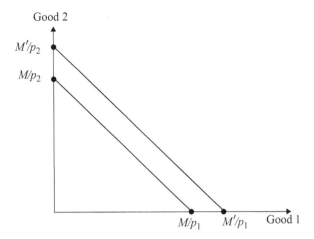

Fig. 3.2. In this figure, income increases from M to M'. The budget line shifts out, parallel to itself. The new intercepts are M'/p_1 and M'/p_2 on the horizontal and vertical axes, respectively.

Figure 3.1, Δx_1 is a positive number (good 1 is increasing) and Δx_2 is a negative number (good 2 is decreasing). If the amount spent on the two goods remains constant, the sum of the increase in money spent on good 1 and the decrease in money spent on good 2 must be zero, or

$$p_1 \Delta x_1 + p_2 \Delta x_2 = 0.$$

This gives

$$-\frac{\Delta x_2}{\Delta x_1} = \frac{p_1}{p_2}.$$

3.3 Shifts of the Budget Line

If the consumer's income changes, or if the prices of the goods change, the budget line moves. Figure 3.2 shows how the budget line shifts if income increases while prices stay constant.

If both prices decrease by the same proportion, the same kind of shift occurs. Suppose the new prices are $p_1' = kp_1$ and $p_2' = kp_2$, where $k < 1$ is the same factor for both prices. Then the new budget line has slope $-p_1'/p_2' = -(kp_1)/(kp_2) = -p_1/p_2$. The new intercept on the horizontal axis is $M/p_1' = M/kp_1 = (1/k)M/p_1$, which is farther out on the axis because $k < 1$.

If income decreases while both prices stay the same, or if both prices rise by the same proportion while income stays constant, the budget line shifts in.

Consider what happens when one price, say p_1, rises, while the other price and income stay the same. Let p_1' be the new price and p_1 the old, with $p_1' > p_1$. If the consumer spends all his income on good 1, he will consume less, because the

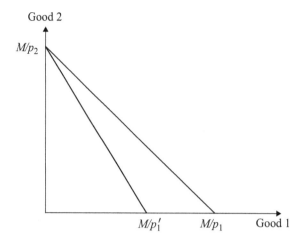

Fig. 3.3. The price of good 1 rises, while the price of good 2, and income, stay the same.

new intercept M/p_1' is smaller than the old M/p_1. The intercept on the good 2 axis does not move. The budget line gets steeper, because the absolute value of the new slope, p_1'/p_2, is greater than the absolute value of the old slope, p_1/p_2. Figure 3.3 shows this important type of budget line shift.

3.4 Odd Budget Constraints

The standard budget constraint described previously assumes first that prices are constant for any quantities of the goods the consumer might want to consume. Second, it assumes that prices do not depend on income. Third, it assumes that nothing constrains the consumer except prices and the money in his pocket. However, the real world often does not follow these assumptions. The real world is full of nonstandard budget constraints; here are two examples.

Example 1: A 2-for-1 Store Coupon. The consumer has one (and only one) coupon from a grocery store, allowing him to buy two units of good 1 for the price of one. The price of good 1 is 1 dollar per unit. In addition, the consumer's income is $M = 5$, and the price of good 2 is $p_2 = 1$. It follows that $p_1 = 1/2$ if $x_1 \leq 2$, and $p_1 = 1$ for $x_1 > 2$. Figure 3.4 illustrates this case. The intercept on the good 2 axis is obviously $M/p_2 = 5$, whereas the intercept on the horizontal axis is, somewhat less obviously, 6.

Example 2: Ration Coupons. In times of war (and other emergencies, real or imagined) governments will sometimes ration scarce commodities (including food, fuel, and so on). This might mean that goods 1 and 2 sell for money at prices p_1 and p_2, but that the purchaser *also* needs a government coupon for each unit of the rationed good (say good 1) that he buys. Suppose the consumer has income of $M = 100$; let $p_1 = 1$, and $p_2 = 2$, and suppose that the consumer has ration

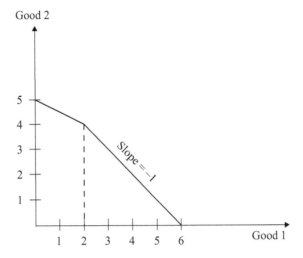

Fig. 3.4. The budget line with a 2-for-the-price-of-1 promotional coupon.

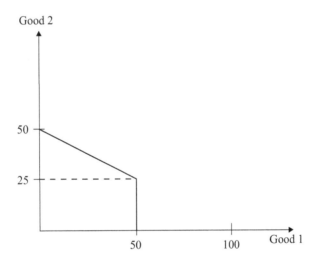

Fig. 3.5. The case of wartime coupon rationing.

coupons for 50 units of good 1. The vertical intercept is $x_2 = 50$ and the slope of the budget line for $x_1 < 50$ is $-1/2$. At the point $(x_1, x_2) = (50, 25)$, the budget line becomes vertical; the consumer cannot buy more than 50 units of good 1 because he has only 50 coupons (see Figure 3.5).

3.5 Income and Consumption over Time

One very crucial type of budget constraint shows the consumer's choices over time. This is called an *intertemporal budget constraint*. For this purpose, we start by assuming that there are two time periods ("this year" and "next year"); we let

x_1 represent consumption this year, and x_2 represent consumption next year. For simplicity, we assume that a unit of the consumption good, called "stuff," has a price of 1, both this year and next year. (Assuming that a unit of a good has a price of 1 is sometimes called *normalizing* the price. A good with a price of 1 is sometimes called a *numeraire* good.) Because we are assuming that the price of a unit of the good is the same this year and next year, we are assuming *no price inflation*. (We will add inflation to the mix in some exercises in this chapter, and again when we revisit this topic in Chapter 5.)

We assume that the consumer has income M_1 this year, and will have income M_2 next year. He could obviously choose $x_1 = M_1$ and $x_2 = M_2$. In this case he is spending everything that he gets this year on his consumption this year, and spending everything that he gets next year on his consumption next year. He is neither borrowing nor saving.

Alternatively, he could save some of this year's income. In this case, he spends some of M_1 on consumption this year, and he sets some aside until next year, when he spends all that remains from this year plus his income from next year. (We assume that he has monotonic preferences; he always prefers more stuff to less, and will therefore end up spending everything available by the end of next year.) Assume for now that what the consumer does not spend this year he hides under his mattress for next year. In other words, he puts the money he does not spend away in a safe place, but he does not get any interest on his savings. His budget constraint now says that what he consumes next year (x_2) must equal what he saved and put under his mattress this year ($M_1 - x_1$) plus his income next year (M_2). This gives

$$x_2 = (M_1 - x_1) + M_2 \qquad \text{or} \qquad x_1 + x_2 = M_1 + M_2.$$

We have written the budget constraint as an equation, rather than as an inequality, because the consumer ultimately spends all that he has.

Next, let us assume that the consumer does not hide his money under his mattress. Instead, whatever he does not spend this year he puts into a bank account (or an investment) that pays a fixed and certain rate of return i (i is for "interest," expressed as a decimal). Now what he saves and puts away in the first year, ($M_1 - x_1$), he gets back with interest (multiply by $(1 + i)$), causing it to grow to $(1 + i)(M_1 - x_1)$ next year. The consumer's budget constraint now becomes

$$x_2 = (1 + i)(M_1 - x_1) + M_2 \qquad \text{or} \qquad (1 + i)x_1 + x_2 = (1 + i)M_1 + M_2.$$

Finally, dividing both sides of the equation by $1 + i$ gives

$$x_1 + \left(\frac{1}{1 + i} \right) x_2 = M_1 + \left(\frac{1}{1 + i} \right) M_2.$$

Economists call the term $1/(1 + i)$ the *discount factor*. In general, the term *present value* means that some future amount, or amounts, or some series of amounts over time, are being converted to the *current time*, or *current year*, equivalent. The term $x_2/(1 + i)$ is called the (year 1) *present value of year 2 consumption*. The term $M_1/(1 + i)$ is called the (year 1) *present value of year 2 income*. The left-hand side of the budget equation, or $x_1 + x_2/(1 + i)$, is called the *present value of the consumer's consumption stream*, and the right-hand side of the equation, or $M_1 + M_2/(1 + i)$, is called the *present value of the consumer's income stream*. Therefore, the budget equation we just derived says that the present value of the consumption stream equals the present value of the income stream.

In the preceding analysis, we assumed that the consumer saves some of his first-year income, M_1, to be able to consume more in the second year than his second-year income, M_2. Now, let us assume he does the reverse. That is, we now assume that he borrows against next year's income to increase this year's consumption. For simplicity, we will assume that the interest rate i is the same for savers and borrowers. (This is, of course, quite unrealistic; in reality, the interest rate paid to savers is normally much less than the interest rate paid by borrowers. To appreciate the difference, compare the interest rate applied to balances on your credit card to the interest rate paid to savers at your bank.)

If the consumer intends to spend less than his income in the second year, then $x_2 < M_2$, or $M_2 - x_2 > 0$. Suppose the consumer goes to his banker in the first year and asks this question: Next year I can pay you back $M_2 - x_2$. How much can you lend me this year, based on this anticipated repayment? The banker reasons to himself: If I make a loan of L this year, I must get all my money back next year, plus interest, or a total of $(1 + i)L$. Therefore, I require $(1 + i)L = M_2 - x_2$. Solving for L then gives $L = (M_2 - x_2)/(1 + i)$. (Of course, this process may be more complicated in the real world. In reality, bankers require either collateral or security for loans – as with real estate mortgages – or, for unsecured loans, they charge interest rates high enough to compensate for defaults.)

We can now lay out the consumer's budget constraint in the case in which he is a borrower. His consumption this year (x_1) is equal to his income this year (M_1), plus the loan he gets from his banker, $(M_2 - x_2)/(1 + i)$. This gives

$$x_1 = M_1 + (M_2 - x_2)/(1 + i),$$

or, rearranging terms,

$$x_1 + \left(\frac{1}{1+i}\right)x_2 = M_1 + \left(\frac{1}{1+i}\right)M_2.$$

This is exactly the same budget equation as in the saver case!

To summarize, we have looked at a consumer who has income this year and income next year, and who will consume some stuff this year and more stuff next year. We assumed that the consumer can save or borrow, and that the interest rate is the same for savers and for borrowers. We have shown that the consumer has a simple budget constraint involving consumption quantities this year and next,

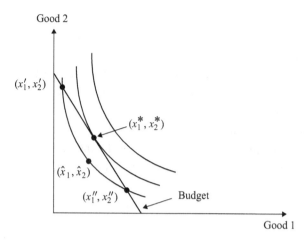

Fig. 3.6. The consumer's optimal choice is (x_1^*, x_2^*).

income this year and next, and the interest rate. We have shown that there is a simple and intuitive interpretation of the budget constraint: The present value of the consumer's consumption stream must equal the present value of his income stream. This is a crucial result for the theory of intertemporal choice. Moreover, the budget constraint we found – and, more generally, the methodology of present values – are crucial in the theory and practice of finance.

3.6 The Consumer's Optimal Choice: Graphical Analysis

As we said when we began the theory of the consumer, the consumer will choose the bundle that he most prefers among those that he can afford. This is his *optimal choice*. To put it another way, he will find the highest indifference curve that is consistent with his budget. Figure 3.6 illustrates this concept.

What conditions must be satisfied by the consumer's optimal choice?

First, at the optimal point, the consumer's indifference curve and budget line are just touching, as we can plainly see in Figure 3.6.

The figure actually shows more than that; it shows the standard case in which the indifference curve and the budget line are in fact tangent at (x_1^*, x_2^*). That is, both slopes are well defined and equal. (Later, we will consider some examples in which the slopes are either not defined, or not equal.) Because the slopes are equal in the figure, the absolute values of the slopes are also equal. The absolute value of the slope of an indifference curve at a point is equal to the MRS, and the absolute value of the slope of the budget line is p_1/p_2. Therefore, for the standard case illustrated in Figure 3.6, we have

$$MRS = p_1/p_2.$$

Recall that the marginal rate of substitution is interpreted as the amount of good 2 the consumer is *just willing* to give up in exchange for getting an increment of good 1, and the price ratio p_1/p_2 is the amount of good 2 that the *market demands* the consumer give up in exchange for an increment of good 1. At the optimal point (x_1^*, x_2^*) of the figure, what the consumer is just willing to do is exactly equal to what the market demands that he do.

Now consider a point at which $MRS \neq p_1/p_2$ – for instance, the bundle (x_1', x_2') in Figure 3.6. At that bundle, consider the possibility of the consumer giving up some of good 2 and getting some of good 1 in exchange. For a given increment of good 1, the consumer would be willing to give up much more of good 2 than the market requires that he give up (the indifference curve is relatively steep and the budget line is relatively flat). Therefore, he would trade according to market prices, move down and to the right on the budget line, and make himself better off. The opposite adjustment would happen at the bundle (x_1'', x_2''); no such adjustment can happen at the optimal bundle (x_1^*, x_2^*).

The optimal point must be on the budget line. That is, it must be the case that

$$p_1 x_1 + p_2 x_2 = M.$$

This is because we are assuming monotonic preferences; the consumer always prefers more to less, and will spend all his income. A bundle such as $(\hat{x}_1, \hat{x}_2)$ in Figure 3.6 is not optimal and would not be chosen by the consumer, because he prefers, and can afford, bundles above and to the right of $(\hat{x}_1, \hat{x}_2)$ – that is, bundles with more of both goods.

The principle behind the consumer's optimal choice is always the same: he wants to buy the most-preferred bundle, or get to the highest indifference curve, that he can afford. However, our marginal rate of substitution condition assumes that the MRS of good 2 for good 1 is well defined, and that the optimal bundle has positive amounts of both goods. What happens to the consumer's optimal choice without these assumptions? Consider the following examples:

- **Marginal rate of substitution not defined.** Suppose $u(x_1, x_2) = \min\{x_1, x_2\}$; $p_1 = 2$ and $p_2 = 1$. When the utility function has this form, we call x_1 and x_2 *perfect complements*. This means a unit of good 1 is always consumed with exactly one unit of good 2. Think, for example, of a left shoe and a right shoe. Unless you are missing a limb, you always want to consume exactly one right shoe with each left shoe. You can check to see that the MRS is not defined when $x_1 = x_2$ because the utility function is not differentiable there. However, it is easy to graph the consumer's choice problem in this case (Figure 3.7).

    Clearly, the budget line equation $p_1 x_1 + p_2 x_2 = M$ still holds because of monotonicity of preferences. The second equation we need in this case is $x_1 = x_2$. It is pointless for this consumer to choose a bundle in which this condition is not met, given his preferences.
- **Corner solution.** Assume $u(x_1, x_2) = x_1 + x_2$. When the utility function has this form, we call x_1 and x_2 *perfect substitutes*. This is like Coke and Pepsi for a consumer who (strangely) cannot taste the difference; a bottle of one soda can be freely substituted for a bottle of the other, with no effect on utility. Clearly, if $p_1 < p_2$, this consumer will spend all his income on good 1. The utility function is differentiable and the MRS is equal

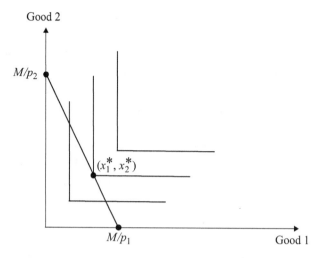

Fig. 3.7. Perfect complements.

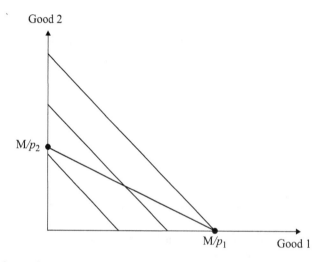

Fig. 3.8. Perfect substitutes. Note that p_1/p_2, the absolute value of slope of the budget line, is now less than 1. This consumer only buys good 1.

to 1 everywhere. If the price ratio $p_1/p_2 \neq 1$, it is impossible to have a tangency of an indifference curve with the budget line (Figure 3.8). This means only, however, that the optimal choice must be at an end point of the budget line; that is, on the good 1 axis or the good 2 axis. (Such an optimal choice is called a *corner solution*.) This consumer would drink only Coke, or only Pepsi, whichever is cheaper.

In most of this book, we construct examples of optimal choices in which indifference curves and budget lines are tangent. We do it this way to make the explanations simpler.

3.7 The Consumer's Optimal Choice: Utility Maximization Subject to the Budget Constraint

As we have said, the consumer will choose the bundle that he most prefers among those that he can afford. This is the consumer's optimal choice. In the last section, we thought of this as finding the highest indifference curve that is consistent with the consumer's budget line. Now we think of the same problem, but this time we think of it as maximizing the consumer's utility function subject to his budget constraint. We assume in this section that the consumer's optimal choice is at a point at which an indifference curve is tangent to the budget line.

The consumer's optimal choice (x_1^*, x_2^*) is the solution to this problem:

$$\text{Maximize } u(x_1, x_2)$$

subject to

$$p_1 x_1 + p_2 x_2 = M.$$

This is a special type of calculus problem; the objective function $u(x_1, x_2)$ is being maximized subject to a constraint. If the constraint were not there, there would be no maximum, given our assumption of monotonicity. Therefore, we cannot try to solve the problem by first maximizing $u(x_1, x_2)$, and then worrying about the constraint. We can solve the problem in one of three ways.

1. **Brute force method.** We could use the constraint to solve for one of the variables, plug the result back into the objective function, and then maximize the objective function, which has been reduced to a function of just one variable. (This function does have a maximum.) That is, we use the constraint to solve for x_2:

$$x_2 = \frac{M - p_1 x_1}{p_2}.$$

We plug this into $u(x_1, x_2)$ giving

$$u\left(x_1, \frac{M - p_1 x_1}{p_2}\right).$$

Note that x_2 has disappeared from the the utility function. We differentiate this function with respect to x_1 and set the result equal to zero. Solving the resulting equation gives x_1^*. We then plug this back into the budget equation, $p_1 x_1^* + p_2 x_2 = M$, and use this to solve for x_2^*.

   The brute force method, as the name suggests, may be rather ugly and difficult, and we try to avoid using it in what follows.

2. **Use-the-graphs method.** We could rely on what we learned from the graphs; at a consumer optimum where an indifference curve is tangent to the budget line, it must be the case that

$$MRS = p_1/p_2.$$

We then combine this equation with the budget constraint equation, $p_1x_1 + p_2x_2 = M$, to solve for the two unknowns (x_1^*, x_2^*). This is the method that we use most often in this book.

3. **The Lagrange function method.** The standard mathematical method for solving a constrained maximization problem is the following. First set up a special function, called the *Lagrange function*, that incorporates both the objective function and the constraint. In our case, the Lagrange function would be

$$L = u(x_1, x_2) + \lambda(M - (p_1x_1 + p_2x_2)).$$

In this function, λ is a special variable called the *Lagrange multiplier*. Next, we proceed to find the first-order conditions for the maximization of L with respect to x_1, x_2, and λ; these boil down to $MRS = p_1/p_2$ and $p_1x_1 + p_2x_2 = M$. Finally, we use the first-order conditions to solve for the optimal quantities of the goods (x_1^*, x_2^*), and for the optimal λ^*. This method is more elegant than methods 1 and 2; furthermore, the Lagrange multiplier has a nice economic interpretation in terms of how much the consumer would value a one-dollar increase in his income. In general, however, we will stick to the use-the-graphs method in this book, as it is simpler than the Lagrange function method. We do describe the Lagrange method in more detail in the appendix to this chapter.

3.8 Two Solved Problems

Problem 1

Part 1. Assume $p_1 = 1$ and $p_2 = 2$, and the consumer has income $M = 10$. Find the consumer's budget constraint. Find utility-maximizing consumption bundles for the following utility functions:

(a) $u(x_1, x_2) = x_1 + x_2$
(b) $u(x_1, x_2) = x_1x_2$

Part 2. Now, assume the prices change to $p_1 = 2$ and $p_2 = 1$. What is the consumer's new budget constraint? What happens to the utility maximizing consumption bundles in the two cases?

Solution to Problem 1

First, note that with these utility functions the consumer will want to spend all his income. He will want to be on his budget line, not below it. The relevant budget constraint is an equation, not an inequality.

Part 1. In general, the budget constraint is $p_1x_1 + p_2x_2 = M$. With prices $(p_1, p_2) = (1, 2)$, this gives $x_1 + 2x_2 = 10$. The budget line has slope $p_1/p_2 = 1/2$ in absolute value, going from intercept $M/p_1 = 10$ on the good 1 (horizontal) axis to intercept $M/p_2 = 5$ on the good 2 (vertical) axis.

(a) If $u(x_1, x_2) = x_1 + x_2$, his indifference curves are straight lines, with slope equal to $MRS = MU_1/MU_2 = 1/1 = 1$ in absolute value. No indifference curve/budget line tangency is possible, because the indifference curves have slope 1 and the budget line has slope 1/2 (both in absolute value). To find the corner solution, we can use a sketch such as Figure 3.8, or we can simply calculate utility levels at the ends of the budget line. If the consumer puts all his income into buying 10 units of good 1, $u(10, 0) = 10$; if he puts all his income into buying 5 units of good 2, $u(0, 5) = 5$. His optimal consumption bundle is therefore $(x_1^*, x_2^*) = (10, 0)$.

(b) If $u(x_1, x_2) = x_1 x_2$, his indifference curves are hyperbolas. The tangency condition is $MRS = p_1/p_2$ or

$$MRS = \frac{MU_1}{MU_2} = \frac{x_2}{x_1} = \frac{p_1}{p_2} = \frac{1}{2}.$$

This gives $x_1 = 2x_2$. His budget constraint is $x_1 + 2x_2 = 10$, and substituting for x_1 gives $4x_2 = 10$. It follows that the solution is $x_1^* = 5$ and $x_2^* = 2.5$.

Part 2. Now, suppose the prices change to $(p_1, p_2) = (2, 1)$. The budget constraint becomes $2x_1 + x_2 = 10$. The budget line now has slope $p_1/p_2 = 2/1 = 2$ in absolute value, going from intercept $M/p_1 = 5$ on the good 1 (horizontal) axis to intercept $M/p_2 = 10$ on the good 2 (vertical) axis.

(a) If $u(x_1, x_2) = x_1 + x_2$, his indifference curves are straight lines, with slope equal to $MRS = MU_1/MU_2 = 1/1 = 1$ in absolute value, and again there is no indifference curve/budget line tangency possible. When we calculate utility levels at the ends of the budget line, we find that the optimal consumption bundle is now $(x_1^*, x_2^*) = (0, 10)$.

(b) If $u(x_1, x_2) = x_1 x_2$, the indifference curves are hyperbolas. The tangency condition is again $MRS = p_1/p_2$, which now leads to

$$MRS = \frac{x_2}{x_1} = \frac{p_1}{p_2} = \frac{2}{1}.$$

This gives $x_1 = x_2/2$. The budget constraint is $2x_1 + x_2 = 10$; substituting for x_1 gives $2x_2 = 10$. It follows that the solution is $x_1^* = 2.5$ and $x_2^* = 5$.

Finally, let us contrast the shifts in the optimal consumption bundles, as p_1/p_2 changes from 1/2 to 2/1 in the cases of the two alternative utility functions. For $u(x_1, x_2) = x_1 + x_2$, the optimal consumption bundle jumps as far as possible, from $(10, 0)$ to $(0, 10)$. For $u(x_1, x_2) = x_1 x_2$, the optimal consumption bundle changes from $(5, 2.5)$ to $(2.5, 5)$.

A moral of this story is that when the slope of the budget line changes, the consumer will substitute one good for the other *dramatically* in the straight-line indifference curve case, but only *moderately* in the curved (hyperbolic) indifference curve case.

Problem 2

The utility function $u(x_1, x_2) = x_1^\alpha x_2^\beta$ is called a *Cobb-Douglas* utility function. (It is named after mathematician Charles Cobb and economist – and Illinois Senator – Paul Douglas. The chapters on the theory of the firm will provide a bit more information.) The constants α and β are both positive. Suppose a consumer is maximizing this utility function subject to the budget constraint $p_1x_1 + p_2x_2 = M$. The consumer will want to spend all his income on his utility-maximizing bundle (x_1^*, x_2^*). Show the following:

$$\text{(a)} \qquad x_1^* = \left(\frac{\alpha}{\alpha + \beta}\right)\frac{M}{p_1}, \text{ and}$$

$$\text{(b)} \qquad x_2^* = \left(\frac{\beta}{\alpha + \beta}\right)\frac{M}{p_2}.$$

Solution to Problem 2

(a) The indifference curves are similar to hyperbolas; however, they are not symmetric around a 45-degree line from the origin when $\alpha \neq \beta$. Note that

$$MU_1 = \alpha x_1^{\alpha-1} x_2^{\beta} \qquad \text{and} \qquad MU_2 = \beta x_1^{\alpha} x_2^{\beta-1}.$$

The tangency condition says that the slope of the indifference curve must equal the slope of the budget line, which leads to

$$MRS = \frac{MU_1}{MU_2} = \frac{\alpha x_1^{\alpha-1} x_2^{\beta}}{\beta x_1^{\alpha} x_2^{\beta-1}} = \frac{\alpha x_2}{\beta x_1} = \frac{p_1}{p_2}.$$

This gives $\beta p_1 x_1 = \alpha p_2 x_2$. It follows that

$$p_1 x_1 = \alpha p_2 x_2 / \beta \qquad \text{or} \qquad p_2 x_2 = \beta p_1 x_1 / \alpha.$$

The budget constraint is $p_1 x_1 + p_2 x_2 = M$.
From $p_2 x_2 = \beta p_1 x_1 / \alpha$ and the budget constraint, we get $p_1 x_1 + \beta p_1 x_1 / \alpha = M$, or $(\alpha p_1 x_1 + \beta p_2 x_2)/\alpha = M$. This gives

$$x_1^* = \left(\frac{\alpha}{\alpha + \beta}\right)\frac{M}{p_1}.$$

(b) From $p_1 x_1 = \alpha p_2 x_2 / \beta$ and the budget constraint, we get $\alpha p_2 x_2 / \beta + p_2 x_2 = M$, or $(\alpha p_2 x_2 + \beta p_2 x_2)/\beta = M$. This gives

$$x_2^* = \left(\frac{\beta}{\alpha + \beta}\right)\frac{M}{p_2}.$$

Exercises

1. The consumer's original budget equation is $p_1x_1 + p_2x_2 = M$, where p_1 and p_2 are the original prices and M is the original income level.
   (a) If p_1 doubles and p_2 falls by half, what is the consumer's new budget equation? How has the slope of the budget line changed?
   (b) If p_1 doubles and M triples, what is the equation for the new budget line? How has the slope of the budget line changed?

$3x_1 + 2x_2 = \}\ v^2$

2. The consumer's utility function is $u(x_1, x_2) = x_1 x_2^2$.

   $9x_1 = 90^2\ x_{1,2}l\ v^0$

   (a) Graph his budget constraint for $p_1 = 3$, $p_2 = 2$ and $M = 900$, and write down the
       equation for his budget line. $x_2 = \dfrac{3}{2}$ $x_2 = 3x_1$

   (b) Using the $MRS = MU_1/MU_2 = p_1/p_2$ tangency condition find his optimal con-
       sumption bundle for these prices and income. $\dfrac{x_2}{2x_1 x_2}$

3. George enjoys apples (a) and bananas (b). If he spends his entire allowance, he can
   afford 10 apples and 30 bananas. Alternatively, he can afford 15 apples and 15 bananas.
   The price of an apple is \$3. $10 P_a + 30 P_b = 15 P_a + 15 P_b$

   (a) Calculate George's allowance, and the price of bananas. $P_a = 3$ $P_b = 1$ Allowance: 10.3

   (b) Assume his utility function is $u(a, b) = a + b$. How many apples and bananas will $+30 \cdot 1$
       he consume. $MRS = \dfrac{MU_a}{MU_b}$ perfect substitute $= 60$

4. There are two goods in the world, pumpkins (x_1), and apple cider (x_2). Pumpkins are
   \$2 each. Cider is \$7 per gallon for the first two gallons. After the second gallon, the
   price of cider drops to \$4 per gallon. $x_2 = -\dfrac{1}{3}x_1 + \dfrac{u}{3}$ $u = 3$

   (a) Peter's income is \$54. Draw his budget line. Solve for the intercepts on the x_1 and
       x_2 axes, and the kink in the budget line. Show these in your graph.

   (b) Peter's utility function is $u(x_1, x_2) = x_1 + 3x_2$. Sketch some indifference curves in
       your graph. Find Peter's optimal consumption bundle (x_1^*, x_2^*). $u = x_1 + 3x_2$ $(20, 2)$

   (c) Paul's income is \$22. Draw his budget line in a new graph. Solve for the intercepts
       on the x_1 and x_2 axes, and the kink in the budget line. Show these in your graph
       for Paul. $u = 3x_1$ $3x_1 < 2x_2$ $3x_1 = y$

   (d) Paul's utility function is $u(x_1, x_2) = \min(3x_1, 2x_2)$. Sketch some indifference
       curves in your graph for Paul. Find Paul's optimal consumption bundle (x_1^*, x_2^*).

5. Olivia gets an allowance of \$50 this week, but it will have to last her for two weeks,
   as Mom pays her *every other week*. Let c_1 be her consumption this week (measured in
   units of stuff), and let c_2 be her consumption next week (measured in the same units).
   The price of one unit of stuff this week is \$1. Next week the price will be higher,
   because of inflation. Assume the inflation rate π is 1 percent per week, or 0.01 per
   week when expressed as a decimal. (About notation: When we use the symbol π in this
   book we do not mean 3.14. In this exercise and in Chapter 5, π means inflation. From
   Chapter 8 onward, π means profit.) Therefore, the price of one unit of stuff next week
   will be \$1$(1 + \pi) = \$1.01$. Olivia can borrow or save at the local bank; whether she is
   borrowing or saving, the interest rate i is 1 percent per week, or 0.01 when expressed
   as a decimal. Olivia's utility function is $u(c_1, c_2) = \ln(c_1) + \ln(c_2)$. $M = 1 \times C_1 + \dfrac{1+\pi}{1+i}C_2$

   (a) Write down Olivia's budget constraint, first in the abstract (with M, π, and i), and
       then with the given values incorporated. $\therefore C_1 + C_2 = 50$

   (b) Find her optimal consumption bundle (c_1^*, c_2^*). $\dfrac{C_2}{C_1} = 1$ $(25, 25)$

   (c) Assume the inflation rate rises to 10 percent, and the interest rate drops to zero. $M = C_1 + 1.1 C_2$
       Find her new optimal consumption bundle. $\dfrac{C_2}{C_1} = \dfrac{1}{1.1}$ $C_1 = 1.1 C_2$ $2.1 C_1 = 50$

6. Sylvester's preferences for consumption this period (c_1) and consumption next period
   (c_2) are given by the utility function $u(c_1, c_2) = c_1^2 c_2$. Suppose the price of consumption $C_2 =$
   this period is \$1 per unit. Assume the interest rate i is 10 percent; and the inflation rate
   π is 5 percent. Sylvester has income of \$100 this period and \$100 next period.

   (a) Write down the equation for his budget line, and show it in a graph. What are the
       intercepts of the budget line on the c_1 and c_2 axes? Label them in your graph. What

$C_1 + \dfrac{1.05}{1.1} C_2 = 200$

is the slope of the budget line? Explain it briefly. Where is the zero savings point? Explain it briefly.

(b) Find Sylvester's optimal consumption bundle (c_1^*, c_2^*). We'll call this S for short. Is Sylvester a saver or a borrower? Show S on your graph, and include the indifference curve passing through it.

(c) Suppose the interest rate i falls to 5 percent. Show the new budget line in your graph. Find Sylvester's new optimal consumption bundle S'.

(d) Is Sylvester better off or worse off at the new point S'?

Appendix. Maximization Subject to a Constraint: The Lagrange Function Method

Joseph Louis Lagrange (1736–1813), an Italian-French mathematician and astronomer, developed a widely used method for maximizing (or minimizing) a function subject to a constraint. Consumers maximize utility subject to budget constraints, and, as we shall see in a later chapter, firms minimize costs subject to output constraints, or maximize profits subject to cost constraints. Therefore, the *Lagrange method*, also called the *Lagrange multiplier method*, is often used by economists. We will illustrate the method for the case of a well-behaved utility function $u(x_1, x_2)$ which a consumer is maximizing subject to a budget constraint $p_1x_1 + p_2x_2 = M$. We assume that the consumer optimum is at a tangency point of an indifference curve and the budget line.

The Lagrange method works as follows. We start with the utility function we want to maximize,

$$u(x_1, x_2).$$

We rewrite the consumer's budget constraint as

$$M - (p_1x_1 + p_2x_2) = 0.$$

We write a new objective function, called the *Lagrange function*, as follows:

$$L(x_1, x_2, \lambda) = u(x_1, x_2) + \lambda(M - (p_1x_1 + p_2x_2)).$$

Here λ is a new variable called the *Lagrange multiplier*. Intuitively, the Lagrange function is formed by taking the original objective function, $u(x_1, x_2)$, and adding to it λ times something that should be zero, at least at the optimal point (i.e., $M - (p_1x_1 + p_2x_2)$). Note that L is a function of three variables, x_1, x_2, and λ.

Then, we maximize L. That is, we derive the first-order conditions for the *unconstrained maximization* of L. It turns out that this process leads to the consumption bundle (x_1^*, x_2^*) that solves the original *constrained maximization* problem. This is because the first-order conditions for the unconstrained maximization of L produce the first-order conditions for the constrained maximization of $u(x_1, x_2)$. Moreover, the process also leads to a λ^* that has a nice intuitive interpretation.

We illustrate with two examples.

Example 1. Let $u(x_1, x_2) = x_1 x_2$. Let $p_1 = 1$, $p_2 = 2$, and $M = 10$, as in the earlier solved problem, part 1(b). The Lagrange function is

$$L = x_1 x_2 + \lambda(10 - (x_1 + 2x_2)).$$

The first-order conditions for the maximization of L are

$$\frac{\partial L}{\partial x_1} = x_2 - \lambda \times 1 = 0,$$

$$\frac{\partial L}{\partial x_2} = x_1 - \lambda \times 2 = 0,$$

and

$$\frac{\partial L}{\partial \lambda} = 10 - (x_1 + 2x_2) = 0.$$

Note that the first two first-order conditions can be combined to get $x_2/x_1 = 1/2$. However, this is exactly the same $MRS = p_1/p_2$ condition we are familiar with from the earlier solved problem, part 1(b). The last condition is, of course, the budget constraint. Solving for the optimal consumption bundle then gives $(x_1^*, x_2^*) = (10/2, 10/4) = (5, 2.5)$. Finally, solving for the optimal Lagrange multiplier gives $\lambda^* = 2.5$.

What is the interpretation of λ^*? First, consider the general description of the Lagrange method. If we were to differentiate the Lagrange function L with respect to money income M, we would get λ. This suggests that λ is the rate of increase in L – and, therefore, in the objective function $u(x_1, x_2)$ – as we relax the budget constraint, that is, as we increase M.

Now, consider our example. Assume we increase M somewhat – say by 1 dollar, to 11. Using the $MRS = p_1/p_2$ condition again gives $x_2/x_1 = 1/2$, and the budget constraint is now $11 - (x_1 + 2x_2) = 0$. Solving both simultaneously gives $(x_1^{**}, x_2^{**}) = (11/2, 11/4)$.

The increase in M results in an increase in utility for the consumer. That change in u is $\Delta u = 11/2 \times 11/4 - 10/2 \times 10/4 = 15.125 - 12.5 = 2.625$. We conclude that

$$\frac{\Delta u}{\Delta M} = 2.625/1 \approx \lambda^*.$$

That is, the Lagrange multiplier λ^* is approximately equal to the consumer's increase in utility when his income rises by 1 dollar. If we let ΔM approach zero, the "approximately equal to" changes to "exactly equal to," or

$$\frac{\partial u}{\partial M} = 2.5 = \lambda^*.$$

That is, *the Lagrange multiplier λ^* equals the consumer's rate of increase in utility as his income rises, or as his budget constraint is relaxed.*

Example 2. Let $u(x_1, x_2) = x_1^2 x_2^3$. Let $p_1 = 2$, $p_2 = 3$, and $M = 10$. The Lagrange function is

$$L = x_1^2 x_2^3 + \lambda(10 - (2x_1 + 3x_2)).$$

The first-order conditions for the maximization of L are:

$$\frac{\partial L}{\partial x_1} = 2x_1 x_2^3 - \lambda \times 2 = 0,$$

$$\frac{\partial L}{\partial x_2} = 3x_1^2 x_2^2 - \lambda \times 3 = 0,$$

and

$$\frac{\partial L}{\partial \lambda} = 10 - (2x_1 + 3x_2) = 0.$$

In the first two first-order conditions, we bring the $-\lambda p_i$ terms to the right-hand sides of the equations, and then we divide each side of the first equation by the corresponding side of the second. This gives

$$\frac{2x_2}{3x_1} = \frac{2}{3}, \text{ and therefore, } x_1 = x_2.$$

Now, we use the last condition – that is, the consumer's budget constraint – to calculate the optimal consumption point $(x_1^*, x_2^*) = (2, 2)$. We finish by calculating $\lambda^* = x_1^*(x_2^*)^3 = (x_1^*)^2(x_2^*)^2 = 2^4 = 16$.

Chapter 4

Demand Functions

4.1 Introduction

Chapter 3 ended with a discussion of the consumer's optimal choice. That is, we learned how the consumer decides how much of good 1 and good 2 she wants to buy, given prices p_1 and p_2, and given her income M. The consumer maximizes her utility $u(x_1, x_2)$, subject to her budget constraint $p_1x_1 + p_2x_2 = M$. We call the utility-maximizing bundle she chooses (x_1^*, x_2^*).

Because this optimal choice can be made for any values of p_1, p_2, and M, we are actually finding two functions: $x_1^* = x_1(p_1, p_2, M)$ and $x_2^* = x_2(p_1, p_2, M)$. These two functions show the amounts of good 1 or 2 the consumer wants to buy, that is, her *demands* for the two goods, given arbitrary values of prices and income. The functions are called her *individual demand functions* for goods 1 and 2, respectively. (For notational ease we will drop the ∗'s for the rest of this chapter.)

We start this chapter with a detailed study of individual demand functions. Each demand function depends on three independent variables. Because of this complication, it would be impossible to graph them in the obvious way. (We would need four dimensions!) Therefore, we will look at how demand changes as we vary one independent variable at a time. This exercise is called *comparative statics*, because we are comparing the consumer's optimal consumption of goods 1 and 2 as one of the exogenous variables – one of the prices, or income – changes from one level to another. From now on, we shall concentrate on the demand function for just one of the goods, say, good 1.

In Section 4.2 we focus on demand as a function of income, holding prices constant. We derive an Engel curve, a graph that shows the desired consumption of a good as a function of income. We distinguish between normal goods (higher income results in higher consumption) and inferior goods (higher income results in lower consumption). In Section 4.3 we focus on demand as a function of price, and we discuss the consumer's standard demand curve (showing

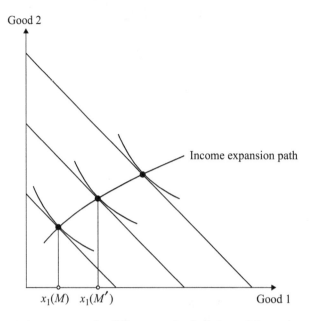

Good 2

Income expansion path

$x_1(M)$ $x_1(M')$ Good 1

Fig. 4.1. The curve that connects the different optimal choices of the consumer for different income levels is called the *income expansion path*.

quantity as a function of price), as well as her inverse demand curve (showing price as function of quantity). In Section 4.4 we analyze the demand for good 1 as a function of the price of good 2, and in Section 4.5 we consider income and substitution effects. An *income effect* is a change in consumption attributable to a change in income, and a *substitution effect* is a change in consumption attributable to a change in relative prices. There are actually several ways to measure the substitution effect; we discuss and graph three alternative methods. In Section 4.6 we discuss compensated demand curves, and in Section 4.7 we develop the idea of *elasticity*, the economist's favored method for measuring the change in one variable (e.g., demand for good 1) in response to the change in another variable (e.g., change in p_1 or change in M). In Section 4.8 we show how the *market demand curve* is found by adding together the demand curves of individual consumers.

4.2 Demand as a Function of Income

Consider the demand function for good 1: $x_1 = x_1(p_1, p_2, M)$. In this section, p_1 and p_2 will remain fixed, so we focus on the function $x_1(M)$. That is, we are now interested in the consumer's demand for a good as a function of the consumer's income.

In Figure 4.1, as income increases (and we move farther out from the origin) the amount of good 1 that the consumer wants to consume increases. A good that

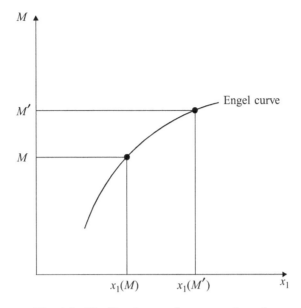

Fig. 4.2. The Engel curve for a normal good.

has this characteristic – as income rises, the consumer demands more – is called a *normal* good. As the word "normal" should suggest, many goods are normal. A richer consumer probably wants to consume a bigger house (more square feet, more bedrooms, more bathrooms, more closets, more counter space, and more cabinets), a bigger yard, and a bigger or better car; she probably wants to travel or vacation more; she may want to consume more clothes or pairs of shoes. (Have you heard of Imelda Marcos? She was the wife of the president of the Philippines, and among other character flaws, she owned thousands of pairs of shoes.) The richer consumer probably also wants to buy more entertainment, more education, and more psychotherapy.

In Figure 4.2, we draw a different picture to summarize this information. We now measure income M on the vertical axis and the desired amount of the good x_1 on the horizontal axis, and we plot the pairs (x_1, M), (x_1', M') from the income expansion path. We connect our points to form a line, which we call an *Engel curve* for good 1. (Ernst Engel (1821–1896) was a German statistician and economist who first studied these curves.)

In the Engel curve, and in other curves we discuss in this chapter, we put the independent variable on the *vertical* axis, and the dependent variable on the *horizontal* axis. This is of course absolutely contrary to standard mathematical custom, which puts the dependent variable on the vertical axis. Economists have been plotting curves the "wrong" way since a great English economist, Alfred Marshall (1842–1924), started doing it in the late nineteenth century. We apologize for Marshall.

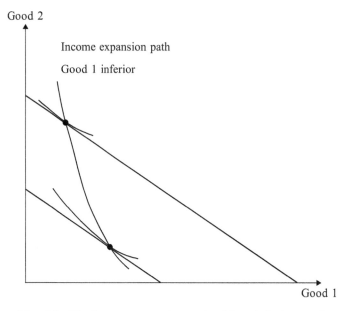

Fig. 4.3. The income expansion path with an inferior good.

Of course there are some goods that the richer consumer wants to consume less of. These are the opposite of normal goods; they are called *inferior goods*. As income rises, the consumer wants to consume less of them. Intercity bus service may be an example: as people become richer, they stop using the bus, and switch to the train, airplane, or their own cars. French fries at McDonald's may also be an inferior good (even though they are yummy!), because a consumer may go less often to McDonald's as her income rises. Figure 4.3 shows the income expansion path for an inferior good. We will not draw the (downward-sloping) Engel curve.

To complicate matters, it is really not possible for a good to be an inferior good for all levels of a consumer's income. If her income is zero, her consumption of good 1 must be zero (because we are assuming goods have positive prices). If her income is just above zero, her desired consumption of any particular good must be greater than or equal to what it was when her income was zero. Therefore, no good can be an inferior good from $M = 0$. Think of those McDonald's French fries. When the consumer is poor, as she gets a little more money, she may well buy more fries at McDonald's. But when she becomes rich enough, she will start to eat fewer and fewer fries at McDonald's. (Perhaps she will then nibble *pommes frites* at Chez Panisse.)

4.3 Demand as a Function of Price

As you recall, the consumer's demand for good 1 depends on the price of good 1, the price of good 2, and her income: $x_1 = x_1(p_1, p_2, M)$. In this section, we assume

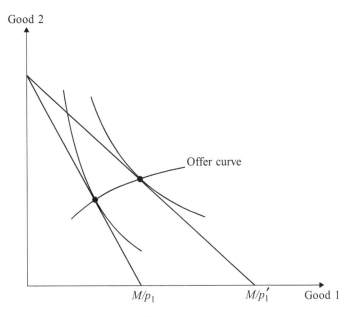

Fig. 4.4. The curve that connects the different optimal choices of the consumer for different prices is called the offer curve. This is the case of an ordinary good.

that M and p_2 are fixed. We focus on the crucial relationship between the price of good 1 and the quantity of good 1 she wants to consume: $x_1(p_1)$. Figure 4.4 shows how the consumer's desired consumption bundle (x_1, x_2) shifts as the price of good 1 falls. This exercise is repeated for various different good 1 prices to get an *offer curve*.

Remember that a "normal" good is one for which the consumer's demand rises as her income rises. We expect a rising *price* to have the opposite effect. That is, as the price of a good rises, the consumer's demand for that good usually falls. If this is true for good 1 – as p_1 rises, x_1 falls – we call good 1 an *ordinary* good.

At this point we will construct a new graph. In Figure 4.5 we again put the independent variable, now the price p_1, on the vertical axis, and the dependent variable, the amount of good 1 the consumer wants, x_1, on the horizontal axis. We plot the points (p_1, x_1), (p_1', x_1'), and so on, corresponding to the consumer's optimal choices, and connect them with a line. The result is the consumer's *demand curve*. Note that price and quantity demanded are inversely related in this graph.

Most goods are ordinary goods. That is, they obey the *law of demand*, which says that as the price goes up, the quantity demanded goes down, and as the price goes down, the quantity demanded goes up. In other words, demand curves are (ordinarily) downward sloping. However, there are examples of goods that are not ordinary, that disobey the law of demand. These are called *Giffen goods*, after Robert Giffen (1837–1910), an English statistician and economist. (Although we continue to call them Giffen goods, the attribution may be incorrect. It may have originated in Alfred Marshall's *Principles of Economics*, 3rd edition, 1895: "As

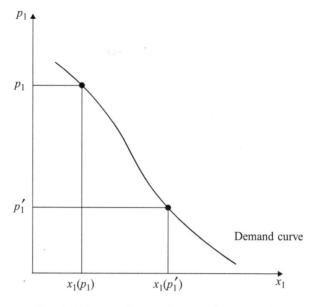

Fig. 4.5. Demand curve for an ordinary good.

Mr. Giffen has pointed out, a rise in the price of bread makes so large a drain on the resources of the poorer labouring families and raises so much the marginal utility of money to them, that they are forced to curtail their consumption of meat and the more expensive farinaceous foods: and, bread being still the cheapest food which they can get and will take, they consume more, and not less of it." In 2009, Wikipedia raised doubts about Marshall's attribution – "scholars have not been able to identify any passage in Giffen's writings where he pointed this out" – but of course others have raised doubts about Wikipedia.)

In any case, whether we call them Giffen goods or Marshall/Giffen goods, these goods violate the law of demand. The very poor consumer eats a lot of bread because she cannot afford to eat much dairy, fish, meat, and vegetables. The price of bread goes up, making her, in effect, poorer. She responds by cutting down even more on the expensive foods (and perhaps on clothing, housing, and so on). As a result, she ends up eating even more bread. In Figure 4.6, we show a Giffen good. The price p_1 rises, but the consumer's demand for good 1 actually rises.

We need to make one last comment before leaving the notion of Giffen goods. Most of us can think of people we know who consume some goods *because* they are expensive in order to show off their wealth. Perhaps this is why some people wear Rolex or Breitling watches, or drive Rolls Royce or Lamborghini cars, or sail thirty-meter yachts. This kind of demand may violate the law of demand; that is, if Rolex watches sold for $20 instead of $2,000, some consumers might want fewer of them. But these are not examples of Giffen goods. They are called *Veblen goods*, after Thorstein Veblen (1857–1929). These examples lie outside the standard economic

Good 2

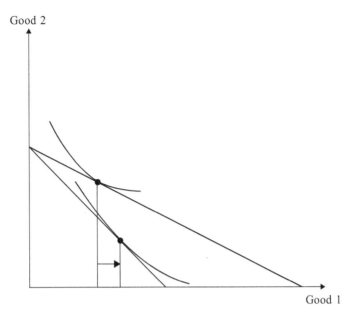

Good 1

Fig. 4.6. Two points on the offer curve, when good 1 is a Giffen good.

model of consumer behavior, in which the consumer's preferences and her utility function depend only on the intrinsic attributes of the goods she consumes, and not directly on the prices of those goods. In particular, the standard economic model does not incorporate a consumer's desire to signal her wealth by buying expensive toys. That would require a different model, and we cannot do everything in such an inexpensive textbook!

Inverse Demand

Consider again the demand curve for an ordinary good (Figure 4.5). We will sometimes want to read each point on the demand curve "vertically," instead of "horizontally" (as we have been doing so far). That is, instead of saying that at each price there is a certain amount demanded, as shown by the demand curve, we may want to say that for each amount demanded, the consumer would be willing to pay a certain price. With ordinary goods, this willingness to pay is decreasing in the amount demanded: for the consumption of a larger amount, the consumer is willing to pay a lower (per-unit) price. A demand curve looked at this way – for each quantity, there is a corresponding price – is called an *inverse demand curve*; it gives price as a function of quantity, which we write $p_1(x_1)$. We will come back to this notion when we introduce the notion of consumer's surplus.

4.4 Demand as a Function of Price of the Other Good

We are still analyzing the demand for good 1 as a function of three underlying variables, the price of good 1, the price of good 2, and the consumer's income;

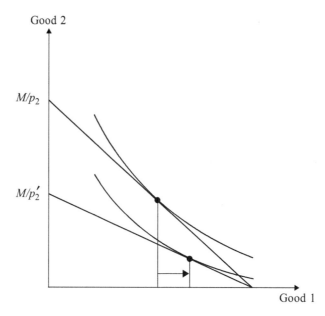

Fig. 4.7. Two points on the offer curve for substitutes; as the price of good 2 rises, the desired quantity of good 1 rises.

that is, $x_1 = x_1(p_1, p_2, M)$. In this section we fix p_1 and M, and focus on the relationship between the demand for good 1 and the price of good 2. Formally, this is $x_1(p_2)$.

Goods 1 and 2 are called *substitutes* if an increase in the price of one causes the demand for the other to increase. As relative prices change, one of the goods is substituted for the other. There are very close substitutes, and not-so-close substitutes. Exxon-Mobil gasoline and Shell gasoline are very close substitutes; the oil companies may claim they are different in some ways, but they are actually almost identical. Competing gas stations selling different brands will find that if one raises its price and the other does not, customers will abruptly shift to the service station with the lower price, whether it is Exxon-Mobil or Shell. Two drugs of the same type, such as Advil and Motrin, are substitutes. Chicken and pork (the "other white meat") are probably substitutes; as the price of one rises, the demand for the other probably increases. Figure 4.7 shows substitutes in the offer curve context. An analogous figure could be constructed in the price/quantity context, with the price of good 2 on the vertical axis and the desired quantity of good 1 on the horizontal. This would be a *cross demand* curve, but we will omit it here.

Goods 1 and 2 are called *complements* if an increase in the price of one causes the demand for the other to decrease. For instance, ink jet printers and ink cartridges are complements, cell phones and ring tones are complements, and (large) autos and gasoline are complements. In 2008, as the price of gasoline soared in the United States, the demand for large SUVs and pickup trucks plummeted, leaving some automakers in dire financial straits. Figure 4.8 shows complements in the offer curve context.

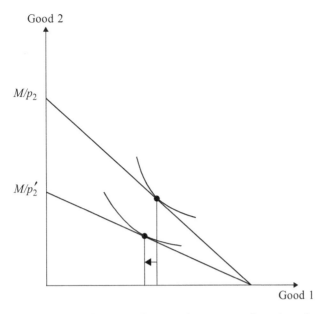

Good 2

M/p_2

M/p_2'

Good 1

Fig. 4.8. Two points on the offer curve for complements; as the price of good 2 rises, the desired quantity of good 1 falls.

A final note about "substitutes" and "complements": saying that goods 1 and 2 are "substitutes" may be trickier than one might think. It is possible, for example, that a consumer's demand for good 1 *rises* as the price of good 2 rises (suggesting that good 1 "substitutes" for good 2), while, at the same time, the consumer's demand for good 2 *falls* as the price of good 1 rises (suggesting that good 2 "complements" good 1). Here is an example. Assume that the consumer's utility function is

$$u(x_1, x_2) = (x_1 - 1)(x_2 + 1),$$

for bundles with $x_1 \geq 1$. Think of good 1 as "food," and assume that $x_1 = 1$ is the subsistence level. With 1 unit of food she is barely alive and has utility of zero; any less food means she is dead. Good 2 is "other stuff." If you sketch a graph of her indifference curves, you will see that they are asymptotic to the line $x_1 = 1$, but intersect the horizontal axis. Note that the marginal utility of good 1 is $x_2 + 1$, and the marginal utility of good 2 is $x_1 - 1$. The marginal rate of substitution is then $(x_2 + 1)/(x_1 - 1)$. Setting this equal to the price ratio gives $p_1(x_1 - 1) = p_2(x_2 + 1)$. Combining this with the standard budget constraint, $p_1 x_1 + p_2 x_2 = M$, leads to the consumer's demand functions for goods 1 and 2. The two demand functions are:

$$x_1(\cdot) = (M + p_1 + p_2)/2p_1$$

and

$$x_2(\cdot) = (M - p_1 - p_2)/2p_2.$$

From the first demand function, for food, as the price p_2 of other stuff rises, the consumer demands more food (suggesting "substitutes"). From the second demand function, for other stuff, as the price p_1 of food rises, she demands less other stuff (suggesting "complements"). The point of this example is that the terms "substitutes" and "complements" are useful for the intuitive understanding they provide. However, they are not mathematically precise terms.

4.5 Substitution and Income Effects

In Section 4.2 we discussed how a change in income affects the demand for good 1. For a normal good, an increase in income will cause an increase in the amount demanded; for an inferior good, it will cause a decrease in the amount demanded. In Section 4.3 we discussed how a change in the price of good 1 affects the demand for good 1. Generally, a decrease in the price will cause an increase in the amount demanded. However, if it is one of those rare Giffen goods, a decrease in the price will cause a decrease in the amount demanded. Let us now think more carefully about what happens to the consumer's demand for good 1 when p_1 falls while p_2 and M stay the same. We realize that there are really two parts to the change in the consumer's demand resulting from a decrease in p_1. First, the *relative price* of good 1 (that is, the price of good 1 compared with the price of good 2, or p_1/p_2) has gone down. By itself, this change should cause the consumer to switch *toward* good 1 and *away from* good 2. Second, because one price has fallen while the other price and income have remained constant, the consumer is, in effect, richer. By itself, this change should cause the consumer to want to consume more of good 1 if it is a normal good, but less of good 1 if it is an inferior good. The first effect – switch toward good 1 because it has become relatively cheaper – is called the *substitution effect*. The second effect – because you are richer, switch toward good 1 if it is normal, and away from it if it is inferior – is called the *income effect*.

In short, we are saying that if a consumer responds to a drop in p_1, that response can be broken down or decomposed into two parts: the substitution effect (the effect of the change in relative prices) and the income effect (the effect of the consumer's having become, in a sense, richer). There are (at least) two ways to approach this decomposition. The first is based on the analysis of Evgeny Slutsky (1880–1948), a Russian economist who wrote a seminal paper on consumer theory in 1915. The second is based on the analysis of the great twentieth-century English economist Sir John Hicks (1904–1989) whose influential book *Value and Capital* was published in 1939. We illustrate Slutsky's breakdown into income and substitution effects in Figure 4.9.

In Figure 4.9, when the price of good 1 falls from p_1 to p_1', the consumer moves from the original point x on the old budget line to the new point y on the new budget line. In Slutsky's decomposition, there is an intermediate (hypothetical) budget line, which has the slope of the new budget line but passes through the

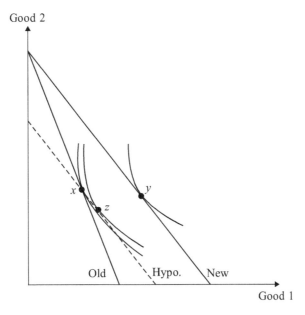

Fig. 4.9. The Slutsky substitution effect is the move from x to z; the income effect is the move from z to y.

original point x. If faced with that hypothetical budget line, the consumer would consume the (hypothetical) bundle z. Slutsky identifies the substitution effect as the move from x to z, and the income effect as the move from z to y. Note that the z-to-y move is a move between budget lines with equal slopes, and therefore, involves no changes in relative prices.

The problem with Slutsky's decomposition, according to Hicks, is this: The consumer does not like x as much as the intervening hypothetical point z. The move from the point x on the original budget line to the point y on the new budget line in effect makes the consumer richer, but this is also true of the move from the point x on the original budget line to the point z on the hypothetical budget line. As Hicks saw it, the decomposition needs a different hypothetical budget line, and a different hypothetical point z, such that the consumer is just indifferent between x and z. The hypothetical budget line should have the same slope as the new budget line, as in Slutsky's analysis. That is, it should be based on the new price ratio, rather than on the old. However, it should be tangent to the original indifference curve. All this gives rise to the next figure, which shows Hicks's breakdown into income and substitution effects. In Figure 4.10, the consumer starts at x and ends up at y. The move from x to y is decomposed into a move from x to z and a move from z to y. The x-to-z move is along the same indifference curve; it reflects a change in relative prices but leaves the consumer exactly as well off as she was before. The z-to-y move reflects a change in income only; it leaves relative prices exactly as they were, but moves the consumer to a higher budget line.

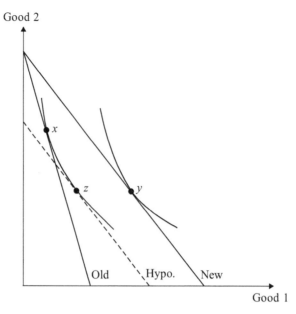

Good 2

Old   Hypo.   New

Good 1

Fig. 4.10. The Hicks substitution effect is the move from x to z; the income effect is the move from z to y.

Either figure can be used to decide whether good 1 is acting as an ordinary good or as a Giffen good. For this purpose, we need to see only whether y is to the right (ordinary good) or to the left (Giffen good) of x. To determine whether good 1 is normal or inferior, look at z compared with y; if y is to the right of z, it is normal; if y is to the left, it is inferior.

Both Slutsky and Hicks decomposed the total change in the amount of good 1 demanded into two parts: the substitution effect, showing the effect of the change in relative prices, and the income effect, showing the effect of the consumer's having become richer (or poorer, if p_1 were to rise instead of fall). Slutsky's method is still used by economists who are constructing price indexes, for example, because it is based on observables, the consumption bundles. However, for economic theorists who are interested in improvements (or reductions) in the welfare levels of consumers, the Hicks approach is better, because the points x and z in the Hicks decomposition figure are on the same indifference curve, and therefore, the move from z to y more accurately reflects the consumer's gain resulting from the price change. We will generally use the Hicks approach in this book.

As a final exercise in this section, we will now draw a substitution effect/income effect figure, Figure 4.11, under the assumption that p_1 rises instead of falls. This means that the price change makes our consumer worse off, as if her income were to fall. To complicate things further, we will show that there are really two ways to do a decomposition in the style of Hicks. In our discussion around Figures 4.9 and 4.10, we constructed a hypothetical budget line that was parallel to the new

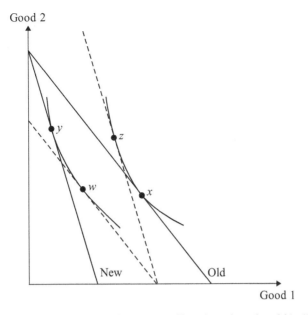

Fig. 4.11. The Hicks version of the substitution effect, based on the old indifference curve, is x to z. The Kaldor variant, based on the new indifference curve, is w to y.

budget line and tangent to the old indifference curve; that is, it incorporated the new price ratio p_1'/p_2. With equally appealing logic we could have constructed the hypothetical budget line parallel to the old budget line and tangent to the new indifference curve; that is, incorporating the old price ratio p_1/p_2. In Figure 4.11, the budget line shifts in, because p_1 rises. The Hicks substitution effect, based on the old indifference curve and the new price ratio, is the move from x to z. The slightly different substitution effect, developed by Nicholas Kaldor (1908–1986), is based on the new indifference curve, and a hypothetical budget line whose slope is given by the old price ratio. The Kaldor substitution effect is the shift from w to y. Which one is right? They both are, even though they give slightly different measurements.

It is easy to see, in any of the substitution effect/income effect figures, that the substitution effect is always negative (or at least less than or equal to zero). That is, as price goes down, quantity demanded via the substitution effect goes up, and as price goes up, quantity demanded via the substitution effect goes down. The income effect, however, can have either sign. If the good is normal, the income effect is negative. That is, as price goes down, quantity demanded via the income effect goes up. On the other hand, if the good is inferior, the income effect is positive. That is, as price goes down, quantity demanded via the income effect goes down. In short, for a normal good, the income and substitution effects work in the same direction. As price goes down, both say: consume more. However, for an inferior good, the substitution effect and the income effect work in opposite directions. As price goes down, the substitution effect says: consume more. The income effect says: consume less. The net effect is then ambiguous; if the income effect (consume less) outweighs the substitution effect (consume more), we have a Giffen good. An exercise at the end of this chapter invites the reader to construct a Hicks-style substitution effect/income effect picture of a Giffen good.

4.6 The Compensated Demand Curve

In Section 4.3 we discussed demand curves. Recall that, in the abstract, demand for good 1 is a function $x_1(p_1, p_2, M)$ of three variables. We fix two of them, p_2 and M, and we focus on how the desired quantity of good 1 depends on its price: $x_1(p_1)$. With standard demand curve analysis, we can graph a demand curve and use it to see how the desired amount of good 1 changes in response to a change in its price. We now realize that the change in the desired quantity of good 1 can be viewed as the sum of a substitution effect change and an income effect change. An alternative tool to measure demand, the *compensated demand curve*, is a modified demand curve that shows how the desired amount of good 1 changes because of the substitution effect alone.

The construction of a compensated demand curve assumes that the consumer maintains the same utility level (or stays on the same indifference curve). That is, we fix the utility level and the price p_2, and we vary the price p_1. To vary p_1 while utility is held constant, we must simultaneously vary M. (To construct a standard demand curve, p_1 is varied while p_2 and M are fixed.) The compensated demand curve construction methodology is illustrated in Figure 4.12. In the figure we show three alternative budget lines; because the absolute value of the slope of a budget line is p_1/p_2, the flattest budget corresponds to the lowest p_1 and the steepest corresponds to the highest p_1.

To construct the compensated demand curve itself (which we have not done in Figure 4.12), we would then plot the pairs (x_1, p_1), for the x_1 in Figure 4.12 and the lowest p_1, the x_1' in the figure and the middle p_1, the x_1'' in the figure and the highest p_1, and so on. It is clear from Figure 4.12 that as p_1 rises, the desired quantity of good 1 must fall. To put this another way, the moves from one desired consumption bundle to another in the figure are substitution effect moves (that is, they are moves resulting from changes in relative prices, as utility is held constant). Moreover, the compensated demand curve must be downward sloping because the substitution effect is negative.

Remember that a standard demand curve may violate the law of demand if a good is a Giffen good, with a positive income effect outweighing the negative substitution effect. A compensated demand curve, in contrast, always obeys the law of demand (it is always downward sloping), because it incorporates only the substitution effect.

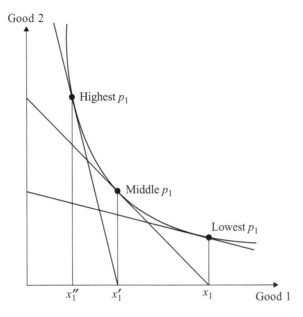

Fig. 4.12. Constructing the compensated demand curve: x_1 is chosen at the lowest p_1, x_1' is chosen at a higher p_1, and x_1'' is chosen at the highest p_1.

4.7 Elasticity

In the previous sections we talked about how the amount of good 1 demanded changes as p_1, M, or p_2 changes. In this section we introduce a standard economists' approach to measuring changes in one variable in response to changes in another variable.

Natural scientists usually measure how changes in one thing bring about changes in another thing by simply looking at ratios of those changes. For instance, if v is velocity, t is time, F is force, and m is mass, $\frac{dv}{dt} = \frac{F}{m}$. You probably remember this familiar equation from high school physics as $F = ma$, Isaac Newton's second law of motion. However, economists have traditionally been reluctant to look at ratios such as dx_1/dp_1 because these ratios are sensitive to units: an equation would change if the measurement of x_1 were changed from ounces to pounds, grams, or kilograms, or if the measurement of dp_1 were changed from U.S. dollars to Australian dollars, euros, or yen. However, if the ratios are of the form (percentage change in x_1)/(percentage change in p_1), they become pure numbers, free of units. The ratios can be used no matter what the commodity units or the currency units may be.

For this reason, economists usually look at what we call *elasticities*. The *elasticity* of A with respect to B is the percentage change in A divided by the percentage change in B. Or, to put it more intuitively, it is the percentage change in A for a 1 percent change in B. We now consider the elasticity of demand for good 1 with respect to the price of good 1, or the price elasticity of demand, for short.

Intuitively, the price elasticity of demand is the percentage change in the amount demanded as the price changes by 1 percent. Because demand goes down as price goes up, if the price increases by 1 percent, the demand will decrease by some percentage. That is, the changes are in opposite directions. To avoid having to worry too much about pluses and minuses, positive and negative changes, we focus on magnitudes, or absolute values. To be precise, then, the price elasticity of demand is the absolute value of the ratio of the percentage increase in the amount demanded to the percentage increase in price. We say that demand is *elastic* if the elasticity is greater than 1. We say that demand is *inelastic* if the elasticity is less than 1.

We start at a point (p_1, x_1) on the demand curve. Let dp_1 represent a change in the price p_1, and let dx_1 represent the resulting change in quantity demanded. Note that if $dp_1 > 0$, then $dx_1 < 0$, and conversely, if $dp_1 < 0$, then $dx_1 > 0$. The percentage change in price is

$$\frac{dp_1}{p_1} \times 100.$$

The percentage change in quantity is

$$\frac{dx_1}{x_1} \times 100.$$

One percentage change will be positive (an increase), and the other will be negative (a decrease). We use the symbol ϵ_{x_1,p_1} for the *price elasticity of demand*. We now have:

$$\epsilon_{x_1,p_1} = \left| \frac{\frac{dx_1}{x_1} \times 100}{\frac{dp_1}{p_1} \times 100} \right| = -\frac{dx_1}{dp_1} \frac{p_1}{x_1}.$$

Clearly, the price elasticity of demand is *related to* the (absolute value of the inverse of the) slope of the demand curve, $(-dx_1/dp_1)$, but it is not *equal to* it. This is because elasticity is a ratio of *percentage* changes, rather than a ratio of changes. We illustrate with the following example.

Example. Consider a very simple linear demand curve (Figure 4.13): $x_1(p_1) = 100 - p_1$. Note that dx_1/dp_1 is constant for any linear demand curve, and equals -1 for this one. It follows that $\epsilon_{x_1,p_1} = \frac{p_1}{x_1}$ will equal 1 at the midpoint (50,50).

Relationship between Price Elasticity of Demand and Consumer's Expenditure on the Good

The amount the consumer spends on good 1 is $E_1(p_1) = p_1 x_1(p_1)$, where $x_1(p_1)$ is the quantity demanded as a function of price. Let's see how the consumer's expenditure on good 1 changes as p_1 increases. We take the derivative of E_1 with

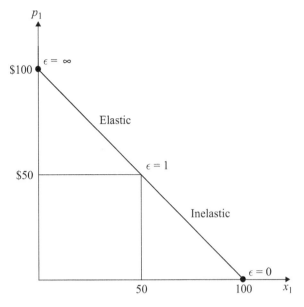

Fig. 4.13. Price elasticity for a linear demand curve. In the elastic region $\epsilon > 1$. In the inelastic region $\epsilon < 1$.

respect to p_1:

$$\frac{dE_1}{dp_1} = x_1 + p_1(dx_1/dp_1) = x_1(1 - \epsilon_{x_1,p_1}).$$

This means that after a price increase, the consumer's spending on a good increases if $\epsilon_{x_1,p_1} < 1$, stays constant if $\epsilon_{x_1,p_1} = 1$, and decreases if $\epsilon_{x_1,p_1} > 1$. When the consumer's demand for a good is inelastic (for instance, a low-wage working person's demand for a very necessary commodity such as bread or fuel), then as the price goes up, the consumer will spend more on that good. However, if the consumer's demand is elastic (for instance, a person's demand for a good that can easily be done without, such as exotic vacation trips), then as the price goes up, the consumer will spend less on that good.

4.8 The Market Demand Curve

Everything we have done so far involves only one consumer. The *market demand* for good 1 is the sum of the demands for good 1 of all the consumers. Suppose, for example, there are 100 people, and they all have the simple linear demand curve described previously, $x_1(p_1) = 100 - p_1$. How would we find the market demand curve? It is very simple: We need to remember only that demand is a function of price, so price is the independent variable and demand is the dependent variable. In other words, given p_1, we need to sum the x_1s, and not vice versa. The market

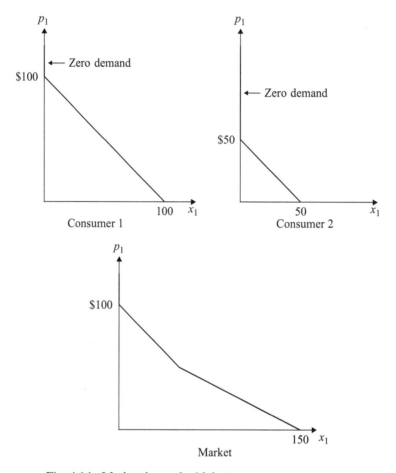

Fig. 4.14. Market demand with heterogeneous consumers.

demand equation is therefore

$$D_1(p_1) = \sum_{i=1}^{100} x_1^i(p_1) = 100(100 - p_1) = 10{,}000 - 100p_1.$$

Because we are putting the dependent variable on the horizontal axis (following Marshall) instead of the vertical axis (the standard mathematical convention), if we are doing the summation graphically, we must be careful to sum the curves horizontally instead of vertically. We must also be careful to remember that a consumer cannot consume a *negative* quantity of good 1, and so, for example, if the demand function is $x_1 = 50 - p_1$ and if $p_1 = 75$, the consumer will not want to consume -25 units of good 1; she will want zero units. The following example (shown in Figure 4.14) illustrates this hazard. Assume there are only two consumers in the market. The first one has demand for good 1 given by $x_1^1 = 100 - p_1$; the second one has demand for good 1 given by $x_1^2(p_1) = 50 - p_1$. Adding together the x_1s is the right thing to do; adding the p_1s would be wrong. (Graphically, add horizontally, not vertically.) This gives

$$D_1(p_1) = x_1^1 + x_1^2 = 150 - 2p_1.$$

This equation is fine if $p_1 \leq 50$. For instance, if $p_1 = 25$, the market demand equation gives $150 - 50 = 100$, which equals consumer 1's demand (75) plus consumer 2's demand (25). However, if you plug $p_1 = 75$ into the market demand equation, you get zero, which is wrong. The difficulty is that when $p_1 = 75$, the second consumer's demand is zero, not -25.

We can avoid all this confusion if we proceed as follows. When there are two (or more) consumers, some of whose demand curves hit the vertical axis, first, carefully sketch the individual demand curves and include, as part of those demand curve graphs, the zero demand part. Second, add the curves horizontally.

4.9 A Solved Problem

Problem

The Cobb-Douglas utility function $u(x, y) = x^a y^{1-a}$, where $0 \leq a \leq 1$, represents a consumer's preferences for tickets to baseball games (x) and football games (y). We'll call our consumer Mr. CD. Suppose that CD's income is M, and that the ticket prices are p_x and p_y.

(a) Derive the demand functions for baseball and football tickets. Indicate whether these goods are normal or inferior, ordinary or Giffen, and whether x and y are complements or substitutes.

(b) Can you describe in words the preferences corresponding to $a = 0$ and $a = 1$? If $a = 1/2$?

The Solution

(a) First we use the utility maximization condition $MRS = MU_x/MU_y = p_x/p_y$. This gives

$$MRS = \frac{MU_x}{MU_y} = \frac{ax^{a-1}y^{1-a}}{(1-a)x^a y^{-a}} = \frac{ay}{(1-a)x} = \frac{p_x}{p_y}.$$

From this we get

$$p_x x = \frac{a}{1-a} p_y y.$$

We then substitute this expression for $p_x x$ into the equation for the budget line, $p_x x + p_y y = M$. This gives

$$\frac{a}{1-a} p_y y + p_y y = \frac{a}{1-a} p_y y + \frac{1-a}{1-a} p_y y = \frac{1}{1-a} p_y y = M.$$

It follows that Mr. CD's demand functions for football tickets and baseball tickets are, respectively,

$$y(\cdot) = (1-a)\frac{M}{p_y} \quad \text{and} \quad x(\cdot) = a\frac{M}{p_x}.$$

This implies that the goods are normal; for each good, as income M goes up, the quantity demanded goes up. Also, the goods are neither complements nor substitutes; the fact that the price of one rises (or falls) has no effect on the demand for the other.

(b) If $a = 0$, Mr. CD gets no utility from x, all he cares about is y, and whatever money he has, he spends on y. If $a = 1$, he cares only about x, and whatever money he has, he spends on x. If $a = 1/2$, he will always spend half his money on x and half on y, no matter what the prices might be.

$$MRS = \frac{x_2}{x_1} = \frac{P_1}{P_2} \qquad x_2 = \frac{P_1 x_1}{P_2}$$

Exercises

$$x_1 = \frac{M}{2P_1}$$

1. Consider the utility function $u(x_1, x_2) = x_1 x_2$.
   (a) Show that the demand function for good 1 is $x_1(p_1, p_2, M) = M/2p_1$.
   (b) Is good 1 normal or inferior? Ordinary or Giffen? Are goods 1 and 2 substitutes or complements? $Income > 0$

2. Consider the utility function $u(x_1, x_2) = x_1 x_2$. Suppose the initial situation is given by $p_1 = 1$, $p_2 = 1$ and $M = 10$.
   (a) If the price of good 1 rises to 2.50, show that the total effect on the consumer's demand for good 1 equals -3.
   (b) Using the Hicks method, show that the total effect can be decomposed into a substitution effect of $-(5 - \sqrt{10})$, and an income effect of $-(\sqrt{10} - 2)$.

3. Suppose the price of a Giffen good falls. Draw a Hicks-style graph showing the income and substitution effects.

4. Professor WL always drinks exactly one cup of coffee (good x) with exactly one spoonful of sugar (good y). He never varies the 1-to-1 proportions. His preferences for the two goods can be represented by the utility function $u(x, y) = \min(x, y)$. (WL stands for Wassily Leontief (1905–1999), an economist who first analyzed functions of this type.) Notice that this utility function is not differentiable when $x = y$. (That is, the partial derivatives of u do not exist if $x = y$). Suppose WL's income is 2, the price of a cup of coffee is 0.20, and the price of a spoonful of sugar is 0.05.
   (a) Find WL's optimal consumption point.
   (b) Suppose that, owing to new import taxes, the prices go up to 0.25 and 0.08 for coffee and sugar, respectively. (The taxes are 0.05 per cup of coffee and 0.03 per spoonful of sugar.) Find WL's new optimal consumption point. How much will he be paying in taxes?
   (c) Derive his demand functions for cups of coffee and spoonsful of sugar. Are the goods normal or inferior, ordinary or Giffen, substitutes or complements?

5. Sammy and Jimmy are twin brothers. Each gets a weekly allowance of $2. Sammy's preferences for baseball cards (good x) and "famous economists" cards (good y) can be represented by the utility function $u(x, y) = xy$. Suppose that both goods are $1 per unit.

$\frac{y}{x} = 1$

$u = 1 \quad x = y = 1$

$\frac{y}{x} = \frac{2}{1}$

$y = 2x$

$x + y = 2$

$x = \frac{2}{3} \quad y = \frac{4}{3}$

(a) Solve for Sammy's optimal consumption bundle.

(b) Suppose p_x rises to $2. What is Sammy's new optimal consumption point?

(c) How much would his parents have to increase his allowance in order to leave him exactly as well off as he was originally?

$2x^2 = 1 \quad x = \frac{\sqrt{2}}{2} \quad y = \sqrt{2} \quad : M = 2\sqrt{2}$

(d) Jimmy's preferences are represented by $v(x, y) = \ln(x) + \ln(y)$. Answer parts (a), (b), and (c) for Jimmy. Comment.

$(1,1) \quad u = 0$

6. Ernie and Bert, Inc., sells cookies (good x) and bananas (good y). They are offering the following deal to their customers. The price of bananas is fixed at $1 each. The first three cookies that a consumer buys are free; after the third cookie, the price of cookies is also $1 each. Cookie Monster's utility function is $u(x, y) = x(y + 3)$ and his income is $5.

(a) Draw Cookie Monster's budget line.

M

(b) Find his optimal consumption point.

AA $\quad \frac{x}{y} = 1$

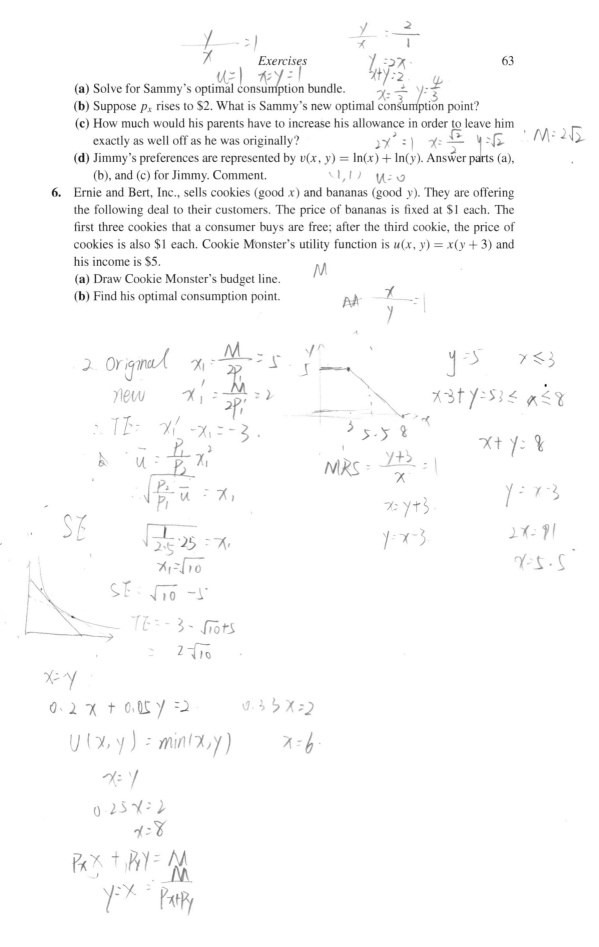

2. Original $x_1 = \frac{M}{2P_1} = 5$

new $x_1' = \frac{M}{2P_1'} = 2$

$\therefore TE = x_1' - x_1 = -3.$

$\frac{-}{u} = \frac{P_1}{P_2} x_1^2$

$\sqrt{\frac{P_2}{P_1} \bar{u}} = x_1$

$\sqrt{\frac{1}{2.5} \cdot 25} = x_1$

$x_1 = \sqrt{10}$

SE $= \sqrt{10} - 5$

$TE = -3 - \sqrt{10} + 5$

$= 2\sqrt{10}$

$y = 5 \quad x \leq 3$

$x - 3 + y = 5 \Rightarrow 3 \leq x \leq 8$

$x + y = 8$

MRS $= \frac{y + 3}{x} = 1$

$x = y + 3.$

$y = x - 3.$

$y = x - 3$

$2x = 11$

$x = 5.5$

$x = y$

$0.2x + 0.05y = 2 \qquad 0.33x = 2$

$U(x, y) = \min(x, y) \qquad x = 6.$

$x = y$

$0.25x = 2$

$x = 8$

$P_x x + P_y y = M$

$y = x = \frac{M}{P_x + P_y}$

Chapter 5

Supply Functions for Labor and Savings

5.1 Introduction to the Supply of Labor

In addition to creating the demand for goods and services, individuals also supply key factors of production to firms. In particular, they supply their labor, and, by saving, they supply capital (i.e., money) to producers. In the first part of this chapter we study the decisions involving consumption and leisure, which are behind the supply of labor. We model the standard budget constraint for the consumption/leisure choice, which involves the wage rate, consumption, and the time spent working versus the time spent on leisure. We also model some special budget constraints, for example, those involving nonlabor income. We analyze the effects of income taxation on the consumer's labor/leisure choice. This analysis has some very interesting implications about the relative desirability of flat and progressive income taxes.

We then turn to the consumer's decisions regarding the supply of savings. We discuss borrowing and saving, and revisit intertemporal budget constraints such as the ones introduced in Chapter 3. Savings flow through the financial system and end up (hopefully) as part of the capital used by firms to produce more goods and services. We model the consumer's savings decision, and show how the amount the consumer saves depends on the interest rate and the inflation rate, as well as on the timing of the consumer's income stream.

5.2 Choice between Consumption and Leisure

We now explain how a consumer decides how much labor to supply. In our simple model, he allocates his time between working and not working. If he works, he earns a wage; with his wage, he can consume. We assume he works to earn money with which to consume. This is, of course, a simplistic model of why people work. Some scholars might say that people work for the sake of working, that working is moral and not working is immoral, and that "idle hands do the devil's work." That is, people should and would work even without pay. (The great English philosopher and logician Bertrand Russell (1872–1970) takes the opposite view in *In Praise of Idleness*, in which he writes, "I hope that, after reading the following pages, the leaders of the YMCA will start a campaign to induce good young men to do nothing. If so, I shall not have lived in vain.") For the most part, economists are on Russell's side; work is not its own reward; "hours of work" is a bad rather than a good. In fact, it is apparent that people usually need to be paid in order to work at least most of the hours they are working.

In our modeling of the decision about how much labor the worker supplies, there are two "goods." One is consumption, and the other is *leisure*, that is, the time spent not working. The worker gets utility from consuming stuff, and from leisure. To consume more stuff he needs to spend more time working, which means less leisure. We let c represent consumption. A unit of consumption is a certain quantity of goods and services. We let p be the price per unit of consumption. We let L represent leisure. (This is leisure per unit time. If the standard time interval is a day, then L is leisure hours per day, e.g., 16 hours.) The consumer's utility depends on (L, c). In the graphs that follow, we will put leisure L on the horizontal axis and consumption c on the vertical axis. We let T represent the number of hours in a standard time interval – for example, $T = 24$ per day. We let l represent hours of work per standard time interval, such as 8 hours per day. The individual looks for his most preferred (L, c) bundle subject to a budget constraint, and this leads to his decision about l; that is, how much time to spend working. Note that we are assuming the consumer can freely choose the number of hours he works. This may not be true if, for example, there is a fixed number of hours in a work day.

The Budget Constraint

Recall the standard budget constraint for a consumer with income M, who is choosing quantities of goods 1 and 2, with prices p_1 and p_2:

$$p_1 x_1 + p_2 x_2 \leq M.$$

To find the budget constraint in our consumption/leisure model, we need one more crucial ingredient. Our consumer earns money by working. We let w represent the *wage rate*, in dollars per hour. If the consumer's income is exclusively from working, it is given by wl. A budget constraint says, "What you spend is less than or equal to what you have." This gives

$$pc \leq wl.$$

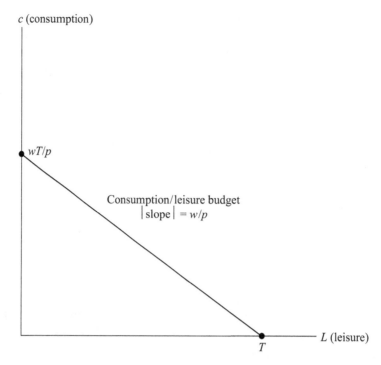

Fig. 5.1. The budget constraint for leisure and consumption.

However, hours of labor plus hours of leisure must equal the total number of hours per standard time interval, or

$$l + L = T.$$

Substituting for l in the budget constraint and rearranging slightly then gives

$$wL + pc \leq wT.$$

This constraint looks very much like the standard budget constraint shown earlier, and has a nice interpretation. It is as if the consumer's total income is what he would get by working all the time available (for example, 24 hours per day). With this total income, the consumer buys stuff c, at a price of p per unit, and also buys leisure, at a price of w per hour. Economists say that the wage rate is the *opportunity cost of leisure*. For each hour of leisure you choose to consume, you forgo w dollars in income, which you would have gotten if you had worked that hour.

Figure 5.1 shows the budget line with L on the horizontal axis and c on the vertical axis.

By construction, the horizontal intercept of the budget line is at T. A consumer at this point is consuming all leisure and no goods; this is the choice of maximum idleness, the *super slacker* choice. The vertical intercept of the budget line is at wT/p; this is the choice of maximum work, the *super go-getter* choice. The absolute value of the slope of the budget line, or w/p, is the relative price of leisure

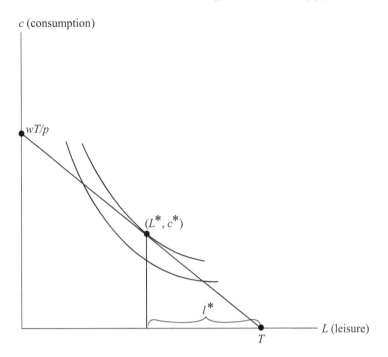

Fig. 5.2. The consumer's optimal choice of leisure and consumption is at (L^*, c^*).

in terms of consumption, or the *real wage*. The real wage is the amount of extra stuff you can consume if you work an extra hour.

Preferences

What about preferences? We continue to make the basic assumptions on preferences that were made in Chapter 2. In particular, both consumption and leisure are considered desirable goods. We assume the usual well-behaved preferences, with downward-sloping and convex indifference curves. Of course, there may be extreme kinds of preferences, such as those of the super go-getter (with horizontal or almost horizontal indifference curves), or those of the super slacker (whose indifference curves are vertical or almost vertical). Figure 5.2 shows the utility-maximizing choice of a typical individual, who spends part of his day working and consumes a positive amount of stuff. The consumer's optimal choice is at the point (L^*, c^*), which means that he wants to work l^* hours, to have L^* hours of leisure, and to consume c^*.

5.3 Substitution and Income Effects in Labor Supply

In Chapter 4 we discussed demand functions. We can do something similar in our consumption/leisure model. We can view w and p as variables, and we can find the corresponding demand functions for utility-maximizing consumption $c^* = c(w, p)$

and leisure $L^* = L(w, p)$. Once we have the leisure demand function, the labor supply function follows easily, because $l^*(w, p) = T - L^*(w, p)$. That is, given the wage rate and price of consumption, we can find the amount of time the consumer wants to spend working. If p is fixed and only w is allowed to vary, then labor supply $l^*(w)$ is simply a function of the wage rate w.

This labor supply function can be graphed in the conventional (for economists) way, with w on the vertical axis and the consumer's labor supply $l^*(w)$ on the horizontal axis. Such a graph is called a *labor supply curve*. Should a labor supply curve have a positive slope (higher wage implies more labor) or a negative slope (higher wage means less labor)? We will answer this question shortly.

In Chapter 4 we also discussed income and substitution effects and normal, inferior, ordinary, and Giffen goods. As the price p_1 of good 1 rises, by the substitution effect, the consumer will want less of it, and by the income effect, he will want less of it, provided it is a *normal good*. The net effect is that as p_1 goes up, x_1^* goes down. The demand curve is downward sloping. If x_1 is an inferior good, then the net effect of a rise in p_1 is ambiguous.

We now turn to a similar analysis. How does the wage rate w affect the consumer's desired consumption of leisure L^*, and his decision about how much time to spend working $l^* = T - L^*$? You might think this discussion should be an easy application of what we already did in Chapter 4. As w goes up, the consumer wants less leisure and wants to supply more labor. However, the analysis we now do is different and slightly complicated, for a mathematically simple reason. Compare the Chapter 4 budget constraint,

$$p_1 x_1 + p_2 x_2 \leq M,$$

with the budget constraint we are now analyzing:

$$wL + pc \leq wT.$$

The reason that what we do now is not an obvious and simple extension of the Chapter 4 analysis is that as w changes, both the left-hand side and the right-hand side of the budget constraint change. With that warning, we can proceed.

Let us assume that we have an initial situation in which the consumer is maximizing utility subject to a budget constraint, as in Figure 5.2. Now, suppose the wage rate goes up, from w to w'. How will this affect his demand for leisure and his supply of labor?

Figure 5.3 shows the substitution effect. When the wage rate rises, the consumer will substitute consumption for leisure; he will want to consume more and spend less time at leisure and more time at work.

However, if leisure is a normal good, as the wage rate rises, the consumer will want to consume more leisure. That is, as w rises and the substitution effect says "consume less leisure," the income effect says "consume more leisure." This is because the right-hand side of the budget constraint, wT, also rises. The net effect

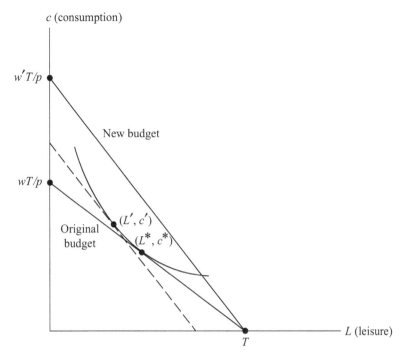

Fig. 5.3. The substitution effect on the demand for leisure, or the supply of labor. When the wage rate rises the consumer wants less leisure (the substitution effect is $L' - L^* < 0$) and he wants to work more hours.

of an increase in w will therefore be ambiguous, and by the same token, the net effect on the consumer's amount of work supplied, l^*, will be ambiguous.

If the substitution effect is larger than the income effect, then a rise in w will lead to the choice of less leisure and more time at work. If this happens, the consumer's labor supply curve is upward sloping (higher w leads to higher l^*). Figure 5.4 shows this case. We will leave it to the reader to draw a graph of the case where the substitution effect is smaller than the income effect, and an increase in w results in a decrease in l^*, so that the labor supply curve is downward sloping.

Some empirical studies find that for low levels of the wage rate, the substitution effect dominates. But as the wage rate (and hence income) increases, the income effect becomes more and more important, and it finally overcomes the substitution effect. In this case, the consumer wants to consume less leisure (and wants to work more) as w rises when w is low, but eventually, when w is high enough, he wants to consume more leisure (and wants to work less) as w rises. This results in what economists call a *backward-bending labor supply curve*.

5.4 Other Types of Budget Constraints

This section is devoted to describing the shapes of more elaborate and more realistic kinds of budget constraints in the consumption/leisure model.

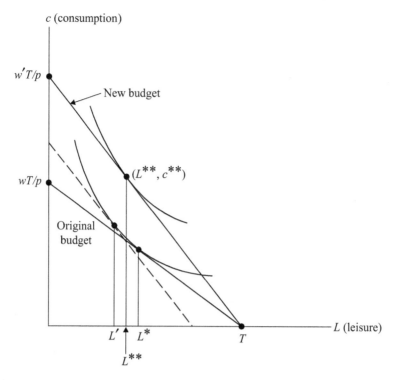

Fig. 5.4. The income effect is outweighed by the substitution effect. By the substitution effect, the consumer wants less leisure ($L' < L^*$) and by the income effect, the consumer wants more leisure ($L' < L^{**}$). But the substitution effect is bigger, so the consumer ends up with less leisure ($L^{**} < L^*$), i.e., with more hours of work.

Nonlabor Income

Suppose the consumer receives nonlabor income of M dollars per time interval. This might be an allowance from his parents, an inheritance, a welfare check, or income from securities or bank accounts. Then, the budget constraint becomes

$$pc \leq w(T - L) + M$$

if $T - L > 0$, and

$$pc \leq M$$

if $T - L = 0$. Rearranging terms in the first equation produces

$$wL + pc \leq wT + M.$$

Figure 5.5 shows this budget constraint.

We can perform a comparative statics exercise to see what happens when M changes. For instance, suppose the consumer originally has zero nonlabor income and then receives an inheritance. What happens to his labor supply? Figure 5.6

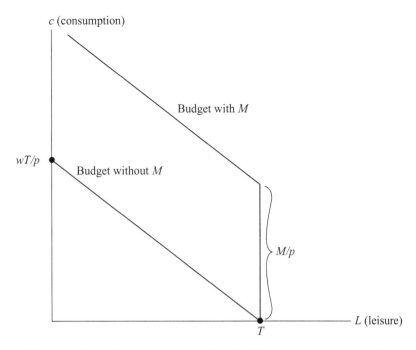

Fig. 5.5. The budget constraint with and without nonlabor income M.

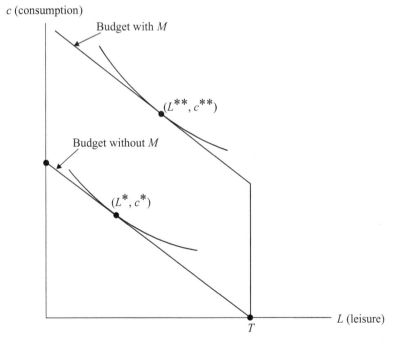

Fig. 5.6. If leisure is normal, the consumer will work less (that is, take more leisure) after receiving an inheritance of M.

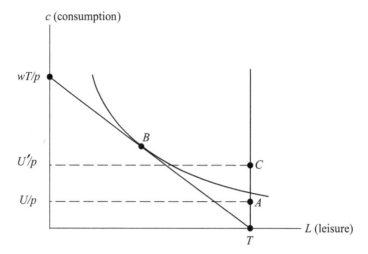

Fig. 5.7. Budget constraints with unemployment benefits. The benefit U has no effect on behavior because the point A is below the indifference curve through B. But U' is large enough to cause the consumer to choose not to work, because the point C is above that indifference curve.

shows the answer; if leisure is a normal good, when $M > 0$ is given to the consumer, he works less.

Unemployment Benefits

Governments often provide unemployment benefits to people who are not working. We start by assuming a fixed unemployment benefit U, provided to the consumer if and only if he is not working; that is, at $L = T$. We will assume no nonlabor income M. The budget constraint is

$$pc \leq w(T - L)$$

if $L < T$, and

$$pc \leq U$$

if $L = T$. Note that the benefit is entirely lost if he does any work at all. In Figure 5.7, with an unemployment benefit equal to U, if the consumer doesn't work, he will be at point A. If he does work, he will be at point B, at the tangency point of his budget constraint and his indifference curve. Note that A is below the indifference curve that goes through B. Therefore, he prefers B to A, so he will work when the benefit is U. But now suppose the unemployment benefit is U'. Because point C is above the indifference curve that goes through B, the consumer prefers C to B. Therefore, he will choose not to work when the benefit is U'. In short, the presence of a large enough unemployment benefit may motivate the consumer to stop working.

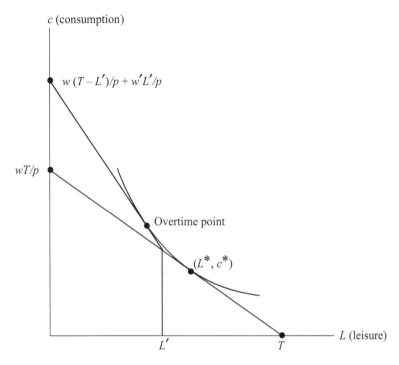

Fig. 5.8. A budget constraint with overtime pay for work hours beyond $T - L'$. Given this overtime rate w', this consumer is indifferent between working overtime (and getting to the "overtime point"), and working no overtime (and getting to the point (L^*, c^*)).

Overtime

Firms (governments and others) often pay overtime to employees who work more than a standard number of hours per week (e.g., more than 40 hours per week). Under these contracts, the wage rate increases after the standard number of hours. For example, it might go from w to $1.5w$. (This would be a 50 percent overtime premium, or "time and a half" for overtime.) Figure 5.8 shows how an overtime premium affects the consumer's budget line. In the figure, the consumer is paid w per hour for up to $T - L'$ hours of work, and $w' > w$ per hour for hours of work beyond $T - L'$. Note that the absolute value of the slope of the budget line is w/p in the part of the budget line without overtime, and w'/p in the overtime part. In the figure, the overtime wage rate w' is just high enough so that this worker is indifferent between working overtime (at the "overtime point") or not working overtime (and ending up at the point (L^*, c^*).

Because the consumer with the indifference curve shown in Figure 5.8 is indifferent between the overtime point and (L^*, c^*), the w' used in the figure must be the minimum wage rate that the consumer has to be offered to get him to work overtime. (Remember we are assuming the consumer can choose the number of hours he works.) At the overtime wage w', the consumer is indifferent between working overtime and not working overtime. At higher overtime wage rates, the consumer will work overtime. We leave it to the reader to draw an example.

5.5 Taxing the Consumer's Wages

The consumption/leisure model reveals some interesting problems with taxation. One of the principal sources of government revenue throughout the world is the taxation of workers' earnings. In the United States, federal income taxes are largely derived from the earnings of employees, and Social Security taxes are largely taxes on wages (and are therefore called *payroll taxes*).

An important characteristic of taxation of earnings in the United States and in most other countries is progressivity. A taxpayer's *average tax* is the fraction of his income that he must pay as tax. A tax on income is said to be *progressive* if, as the taxpayer's income rises, his average tax rises. In the United States, for instance, the federal income tax involves brackets with increasing rates. For a single individual in 2011, the first $8,500 in taxable income is taxed at a rate of 10 percent (i.e., each additional dollar adds $0.10 to one's tax bill), the next $26,000 is taxed at a rate of 15 percent (i.e., each additional dollar adds $0.15 to one's tax bill), and so on. There are six tax brackets, with the bracket rates rising from a low of 10 percent at the lowest bracket to a high of 35 percent at the highest bracket (which starts when taxable income is $379,150). The increasing bracket rates produce a progressive tax, once the taxpayer goes beyond the first bracket.

Social Security taxes in the United States, however, are not progressive. For Social Security, all wages up to a certain ceiling ($106,800 in 2011) are subject to the same flat rate; beyond the ceiling, the tax stops. Once the taxpayer's income has risen beyond the ceiling, the Social Security tax is *regressive*, which means that as income rises, his average tax falls. (This does not mean that the Social Security system as a whole – taxes plus benefits financed by those taxes – is regressive. In fact, the system as a whole, taxes plus benefits, is very progressive.) Medicare taxes in the United States provide a good example of a *flat tax*; all the worker's earnings are taxed at the same rate for Medicare, from the first dollar to the billionth and beyond. (For a typical employed person, both the Social Security tax and the Medicare tax are split equally between the employee and the employer, with the total rate, of Social Security tax plus Medicare tax, for someone whose wages do not exceed the Social Security ceiling, equal to 15.3 percent since 1990. (In 2011 and 2012, there was a temporary 2 percent cut in the employee rate.)

Obviously, whether taxes are progressive, flat, or regressive is vitally important to workers, to the government, to the economy, and to society. This is an important political issue, and always will be. We can illustrate some parts of the controversy with our model.

Let us now assume a very simple progressive tax system with only two brackets: 0 percent for income below a certain threshold, and 50 percent for all income above the threshold. Let us set the threshold so that our consumer must work exactly $T/3$

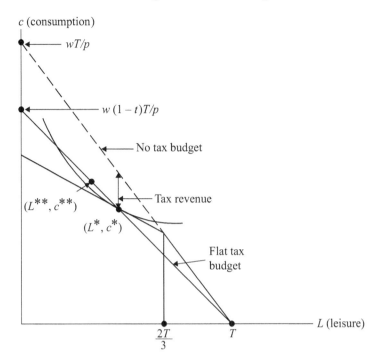

Fig. 5.9. Budget constraint with progressive tax (two brackets), showing that the flat tax is better for this consumer, better for the government, and results in more hours of work by the consumer.

hours per standard time interval to reach it. (For instance, if the standard time interval is a day, so $T = 24$ and $T/3 = 8$, and w is the hourly wage rate, the threshold is at $8w$ dollars per day. If $w = \$15$, and a worker works 5 days per week and 52 weeks per year, then we are assuming the threshold income is at $8 \times 15 \times 5 \times 52 = \$31{,}200$ per year. With these numbers, the consumer would pay no income tax on the first \$31,200 in (annual) income, and \$0.50 in income tax on each dollar above \$31,200.)

In Figure 5.9, we show the consumer's budget constraint, and a choice (L^*, c^*) that involves his earning enough that he is subject to the income tax. Now consider what would happen to this particular consumer if the two-bracket tax is replaced with a flat tax, at a rate t. With such a tax, the consumer's budget constraint is replaced by a straight line, with intercept T on the horizontal axis and $w(1 - t)T/p$ on the vertical axis. The slope of this budget line is $w(1 - t)/p$ in absolute value. Now assume that the rate t is so cleverly chosen that the new straight-line budget constraint goes exactly through the point (L^*, c^*). This makes the transition from the progressive tax to the flat tax *neutral* for this consumer, in the sense that if he wanted to, he could continue to consume exactly the same leisure/consumption combination that he used to consume.

Looking at Figure 5.9, three remarkable conclusions become apparent: (1) This consumer is better off when the two-bracket progressive tax is replaced by the flat tax. (2) This consumer works more hours after the change. (3) The government collects more income tax from this consumer after the change.

Conclusion (1) is because the flat tax budget line must cross the consumer's indifference curve at (L^*, c^*). Therefore, the consumer can find a new optimum on a higher indifference curve. Conclusion (2) is because the chosen point under the flat tax, call it (L^{**}, c^{**}), must lie to the left of (L^*, c^*). Therefore, $L^{**} < L^*$, and it follows that $l^{**} > l^*$. For conclusion (3), note that for any given L and $l = T - L$, going straight up to the no-tax budget line gives wl/p, the consumer's gross earnings expressed in units of consumption. And going straight up to the flat-tax budget line gives the consumer's net-of-flat-tax earnings $w(1 - t)l/p$, expressed in units of consumption. The vertical difference between the no-tax budget and the flat-tax budget, for a given L and $l = T - L$, is therefore wtl/p, or how much the government is collecting from this consumer, measured in units of consumption. This vertical difference increases as we move to the left.

Given this remarkable triplet of conclusions, that the consumer is better off, works more, and pays more taxes under flat taxes, why haven't all progressive taxes in the world been abandoned? One answer is that although Figure 5.9 is a convincing argument for one person, it is an argument for *just one person*. Imagine a second consumer, similar to the one whose budget appears in Figure 5.9, but one who earns half the wage. Under the progressive two-bracket tax, person 2 would most likely pay no income taxes at all (unless he worked more than 16 hours per day, which would be unusual). The introduction of the flat tax would therefore make him worse off. The conclusion is that although replacing progressive taxes with flat (or flatter) taxes is desirable for high earners and even average earners (possibly causing high earners to work more hours, and possibly causing government revenues to increase), it may make low earners worse off.

5.6 Saving and Borrowing: The Intertemporal Choice of Consumption

In the previous sections of this chapter, we analyzed a consumption/leisure model of consumer behavior to draw conclusions about a consumer's decision to supply his time and labor. He sells his labor for wages in the *labor market*. In the following sections, we consider how the consumer interacts with the *capital market*. This is the market (or markets) where the consumer puts his savings, or where he goes to borrow. We will show how the consumer decides how much money to save and lend to others (his *supply of savings*), or how much money to borrow from others. To do this, we revisit the discussion of budget constraints over time laid out in Section 3.5. A budget constraint over time is called, more elegantly, an *intertemporal budget constraint*. It shows how much a consumer can consume today, and how much he can consume in the future. That is, it shows the tradeoff between consumption this year and consumption next year. The consumer's decision about this tradeoff will immediately lead to his decision about how much to save, or how much to borrow.

We start by assuming that there are two time periods, which can be called "today" and "tomorrow," "this year" and "next year," or "year one" and "year two." In Chapter 3, we had labeled consumption in the two years x_1 and x_2, respectively, but in this chapter we will use c_1 and c_2 to make the notation similar to that used in our discussion of the consumption/leisure model. Thus, c_1 is the number of units of goods and services, or "stuff," that our person consumes this year, and c_2 is the number of units he consumes next year. A unit of stuff this year is the same amount of stuff as a unit next year; the only difference is the timing.

We will again assume, as we did in Chapter 3, that a unit of stuff this year costs \$1, or $p_1 = 1$. Now, however, we will allow for inflation. The inflation rate is π, expressed as a decimal. (We use π for inflation in this chapter, but in Chapter 8 and later chapters it will be used for profit.) Therefore, the price of a unit of stuff next year is $p_2 = 1 + \pi$. In most of Chapter 3, we assumed no inflation, and the price of stuff this year and next year were equal, at \$1 per unit. In this chapter that is no longer true.

We will let M_1 represent the consumer's income this year, in dollars, and M_2 represent his income next year, in dollars. In Chapter 3, in which we assumed no inflation, a dollar this year was equal to a dollar next year, in terms of its buying power. In this chapter, because we allow inflation, that is no longer true. Therefore, we must be careful to remember that M_1 dollars in income this year will buy M_1 units of stuff this year, but because of inflation, M_2 dollars in income next year will buy only $M_2/(1 + \pi)$ units of stuff next year.

The Budget Constraint

The consumer with income M_1 this year and M_2 next year could obviously consume $c_1 = M_1$ units of stuff this year, and $c_2 = M_2/(1 + \pi)$ units of stuff next year. Therefore, $(M_1, M_2/(1 + \pi))$ satisfies his budget constraint. If he did this, he would not be going to the capital market; he would neither save part of his first-year income and lend it to others, nor would he borrow from others against his anticipated second-year income.

We will call the point $(M_1, M_2/(1 + \pi))$, which is always available to the consumer, the *zero savings point*. This is the point on the budget constraint recommended by Polonius, a character in William Shakespeare's tragedy *Hamlet* (1603): "Neither a borrower nor a lender be; for loan oft loses both itself and friend, and borrowing dulls the edge of husbandry." (Like most of the characters in the play, Polonius came to a bad end.)

On the other hand, our consumer might want to consume less than M_1 this year, in which case he can set money aside, and then consume more than $M_2/(1 + \pi)$ next year. The amount he saves is $M_1 - c_1$. We assume, as in Chapter 3, that if the consumer saves some money, he earns interest on his savings at a rate of i per period. We will also assume that $i \geq 0$. (This is almost always true for *nominal* interest rates – that is, interest rates from which inflation rates have not been subtracted. However, during the panic of 2008–09, interest rates on U.S. Treasury bills actually became slightly negative.) The budget constraint for the consumer who is saving money this year says that his spending on stuff next year has to be less than or equal to his income next year plus what he saved this year, with interest. This gives

$$(1 + \pi)c_2 \leq M_2 + (1 + i)(M_1 - c_1).$$

Rearranging terms leads to

$$(1 + i)c_1 + (1 + \pi)c_2 \leq (1 + i)M_1 + M_2,$$

and dividing both sides by $1 + i$ gives

$$c_1 + \left(\frac{1 + \pi}{1 + i}\right)c_2 \leq M_1 + \left(\frac{1}{1 + i}\right)M_2.$$

This is almost the same constraint as we found in Chapter 3. The differences are that (1) here we have an inequality (for the *budget constraint*) rather than an equality (for the *budget line*), (2) we have replaced x's with c's, and (3) we have allowed for inflation with π.

We will assume here, as we did in Chapter 3, that the interest rate paid by a borrower is the same as the interest rate paid to a saver, that is, i. This is obviously an unrealistic assumption, but it is easy to modify later, and we will do so in an exercise. The consumer who borrows this year and pays off his loan next year consumes more than his income in the first year; he borrows $c_1 - M_1$. Next year he must pay back this amount with interest. His budget constraint says that his spending on stuff next year must be less than or equal to his income next year minus what he borrowed this year, plus interest. This gives

$$(1 + \pi)c_2 \leq M_2 - (1 + i)(c_1 - M_1).$$

This leads to exactly the same formula as the one for the saver. The equation for the intertemporal budget line, for the lender, the borrower, or the consumer who neither lends nor borrows, is

$$c_1 + \left(\frac{1 + \pi}{1 + i}\right)c_2 = M_1 + \left(\frac{1}{1 + i}\right)M_2.$$

In Figure 5.10, we show an intertemporal budget line. It goes through the zero savings point $(M_1, M_2/(1 + \pi))$, which represents the consumer's consumption bundle if he neither saves nor borrows. Its intercept on the horizontal axis is $M_1 + (1/(1 + i))M_2$. This is the *present value of the consumer's income stream*. If the super-impatient consumer decided to consume everything this year and nothing next year, this is how much stuff he could consume. The intercept on the vertical axis

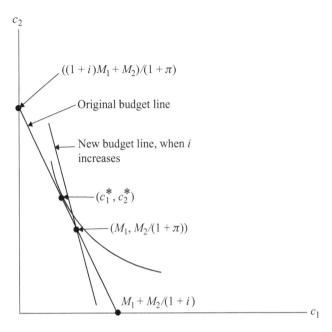

Fig. 5.10. The intertemporal budget constraint for a saver, and a new budget constraint showing what he can consume when the interest rate increases.

is $((1 + i)M_1 + M_2)/(1 + \pi)$. This is how much stuff the super-patient consumer could consume if he consumed nothing this year, and everything next year. The slope of the intertemporal budget line, in absolute value, is $(1 + i)/(1 + \pi)$.

This ratio is the relative price of current consumption, or the amount of future stuff that could be exchanged for one unit of current stuff. If the ratio is high, current consumption is relatively expensive. On the other hand, if the ratio is low, current consumption is relatively cheap. The ratio also has another important interpretation. Economists define the *real interest rate*, or δ, with the equation

$$\frac{1}{1 + \delta} = \frac{1 + \pi}{1 + i}.$$

This gives $\delta = (1 + i)/(1 + \pi) - 1$; this makes δ approximately equal to $i - \pi$. (Therefore, the real interest rate is roughly the nominal interest rate minus the inflation rate.) It follows immediately from the definition of δ that the slope of the intertemporal budget line, in absolute value, equals $1 + \delta$.

Given the budget constraint, which tells the consumer what is possible, he chooses the combination of current consumption and future consumption that gets him to the highest indifference curve, or maximizes his utility. Figure 5.10 also shows an indifference curve for the consumer; given this indifference curve and the "original" budget line shown, he chooses to consume (c_1^*, c_2^*) and to save an amount $M_1 - c_1^*$. The figure also shows an alternative "new" budget line based on an increase in i.

5.7 The Supply of Savings

In response to given M_1, M_2, π, and i, the consumer will decide on utility-maximizing c_1^* and c_2^*. We call his chosen savings level s^*, defined by $s^* = M_1 - c_1^*$. If $s^* > 0$, then he really is *saving*; if $s^* < 0$, he is actually *borrowing*, and if $s^* = 0$, he is at the zero savings point, and is neither saving nor borrowing. The consumer's supply of savings is a function of the underlying variables M_1, M_2, π, and i, and also depends, of course, on the consumer's preferences or utility function. We now consider how s^* depends on the interest rate i.

We start by assuming that consumption this year and consumption next year are both normal goods. That is, if the consumer's budget line shifts out, but the slope of the budget line, $(1 + i)/(1 + \pi)$ in absolute value, does not change, then the consumer wants to consume more of both goods – more stuff this year and more stuff next year. This kind of shift would result, for example, from an increase in both M_1 and M_2.

Next, consider a saver, such as the one whose budget line is shown in Figure 5.10. Suppose all variables are constant except for i; assume that i rises a bit. Now there is a new budget line. It still goes through the point $(M_1, M_2/(1 + \pi))$, but it is now steeper, and the point (c_1^*, c_2^*) now lies below it. The increase in i has an income effect and a substitution effect. Because (c_1^*, c_2^*) lies below the new budget line, our consumer, who is a *saver*, welcomes the increase in the interest rate; he can now afford more stuff this year and more stuff next year – he is richer. By the income effect, his desired consumption of stuff this year rises. Therefore, his desired savings (income minus current consumption) falls by the income effect.

However, the new budget constraint is also steeper. Its slope (in absolute value), $(1 + i)/(1 + \pi)$, is the relative price of current consumption. Because consumption this year has become relatively more expensive, by the substitution effect the consumer's desired consumption of stuff this year falls. Therefore, by the substitution effect, his desired savings (income minus current consumption) rises.

In short, for the saver, when i increases, the income effect says "consume more and save less," but the substitution effect says "consume less and save more." Therefore, the net effect of an increase in i on desired consumption this year, and on desired savings, is ambiguous. When i rises, the saver might save more (if the substitution effect prevails), or he might save less (if the income effect prevails).

In Figure 5.11, we show an enlarged and enhanced view of the crucial region of Figure 5.10. We add a hypothetical budget line with the same slope as the new budget line, as well as a new optimal point (c_1^{**}, c_2^{**}) on a new indifference curve. The substitution effect is the dashed arrow from the original consumption point (c_1^*, c_2^*) to a tangency point between the original indifference curve and the hypothetical budget line. The income effect is the dashed arrow to the new consumption point (c_1^{**}, c_2^{**}). The new consumption point (c_1^{**}, c_2^{**}) might lie to

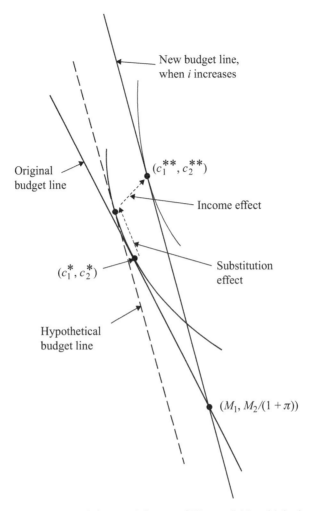

Fig. 5.11. An enlarged view of the crucial area of Figure 5.10, which shows income and substitution effects. By the substitution effect, when the interest rate rises the saver wants to save more; by the income effect, he wants to save less. The net effect is ambiguous.

the right or to the left of the original consumption point (c_1^*, c_2^*). Therefore, the net effect of an increase in i, on current consumption and on savings, is ambiguous.

In the preceding analysis, we considered the effects of an increase in i on a saver.

We now turn to the same kind of analysis, but for a borrower. Figure 5.12 shows the case for a borrower. Note that the indifference curves and zero savings points in Figure 5.10 and Figure 5.12 are very similar. The only important difference between the figures is that in Figure 5.10 both the original and the new budget lines are relatively steep, and in Figure 5.12 both the original and the new budget lines are relatively flat. The figures represent very similar consumers; one is a saver, in Figure 5.10, because interest rates are high, and one is a borrower, in Figure 5.12, because interest rates are low.

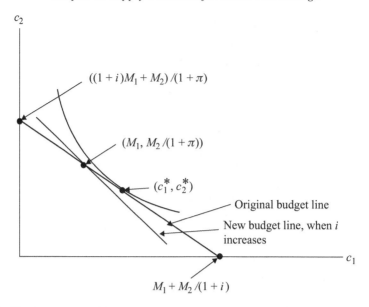

Fig. 5.12. The intertemporal budget constraint for a borrower, and a new budget constraint showing what he can consume when the interest rate increases.

We consider again a small increase in i, which modifies Figure 5.12. There is a new budget line. It still goes through the point $(M_1, M_2/(1 + \pi))$, but it is now steeper, and the point (c_1^*, c_2^*) now lies *above* it. Because (c_1^*, c_2^*) lies above the new budget line, our consumer, who is a borrower rather than a saver, is hurt by the increase in the interest rate; he can no longer afford the combination of stuff this year and stuff next year that he used to consume – he is poorer. By the income effect, his desired consumption of stuff this year falls. Therefore, his desired savings $s^* = M_1 - c_1^*$ rises by the income effect. (Remember that s^* is a negative number for the borrower; when we say he saves more, we mean he borrows less.)

The new budget line is steeper than the original. By the same argument made in the case of the saver, the borrower's savings rise as a consequence of the substitution effect. (A steeper budget line indicates that current consumption is relatively more expensive, which implies less current consumption, which implies more savings.) In the case of the borrower, therefore, the net effect of an increase in i on desired consumption this year, c_1^*, and on desired savings, $s^* = M_1 - c_1^*$, is unambiguous. As i rises, the borrower will want to consume less this year, and he will want to save more, that is, borrow less.

The upshot of what we have done so far is that an increase in i has an ambiguous effect for the saver but an unambiguous effect for the borrower. For the borrower, higher i means save more; that is, borrow less. On the other hand, for the saver, higher i might result in more savings or less savings.

We finish this discussion by emphasizing that the same consumer, with the same income stream and the same preferences, should sometimes choose to be a saver and sometimes choose to be a borrower. Whether a person chooses to be a saver or chooses to be a borrower depends on how steep the intertemporal budget line is; that is, it depends on $(1 + i)/(1 + \pi)$. The crucial difference between Figures 5.10 and Figure 5.12 was the initial i. For a given π, the consumer will borrow the most when $i = 0$. (Remember that we are assuming the interest rate cannot be negative. Therefore, the flattest possible intertemporal budget line has slope $(1 + 0)/(1 + \pi)$ in absolute value.) As i rises from 0, borrowing will decline monotonically (that is, negative savings will increase monotonically) until a "crossover" i is reached, at which point the consumer neither saves nor borrows. As i rises above the crossover, the consumer will have positive savings. However, with further increases he may reach a point of maximum savings, after which his savings may actually decline. That is, for i above the crossover point, when the consumer is saving, there is no longer a monotonic relationship between i and s^*.

The interested reader is invited to sketch a savings supply curve, showing i on the vertical axis and desired savings s^* on the horizontal axis. Remember to allow for positive s^* for the saver case and negative s^* for the borrower case, and show the "crossover" i.

5.8 A Solved Problem

The Problem

Penny is deciding how much money to allocate to consumption today and to consumption tomorrow, c_1 and c_2. Penny's utility function is $u(c_1, c_2) = c_1 c_2$. She will receive income of $M_1 = \$100$ today and $M_2 = \$100$ tomorrow. Suppose the interest rate is 10 percent ($i = 0.10$). Assume that today's price of stuff is \$1 per unit, and the inflation rate is 5 percent ($\pi = 0.05$). Assume that Penny can either save or borrow at a bank, at the given interest rate. Of course, she can borrow only up to a maximum of $100/(1 + i)$, the present value of tomorrow's income.

(a) Write down the equation for Penny's budget line.
(b) Calculate Penny's optimal (c_1^*, c_2^*). How much does she save or borrow today?
(c) How does your answer to (b) change if the inflation rate goes up to 10 percent?
(d) Answer parts (a) and (b) for Milly, Penny's friend, who has the same income stream and whose utility function is $u(c_1, c_2) = \sqrt{c_1} + c_2$.

The Solution

(a) An intertemporal budget constraint says that the present value of the consumption stream must be less than or equal to the present value of the income stream. On the budget line, the present values must be equal. The present value of consumption is $c_1 + ((1 + \pi)/(1 + i))c_2$. The present value of income is $M_1 + (1/(1 + i))M_2$. Therefore, her budget line equation is

$$c_1 + \frac{1 + \pi}{1 + i}c_2 = M_1 + \frac{1}{1 + i}M_2 \quad \Leftrightarrow \quad c_1 + \frac{1.05}{1.10}c_2 = 100 + \frac{100}{1.10}.$$

Note that the slope of the budget line, in absolute value, is $(1 + i)(1 + \pi) = 1.10/1.05$.

(b) Next we use the tangency condition, which says that the MRS should equal the absolute value of the slope of the budget line. This gives $MRS = MU_1/MU_2 = (1 + i)/(1 + \pi) = 1.10/1.05$. Because her utility function is $u(c_1, c_2) = c_1 c_2$, $MU_1 = c_2$ and $MU_2 = c_1$. Therefore, the tangency condition is

$$\frac{c_2}{c_1} = \frac{1+i}{1+\pi} = \frac{1.10}{1.05},$$

which gives $c_1 = (1.05/1.10)c_2$. When we plug this into the budget line equation, we get

$$\frac{1.05}{1.10}c_2 + \frac{1.05}{1.10}c_2 = 100 + \frac{100}{1.10}.$$

It follows that the optimal quantities are $c_1^* = (1.05/1.10)100 = 95.455$ and $c_2^* = 100$.

(c) If π rises from 5 percent to 10 percent, the budget line equation changes to

$$c_1 + \frac{1.10}{1.10}c_2 = 100 + \frac{100}{1.10}.$$

The tangency condition changes to

$$\frac{c_2}{c_1} = \frac{1+i}{1+\pi} = \frac{1.10}{1.10} = 1,$$

which gives $c_1 = c_2$. Plugging this into the budget line equation leads directly to $c_1^* = 95.455$ and $c_2^* = 95.455$. Note that the increase in inflation has made Penny worse off, and she has reacted by cutting back on her consumption tomorrow, which has become relatively more expensive.

(d) Milly's utility function is $u(c_1, c_2) = \sqrt{c_1} + c_2$. It is clear that she is going to favor consumption tomorrow over consumption today, because c is usually much bigger than $\sqrt{c}$. However, she will not ignore consumption today entirely. Her marginal utility of consumption today is $\frac{1}{2}c_1^{-1/2}$. Her marginal utility of consumption tomorrow is 1. Therefore, her tangency condition is

$$\frac{MU_1}{MU_2} = \frac{\frac{1}{2}c_1^{-1/2}}{1} = \frac{1+i}{1+\pi} = \frac{1.10}{1.05}.$$

This gives $c_1^{-1/2} = 2.20/1.05$. Therefore, $c_1^* = (1.05/2.20)^2 \approx 0.2278$. Her budget line equation is the same as Penny's:

$$c_1 + \frac{1.05}{1.10}c_2 = 100 + \frac{100}{1.10}.$$

We now plug in $c_1^* \approx 0.2278$ and get $c_2^* \approx 199.7614$.

Exercises

1. In the consumption/leisure model, let the consumer's utility function be $u(L, c) = Lc$. Suppose the price of stuff is $p = 1$. Can you show that the daily labor supply curve is $l^*(w) = 12$ hours? (That is, this consumer's preferences are such that, regardless of the wage rate, he wants to work exactly half his day.)

2. Humpty Dumpty receives some nonlabor income and decides not to work. Draw a graph with leisure on the horizontal axis and consumption on the vertical axis, showing his preferences, budget constraint, and the optimal consumption bundle. Label the intercepts and the optimal bundle.

3. Suppose the interest rate for savers is i_1 and the interest rate for borrowers is i_2, with $i_1 < i_2$.

   (a) Sketch the consumer's intertemporal budget line.

   (b) Now assume $i_1 > i_2$. Show with a graph that the consumer might be indifferent between borrowing a large amount of money and saving a large amount of money.

4. Mr. A's preferences for present consumption (c_1) and future consumption (c_2) are given by the utility function $u(c_1, c_2) = c_1^{1/3} c_2^{2/3}$, whereas Mr. B's are given by $v(c_1, c_2) = c_1^{2/3} c_2^{1/3}$. Suppose that the price of current consumption is 1, and that the interest rate and the inflation rate both equal 5 percent. Finally, both Mr. A's income and Mr. B's income is \$100 per period, today and tomorrow.

   (a) Write down the equation of the budget line and show it graphically, labeling the two intercepts with the axes, the slope, and the zero savings point. Comment on each of these values.

   (b) Solve for Mr. A's and Mr. B's optimal consumption bundles. Can you say whether they are lenders or borrowers?

   (c) For those values of income, price, and the inflation rate, find Mr. A's and Mr. B's savings supply curves. Next, suppose they are the only consumers in the economy. Find the aggregate supply of savings of this economy. Represent the three curves graphically.

   (d) Assume that the interest rate goes up to 10 percent. Find the new consumption bundles of the two consumers. Are they better or worse off than in the initial situation? Discuss.

5. Sketch a consumer's savings supply curve, with i on the vertical axis and s^* on the horizontal axis. Be sure to show s positive for one range of i and negative for another, and show the critical i where the consumer crosses over from being a borrower to being a saver.

6. Analyze the effect of a decrease in π on the saver's choice of current consumption c_1^* and savings s^*. Is the effect the same as an increase in i? In your analysis, be careful to consider the saver's budget constraint, and how decreasing π or increasing i affects that constraint.

Chapter 6

Welfare Economics 1: The One-Person Case

6.1 Introduction

This chapter is part of welfare economics. Welfare economics is about the well-being of society: which institutions, which policies, which market structures, which distributions of goods or wealth make society better or worse off. This type of question has interested economists since the time of Adam Smith (1723–1790), whose *The Wealth of Nations* was published in the same year (1776) as the American Declaration of Independence. Welfare economics is easy if society can be modeled as just one person, plus a government deciding on something like a tax policy, and the only question is whether that one person would be better off with policy A or policy B. This is the kind of analysis we will do in Sections 6.2 and 6.3. The appendix to this chapter covers the theory of *revealed preference* and relates it to some of the Section 6.2 material.

Welfare economics is somewhat more difficult if we want to know *how much* that one individual prefers policy A to policy B. We look at this issue in Section 6.4.

Welfare economics is complicated if there are two or more people in society, and if we are trying to determine whether policy A is better for the many-person society than policy B. In Section 6.5 we provide an example that touches on the problem, but the many-person model is discussed mainly in the following chapter. A different branch of welfare economics explores the connections between competitive markets and what economists call *Pareto efficiency* or *Pareto optimality*. We will do this later, in our chapters on exchange and production economies.

6.2 Welfare Comparison of a Per-Unit Tax and an Equivalent Lump-Sum Tax

We now focus on one consumer, who we will call the *typical consumer* or *Ms. Typical*. We assume she has income M, and that there are two goods, with prices p_1

and p_2. We assume that Ms. Typical has well-behaved preferences and a standard utility-function that depends on the quantities (x_1, x_2). Her utility-maximizing bundle is $x^* = (x_1^*, x_2^*)$. This point is the solution to

$$\max u(x_1, x_2) \quad \text{subject to} \quad p_1 x_1 + p_2 x_2 \leq M.$$

Note that (x_1^*, x_2^*) is on the budget line, and is a point of tangency between the budget line and an indifference curve, so that $MRS = p_1/p_2$.

Now, suppose a per-unit tax on good 1 is introduced. A *per-unit tax* on good 1, also sometimes called a *specific tax*, is a fixed amount of money that the consumer must pay to the government for each unit of good 1 that she consumes. For instance, a state gasoline tax in the United States is a per-unit tax; it is figured as cents per gallon. A per-unit tax is different from a *percentage* or *ad valorem* tax, which is figured as a *percentage of the price*, rather than as a fixed amount of money per unit. For example, state (and city and county) sales taxes in the United States are typically percentage taxes. In 2010, U.S. sales taxes (state plus city and county) ranged between a low of 0 percent in Delaware, New Hampshire, and Oregon and a high of more than 9 percent in California, Illinois, and Tennessee. (Value-added taxes in the European Union are also percentage taxes, but unlike U.S. sales taxes, these percentage taxes are paid several times at steps along the production process, when inputs or unfinished goods are being sold from firm to firm, as well as when the final product is sold by the last firm to the consumer. At each step, the tax is calculated by multiplying the given percentage by the value added by the producer at the current step, that is, price minus cost of materials and other inputs.)

We now model a per-unit tax. We will let t represent the per-unit tax on good 1. With the introduction of the tax, the cost of a unit of good 1 to the consumer rises from p_1 to $p_1 + t$. Her budget constraint becomes $(p_1 + t)x_1 + p_2 x_2 \leq M$. She solves the maximization problem

$$\max \ u(x_1, x_2) \quad \text{subject to} \quad (p_1 + t)x_1 + p_2 x_2 \leq M.$$

Let us call the solution $x^{**} = (x_1^{**}, x_2^{**})$. Notice that the government tax revenues must be equal to $t x_1^{**}$.

In contrast to per-unit taxes or ad valorem (percentage) taxes, we can think of a tax on Ms. Typical's income M. In this chapter, we have not discussed how she came by that income (for instance, by working a number of hours at a wage rate, by inheritance, and so on). Nor do we want to worry about this significant issue. We will simply assume that somehow the government takes a sum of money out of her pocket, without creating incentives or disincentives for her to earn the money in the first place. This kind of tax acts as an unavoidable, and perhaps unanticipated, wallet lightening. A tax that a consumer must pay, but that is independent of any decision she might make, is called a *lump-sum tax*. Lump-sum taxes are actually rather unusual in the real world. So-called *poll taxes* are examples; a poll tax is a

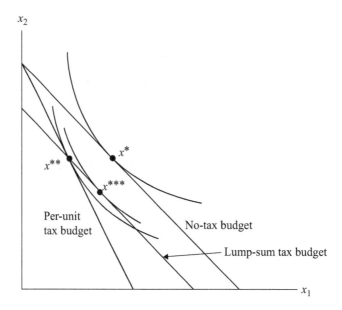

Fig. 6.1. Comparison of a per-unit tax and a lump-sum tax on income.

fixed tax imposed on every person or every adult in a given community; that is, a *per-head* tax. Poll taxes were once used in southern U.S. states to limit voting by blacks and poor whites, and they are now generally viewed as unconstitutional in the United States.

We now let T represent the lump-sum tax. With this tax in place, and no per-unit tax, Ms. Typical's budget constraint becomes $p_1 x_1 + p_2 x_2 \leq M - T$. Let us also assume that the lump-sum tax T is chosen so that the tax revenue generated is the same as with the per-unit tax. That is, $T = t x_1^{**}$. Which of these two taxes would our typical consumer prefer? With the lump-sum tax, she would solve this problem:

$$\max \ u(x_1, x_2) \quad \text{subject to} \quad p_1 x_1 + p_2 x_2 \leq M - T = M - t x_1^{**}.$$

The bundle $x^{**} = (x_1^{**}, x_2^{**})$ is still feasible for the consumer, as it was feasible under the per-unit tax. That is, x^{**} is on the lump-sum tax budget line. But the lump-sum tax budget line has slope p_1/p_2, and at the point x^{**}, Ms. Typical's $MRS = (p_1 + t)/p_2$. Therefore, her indifference curve must cross the lump-sum tax budget line at that point, and so she will choose something else she prefers. (See Figure 6.1.) Let us call the something else she prefers $x^{***} = (x_1^{***}, x_2^{***})$. The moral of this story is that with the lump-sum tax, which raises the same revenue as the per-unit tax, the consumer ends up at a point x^{***}, which she likes better than the point she ends up with under the per-unit tax. In short, an equivalent lump-sum tax is better for the consumer than a per-unit tax, and raises the same amount of money for the government. This result is shown in Figure 6.1.

Why is the lump-sum tax better? In a sense, the typical consumer's decision is affected less by the lump-sum tax than by the per-unit tax. With the lump-sum tax, she has $T = tx_1^{**}$ less to spend on all goods, and so she is poorer; but with her reduced income, she faces undistorted market prices. On the other hand, with the per-unit tax, she is again poorer in the sense that she cannot afford her no-tax bundle of goods, and, in addition, the per-unit tax causes her to inappropriately substitute good 2 for good 1, because the relative prices are distorted by the tax.

Finally, let us think about this question: The lump-sum tax would make the consumer better off than the per-unit tax. But by how much? We will come back to this in Section 6.4.

6.3 Rebating a Per-Unit Tax

Occasionally a government may impose a per-unit tax on a commodity, say caviar, perhaps because it thinks consuming caviar is an immoral extravagance. However, it may want to compensate the typical consumer for the caviar tax by rebating the revenue in some other way. For instance, the government may decide to send a check to Ms. Typical at the end of the year, equal to the amount of caviar taxes she paid. Would this policy make her better off, the same, or worse off? For the purposes of this analysis, we assume that Ms. Typical does not connect the total per-unit tax paid over the course of the year for her caviar purchases with the rebate check received at the end of the year. That is, the rebate is a lump-sum rebate.

Before the government sets up the per-unit tax/lump-sum rebate scheme, Ms. Typical is maximizing utility subject to prices (p_1, p_2) and income M. That is, she is solving the problem:

$$\max \ u(x_1, x_2) \quad \text{subject to} \quad p_1 x_1 + p_2 x_2 \le M.$$

We let the bundle $x^* = (x_1^*, x_2^*)$ represent her choice absent the scheme. This point is shown in Figure 6.2.

Now, the government imposes the per-unit tax on good 1, caviar, and rebates the proceeds in a lump sum. The cost of a unit of good 1 to Ms. Typical becomes $p_1 + t$, where t is the per-unit tax. The government is collecting t times the number of units of caviar she consumes, and simultaneously rebating her what it collects. We let R be the lump-sum rebate. Also, we let $x^{**} = (x_1^{**}, x_2^{**})$ represent her new chosen point. This is the solution to the following utility maximization problem:

$$\max \ u(x_1, x_2) \quad \text{subject to} \quad (p_1 + t)x_1 + p_2 x_2 \le M + R,$$

Note that $R = tx_1^{**}$, but the consumer does not act on this information. That is, she does not plug the formula for R into the budget constraint and thereby "solve

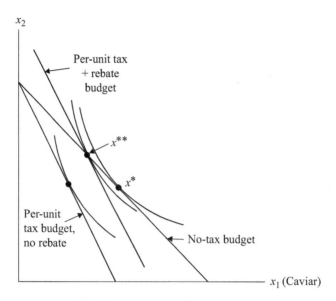

Fig. 6.2. Rebating a per-unit tax.

out" the tx_1 term. However, *we* know that $R = tx_1^{**}$, and therefore, at (x_1^{**}, x_2^{**}), the following must be true:

$$(p_1 + t)x_1^{**} + p_2 x_2^{**} = M + t x_1^{**}.$$

Therefore,

$$p_1 x_1^{**} + p_2 x_2^{**} = M.$$

In short, the point x^{**} satisfies her original budget constraint. That is, it was affordable when the consumer chose x^*. Therefore, the consumer must be worse off at x^{**} than at x^*. All this is shown in Figure 6.2.

Schemes such as this are quite common in the real world, although the real-world schemes usually have a serious and important reason for the government's action. (In our example, the government's rationale, discouraging the immoral extravagance of eating caviar, obviously was not serious.) As an example of a real-world scheme of this type, but one with a serious reason behind it, consider the following. In early 2009, members of the U.S. Congress proposed a carbon emissions tax (which would ultimately be paid by users of electricity, gasoline, and so on). To mitigate the negative impact on Ms. Typical, payroll taxes would simultaneously be reduced. For the typical consumer, the burden of the new taxes on electricity and fuel would be just offset by the reduction in payroll taxes. Our previous analysis suggests that this would be a bad thing for Ms. Typical, but when the benefits of reduced carbon emissions are factored in, a bad thing might become a good thing. (The proposal failed in Congress.)

We will discuss pollution-based externalities in Chapter 17.

6.4 Measuring a Change in Welfare for One Person

Our previous discussion of per-unit taxes and lump-sum taxes made no attempt to measure *how much* Ms. Typical might like one policy more than another. We will now turn to that question. We continue to assume that there is just one person.

Recall our comparison of a per-unit tax and an equivalent lump-sum tax, illustrated in Figure 6.1. We learned from that comparison that the consumer prefers the lump-sum tax, which gets her to x^{***}, to the per-unit tax, which gets her to x^{**}. This is because x^{***} is on a higher indifference curve than x^{**}. If we were asked "By how much does she prefer x^{***}?", we might give an answer along these lines: "Her utility levels at the two points are $u(x^{**}) = 7$ and $u(x^{***}) = 9$, and therefore, she likes x^{***} exactly 2 utility units more than x^{**}." (Because we did not specify a utility function in this example, we just made up the 7 and the 9.)

The problem with this answer is that although it might be true, it means only that she prefers x^{***} to x^{**}. That is, because utility functions are ordinal, a 2-utility-unit preference for one point over another means no more and no less than a 0.2-utility-unit preference or a 200-utility-unit preference.

To get a meaningful idea of how much Ms. Typical prefers one point to another, we need a measurement in more tangible units, such as units of goods, or units of money. A measurement in units of utility will not do.

In Chapter 4, in our discussion of the Hicks substitution effect, we developed the means for transforming utility unit gains and losses into corresponding dollar gains and losses. The reader might look back at Figure 4.10 to recall how Hicks decomposes a move from an initial consumption bundle to a new consumption bundle into an income effect and a substitution effect. The substitution effect shows how the consumer's consumption bundle shifts because of a shift in prices, holding utility constant, whereas the income effect shows how the consumer's consumption bundle shifts because her income has in effect changed; she has, in effect, become richer or poorer. The income effect abstracts away the change in relative prices, and makes the shift from a point on an old indifference curve to a point on a new indifference curve a consequence of a change in income alone (measured in dollars). This gives us an easy and objective way to measure a consumer's gain or loss from a shift in consumption: figure the dollar amount of the income effect.

Also recall that in Figure 4.11, we indicated there are really two ways to do an income/substitution effect decomposition in the Hicks style; one proposed by Hicks himself and an alternative proposed by Kaldor. The Hicks version uses relative prices at the new point to produce a hypothetical budget line tangent to the old indifference curve, whereas the Kaldor variant uses relative prices at the old point to produce a hypothetical budget line tangent to the new indifference curve.

Before proceeding, let us lay out some terminology. Suppose a consumer shifts from one consumption point to another. We know that her move can be decomposed into a substitution effect and an income effect, using either the Hicks decomposition or the Kaldor decomposition. Whichever decomposition we use, the income effect is a move from one bundle to another bundle, and at each of these bundles there is a budget line (one real and one hypothetical) tangent to an indifference curve. The two budget lines are parallel; they are based on the same prices. The *dollar amount* or *dollar value of the income effect* is the dollar difference between the two parallel budget lines; that is, the dollars it would take to get from one budget line to the other. The *compensating variation measure of the consumer's gain* (or loss, if negative) is the dollar amount of the Hicks income effect, the income effect based on the new prices. The *equivalent variation measure of the consumer's gain* (or loss if negative) is the dollar amount of the Kaldor variant income effect, the income effect based on the old prices.

We now turn to an algebraic example, which will make everything crystal clear.

Example 1. Measuring one consumer's welfare change in dollars, when p_1 rises, for a simple product utility function.

Let us assume that a consumer has a utility function $u(x) = u(x_1, x_2) = x_1 x_2$. Assume that her income is $M = 18$, and the prices at the start are $p_1 = 1$ and $p_2 = 1$. To maximize her utility subject to her budget constraint, she sets her MRS equal to the price ratio p_1/p_2. This gives

$$MRS = \frac{MU_1}{MU_2} = \frac{x_2}{x_1} = \frac{p_1}{p_2}.$$

Therefore, $p_1 x_1 = p_2 x_2$. Because her budget constraint is $p_1 x_1 + p_2 x_2 = M$, we get $2 p_1 x_1 = M$. Therefore, her demand function for good 1 is

$$x_1 = \frac{M}{2 p_1}.$$

At the initial prices of $(p_1, p_2) = (1, 1)$, and because $M = 18$, her utility-maximizing bundle is $x^* = (x_1^*, x_2^*) = (9, 9)$. Her initial utility level is $u(x^*) = 9 \times 9 = 81$.

Now, let us assume the price of good 1 rises to $p_1 = 2.25$, while M and p_2 remain the same. The consumer is worse off, as she can no longer afford the bundle she had been consuming.

We want to measure her loss.

We first use the demand function to find her new desired quantity of good 1: $x_1^{**} = M/2p_1 = 18/(2 \times 2.25) = 18/4.5 = 4$. Then we use the budget constraint to find $x_2^{**} = 9$. Therefore, her new utility-maximizing bundle is $x^{**} = (x_1^{**}, x_2^{**}) = (4, 9)$. Her new utility level is $u(x^{**}) = 4 \times 9 = 36$.

We use Table 6.1 to record the quantity and cost variables we are calculating. In the table, we have columns identifying the original ("old") prices (1, 1), as well as the revised ("new") prices (2.25, 1). The original utility-maximizing bundle x^* is shown on line 1 of the table, and the new utility-maximizing bundle x^{**} is shown on line 2. Entries under the "old" and "new" price columns are the dollar costs of

Table 6.1. *Figuring compensating and equivalent variation*

		Old prices $(p_1, p_2) = (1, 1)$	New prices $(p_1, p_2) = (2.25, 1)$
1.	$x^* = (9, 9)$	$18	
2.	$x^{**} = (4, 9)$		$18
3.	$y = (6, 13.5)$		$27
4.	$z = (6, 6)$	$12	
5.	y to x^{**} (C.V.)		minus $9
6.	x^* to z (E.V.)	minus $6	

the given bundles at those prices. For example, the cost of x^* at the old prices is $18. The cost of x^{**} at the new prices is also $18.

In the move from the old optimal point x^* to the new optimal point x^{**}, the consumer's utility drops by $81 - 36 = 45$ utility units. But this information is not particularly helpful, because utility functions are ordinal.

Also, in the move from x^* to x^{**}, the consumer's income stays constant, at $18. This suggests a loss of $18 - $18 = $0. But only a fool would say she has lost nothing.

How, then, do we measure her loss in dollars? We decompose the move from x^* to x^{**} into income and substitution effects, and then use the dollar value of the income effect. There are two very similar ways to do the decomposition: the compensating variation (Hicks) method is based on a hypothetical budget line that is tangent to the original indifference curve but with a slope based on the new prices; the equivalent variation (Kaldor variant) method is based on a hypothetical budget line that is tangent to the new indifference curve but with a slope based on the old prices.

We illustrate the two methods in Figure 6.3. The original consumer optimum is at $x^* = (9, 9)$ and the new consumer optimum is at $x^{**} = (4, 9)$. To get the *compensating variation* measure, we draw a hypothetical budget line, tangent to the old indifference curve, but with a slope of $2.25/1 = 2.25$ in absolute value, based on the new prices. This is the hypothetical budget $B1$ in the figure. The substitution effect is the x^* to y shift, and the income effect is the y to x^{**} shift. To find y, we use the fact that $y = (y_1, y_2)$ is on the old indifference curve, so $y_1 y_2 = 81$; we also use the fact that the slope of the indifference curve at y, in absolute value, must equal 2.25. This gives $MRS = y_2/y_1 = 2.25$, or $y_2 = 2.25 y_1$. Putting these two equations together gives $2.25 y_1^2 = 81$, or $y_1^2 = 81/2.25 = 36$. Therefore, $y_1 = 6$ and $y_2 = 13.5$. (This is Table 6.1, line 3.) At the new prices $(p_1, p_2) = (2.25, 1)$, y would cost $2.25 \times 6 + 1 \times 13.5 = 27$; at the new prices x^{**} costs 18. Therefore, the dollar value of the income effect is $18 - 27 = -9$ (Table 6.1, line 5). That is, using the compensating variation measure, the move from the old point x^* to the new point x^{**} is equivalent to the consumer losing $9.

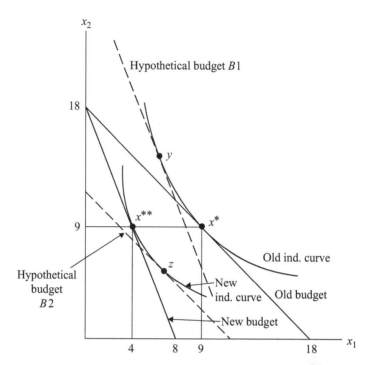

Fig. 6.3. There are two ways to measure the consumer's loss in dollars. Compensating variation is the dollar value of the y to x^{**} income effect (based on the new prices); equivalent variation is the dollar value of the x^* to z income effect (based on the old prices). Positions of y and z are approximate.

To get the equivalent variation measure, we draw a hypothetical budget line, tangent to the new indifference curve, but with a slope of $1/1 = 1$ in absolute value, based on the old prices. This is the hypothetical budget $B2$ in the figure. The substitution effect is now the z to x^{**} shift, and the income effect is the x^* to z shift. To find z, we use the fact that $z = (z_1, z_2)$ is on the new indifference curve, so $z_1 z_2 = 4 \times 9 = 36$; and we also use the fact that the slope of the indifference curve at z, in absolute value, must equal 1.0. This gives $MRS = z_2/z_1 = 1$, or $z_2 = z_1$. Putting these two equations together gives $z_1^2 = 36$. Therefore, $z_1 = 6$ and $z_2 = 6$. (This is Table 6.1, line 4.) At the old prices $(p_1, p_2) = (1, 1)$, z would cost $1 \times 6 + 1 \times 6 = 12$; at the old prices x^* costs 18. Therefore, the dollar value of the income effect is $12 - 18 = -6$. (Table 6.1, line 6.) That is, using the equivalent variation measure, the move from the old point x^* to the new point x^{**} is equivalent to the consumer losing \$6.

At this point, we can say the following: Our consumer's move from x^* to x^{**} has made her worse off. She has lost 45 utility units, which means she is worse off, but the number "45" doesn't mean anything in particular. However, the move has an effect that can be measured in dollars; measured in the compensating variation (Hicks income effect) fashion, the result is $-\$9$; measured in the slightly different equivalent variation (Kaldor variant income effect) fashion, the result is $-\$6$.

Before leaving this section, we must point out a disturbing peculiarity of the compensating variation and equivalent variation measures. Take another look at Figure 6.3. Now, instead of assuming that the consumer starts at x^* and finishes at x^{**}, suppose she starts at x^{**} and finishes at x^*. In other words, we reverse the direction of the move. Then what had been new is now old, and what had been old is now new. Therefore, for this shift, by the compensating variation measure, the consumer has gained \$6 (the dollar value of the z to x^* income effect). For this shift, by the equivalent variation measure, the consumer has gained \$9 (the dollar value of the x^{**} to y income effect). This is all very confusing, but here's the worst part.

Now consider a round trip, from x^* to x^{**}, and then back, from x^{**} to x^*. According to the compensating variation measure, the consumer in effect loses \$9 on the x^* to x^{**} leg. According to the compensating variation measure, she in effect gains \$6 on the return leg. Therefore, by the compensating variation measure, starting at x^* and ending back up at x^*, the consumer's has a *net loss of \$3*. But this is absurd, a paradox, because she ends up at the same point at which she started!

We have shown that compensating variation and equivalent variation measures of one consumer's gains (or losses) from a move from one consumption bundle to another are useful gauges of how much the consumer gains or loses. This is because they are dollar measures of the gains (or losses), and therefore, much more tangible than utility measures of those gains or losses. On the other hand, at least for some utility functions, these measures may produce strange results. The reason is the ambiguity of income effects, which makes things quite tricky.

6.5 Measuring Welfare for Many People; A Preliminary Example

We now turn to another example that illustrates how choices between policies or programs might be made by a government. In this example we assume that there are many people in society, instead of just one. In other words, we are no longer thinking of alternative government policies and how they might affect Ms. Typical. We are now thinking of alternative government policies and how they affect a population of consumers with different preferences and different utility functions.

In the last section, we carefully discussed compensating and equivalent variation measures of one consumer's gain or loss from a change in a budget constraint variable, the price of one good. Both these measures in effect converted utility changes into dollar equivalents. In the following example, we use a similar, although less carefully defined, measure of welfare: willingness to pay. We assume that various consumers are being offered a choice between two different policies (or "programs") by their government, and each consumer (or "family") would be willing to pay, at most, a certain dollar amount for each policy. This example is simpler than the last example in the sense that there is no change in relative prices.

The example shows that if the government makes choices by adding together the willingness-to-pay numbers of the various families, it risks putting too much importance on the preferences of the rich.

Example 2. Measuring society's preference for one program over another, in dollars. Should schools teach music or art (if they cannot afford both)?

Suppose there are two regions of the country, the East and the West. People in the East love music and are less interested in the visual arts. People in the West love the visual arts and are less interested in music. Assume there are equal numbers of families in the two regions. There is a public school system that educates children in both regions. The school system is short of funds and can afford to provide only a music education program, or an art education program, but *not both*. Nor can it afford to provide music in one region and art in the other. Policy M is to teach music in all schools in the country; policy A is to teach art in all schools in the country. Assume that each family in each region would be willing to pay up to 2 percent of family income each year for the type of education (music or visual arts) they like more, and up to 1 percent of family income each year for the type of education they like less.

Now, suppose that social welfare for each education program is measured simply by summing each family's willingness to pay, over all families in the country. Assume that the government opts for the education program that maximizes aggregate willingness to pay. We might call this the *naive willingness-to-pay approach*. It is "naive" in the Webster's dictionary sense, of being too simple, too deficient in worldly wisdom.

Here is the problem with measuring society's preference this way: The decision will simply depend on aggregate family income in the two regions of the country. If the East is richer, the decision will be M; if the West is richer, it will be A. The government will provide the program preferred by the richer region. Even worse, if every family in the country is middle-income except for one super-rich family, the decision will depend only on whether the super-rich family lives in the East or in the West. Many economists would reject this approach.

Should we then abandon the naive willingness-to-pay approach and just use compensating variation, or equivalent variation, or some similar measure? This might produce paradoxes and inconsistencies like those in Example 1 – which was about one person – compounded in a world with many people. In the following chapter we will continue to discuss these problems. We will introduce an assumption, called *quasilinearity*, which will prevent the paradox of Example 1 and prevent the unpalatable outcome of Example 2.

6.6 A Solved Problem

The Problem

The King of Phoenicia wants to build a new university, which will cost roughly $100 million. To pay for it, he will tax the people of Phoenicia. There are 1 million people in the country, and they are all alike. They consume only two goods, fruits (f) and nuts (n). They all have the same utility function, $u(f, n) = f(n + 2)$, and they all have the same income, $M = \$1,000$. The prices of fruits and nuts are $p_f = \$4$ and $p_n = \$4$. The King's Council of Economic Advisors presents him with three alternative proposals:

(1) Impose a per-unit tax of $1 on fruits.
(2) Impose a per-unit tax of $1 on nuts.
(3) Impose a lump-sum tax of $100 on each person.

How do these proposals effect the citizens of Phoenicia? How much revenue will each proposal raise?

The Solution

With no tax, each citizen's budget constraint is $4f + 4n = 1,000$. The tangency condition for utility maximization is

$$MRS = \frac{MU_f}{MU_n} = \frac{n + 2}{f} = \frac{p_f}{p_n} = \frac{4}{4} = 1.$$

This gives $n = f - 2$. Plugging this into the budget constraint gives the optimal consumption bundle $(f^*, n^*) = (126, 124)$. Utility with no tax is $u(f^*, n^*) = 126(124 + 2) = 15,876$.

(1) With a per-unit tax of $1 on fruits, the consumer must pay $4 + \$1 = \$5$ for each unit of fruit she consumes. The budget constraint is now $5f + 4n = 1,000$. The tangency condition is now

$$MRS = \frac{n + 2}{f} = \frac{5}{4}.$$

This gives $n = (5/4)f - 2$. Plugging this into the budget constraint gives the optimal consumption bundle $(f^*, n^*) = (100.8, 124)$. Utility with the per-unit fruit tax is $u(f^*, n^*) = 100.8(124 + 2) = 12,701$. Tax revenue from one consumer is $\$1 \times 100.8 = \$100.8$, and total tax revenue is 1 million times this, or $100.8 million.

(2) With a per-unit tax of $1 on nuts, the consumer must pay $4 + \$1 = \$5$ for each unit of nuts he consumes. The budget constraint is now $4f + 5n = 1,000$. The tangency condition is now

$$MRS = \frac{n + 2}{f} = \frac{4}{5}.$$

This gives $n = (4/5)f - 2$. Plugging this into the budget constraint gives the optimal consumption bundle $(f^*, n^*) = (126.25, 99)$. Utility with the per-unit nut tax is $u(f^*, n^*) = 126.25(99 + 2) = 12,751$. Tax revenue from one consumer is $\$1 \times 99 = \$99$, and total tax revenue is 1 million times this, or $99 million.

(3) With a lump-sum tax of $100, the prices stay the same, $(p_f, p_n) = (4, 4)$. However, the consumer's income drops by $100. The budget constraint is now $4f + 4n = 900$.

The tangency condition is

$$MRS = \frac{n+2}{f} = \frac{4}{4} = 1.$$

This gives $n = f - 2$. Plugging this into the budget constraint gives the optimal consumption bundle $(f^*, n^*) = (113.5, 111.5)$. Utility with the lump-sum tax is $u(f^*, n^*) = 113.5(111.5 + 2) = 12,882$. Tax revenue from one consumer is $100, and total tax revenue is 1 million times this, or $100 million.

We conclude that all three proposals raise roughly $100 million. However, the citizens prefer proposal 3 over proposal 2 over proposal 1. The king has heard about the Arab Spring uprisings of 2011, so he goes with the lump-sum tax.

Exercises

1. Leah spends $200 a month on berries ($b$) and cream ($c$). Her utility function is $u(b, c) = bc$. Berries cost $4 a pint and cream costs $2 a pint.
    (a) Find Leah's optimal consumption bundle, and calculate her utility at that bundle.
    (b) Suppose a 25 percent tax on cream is imposed. What is Leah's optimal consumption bundle?
    (c) The government is contemplating a subsidy on berries. What would the net price of berries have to be, so that with the 25 percent tax on cream and the subsidized berry price, Leah ends up with the same utility as in (a)?

2. Rachel gets a weekly allowance of $45, which is spent on milk (m) and cookies (c). Her utility function is $u(m, c) = mc^2 + 100$. A glass of milk is $1 and a cookie is $3.
    (a) Find Rachel's optimal consumption bundle, and calculate her utility at that bundle.
    (b) Suppose the government taxes Rachel $1 for each cookie consumed. At the end of the week, the government sends Rachel a rebate check equal to the amount of cookie taxes she paid. Rachel, however, does not connect the rebate check with the cookie taxes she paid. Find Rachel's new consumption bundle, and show that she is worse off than in (a).

3. There are two goods in the world, x and y. William's utility function is $u(x, y) = \min(x, y)$ and Mary's utility function is $v(x, y) = x + y$. If a tax is imposed on good x, how does William's utility change? How about Mary's utility?

4. Louis's utility function for champagne (c) and soda (s) can be written as $u(c, s) = 10c^4 s$. A bottle of champagne is $32 and a bottle of soda is $1. His monthly budget for champagne and soda is $80.
    (a) Find Louis's optimal consumption bundle, (c^*, s^*), and his utility level at this bundle.
    (b) Suppose a new study shows that champagne has tremendous health benefits, and a bill subsidizing the consumption of champagne is passed. The net price of champagne with the subsidy is $16. Find Louis's new consumption bundle, (c^{**}, s^{**}), and his utility level at this bundle.
    (c) Using the Hicks notion of income and substitution effects, calculate the dollar value of the income effect.

5. A couple's utility function for condominiums (good x measured in square feet) and other stuff (good y) is given by $u(x, y) = x^2 y$. Suppose that the couple's income is $30,000, the initial price of x is $100, and the price of y is $1. The local government offers the following alternative housing programs. Which program does the couple prefer? How much would each program cost the government? Comment briefly.

   (a) A lump-sum subsidy of $3,000, independent of the size of the condominium purchased.

   (b) A subsidy on the price of condominiums such that the net price per square foot is $80.

6. President Clinton has appointed you as her secretary of the economy. Assume that goods may be classified into just two types (x and y), and that the preferences of all consumers are $u(x, y) = \min(x, y)$. Let x^* and y^* be the initial amounts demanded. Suppose $p_x = 10$ and $p_y = 10$. A third of the consumers, Group A, earn $500 each; a third of the consumers, Group B, earn $400 each; and a third of the consumers, Group C, earn $300 each. You present the following plan to Congress:

   (a) Lump-sum income taxes will be levied on everyone. Consumers in Group A pay a tax of $68 each, consumers in Group B pay a tax of $40 each, and consumers in Group C pay a tax of $12 each.

   (b) The two goods will have per-unit subsidies of $s_x = 1$ and $s_y = 1$. The subsidies are chosen so that the new (net-of-subsidy) prices $p_x - s_x$ and $p_y - s_y$ satisfy $s_x x^{**} + s_y y^{**} = T$ and $(p_x - s_x)/(p_y - s_y) = p_x/p_y$, where p_x and p_y are the initial prices, x^{**} and y^{**} are the amounts demanded after the policy intervention, and T is the total tax collected.

   Members of Congress argue that the plan should be rejected on the grounds that it worsens the welfare of the median consumer. Can you show that their argument is wrong? Who would be better off and who would be worse off if the policy were implemented? Calculate each group's optimal consumption bundle and utility pre-policy and post-policy.

Appendix. Revealed Preference

In our approach to the theory of the consumer, starting in Chapter 2, we began by assuming that the consumer has preferences. We made certain assumptions about preferences and the utility functions that represent preferences. From the preferences, the utility functions, and the budget constraints, we derived demand curves, and we discussed the properties those demand curves should have. This line of reasoning started with the properties of preferences or utility, which generally are not directly observable, and moved to the properties of demand, which are directly observable.

In the 1930s and 1940s, the great twentieth-century American economist Paul Samuelson (1915–2009) developed a different sort of theory, which started with the properties of demand, rather than the properties of preferences or utility. Because it started with demand, which is observable, it was in a sense more empirical than classical consumer theory. Samuelson (and others) worked out the assumptions about consumer choice that would produce the same kind of logical structure as the standard preference-based consumer theory.

The essential idea of Samuelson's theory is this. Suppose a consumer chooses a bundle of goods (x_1, x_2), when she could have chosen a different bundle (y_1, y_2), given the prices of the goods and her income. Then she has directly demonstrated that she prefers (x_1, x_2) to (y_1, y_2), or *directly revealed a preference* for (x_1, x_2) over (y_1, y_2). Samuelson then proposed a basic assumption about the bundles that the consumer chooses: *if the consumer directly reveals a preference for (x_1, x_2) over (y_1, y_2), then she should not directly reveal a preference for (y_1, y_2) over (x_1, x_2).* This assumption, although it incorporates the word "preference," is purely a statement about what bundles of goods the consumer does or does not choose. That is, it is a statement about bundles the consumer chooses, which are observable, and not about preference relations or a utility functions, which are not observable.

Samuelson's basic assumption about choice is now called the *weak axiom of revealed preference (WARP)*. Figure 6.4 shows two pairs of budget lines in two graphs. In both graphs, the consumer chooses the point (x_1, x_2) when her budget line is B_x. In each graph, there is an alternative budget line B_y, flatter than B_x, under which the consumer chooses a different bundle (y_1, y_2). In both graphs, (y_1, y_2) lies on B_x, which means the consumer could have chosen (y_1, y_2) when she in fact was choosing (x_1, x_2). The upper graph is consistent with the weak axiom of revealed preference, but the lower graph is not.

That is, in the upper graph, the consumer is directly revealing her preference for (x_1, x_2), but she is not (illogically) also directly revealing her preference for (y_1, y_2) over (x_1, x_2). On the other hand, in the lower graph, the consumer is directly revealing her preference for (x_1, x_2) over (y_1, y_2), and, simultaneously, illogically, she is directly revealing her preference for (y_1, y_2) over (x_1, x_2).

In some applications, the weak axiom of revealed preference is strengthened to what is now called the *strong axiom of revealed preference (SARP)*. The idea of SARP is the following: we say a consumer *indirectly reveals a preference* for (x_1, x_2) over (y_1, y_2) if there is some string of alternative bundles (call them AB_1, AB_2, and so on), such that she directly reveals a preference for (x_1, x_2) over AB_1, and she directly reveals a preference for AB_1 over AB_2, and so on, until she directly reveals a preference for the last in the string of alternative bundles, say, AB_k, over (y_1, y_2). The assumption of SARP says that *if the consumer indirectly reveals a preference for (x_1, x_2) over (y_1, y_2), then she should not indirectly reveal a preference for (y_1, y_2) over (x_1, x_2).*

In Figure 6.5, we show three bundles and the associated budget lines that give rise to their choice. The consumption bundles are (x_1, x_2), (y_1, y_2), and (z_1, z_2), and the corresponding budget lines are labeled B_x, B_y, and B_z. The figure illustrates the idea of SARP, because (x_1, x_2) is indirectly revealed preferred to (z_1, z_2), but (z_1, z_2) is not indirectly revealed preferred to $x_1, x_2)$.

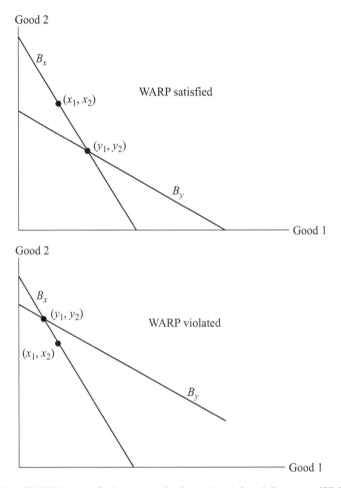

Fig. 6.4. When WARP is satisfied (top), and when it is violated (bottom). With budget B_x, the consumer chooses (x_1, x_2); with B_y she chooses (y_1, y_2).

We end this section with some hints about how revealed preference theory might be merged into the welfare economics analysis we have been doing in this chapter, as well as the consumer theory we did in the previous chapters.

First, consider the welfare comparison of a per-unit tax and the equivalent lump-sum income tax, which we discussed in the second section of this chapter, particularly in Figure 6.1. To understand how revealed preference relates, take another look at Figure 6.1, focusing on the three points (x_1^*, x_2^*), (x_1^{**}, x_2^{**}), and (x_1^{***}, x_2^{***}), and the three budget lines in the figure, labeled "no tax," "per-unit tax," and "lump-sum tax." Try to ignore the indifference curves in the figure. Obviously, the consumer is revealing her preference for the no-tax consumption bundle (x_1^*, x_2^*) over the other two bundles. Moreover, as Figure 6.1 is drawn, the consumer is directly revealing her preference for (x_1^{***}, x_2^{***}) over (x_1^{**}, x_2^{**}). Therefore, the lump-sum tax policy is better than the per-unit tax policy. Finally, the

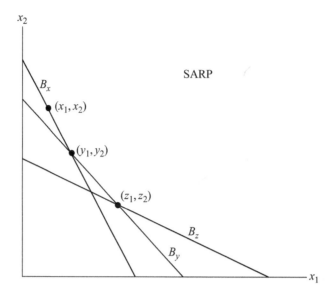

Fig. 6.5. Illustrating SARP. The bundle (x_1, x_2) is indirectly revealed preferred to (z_1, z_2), but not vice versa.

point (x_1^{***}, x_2^{***}) must lie where it does, to the right and below (x_1^{**}, x_2^{**}), because if it were to the left and above, WARP would be violated. The reader should figure out why.

Second, consider the discussion of the Slutsky substitution effect, from Section 4.5, particularly in Figure 4.9. A quick look back at that figure should convince the reader that the figure is virtually identical to Figure 6.1 and very close to Figure 6.4, top. Consequently, revealed preference analysis can be applied there as well. In particular, we can easily establish, without relying on indifference curves, that WARP implies that the Slutsky substitution effect is negative.

Chapter 7

Welfare Economics 2: The Many-Person Case

7.1 Introduction

Most of the last chapter was about the well-being of a one-person society. It is appropriate to model society as having just one person (our Ms. Typical) if, for example, we want to decide between alternative tax policies that impact a homogeneous population (made up of many Ms. Typicals) in a uniform fashion. However, if people are very different (with different preferences and income levels, for instance), and are differently affected by any particular policy choice, it may be wrong to model society this way.

In this chapter, we assume that there are two or more people. How do we determine whether policy A is better than policy B if various people are affected by those policies, in various different ways? This is the crucial problem we now face. We touched on this problem in Section 6.5, but now we explore it further.

We know from Chapter 2 that utility is an ordinal measure, so it probably makes no sense to add together the utility levels of two or more people to get a social utility measure. However, if this is so, is it possible to judge alternative government policies, institutions, or market structures by adding together numbers that in some way represent individual assessments of those alternatives?

Economists use the idea of *consumers' surplus* to do this, and we explore consumers' surplus in this chapter. We start off by quickly revisiting problematic Examples 1 and 2 from the last chapter, and then we introduce an assumption, called *quasilinear preferences* or *quasilinearity*, that rules them out. We then carefully define *consumer's* surplus for a single individual. We show that under the quasilinearity assumption, a consumer's change in welfare as measured by compensating variation, equivalent variation, or the change in consumer's surplus, all agree (which rules out Example 1). We show that under the quasilinearity assumption, the consumer's demand for good 1 is independent of income (which rules out Example 2). Then we define *consumers'* surplus, for two or more individuals, and present an example. We conclude with some comments on the restrictiveness of the quasilinearity assumption: although it is sometimes a good approximation to reality – for instance, when the good under study is subject to small income effects – at other times it is an unrealistic and inappropriate assumption.

7.2 Quasilinear Preferences

Recall that Chapter 6 ended with two examples that were slightly unsettling. To recapitulate, they were:

Example 1. Measuring one consumer's welfare change in dollars, when p_1 rises, for a simple product utility function. The consumer has utility function $u(x) = x_1 x_2$. Her income is $M = 18$, and the prices at the start are $p_1 = 1$ and $p_2 = 1$. Based on these prices, she chooses a utility-maximizing bundle x^*. Suppose the first price rises to $p_1 = 2.25$. Now, she chooses a utility-maximizing bundle x^{**}. She is worse off; her utility change is -45. By the compensating variation measure, she is worse off by $9. By the equivalent variation measure, she is worse off by $6. Thus, the dollar measures of her welfare loss are somewhat inconsistent, and this can lead to paradoxical conclusions. These inconsistencies suggest potential measurement errors, and as will be explained later, can be traced back to the presence of income effects.

Example 2. Measuring society's preference for one program over another, in dollars. Should schools teach music or art (if they cannot afford both)? The government must choose between policy M (music education) and policy A (art education). There are two regions of the country, the East and the West. Preferences are different for M and A in the two regions. Social welfare from the alternative policies is measured by aggregating naive willingness to pay. We call this "naive" because it is too simple, too deficient in informed judgment. Naive willingness to pay depends only on income levels; each family is willing to pay 2 percent of its income for the program it likes more, but only 1 percent of its income for the program it likes less. The problem is that this social welfare measure is too dependent on the income distribution. Society's choice between M and A will only depend on whether wealthy people live in the East or the West.

We now turn to an important assumption that prevents problems such as these. There are situations in which this assumption will be a good approximation of reality, but there will be others when it won't be; Section 7.6 elaborates on this.

The key is to assume that the goods available to consumers in society, and the utility functions of those consumers, have a special property. There is one good that enters everyone's utility function in the same way, and the way it enters it is as a simple additive term. For example, if the special good is apples, then each person's utility can be written as

$$u_i(\text{everything}) = v_i(\text{everything except apples}) + \text{apples}.$$

Here the v_i function represents person i's utility from everything *except* apples. If this is the case, we can measure a change in i's utility as an apple equivalent, and there is no problem in measurement, because an apple is an apple. (Speaking loosely, we do know about Macintosh versus Red Delicious, fresh versus rotten!) Moreover, if we measure apples in one-dollar units, then a change in i's utility becomes a dollar equivalent, and there is again no problem in measurement, because a dollar is a dollar.

Finally, if we are looking at social welfare rather than the welfare of one individual, instead of summing over utilities for the various people, which is not legitimate, we can sum over quantities of apples or quantities of dollars for the various people, which is perfectly legitimate.

More formally, we proceed this way. We assume that there are two goods. The first good enters the utility functions of different people in different ways; opinions are divided about it. However, the second good enters everybody's utility function as a simple additive term. We assume that the second good is measured in one-dollar units, so $p_2 = 1$. (When we measure a good in units chosen so that 1 unit costs 1 dollar, we call it a *numeraire good*.) Although good 2 should be viewed as a real "good," that is, as something the consumer consumes, it may also be a composite of various other things whose relative prices do not change. We will call it the *money good*, although it should not be mistaken for the consumer's income M.

Now, let us focus on one consumer. When we are considering just one person, we do not need a subscript i to identify her. Her utility u is a function of the quantities of the two goods that she consumes, (x_1, x_2). We say that she has *quasilinear preferences* if her utility function can be written as

$$u(x_1, x_2) = v(x_1) + x_2.$$

Here, v is an increasing and concave function of x_1. Note that x_2 enters our consumer's utility function as a simple additive term.

We say that the utility functions of the various individuals, as a group, satisfy *quasilinear preferences* if they can all be written in this form, with the quantity of the second good entering in the same way in every utility function, but with the $v(x_1)$ terms generally differing between consumers.

At this point we can note that the quasilinearity assumption would rule out the simple product utility function used in Example 1.

7.3 Consumer's Surplus

Note the location of the apostrophe in the heading of this section; we are again focusing on one person. Our consumer wants to maximize her utility subject to her budget constraint:

$$\max \; u(x_1, x_2) = v(x_1) + x_2 \quad \text{subject to} \quad p_1 x_1 + x_2 = M.$$

The two equations that describe her choice are the budget line equation and the tangency condition $MRS = v'(x_1)/1 = v'(x_1) = p_1/p_2 = p_1$.

We assumed earlier that the function v is concave. This assumption guarantees that the consumer's preferences are convex; that is, the consumer's indifference curves have the standard curvature. If we move to the right on any indifference curve, the curve must get flatter and flatter. But quasilinearity implies much more: it implies that the consumer's indifference curves have some very special properties. If we fix x_1, the consumer's marginal rate of substitution is constant, equal to $v'(x_1)$, the marginal utility of the first good at x_1. Therefore, if we graph some indifference curves in an x_1, x_2 picture, and if we go straight up from a fixed x_1, (1) the slopes of the indifference curves above the given x_1 are constant. It is also the case that (2) if we take any two different indifference curves, the vertical gap between them is constant, no matter what x_1 might be. That is, under quasilinearity, *any two indifference curves are vertical translations of each other.* We say, somewhat loosely speaking, that the indifference curves are "parallel." (The quotation marks are there because being parallel is usually defined as a geometric property of straight lines.) Showing point (2) will be left as an exercise at the end of this chapter. Figure 7.1 shows a consumer's indifference curves under the assumption of quasilinear preferences.

Recall that in Example 1, as the consumer moves from x^* to x^{**}, her compensating variation loss (of \$9) and her equivalent variation loss (of \$6) are *different.* This leads to a worrisome paradox. We have already noted that the quasilinearity assumption rules out the product utility function used in Example 1. But quasilinearity does more than ruling out the Example 1 utility function; quasilinearity rules out the possibility of any difference between compensating variation and equivalent variation. Therefore, it rules out the type of paradox encountered in Example 1. We show this in Figure 7.2.

Figure 7.2 is based on the income and price assumptions of Example 1. However, we now assume a quasilinear utility function $u(x_1, x_2) = v(x_1) + x_2$. In Figure 7.2, as in Figure 6.3, compensating variation is the y to x^{**} income effect move, based on the new prices, whereas equivalent variation is the x^* to z income effect move, based on the old prices. Because of quasilinearity, y is directly above x^{**}, and x^* is directly above z. Also because of quasilinearity, the vertical gap between the two indifference curves in the figure is constant. Because $p_2 = 1$ and because the

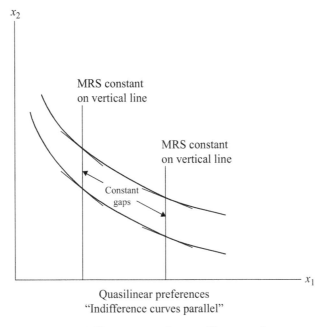

Fig. 7.1. Indifference map for quasilinear preferences.

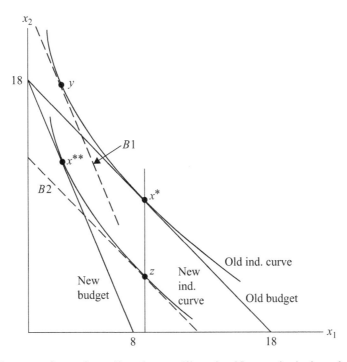

Fig. 7.2. The move from x^* to x^{**} under quasilinearity. No paradoxical result is possible.

vertical gaps between y and x^{**} and between x^* and z are equal, compensating variation must equal equivalent variation, and the Example 1 paradox is impossible.

At this point we derive a consumer's demand function under the quasilinearity assumption. The consumer wants to maximize $v(x_1) + x_2$, subject to $p_1 x_1 + x_2 = M$. (We are assuming $p_2 = 1$.) From the tangency condition, we get $v'(x_1) = p_1$. We let v'^{-1} represent the *inverse* of the v' function. Therefore, $x_1 = v'^{-1}(p_1)$ shows the consumer's desired consumption of good 1, contingent on the price p_1. That is, v'^{-1} is the consumer's *demand function* for good 1. Her demand for good 2 is given by $x_2 = M - p_1 x_1$. We assume for simplicity that the consumer's income M is large enough such that she spends positive amounts on both goods.

Now note that under quasilinearity, the consumer's demand for good 1 is independent of her income M; her demand for good 1 depends only on p_1, the price of good 1 (or, more generally, on the relative price of good 1, p_1/p_2). This rules out the objectionable outcome of Example 2.

We can easily draw the consumer's demand curve for good 1. We simply graph the equation for the demand function, $x_1 = v'^{-1}(p_1)$, or equivalently, we graph the equation for the inverse demand function, $p_1 = v'(x_1)$. (There is just one graph for demand and for inverse demand, the only difference is that demand is read from vertical (price) to horizontal (quantity), and inverse demand is read from horizontal (quantity) to vertical (price).) See Figure 7.3, in which we also include a horizontal line at a particular price p_1^*. When we read the graph from vertical to horizontal, it shows the amount of good 1 the consumer wants to consume at any particular price. When we read the same graph from horizontal to vertical, it shows, for each x_1, the corresponding $p_1 = v'(x_1)$. But $v'(x_1) = MRS$. So, for a given x_1, the height of the (inverse) demand curve is the number of dollars or units of good 2 (remember we are assuming $p_2 = 1$), that the consumer would be willing to give up in exchange for one more unit of good 1. (The "one more unit" is what economists often call the *marginal unit*; it is the additional or incremental unit.) Naturally, we call the height of the (inverse) demand curve the consumer's *willingness to pay* for a marginal unit of good 1.

It is important to note that the equation $v'(x_1) = p_1$ does not include the terms M or x_2. Therefore, neither the consumer's demand for x_1 (contingent on p_1) nor her willingness to pay for an additional unit of good 1 (contingent on x_1) depends on how much income she has, or on how much good 2 she is consuming. Consequently, willingness to pay, as we use it here and in the rest of this chapter, avoids the bad implications of naive willingness to pay as described in Example 2.

Now consider the horizontal line in Figure 7.3. It crosses the demand curve at the point (x_1^*, p_1^*). When the consumer is paying a price of p_1^* and consuming x_1^* units of good 1, her willingness to pay is p_1^* for the additional or marginal unit; that is, for the x_1^*th unit. However, for any $x_1 < x_1^*$, the willingness to pay is higher. For the first unit, the second unit, and so on, her willingness to pay is the height of the demand curve at each of those points. In a sense, when she is buying x_1^* at price p_1^*,

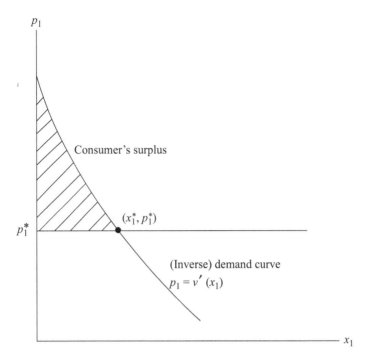

Fig. 7.3. The consumer's willingness to pay for good 1, and the consumer's surplus.

she is getting a real bargain, because she is getting the first unit, the second unit, and so on, at lower prices than what she is willing to pay. This is true for every bit of good 1 that she is consuming up to the marginal unit, the x_1^*th.

We can now suggest a way to measure our consumer's benefit from the situation at hand, of being able to buy and consume x_1^* units of good 1 (and simultaneously, buy and consume $M - p_1^* x_1^*$ units of good 2). *Consumer's surplus* is the aggregate amount, over all units consumed, of the consumer's willingness to pay for the additional units, minus the amount actually paid. This is the area in Figure 7.3 under the demand curve and above the horizontal line at p_1^*. Under the assumption of quasilinearity, the consumer's surplus is not sensitive to income levels or levels of consumption of the other good(s). Finally, note that the consumer's surplus is measured in dollars (or in units of good 2), rather than in utility units for our particular consumer. This will allow us to add together the consumer's surpluses of two different consumers.

7.4 A Consumer's Surplus Example with Quasilinear Preferences

We will now work out an example similar to Example 1, but with quasilinear preferences. Remember that Example 1 produced a disturbing inconsistency between compensating variation and equivalent variation, and a strange paradox. In the example to which we now turn, we will see that the compensating variation and equivalent variation measures are exactly equal (making inconsistencies and para-doxes impossible), and that they are precisely equal to the change in the consumer's surplus.

Example 3. A quasilinear utility function, with a rise in p_1. Compensating variation, equivalent variation, and the change in consumer's surplus. As in Example 1, we assume that the consumer's income is $M = 18$, and the prices at the start are $p_1 = 1$ and $p_2 = 1$. As before, the change will be an increase in the price of good 1, to $p_1 = 2.25$. In contrast to Example 1, we now assume the utility function is

$$u(x_1, x_2) = \ln x_1 + x_2.$$

Note that $u(x_1, x_2)$ is quasilinear. Setting MRS equal to the price ratio gives

$$MRS = \frac{MU_1}{MU_2} = \frac{1}{x_1} = \frac{p_1}{p_2} = p_1.$$

Therefore, the consumer's demand function for good 1 is $x_1 = 1/p_1$.

Note that the consumer's demand for good 1 is independent of her income M. At the start, when $p_1 = 1$ and $p_2 = 1$, she will choose $x_1^* = 1$; because her budget constraint is $x_1 + x_2 = M = 18$, $x_2^* = 17$. That is, her initial utility-maximizing bundle is $x^* = (x_1^*, x_2^*) = (1, 17)$. Her initial utility level is $u(x^*) = \ln 1 + 17 = 17$.

Now, we assume that the price of good 1 rises to $p_1 = 2.25$, while M and p_2 remain the same. The consumer is worse off, as she can no longer afford the bundle she had been consuming before.

We first use the demand function to find her new desired quantity of good 1: $x_1^{**} = 1/p_1 = 1/2.25 = 4/9$. Then we use the budget constraint, $2.25(4/9) + x_2 = 18$, which gives $x_2^{**} = 17$. Therefore, her new utility-maximizing bundle is $x^{**} = (x_1^{**}, x_2^{**}) = (4/9, 17)$. Her new utility level is $u(x^{**}) = \ln(4/9) + 17 = 17 - \ln(9/4) = 16.19$. In the move from the old point x^* to the new point x^{**}, her utility drops by $17 - 16.19 = 0.81$ utility units. As was the case with Example 1, this information is not particularly helpful, because we do not know how to interpret a utility unit.

We now want to measure the consumer's welfare change in terms of the com-pensating variation measure (the income effect based on the new prices) and the equivalent variation measure (the income effect based on old prices). It will help to refer to Figure 7.2, which shows all the relevant points and lines, although the horizontal and vertical coordinates are off because that figure was not drawn for this particular quasilinear utility function.

The original consumer optimum is at $x^* = (1, 17)$ and the new consumer opti-mum is at $x^{**} = (4/9, 17)$. To find the compensating variation measure of the consumer's loss, we need to find the point corresponding to y in Figure 7.2. We know that y is on the old indifference curve, so $\ln y_1 + y_2 = u(x^*) = 17$. We also know that y is directly above x^{**}, so $y_1 = x_1^{**} = 4/9$. Therefore, the vertical coordinate of y is $y_2 = 17 - \ln(4/9) = 17 + \ln(9/4)$, and the vertical gap between y and x^{**} equals $17 + \ln(9/4) - 17 = \ln(9/4) = 0.81$. Because $p_2 = 1$, the compensating variation measure of the consumer's loss is \$0.81.

The equivalent variation measure is based on the vertical gap between x^* and z in Figure 7.2. We will not go over the detailed calculations, which are obviously very similar to what we just did. Remember, though, that under the quasilinearity assumption, the vertical distance or gap between two indifference curves is constant as x_1 varies. In short, the equivalent variation measure of the consumer's loss is also $\ln(9/4)$, or \$0.81.

Next, we figure out the consumer's loss of consumer's surplus as p_1 changes from 1.0 to 2.25. Figure 7.3 shows the consumer's surplus as the area under a demand curve (or, more precisely, an inverse demand curve) but above p_1^* for a consumer consuming x_1^* units of good 1 when the price is p_1^*. Figure 7.4 applies this method to our Example 3 consumer, whose inverse demand function is $p_1 = 1/x_1$.

In Figure 7.4, when the price is $p_1 = 1$, the consumer's surplus is the area under the inverse demand curve but above $p_1 = 1$. When the price is $p_2 = 2.25$, the consumer's surplus is the area under the inverse demand curve but above $p_1 = 2.25$. The *change in consumer's surplus* is therefore the roughly trapezoidal difference between these two areas, shown with cross-hatching in the figure. We need to find the area of the cross-hatched region. Let's call it CS. Note first that CS is the sum of the area of a (cross-hatched) rectangle and the area of a (cross-hatched) roughly triangular region ABC. The area of the cross-hatched rectangle is $(4/9) \times (9/4 - 1) = (4/9) \times (5/4) = 5/9$.

To find the area of the ABC rough triangle in Figure 7.4, we first take the integral of the inverse demand function, going from $x_1 = 4/9$ to $x_1 = 1$. This gives us the area below the inverse demand curve, down to the horizontal axis, between $x_1 = 4/9$ and $x_1 = 1$. Then we subtract the area of the rectangle immediately below the ABC rough triangle, which is $(5/9) \times 1 = 5/9$.

In short, CS will equal the integral of the inverse demand curve from $x_1 = 4/9$ to $x_1 = 1$, minus $5/9$ (for the area of the non–cross-hatched rectangle below ABC), plus $5/9$ (for the area of the cross-hatched rectangle to the left of ABC). That is, CS equals the integral of the inverse demand curve from $x_1 = 4/9$ to $x_1 = 1$. We now have

$$CS = \int_{x_1=4/9}^{x_1=1} \frac{1}{x_1} \, dx_1 = \ln 1 - \ln\left(\frac{4}{9}\right) = 0 + \ln\left(\frac{9}{4}\right) = 0.81.$$

We conclude that when p_1 rises from 1 to 2.25, our consumer with quasilinear preferences suffers a loss. Whether we calculate her loss using the compensating variation measure, the equivalent variation measure, or the consumer's surplus measure, we get the same answer, \$0.81. And 0.81 is also her loss in utility units.

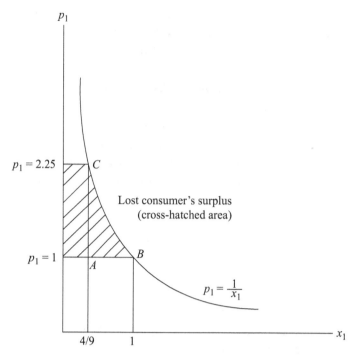

Fig. 7.4. The cross-hatched area is the loss of consumer's surplus when p_1 rises from 1 to 2.25. For this quasilinear preferences example, compensating variation, equivalent variation, and consumer's surplus all agree.

7.5 Consumers' Surplus

Note the changed location of the apostrophe. We are now discussing a *social measure*, and allowing for many people.

Suppose we have a group of consumers with quasilinear preferences. For each consumer, separately, we do the exercise described previously. This will produce a demand curve for each consumer, showing consumer i's demand for good 1, contingent on p_1, the price of good 1. We write this as $x_{i1} = v_i'^{-1}(p_1)$. We then add all the demand functions together. That is, for each p_1, we add together the amounts demanded by the various consumers. (Because economists put good 1 on the horizontal axis and p_1 on the vertical axis, this is sometimes called "adding the demand curves horizontally." See Chapter 4.) Let $X_1(p_1)$ be the resulting *market demand* curve. Based on the assumptions we have been making in this section, the market demand curve is independent of the incomes of the various consumers and of their consumption levels for the other good.

As was the case with individual demand curves, we can read points on the market demand curve $X_1(p_1)$ in two ways. We can read them from the vertical coordinate (price) to the horizontal coordinate (quantity). This reading says that at each price p_1, there is a market demand $X_1(p_1)$ that is the sum of the individual demands of all the consumers: $X_1(p_1) = x_{11}(p_1) + x_{21}(p_1) + \cdots$. Or we can read them from the horizontal coordinate (total quantity demanded) to the vertical coordinate (price), with the understanding that the total demand is based on particular amounts demanded by consumer 1, consumer 2, and so on. With this reading, for a given X_1, there is an underlying list of desired quantities of good 1 for the various consumers, which sum to X_1. In this list, consumer 1's willingness to pay for an additional unit is equal to p_1, consumer 2's willingness to pay for an additional unit is also equal to p_1, and so on, for all the consumers.

Now, fix the price p_1 at p_1^*. There is a corresponding market demand X_1^*. For each of the consumers, there is an individual demand curve, and an amount of consumer's surplus associated with the consumer being able to buy her desired amount of good 1 at the price p_1^* per unit. That amount of consumer's surplus for consumer i is in money units or units of good 2. Adding together money amounts of consumer's surplus over all the consumers makes perfectly good sense. Doing so produces the *consumers' surplus*, which is simply aggregated consumer's surpluses.

Finally, the economist can find consumers' surplus in a simple graphical way without looking at the separate demand curves of the various consumers. For the fixed p_1^*, simply find the area under the market demand curve, above the horizontal line at p_1^*. That is, take the market demand function, reading it from the horizontal axis (quantity) to the vertical axis (price), and integrate it from $X_1 = 0$ to $X_1 = X_1^*$. Then subtract $p_1^* X_1^*$. The result is *consumers' surplus*.

The formal mathematical definition is as follows. Let $X_1(p_1)$ represent the market demand function (reading from price to market quantity), and let $V_1(X_1)$ represent the inverse market demand function (reading from market quantity to price). Let p_1^* be a given market price, and suppose X_1^* is the corresponding market quantity. We abbreviate consumers' surplus CsS (note the plural "consumers"). Consumers' surplus, given (p_1^*, X_1^*), is now defined as:

$$CsS = \int_{X_1=0}^{X_1=X_1^*} V_1(X_1) dX_1 - p_1^* X_1^*.$$

In Figure 7.5, we show two consumers' individual demand curves for good 1, assumed here for the sake of simplicity to be linear, and we show a market demand curve, which is drawn as the (horizontal) sum of the two individual demand curves. The market price is at p_1^*. Consumers' surplus is shown in the graph of the market demand curve. We leave it as an exercise for the student to show that in Figure 7.5, consumers' surplus equals consumer 1's surplus plus consumer 2's surplus.

Example 4. Build a bridge? Here is a rather typical application of consumers' surplus.

Suppose the government is considering building a bridge. There is just one size, and it will either be built or not be built. It will cost $1 million (per unit

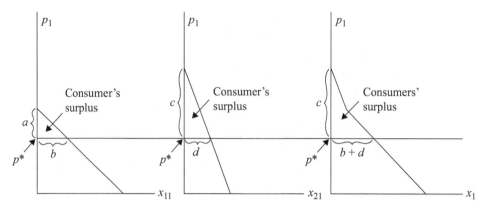

Fig. 7.5. Consumer's surplus for two consumers, and consumers' surplus.

time) if built, and nothing if not built. Assume quasilinear preferences. Local econometricians have estimated a market demand curve for the bridge, given by $X(p) = 1,000,000 - 200,000p$, where p is the price charged by the government for use of the bridge, per unit time, or the *user fee*. The government wants to build the bridge if it is socially worthwhile to do so. Building the bridge is socially worthwhile if and only if the *net social benefit* is nonnegative; that is, if and only if consumers' surplus given the price, plus the net profit to the government (revenue minus cost, or $pX(p) - \$1,000,000$) is greater than or equal to zero. Should the bridge be built? If so, what price should be charged?

To determine whether the bridge should be built, we can calculate consumers' surplus at the user fee that maximizes the consumers' surplus, namely, $p = 0$. The consumers' surplus triangle at $p = 0$ has a height of $5 and a base of 1,000,000, and therefore, an area (one-half base times height) of $2,500,000. This far exceeds the cost of building the bridge, so the bridge certainly should be built.

However, the government might be reluctant to build the bridge and charge a user fee of $0. What if it requires a p just high enough to cover its cost of building the bridge? In that case, it requires that the fee revenue cover costs, or $pX(p) = 1,000,000$. This leads to $5p - p^2 = 5$, which gives $p = (5 - \sqrt{5})/2 = 1.382$.

But is charging $p = \$1.382$ the best policy? We leave it as an exercise for the student to compare the net social benefit (consumers' surplus plus government revenue minus the cost of the bridge) under three alternative policies: build the bridge and charge a user fee of $p = \$0$, or build the bridge and charge a user fee of $p = \$1.382$, or build the bridge and charge the user fee that maximizes government revenue.

7.6 A Last Word on the Quasilinearity Assumption

Our measures of consumer's surplus (one person) and consumers' surplus (many people) make good sense under the assumption of quasilinearity, but may be objectionable without that assumption. We should not be complacent about this, and should not take the quasilinearity assumption lightly, because many plausible utility functions are not quasilinear. For example, the utility function we used in Example 1, $u(x_1, x_2) = x_1 x_2$, is not quasilinear, and neither are commonly used variations on the same theme, such as $u(x_1, x_2) = x_1^\alpha x_2^\beta$. (This is called a Cobb-Douglas utility function.) These utility functions, and many others, simply cannot be rewritten as $v(x_1) + x_2$, and indifference curves for these utility functions do not have the indifference curve properties for quasilinear utility functions that we used in this chapter, namely, that the MRS is constant for fixed x_1, and that for any two indifference curves, the vertical gap between them is constant as x_1 varies. For utility functions such as these, income effects on good 1 are not zero. Then, as Example 1 showed, compensating variation and equivalent variation measures produce paradoxical results, and demand functions for good 1 depend on income M. In short, quasilinearity is a big assumption, which is not likely to be true for a utility function blindly picked out of a hat, and we should not take it lightly.

Economists sometimes try to avoid the quasilinearity assumption by measuring consumer's surplus and consumers' surplus with *compensated demand curves*. With such demand curves, the income effects have already been teased out, so the objectionable results of Examples 1 and 2 may be avoided. In a similar fashion, economists may try to avoid problems in the logic of the consumer's and consumers' surplus by focusing on goods for which income effects are minor (goods such as zucchini, apples, toothpaste, or the services of a bridge used in the commute to work). However, we should be aware of the limitations of the concept when applying it to markets with significant income effects (such as housing, health care, and the like). To return to the issue raised in Example 2, the quasilinearity assumption makes our conclusions independent of the income distribution. Quasilinearity makes demand independent of income, and in effect makes the marginal utility of income equal to 1 for every consumer. But are we really willing to say that an additional dollar of income is valued the same by Bill Gates and by the poorest person in your hometown?

7.7 A Solved Problem

The Problem

The small state of Rhode Island in the United States is planning to build a state-of-the-art highway from Providence to Newport. The aggregate demand for highway services between the two cities is given by $x = 100,000 - 20,000P$, where x measures the number of cars and P the toll charged to the user. Assume quasilinear preferences. The total cost of the highway is estimated as $300,000. (All prices and costs quoted are per unit time.) The state has decided not to charge a toll on this road. The project will go ahead if consumers' surplus covers at least the total cost of the project.

(a) Should the highway be built?
(b) Newport plans an advertising campaign ("Come to Newport – The City by the Sea!") that will cost $10,000, and will cause the highway demand to double to $x = 200,000 - 40,000P$. Should the ad campaign *and* the highway project be carried out?

The Solution

(a) The demand curve is linear. Its vertical intercept is $P = 100,000/20,000 = 5$, and its horizontal intercept is $x = 100,000$. Consumers' surplus is the area under the demand curve and above the horizontal axis (where $P = 0$). Therefore, consumers' surplus is the area of a triangle with height 5 and base 100,000, or $\frac{1}{2} \times 5 \times 100,000 = \$250,000$. Therefore, the highway should not be built.
(b) If the advertising campaign happens, the demand curve will shift out. The new vertical intercept is $P = 200,000/40,000 = 5$, which is the same as the old intercept, and the new horizontal intercept is $x = 200,000$. The new consumers' surplus is the area of a triangle with height 5 and base 200,000, or $\frac{1}{2} \times 5 \times 200,000 = \$500,000$. Because $\$500,000$ is greater than the sum of the cost of the highway ($\$300,000$) and the cost of the advertising campaign ($\$10,000$), both the ad campaign and the highway project should be carried out.

Exercises

1. Assume a consumer has quasilinear preferences. Consider two of her indifference curves, corresponding to $u(x_1, x_2) = 5$ and $u(x_1, x_2) = 10$. Show that the vertical distance between the two indifference curves remains constant, no matter what x_1 might be.
2. In Example 3, compensating variation, equivalent variation, and the change in consumer's surplus were all equal to $-\$0.81$. The change in utility was -0.81 utility units. Can you explain why the change measured in utility units was identical to the change measured in dollars?
3. In Figure 7.5, prove (using simple geometry) that consumers' surplus equals consumer 1's surplus plus consumer 2's surplus.
4. Consider again the story of the bridge in Example 4.
    (a) Calculate the net social benefit when $p = 0$ and when $p = (5 - \sqrt{5})/2 = 1.382$.
    (b) Find the price that would maximize government revenue from the bridge, $pX(p)$. If the government chooses the price that maximizes revenue, what is the net social benefit?
    (c) Explain this claim: because the cost of the bridge is fixed at $\$1,000,000$, the net social benefit must be maximized when $p = 0$. Can you find a formula for the net social benefit?
5. Consider the utility function of Example 1, $u(x) = u(x_1, x_2) = x_1 x_2$. Assume again that the consumer has $M = 18$, that the prices are $p_1 = 1$ and $p_2 = 1$ to start, and that the price of good 1 rises to $p_1 = 2.25$. Recall that the consumer's demand function for

good 1 is $x_1 = M/2p_1$. Find the loss of consumer's surplus resulting from the rise in p_1. (Hint: Look at the methodology of Example 3, sketch a picture similar to Figure 7.4, and integrate.)

6. Carter's utility function is $u(x, y) = 10x + \frac{1}{3}x^3 + y$.

   (a) Find his demand function for x, $x(p_x)$. How many units of x does he demand when $p_x = 1$ and $p_y = 1$?

   (b) Find his inverse demand function for x, $p_x(x)$. What is his consumer surplus?

   (c) Suppose the price of x rises to $p_x = 6$ while p_y is unchanged. How many units of x does he demand now? What is his new consumer surplus?

Part II

Theory of the Producer

Chapter 8

Theory of the Firm 1: The Single-Input Model

8.1 Introduction

Production is the transformation of inputs into outputs. The production process typically takes place within firms. They buy or hire various inputs and combine them, using available technology, to produce various outputs of goods and services. Then they sell the outputs they produce. For example, a firm that makes video games hires different kinds of labor (game experts, programmers, salespeople, accountants, lawyers, and so on) and buys or rents various capital goods (office space, computer equipment, Internet access, furniture, and so on) to make and market games. A farm, whose land and machinery are more or less fixed in the short term, employs labor to produce corn. In the farm example, it is plausible to think of the production process as one that uses one input to produce one output.

In this chapter, we develop a simple production model with just one input and one output; we call it the *single-input/single-output model*. At the end of the chapter we briefly describe a model with a single input and multiple outputs – most firms in reality have many outputs – and we will provide techniques for solving its profit maximization problem. Later, in the next chapter, we will move on to the case of the production of a single output with multiple inputs, the *multiple-input/single-output model*.

Focusing on the simple single-input/single-output model is definitely not the usual textbook approach. Most books on microeconomics start with a two-input/one-output model, the kind that we will cover in our next chapter. We think that either approach – single-input/single-output or multiple-input/single-output – can be used to introduce a reader to the most important implications of the theory of the firm. In this book we give the reader a choice.

When we developed the theory of the consumer in Chapters 2 and 3, we modeled his or her goals (finding a most-preferred bundle, or maximizing utility) and his or her constraints (the budget constraint). Similarly, we will now model the goals and the constraints for a typical firm. As for goals, we will assume that the firm wants to maximize its profit, that is, revenue minus the cost of production. There may be some debate about this assumption. For instance, some analysts assume that firms want to maximize market shares, rather than profits, or that the managers of some firms may be more interested in maximizing their own compensation levels, rather than their firms' profits. Moreover, many important institutions in society are explicitly nonprofit, including most government institutions and many schools, charities, universities, and hospitals. Our model may not fit them well at all. However, economists feel that the profit motive – money, money, money – usually motivates private firms that are in the business of producing and selling goods and services.

What about the firm's constraints? There are two kinds. First, there are technological constraints. This means that the firm must work with an existing body of scientific and technical knowledge, and the restrictions imposed by nature. For example, it is impossible for Federal Express, no matter how effectively managed, to deliver a package on the day before it was sent. That is due to a law of nature. And it is impossible for Pfizer (currently the world's largest pharmaceutical firm) to make a pill that cures all forms of cancer. That is because it cannot be done, given the reality of current science and technology. Such restrictions are embodied in the idea of a *production function*. A production function is a mathematical description of how the firm can transform inputs into outputs, given the technological constraints. Second, there are market constraints. These are the constraints on the prices and quantities of the inputs the firm uses, and on the prices and quantities of the outputs the firm sells.

We start this chapter by describing the single-input/single-output model. In Section 8.2, we assume that the firm's output is its choice variable, and in Section 8.3, we will assume the firm's input is its choice variable. In Section 8.2, we derive the firm's supply function for its output, or its supply curve, and in Section 8.3, we derive the firm's demand function for its input, or its demand curve. In Section 8.4, we consider the case of many outputs – that is, the single-input/multiple-output model.

8.2 The Competitive Firm's Problem, Focusing on Its Output

The Production Function

We assume now that the firm produces one output using one input. The output quantity is y; the input quantity is x. (For instance, the farm produces y bushels of corn using x units of labor.) The technological constraints on the firm are represented by its *production function* $y = f(x)$. The function shows the maximum output y that the firm can produce if it uses x units of the input.

The first basic assumption we make about the production function is *monotonicity*. This means that as x increases, y also increases. Formally, the first derivative of the production function, $f'(x)$, is positive. This is a very plausible assumption in most situations. Think of the farm that grows corn – more labor on the farm means more corn. Of course, if the farm is 10 acres, and the farm already employs so many workers that they cannot physically fit on 10 acres, then monotonicity is implausible. But we assume that firms try to make money, and a firm interested in making money would never use so many workers that an additional unit of labor produces negative additional output.

The second basic assumption that we make about the production function has to do with its curvature. We have two alternative versions of this assumption: a simple version and a more realistic version. The simple assumption is *concavity*. Concavity says that, whereas increases in x lead to increases in y, the increases get smaller and smaller as x gets bigger and bigger. Mathematically, whereas the first derivative of the production function, $f'(x)$, is positive, the second derivative, $f''(x)$, is negative. This is sometimes described as the assumption of *diminishing returns*. Think of that 10-acre farm. Suppose there are n workers, and one worker is added. This will result in some increment of corn, say 100 bushels. But going from $n + 1$ to $n + 2$ workers will result in a smaller increment of corn, say 90 bushels, and so on.

David Ricardo (1772–1823), a descendant of Sephardic Jews from Portugal and an eloquent member of the British Parliament, was one of the great classical economists (along with Adam Smith (1723–1790) and Thomas Malthus (1766–1834)). He once gave a speech against the corn laws, which put tariffs on grain imports to Britain. In the speech, he justified the assumption of diminishing returns. He argued that if it were not for diminishing returns, one could feed all of England, and all the world for that matter, simply by putting more and more labor into raising grain planted in one flower pot. His *reductio ad absurdum* argument convinced his opponents that diminishing returns are real, but the corn laws lived on until 1846.

The more realistic curvature assumption is that the production function is convex at first, and then turns concave. More formally, $f'(x)$ is always positive, but $f''(x)$ is at first positive, passes through zero, and then becomes (and stays) negative. That is, when x is small, $f'(x)$ is increasing as x increases, but when x is big, $f'(x)$ is decreasing. This is sometimes described as "increasing returns" when the firm is small, followed by "diminishing returns" when the firm is large. The firm becomes more and more efficient as it grows from size zero, in the sense that, if x is the number of workers, the incremental output of an additional worker gets greater and greater, until the firm reaches maximal efficiency, in the sense that the incremental output of an additional worker is maximized, after which the incremented output gets smaller and smaller. Many real production functions have this property, so we will call it the *real-world convexity/concavity* assumption, or the *real-world* assumption for short. For reasons that will soon become clear, this is also called the *U-shaped average cost curve* assumption.

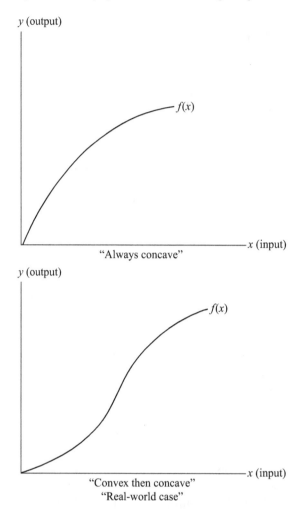

Fig. 8.1. Two production functions: (a) the always-concave case and (b) the real-world case.

In Figure 8.1 we draw two production functions. The first is always concave; the second shows the real-world case, with a production function that is convex at first and then becomes concave.

We will also assume $f(0) = 0$. This means that our firm has the option of choosing to use no input x and produce no output y. That is, our firm can shut down, hire no input, and sell nothing. If it does this, it has zero profit.

Price or Market Constraints

So far we have talked about the technological constraints. We now turn to the market constraints. At this point we assume that our firm operates in perfectly competitive markets. When we say that a firm (or, for that matter, a consumer) operates in a *competitive market*, we mean that the firm (or the consumer) takes the price as given. We assume that our firm is competitive in the market where it buys or hires its input x, and that it is competitive in the market where it sells its output y. Let w represent the input price (w suggesting "wage") and let p represent the output price. Our competitive firm takes both w and p as given and fixed; that is, beyond its control. The firm acts as a price taker when it is deciding how to maximize profits. The assumption that the firm is competitive in the markets for its input and for its output is especially reasonable for small firms (small in the sense that they use only a small fraction of the input good sold to various firms, and provide only a small fraction of the output good sold by the various firms that sell the same good). For instance, a corn farmer in the midwestern United States, even one with a 1,000-acre farm, will produce only a minute fraction of the corn produced each year for the U.S. market. It will be competitive in the market for its output. It will also probably use only a small part of the labor input available in the local labor market. Thus, the small farmer is competitive in its input market and in its output market. On the other hand, there are some very large firms that *buy* corn, and some of them may be so large that their decisions about how much to buy will affect the market price for corn. We would not call them competitive in the corn market. Note that this example illustrates that in any market there are buyers and there are sellers, and there may be competitive behavior or noncompetitive behavior on either side of the market.

Profit

Let us now think more carefully about profit. *Profit* is the difference between revenue and cost. We will write π for profit. (In Chapters 3 and 5 the symbol π was used for inflation. In this and later chapters π means profit.) Profit is usually measured as money per unit time, or what is called a *flow*, such as "$500 per month" or "$1 billion per year." However, we drop the time reference when no confusion results. *Revenue* is the money that comes into the firm from the sale of its output. In our case, revenue is $py(x)$. *Cost* is the money that goes out of the firm because of its purchase of its input. In our case, cost is wx. Like profit, revenue and cost are both money amounts per unit time, but we will usually drop the time reference.

Our firm wants to select the input quantity x, and/or the output quantity y, that will maximize profit:

$$\pi = py - wx.$$

We can substitute $y(x)$ for y in the above equation, in which case we are left with the simple problem of finding the x that maximizes profit, as a function of x:

$$\pi(x) = py(x) - wx.$$

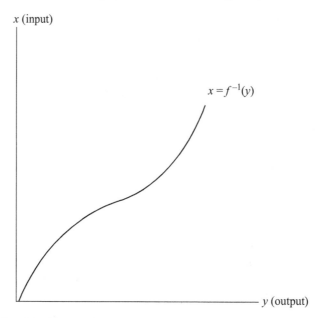

Fig. 8.2. The conditional factor demand in the real-world case.

Alternatively, we can look at the inverse of the production function $x = f^{-1}(y)$. We can use this function to substitute for x in the expression for profit, and then we are left with the simple problem of finding the y that maximizes profit, as a function of y:

$$\pi(y) = py - wf^{-1}(y).$$

In this section, we take the second approach. We "solve out" the input variable x, treat profit as a function of output y, and solve the profit maximization problem by finding the y that maximizes $\pi(y)$.

Consider again the inverse of the production function $x = f^{-1}(y)$. For a given output level y, it shows the amount of the input x that the firm must use to produce y. When there is only one input, the firm doesn't have much to think about. If it wants to produce and sell y, it must use $x = f^{-1}(y)$. However, when we analyze the behavior of the firm that uses two or more inputs, then this stage of the decision making will become much more interesting and complicated, because the firm will have to decide, for a given level of output y, what combination of inputs will produce that output at least cost. We put off this question to the next chapter.

For now, if the firm is to produce and sell y, it must buy or hire x. Looked at this way, the function $f^{-1}(y)$ shows what's called the firm's *conditional input demand* or *conditional factor demand*. Figure 8.2 shows this factor demand function for the real-world case of a production function that is convex at first, and then turns concave. The function shown in Figure 8.2, which is the inverse of the second

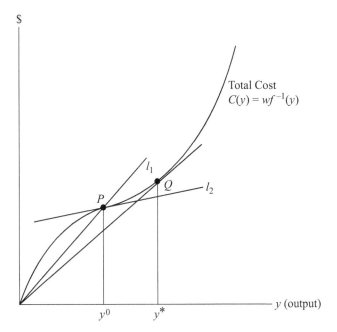

Fig. 8.3. The total cost curve in the real-world case.

function shown in Figure 8.1, can be found by flipping the axes in Figure 8.1 – just put x on the vertical axis and y on the horizontal axis. Also note that this function starts out concave, and then turns convex.

Total Cost, Average Cost, and Marginal Cost

Let us go back to the problem at hand, which is to maximize the firm's profit (as a function of y) – that is, to maximize $\pi(y) = py - wf^{-1}(y)$. We call $wf^{-1}(y)$ the firm's *total cost function* and write it as $C(y)$. This is the cost in dollars – or currency – that the firm must pay if it wants to produce y units of the output. We show a graph of the total cost function, or the total cost curve, in Figure 8.3. Notice that the total cost curve is simply a translation of the conditional input demand curve in this simple single-input model. In Figure 8.3, we also show a point P on the total cost curve, and, at P, a ray from the origin through P, labeled l_1, and a line l_2 that is tangent to the total cost curve at P. The horizontal component of P is identified as y^0. The point Q in the graph, corresponding to output y^*, is where a ray from the origin is tangent to the total cost curve.

Now, consider the straight lines in Figure 8.3. First, look at l_1. The slope of l_1 is important; it equals the height of P, which is the total cost of producing the quantity y^0, divided by the horizontal coordinate of P, which is y^0. That is, the slope of l_1 is the total cost of producing the given amount, divided by that amount. In short, it is the *average cost* of producing the given amount. Next, consider the slope

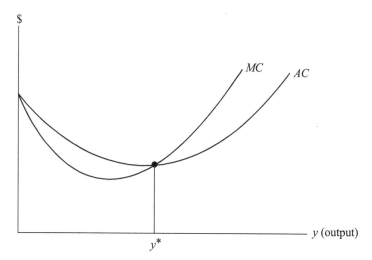

Fig. 8.4. Marginal and average cost curves in the real-world case. The minimum of the average cost curve is at y^*.

of l_2 at P. This is the slope of a tangent line to the total cost curve, or the slope of the total cost curve itself. It is the rate of change of total cost as the quantity changes, or intuitively, the extra cost of producing an additional unit, given that the firm is at the point P. This is the *marginal cost* at the given quantity.

More formally, for any quantity y, *average cost*, written $AC(y)$, is defined by

$$AC(y) = \frac{C(y)}{y}.$$

For any quantity y, *marginal cost*, written $MC(y)$, is defined as the derivative of total cost at y, or

$$MC(y) = C'(y) = \frac{dC(y)}{dy}.$$

Looking at Figure 8.3, and focusing on the slopes of the lines l_1 and l_2, should convince the reader of several important things. First, average cost starts as a large positive number (the slope of the total cost curve at or near the origin), then declines monotonically until it reaches a minimum at the point Q in the figure (corresponding to output y^*). After that, it rises monotonically. Second, marginal cost starts as a large positive number (again, the slope of the total cost curve at or near the origin), declines monotonically until it reaches a minimum (in Figure 8.3, at the point P), and then rises monotonically. Third, at the point at which average cost reaches its minimum (that is, at the point Q), average cost and marginal cost must be equal. Fourth, to the left of that point, average cost exceeds marginal cost, and to the right of that point, average cost is less than marginal cost.

Based on these observations about the important real-world case, we can draw the average cost and marginal cost curves of Figure 8.4.

The relationship between average cost and marginal cost in the real-world case can be easily derived mathematically. Recall that $AC(y) = C(y)/y$. Differentiating gives

$$\frac{dAC(y)}{dy} = \frac{yC'(y) - C(y)}{y^2}.$$

At the bottom of the average cost curve, this derivative has to be zero, which gives

$$\frac{yC'(y) - C(y)}{y^2} = 0,$$

or

$$MC(y) = C'(y) = C(y)/y = AC(y).$$

Therefore, when average cost is at its minimum, average cost is equal to marginal cost. To the left of the average cost minimum point, average cost is declining as y increases, or

$$\frac{dAC(y)}{dy} = \frac{yC'(y) - C(y)}{y^2} < 0.$$

This leads immediately to $C'(y) < C(y)/y$, or marginal cost is less than average cost. To the right of the average cost minimum point, we easily see from an almost identical argument that marginal cost is greater than average cost.

Profit Maximization with Output as the Choice Variable

We are now ready to solve the profit maximization problem for the competitive firm:

$$\max \ \pi(y) = py - wf^{-1}(y) = py - C(y).$$

Note that y is constrained to be greater than or equal to zero; furthermore, remember that we are assuming that the firm has the option of choosing $x = 0$, in which case $y = 0$, and therefore, $\pi = 0$.

Once we have found the solution to this problem for every output price p, we will have the supply curve of the firm; that is, for each p, we will have the output y that the firm will supply to the market. We start by observing that because the firm can choose $\pi = 0$, the y it chooses must produce nonnegative profits. Therefore,

$$\pi(y) = py - C(y) \geq 0.$$

Dividing both sides of the inequality gives $p \geq AC(y)$, which in turn implies

$$p \geq \min AC(y).$$

We conclude that if the market price p for the output does not even cover the firm's minimum average cost of producing its output, the firm will not produce anything.

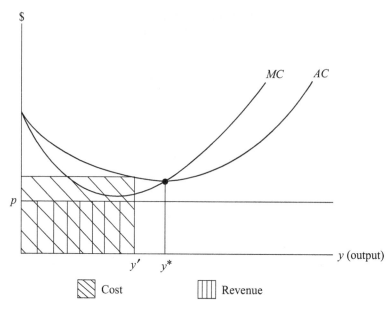

Fig. 8.5. $p < \min AC(y)$ leads to zero supply. Given the price p, at output y' the firm would lose money. This is true for any y', and so the firm produces nothing.

In Figure 8.5, we show a "produce-nothing" situation. In the figure, we consider the possible choice of an arbitrarily chosen y', but at that point (as at all the points), the price p is less than average cost.

Now, we assume that the market price p is high enough to cover minimum average cost. How much output should the firm produce? The first-order condition for maximizing profit says that the derivative of $\pi(y)$ should be zero. Of course, setting the derivative of a function equal to zero will find the function's minima as well as its maxima. To find the maximum of a function, we set the first derivative equal to zero (the first-order condition), and we also require the second derivative to be less than or equal to zero (the second-order condition). The first-order condition for profit maximization is

$$\frac{d\pi(y)}{dy} = p - \frac{dC(y)}{dy} = p - MC(y) = 0.$$

This gives the crucial basic rule for profit maximization for a competitive firm: price equals marginal cost, or

$$p = MC(y).$$

The second-order condition for profit maximization is

$$\frac{d^2\pi(y)}{dy^2} = \frac{d(p - MC(y))}{dy} \leq 0,$$

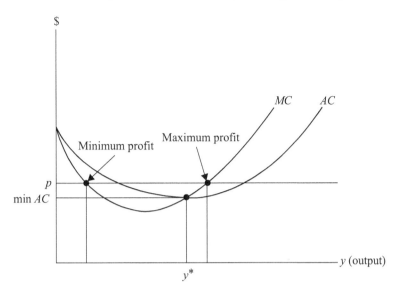

Fig. 8.6. Supply the quantity for which $p = MC(y)$ and the slope of $MC(y)$ is nonnegative.

and this leads directly to

$$\frac{dMC(y))}{dy} \geq 0.$$

In short, at a profit-maximizing point, price equals marginal cost, and marginal cost is rising (or at least not falling). The marginal cost curve cannot be downward sloping at the point of maximum profit.

In sum, profit maximization for a competitive firm implies the following: (1) If p is less than the minimum of average cost, the firm produces nothing. (2) If the firm is producing something, it will choose an output level y at which $p = MC(y)$, and at which marginal cost is rising (or at least not falling).

In Figure 8.6, we show average cost and marginal cost curves for the real-world case, and a horizontal line at price p. The line passes through the marginal cost curve at two points; one intersection represents the profit minimum, and the other represents the profit maximum. At the point labeled "minimum profit," the price p is less than average cost, which implies that profits are negative. In addition, at the "minimum profit" point, marginal cost is declining, indicating that this point fails the second-order condition for a maximum. (It actually satisfies the second-order condition for a profit *minimum*.)

Now, let us describe the supply curve for our competitive firm in the real-world case. As long as $p < \min AC(y)$, the firm supplies zero. That is, in Figure 8.6, if the market price is less than $\min AC(y)$, the supply curve coincides with the vertical axis. If $p \geq \min AC(y)$, the firm will find the y at which $p = MC(y)$ and at which $MC(y)$ is rising (or at least not falling). That is, in Figure 8.6, if $p \geq \min AC(y)$,

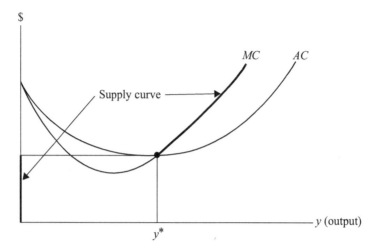

Fig. 8.7. The competitive firm's supply curve. When $p < \min AC(y)$, supply is zero. When $p = \min AC(y)$, supply jumps to y^*. When $p > \min AC(y)$, supply coincides with the MC curve.

the supply curve will coincide with that part of the $MC(y)$ that lies *above* the $AC(y)$ curve. Figure 8.7 shows the competitive firm's supply curve.

8.3 The Competitive Firm's Problem, Focusing on Its Input

Remember that the firm chooses its output y and/or its input x to maximize its profit $\pi = py - wx$, given its production function $y = f(x)$. In Section 8.2, we substituted for x using the inverse of the production function and maximized

$$\pi(y) = py - wf^{-1}(y).$$

That is, we viewed profit as a function of output quantity, we found important conditions for profit maximization, and we derived the firm's supply function for the output. Now we will do it the other way; that is, we will treat profit as a function of *input quantity*, we will find new and equally important conditions for profit maximization, and we will derive the firm's demand function for the input.

In other words, in this section we consider how to maximize profit, given by

$$\pi(x) = pf(x) - wx.$$

Marginal Product and Average Product

Before proceeding, we need to introduce a few concepts related to the production function $f(x)$. First, consider increasing x by a small amount; say, one unit. Then, output y goes up by some amount. Somewhat loosely speaking, the extra output resulting from another unit of input is called the marginal product of the input. For example, one extra worker on the farm might produce another 100 bushels of corn. More precisely, the *marginal product* of the input is defined as the derivative of the production function, or

$$MP(x) = \frac{df(x)}{dx} = f'(x).$$

Of course we are already familiar with this function, having discussed it when we were describing the curvature of the production function.

Marginal product is, intuitively, the extra output from one extra unit of input. This is generally quite different from the average output from all the units of input. The *average product* is defined, quite simply, as the average output of all those input units:

$$AP(x) = \frac{f(x)}{x}.$$

Given the curvature assumptions we have made for the production function in the real-world case, both $MP(x)$ and $AP(x)$ are at first increasing as x increases, and then switch to decreasing as x increases. To see this, refer back to Figure 8.1, showing the production function. In the "real-world" panel, where marginal product would be the slope of a tangent to the $f(x)$ function, and where average product would be the slope of a ray from the origin to the $f(x)$ function, it is clear that $MP(x)$ (the slope of a tangent line) rises and then falls, and that $AP(x)$ (the slope of a ray from the origin) also rises and then falls. It is also clear that marginal product and average product start out equal at $x = 0$ (where they both equal the slope of the production function at the origin). Marginal product must reach its maximum first (at the point of inflection of the $f(x)$ function in Figure 8.1), and average product reaches its maximum second (at the input level where a ray from the origin is tangent to $f(x)$). Finally, it is clear from Figure 8.1 that at the point at which average product is maximized, $AP(x)$ is equal to $MP(x)$. All this leads to Figure 8.8, which shows the marginal and average product curves for the real-world firm.

Marginal product and average product are measured in units of output. To convert the measures into dollars, we simply multiply by the output price p. This produces what we call the *value of marginal product* (*VMP*), and the *value of average product* (*VAP*), respectively. The simple definitions are

$$VMP(x) = pMP(x) \quad \text{and} \quad VAP(x) = pAP(x).$$

To graph these functions, simply take the graphs shown in Figure 8.8, and shift all points upward by multiplying by p. This will be done in Figures 8.9 and 8.10.

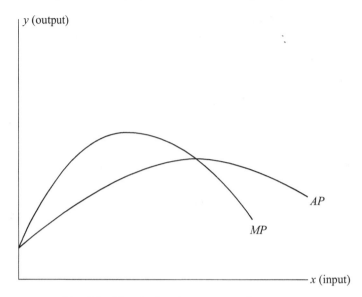

Fig. 8.8. Marginal and average product curves.

Profit Maximization with Input as the Choice Variable

We can now return to the profit-maximization problem. The firm wants to maximize $\pi(x) = pf(x) - wx$, and we know that if it chooses $x = y = 0$, profit will be zero, so it will not accept negative profit. Given that it will not accept negative profit, it will choose an $x > 0$ only if $\pi(x) = pf(x) - wx \geq 0$. Therefore, $pf(x)/x \geq w$, or $VAP(x) \geq w$. This leads to a condition that must hold if the firm is to use any input:

$$\max VAP(x) \geq w.$$

To put it another way, the input price w must be less than or equal to the maximum of the VAP curve.

   If this condition is met, we can use the first- and second-order conditions to see how much x the firm wants to hire in order to maximize profit. The first-order condition says that the derivative of $\pi(x)$ should be zero, and the second-order condition says that the derivative should be falling (or at least not rising) at the profit-maximizing x. The first-order condition is:

$$\frac{d\pi(x)}{dx} = p\frac{df(x)}{dx} - w = VMP(x) - w = 0.$$

This yields a simple expression:

$$VMP(x) = w.$$

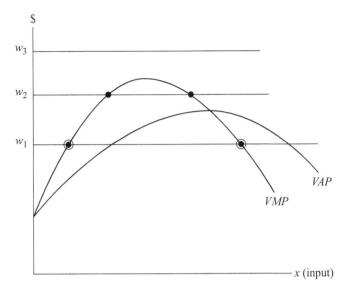

Fig. 8.9. Choosing x to maximize profits. Choose the one where $VMP(x)$ is downward sloping.

The second-order condition says that the derivative of $d\pi(x)/dx$ should be less than or equal to zero:

$$\frac{d^2\pi(x)}{dx^2} = \frac{dVMP(x)}{dx} \leq 0.$$

That is, the $VMP(x)$ curve should be downward sloping (or at least not upward sloping).

Figure 8.9 shows $VMP(x)$ and $VAP(x)$ curves, and is based on Figure 8.8, with the curves scaled up by a multiplicative factor p. In Figure 8.9, we also show three possible input prices, w_1, w_2, and w_3. At both w_2 and w_3, the input price is too high, above the maximum of the $VAP(x)$ curve. Therefore, the firm would opt for $x = y = 0$ and $\pi = 0$ under either of these prices. At the price w_1, however, there are many xs for which $VAP(x) \geq w_1$. The firm would choose the profit-maximizing x by using the first-order condition, $VMP(x) = w_1$. That condition leads to two points, which are circled. However, only the point on the right satisfies the second-order condition, which requires the $VMP(x)$ curve to be downward sloping.

Repeating what was done in Figure 8.9 for all possible levels of the input price w gives us the firm's demand curve for its input. This is shown in Figure 8.10. This input demand curve should not be confused with the firm's *conditional* input demand, which shows how much x the firm needs in order to produce a given level of output y. The demand curve we are now considering shows the quantity x of the input the firm wants to employ, for a given input price w, to maximize profits. As Figure 8.10 shows, for w above the maximum of the VAP curve, the

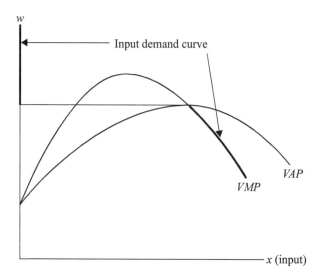

Fig. 8.10. The profit-maximizing firm's input demand curve.

firm will use none of the input good, because if it did use any, it would end up with negative profit. Once the input good price falls below the maximum of the VAP curve, however, the firm can make positive profits. The quantity of the input good it buys or hires is found on the VMP curve (first-order condition), but only on the downward-sloping part of that curve (second-order condition).

8.4 Multiple Outputs

Most firms in the real world produce multiple outputs. In this section, we model a firm with one input and multiple outputs, to show how the conditions we have derived in earlier sections of this chapter might be generalized. As before, the analysis can be done by focusing on the outputs, or by focusing on the input. Focusing on the input involves techniques that are similar to the multiple-input/single-output case that will be developed in the next chapter, and will be left as an exercise at the end of that chapter. At this point we focus on the outputs.

Suppose, then, that the firm produces two different outputs, y_1 and y_2, using one input x. In Section 8.2, where there was one output y, we started with the production function $y = f(x)$, and then we used its inverse $x = f^{-1}(y)$ to derive profit-maximization conditions involving y, such as $p = MC(y)$. We do something similar here. However, there is one small complication. When there are two (or more) outputs, it would be wrong to write a production function $(y_1, y_2) = f(x)$. Why would this be wrong? Simply because for any fixed level of the input x, there are many combinations of y_1 and y_2 that the firm might be able to produce. On the other hand, the *inverse production function* f^{-1} does make perfect sense. Writing $x = f^{-1}(y_1, y_2)$ simply means that if the firm is going to produce y_1 units of output

1 and y_2 units of output 2, it needs to employ x units of the input. Therefore, in this section, we will use the inverse production function f^{-1} to represent the firm's technological constraint, and we will use this notation even though the production function $f(x)$ itself is not defined.

In Section 8.2, when there was one output, we assumed monotonicity. This meant that as x increases, y also increases, or $dy/dx = df(x)/dx > 0$. Here we make a similar assumption, but on the inverse production f^{-1}, and for one output at a time. We assume that $\partial x/\partial y_i = \partial f^{-1}(y_1, y_2)/\partial y_i > 0$ for $i = 1$ and 2. That is, if the firm wants to increase its production of one of the outputs, while keeping the other constant, it will have to hire more units of the input.

Also recall that in Section 8.2, the second basic assumption we made about the production function involved its curvature. The simple version of that assumption was that the production function is concave; the real-world assumption was that it is first convex and then concave. Concavity of a production function translates into convexity of its inverse. (A quick look at the graph of a concave production function in Figure 8.1 should convince you of this.) Therefore, in this section, for the simple version, we shall assume that f^{-1} is a (*strictly*) *convex* function. Somewhat loosely speaking, strict convexity of f^{-1} means the following. Suppose $x^0 = f^{-1}(y_1^0, y_2^0)$ and $x^1 = f^{-1}(y_1^1, y_2^1)$. Consider the average of the two output vectors: $(0.5y_1^0 + 0.5y_1^1, 0.5y_2^0 + 0.5y_2^1)$. To produce this combination of outputs, it would take less than the average of the input quantities, $0.5x^0 + 0.5x^1$. In a sense, the firm gains by averaging output vectors, perhaps because it can profitably rearrange the units of the inputs going to each output.

Finally, we assume, similar to what we assumed before, that if the firm hires no input, it produces zero of both outputs.

With respect to the firm's market constraints, we continue to assume that the firm is competitive in all markets in which it operates. That is, it acts as a price taker in both of the output markets, and in the input market. Let p_1 and p_2 be the output prices, and let w be the input price. The firm wants to maximize profit, given by

$$\pi(y_1, y_2) = p_1 y_1 + p_2 y_2 - wx = p_1 y_1 + p_2 y_2 - wf^{-1}(y_1, y_2)$$

subject to the constraint that $\pi(y_1, y_2) \geq 0$. (Remember that the firm can hire no x and produce no outputs, giving $\pi = 0$.)

Assuming that profit is nonnegative and that the firm is operating, how much of each output should it produce? The first-order conditions for profit maximization are now

$$\frac{\partial \pi}{\partial y_1} = p_1 - w \frac{\partial f^{-1}(y_1, y_2)}{\partial y_1} = 0$$

and $$\frac{\partial \pi}{\partial y_2} = p_2 - w \frac{\partial f^{-1}(y_1, y_2)}{\partial y_2} = 0.$$

But what is $w\partial f^{-1}(y_1, y_2)/\partial y_i$? It is the price of x times the extra amount of input x required to produce another unit of output i, while holding output j constant. That is, it is the *marginal cost of output i* or MC_i. Therefore, the two first-order conditions for profit maximization say that

$$p_1 = MC_1 \quad \text{and} \quad p_2 = MC_2.$$

These conditions are exactly parallel to the $p = MC$ condition of the single-output case. To maximize profit, the firm will produce an amount of *each* output that equates price and marginal cost. Finally, provided the nonnegative profit condition is met, the solution to this set of equations gives the firm's *supply functions* for outputs 1 and 2. In general, each of these will depend on both prices; that is, they would be written $y_1^*(p_1, p_2)$ and $y_2^*(p_1, p_2)$.

Given our assumption of convexity for f^{-1}, it is not necessary to check the second-order profit-maximization conditions. However, in more general cases such as the real-world case described in Section 8.2, we would have to check them. The second-order conditions would be generalizations of the nondecreasing marginal cost conditions, also described earlier in Section 8.2.

8.5 A Solved Problem

The Problem

A competitive firm's production function is $y = 10 + (x - 1{,}000)^{1/3}$. The price of the input x is $w = 1$.

(a) Show that the firm's total cost curve is $C(y) = 1{,}000 + (y - 10)^3$.
(b) Show that the minimum of the marginal cost curve is at $y = 10$, and the minimum of the average cost curve is at $y = 15$.
(c) Finally, show that the firm supplies zero when $p < 75$, and the firm supplies $y(p) = 10 + \sqrt{p/3}$ when $p \geq 75$.

The Solution

(a) First, we solve for x as a function of y. We rewrite the production function as

$$y - 10 = (x - 1{,}000)^{1/3}.$$

Then we cube both sides:

$$(y - 10)^3 = (x - 1{,}000),$$

which gives the inverse of the production function:

$$x = 1{,}000 + (y - 10)^3.$$

Because cost is wx and $w = 1$, the cost function is $C(y) = 1{,}000 + (y - 10)^3$.

(b) Marginal cost is the derivative of the cost function:

$$MC(y) = \frac{dC(y)}{dy} = 3(y - 10)^2.$$

To find the minimum of the marginal cost curve, we differentiate $MC(y)$ and set the result equal to zero:

$$\frac{dMC(y)}{dy} = 6(y - 10) = 0.$$

This gives $y = 10$.
Average cost is

$$AC(y) = \frac{C(y)}{y} = \frac{1,000 + (y - 10)^3}{y}.$$

Differentiating $AC(y)$ and setting the result equal to zero gives

$$\frac{dAC(y)}{dy} = \frac{y(3(y - 10)^2) - (1,000 + (y - 10)^3)1}{y^2} = 0.$$

This leads to

$$3y(y - 10)^2 = 1,000 + (y - 10)^3,$$

which simplifies to

$$(2y + 10)(y - 10)^2 = 1,000,$$

which yields $y = 15$. Consequently, average cost is minimized at $y = 15$.
(c) At $y = 15$, the point at which average cost is minimized, average cost is

$$AC(15) = \frac{1,000 + (y - 10)^3}{y} = \frac{1,000 + 125}{15} = 75.$$

Therefore, for any price $p < 75$ and any $y > 0$, price is less than average cost. If $p < 75$, the firm will produce $y = 0$. For $p \geq 75$, the firm will maximize profit by setting price equal to marginal cost, which gives

$$p = MC(y) = 3(y - 10)^2.$$

Solving this equation for y as a function of p leads to $y(p) = 10 + \sqrt{p/3}$.

Exercises

1. Let the production function be $y = x^{1/2}$.
   (a) Show that the production function $y(x)$ is concave.
   (b) Suppose the price of x is $w = 1$. Find the firm's total cost curve $C(y)$, average cost curve $AC(y)$, and marginal cost curve $MC(y)$.
   (c) Find the firm's supply curve $y^*(p)$.
   (d) Suppose the price of y is $p = 10$. Calculate the firm's profit.

2. Assume the production function is $y = 5x^{1/3} - 30$, and the price of x is $w = 1$.

   (a) Derive the firm's total cost curve $C(y)$, average cost curve $AC(y)$, and marginal cost curve $MC(y)$.

   (b) What is the firm's supply curve $y^*(p)$?

3. Consider the production function from question 1, $y = x^{1/2}$. Assume $x \geq 1$.

   (a) Show that the inverse production function $x(y)$ is convex.

   (b) The price of y is $p = 10$. Find the firm's marginal product $MP(x)$ and average product $AP(x)$.

   (c) Find the firm's value of marginal product $VMP(x)$ and value of average product $VAP(x)$.

   (d) Find the firm's input demand curve $x^*(w)$.

   (e) Suppose the price of x is $w = 1$. Calculate the firm's profit.

4. Suppose the production function is $y = x^{2/3} + \frac{1}{3}x$, and the price of y is $p = 6$. Assume $x \geq 1$.

   (a) Find the firm's marginal product $MP(x)$ and average product $AP(x)$.

   (b) Derive the firm's value of marginal product $VMP(x)$ and value of average product $VAP(x)$.

   (c) What is the firm's input demand curve $x^*(w)$?

5. Consider the single-input/multiple-output model. Recall that $x = f^{-1}(y_1, y_2)$, the inverse production function, represents the firm's technological constraint. Can you solve the profit maximization problem for this firm by focusing on the input variable? **Hint:** Do it with the following four steps. (Note: Because we have not specified the f^{-1} function, this is a graphical exercise, without specific functional or numerical solutions.)

   (a) An *isofactor curve* is a locus of output combinations that use the same level of input. In a graph of the (y_1, y_2)-quadrant, sketch some isofactor curves, assuming f^{-1} is convex.

   (b) An *isorevenue line* is a locus of output combinations that yield the same total revenue. Plot several isorevenue lines on the same graph as the isofactor curves.

   (c) Solve the revenue maximization problem for a fixed level of input. This will yield the conditional output supply curves $y_1(p_1, p_2, x)$ and $y_2(p_1, p_2, x)$.

   (d) Finally, write down the profit maximization problem, making profit a function of the single variable x.

6. The inverse production function with one input and two outputs is $x = y_1^2 + y_2^2 + y_1 y_2$. Assume the price of x is $w = 1$.

   (a) Find the firm's total cost curve $C(y_1, y_2)$ and marginal cost curves $MC_1(y_1)$ and $MC_2(y_2)$.

   (b) Find the firm's supply curves $y_1^*(p_1, p_2)$ and $y_2^*(p_1, p_2)$, subject to the nonnegative profit condition.

   (c) Suppose $p_1 = 1$ and $p_2 = 1$. Calculate y_1^* and y_2^*. What is the firm's profit?

   (d) Suppose p_2 rises to 2. Recalculate y_1^* and y_2^*. How has the firm's profit changed?

Chapter 9

Theory of the Firm 2: The Long-Run, Multiple-Input Model

9.1 Introduction

In most of the last chapter we modeled a firm with one input and one output. However, assuming one input is unrealistic; most goods and services are produced by firms with a variety of different inputs. The production of something as simple as corn really requires land, labor, trucks, tractors, combines, fertilizer, pesticides, possibly irrigation, and so on. Moreover, the single-input model fails to capture a basic economic problem. Normally there are many ways to combine inputs to produce a desired level of the output; some of the ways are expensive and some are cheap. How does the firm combine various inputs to produce a given level of output at the least cost? In this chapter, we assume there are two or more inputs that the firm combines in some way to produce its output. We analyze how the firm decides how much output to produce, and how much of each input to use, to minimize its costs and maximize its profits. That is, we will now develop the *multiple-input/single-output model*.

As we indicated in the introduction to the last chapter, it is possible to learn about the most important results in the theory of the firm by studying either the single-input/single-output model or the multiple-input/single-output model. (The only important topic that the single-input/single-output model cannot handle is cost minimization.) This book differs somewhat from the typical textbook on microeconomics because it gives the reader the choice between these two models. We now turn to the second model.

In the last chapter, x was the quantity of the (single) input and y was the quantity of the output. The production function was $y = f(x)$. Now we assume there are two or more inputs. We let x_1 represent the quantity of input 1 used by the firm, x_2 the quantity of input 2, x_3 the quantity of input 3, and so on. The production function now becomes $y = f(x_1, x_2, x_3, \ldots)$. Most of the important implications of profit maximization with two or more inputs can be seen with just two inputs, so we will focus on that case. In short, in this chapter the production function is assumed to be

$$y = f(x_1, x_2).$$

The function $f(x_1, x_2)$ represents the technological constraints facing the firm, as did the function $f(x)$ in the last chapter. The firm must work within the constraints imposed by nature, science, and technology. The firm also faces market constraints, involving the price of its output p, and the prices of its inputs w_1 and w_2.

We consider another kind of constraint in this chapter and the next, having to do with the variability of the firm's inputs. Some input quantities can be changed quickly and easily; others cannot. For example, if the firm's inputs are electricity or phone service, the quantities used can easily be varied hour by hour, even minute by minute. However, if the inputs are, for example, acres of farmland planted in corn, or pharmaceutical research to develop new drugs, the input quantities can be varied only over periods of months, years, or even decades. Thus, time horizons and the degrees of variability of input levels within those time horizons create a new type of constraint on the firm.

In this chapter we assume that the inputs are both (or all) freely variable. In the next chapter we will assume one or more of the inputs is fixed over the underlying time horizon, while one or more of the inputs is variable. Economists call a period of time that is so long that all of the firm's inputs are freely variable the *long run*, and they call a period of time that is so short that one or more inputs is fixed the *short run*. Therefore, this chapter is about the theory of the firm in the long run. The next chapter is about the theory of the firm in the short run. We are doing the long-run theory first because it is simpler and more elegant than the short-run theory.

We apologize for the inescapable vagueness about how long a time is long run, and how short a time is short run, but the study of economics is different from the study of, say, chemistry or physics. Moreover, as the great economist John Maynard Keynes (1883–1946) once quipped, "The long run is a misleading guide to current affairs. In the long run we are all dead." (Keynes was writing about macroeconomic policy, rather than microeconomic theory, when he created that gem.) A complication of the long-run/short-run dichotomy is the possibility of bankruptcy. For example, in 2009, American automobile companies General Motors and Chrysler went through what is called Chapter 11 bankruptcy to escape the burdens of debt and union contracts, both of which create massive costs that are impossible to escape in the short run. Government aid facilitated the bankruptcy. Chapter 11 allows a firm to shield itself from its creditors in a court; the court has the power to rewrite or erase the firm's contractual obligations and thus, modify or end such costs. In standard microeconomic theory, the long run is a period of time long enough to modify all the firm's costs. In the real world, bankruptcy is another way to modify costs, and it may be faster than the "long run." We end this very brief discussion of bankruptcy by paraphrasing Keynes: In the long run we are all dead, and if not dead, perhaps bankrupt.

9.2 The Production Function in the Long Run

We are now assuming that $y = f(x_1, x_2)$, and that both inputs are free to vary. Suppose a firm can produce 1 unit of its output by using 2 units of input 1, which we will call "workers," and 3 units of input 2, "raw materials." If 2 workers and 3 units of raw materials can produce 1 unit of the output, it is easy to imagine that 3 workers and 3 units of raw materials can also produce 1 unit of output. Just ask the third worker to sit at a table in the shop or office and send text messages to her children, while the original 2 workers make the 1 unit of output! Naturally, we want to refine our notion of the production function to rule out this possibility, so we will impose the assumption of *technological efficiency*.

When various combinations of inputs produce the same level of output, we call such combinations *production techniques*. For instance, in the preceding example, $(x_1, x_2) = (2, 3)$ and $(x_1, x_2) = (3, 3)$ are alternative production techniques, both resulting in output $y = 1$. We will say that a production technique is *technologically inefficient* if there is another production technique (or combination of techniques) that results in the same level of output, but uses less of one of the inputs and no more of the other input or inputs. Otherwise, it is *technologically efficient*. In our example, $(3, 3)$ is technologically inefficient. Because firms generally have to pay for the inputs they use, they do not want to use technologically inefficient production techniques. Therefore, we will confine the application of the production function f to efficient production techniques. That is, when we write $y = f(x_1, x_2)$ in what follows, it is understood that (x_1, x_2) is an efficient production technique.

We now define an *isoquant*. The prefix "iso" is Greek for "the same" or "equal," and "quant" is short for "quantity." An *isoquant* is a set of efficient production techniques that result in the same quantity of output. To graph an isoquant, we start with a picture that has quantities of the inputs x_1 and x_2 on the horizontal and vertical axes, respectively, and we identify a locus of points (x_1, x_2) that all produce a fixed quantity of output y. When we do this for different y's, we get different isoquants. Isoquants for $y = 1, 2,$ and 3 are shown in Figure 9.1. The isoquants in Figure 9.1 also happen to be "evenly spaced"; we will explain the meaning of this later.

The reader may think that isoquants look vaguely familiar – and so they should. Isoquants in the theory of the firm play a role very similar to that of indifference curves in the theory of the consumer, introduced back in Chapter 2.

Recall that a consumer wants to get to higher and higher indifference curves, all else being equal. Similarly, a firm wants to get to higher and higher isoquants, all else being equal. (Of course, the exact meanings of these statements depends on what we mean by "all else being equal.") There is, however, one important

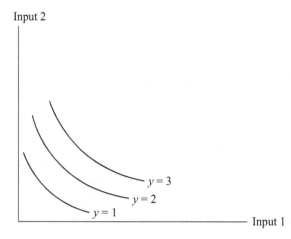

Fig. 9.1. A map of isoquants.

difference between isoquants and indifference curves, which we should point out immediately. In consumer theory, utility is an *ordinal* measure; only relative utilities matter, and in the statement "I am on the indifference curve for $u = 3$," the number 3 has no intrinsic meaning. On the other hand, in the theory of the firm, output is a *cardinal* measure. In the statement "the firm is at $y = 3$," the number 3 does have significance. It means that the firm is producing 3 cars, or 3 bushels of wheat, or 3 units of whatever the firm produces. Moreover, the $u = 6$ indifference curve is better for the consumer than the $u = 3$ indifference curve, but not twice as good. In contrast, the $y = 6$ isoquant really does produce twice the output of the $y = 3$ isoquant.

Marginal Products of the Inputs and Assumptions about Production Functions and Isoquants

In Chapter 8, on the single-input/single-output model, we defined the marginal product of the input. Intuitively, the marginal product is the extra output resulting from another unit of the input. Formally, it is the derivative of the production function $f(x)$ with respect to x. When there are two (or more) inputs, the definition is quite similar. Intuitively, the marginal product of input 1, for instance, is the extra output resulting from an additional unit of input 1 and zero additional units of input 2. Formally, *the marginal product of input 1* is the derivative of the production function with respect to x_1, holding x_2 constant, or the partial derivative of $f(x_1, x_2)$ with respect to x_1. That is,

$$MP_1 = \frac{\partial f(x_1, x_2)}{\partial x_1}.$$

This may also be written as $\partial f/\partial x_1$, or $\partial f(x_1, x_2)/\partial x_1$, or $f_1(x_1, x_2)$. If we need to emphasize where the partial derivative is being computed, we will write $MP_1(x_1, x_2)$ if it is being evaluated at (x_1, x_2).

The marginal product for input 2 is defined similarly.

Note the strong resemblance between the marginal product of input 1 in the theory of the firm, and the marginal utility of good 1 in the theory of the consumer, as defined in Chapter 2. The reader may remember that, in the theory of the consumer, the marginal rate of substitution was equal to the marginal utility of good 1 divided by the marginal utility of good 2. As we shall see, there is a close parallel in the theory of the firm.

We will now turn to the assumptions we make about the production function and its associated isoquants.

Assumption 1: *Monotonicity.* If a firm increases one input without decreasing the other, output increases. That is, the marginal products $MP_1 = \partial f(x_1, x_2)/\partial x_1$ and $MP_2 = \partial f(x_1, x_2)/\partial x_2$, or the partial derivatives of f with respect to x_1 and x_2, are both positive. This rules out instances of technological inefficiency such as that described in the earlier example. It also rules out the possibility of "fat" isoquants; that is, isoquants that are other than thin lines. And it rules out isoquants that are horizontal, vertical, or upward sloping. That is, it forces isoquants to be downward sloping.

Assumption 2: *Convexity.* The isoquants are convex. There are several reasons why this is a plausible assumption.

First, in many cases, it is reasonable to assume that production techniques can operate at different levels, with output levels scaled proportionately, and that a firm can use two or more production techniques simultaneously, without the techniques interfering with one another. For instance, suppose $(x_1, x_2) = (2, 3)$ is an efficient production technique that gives $y = 1$, and suppose $(x_1, x_2) = (3, 2)$ is another efficient technique that gives $y = 1$. Consider running the first technique at half level, and the second also at half level. It is reasonable to assume that this would produce at least $1/2 + 1/2 = 1$ unit of output. Running the two techniques at these levels would require $(1/2)(2, 3) + (1/2)(3, 2) = (2.5, 2.5)$ units of inputs 1 and 2. Now think of the $y = 1$ isoquant. It has to pass through $(2, 3)$ and $(3, 2)$. It would *fail to be convex* if it passed *above* the point midway between these two points – that is, $(2.5, 2.5)$. However, it cannot pass above $(2.5, 2.5)$, because at that point the firm can produce at least $y = 1$ just by running those two production techniques at half level. There are likely to be other techniques available that would transform inputs of $(2.5, 2.5)$ into output of $y > 1$. This implies that the isoquant running through $(2, 3)$ and $(3, 2)$ should pass *below* the point $(2.5, 2.5)$. This would mean that the isoquant is (strictly) convex.

Second, if isoquants are not convex, a firm will use "extreme" input bundles (extreme in the sense that one of the input levels is zero). That is, the inputs would not be used in combination. Because we observe firms using combinations of inputs, it is plausible to assume convexity.

Technical Rate of Substitution

The reader will recall that in the theory of the consumer, a crucial concept is the marginal rate of substitution of good 2 for good 1, or MRS_{x_1,x_2}, or MRS for short. The intuition is this: If the consumer gives up a unit of good 1, how much good 2 does he need to replace it, and remain on the same indifference curve? The marginal rate of substitution of good 2 for good 1 is minus 1 times the slope of an indifference curve. Also recall from Chapter 2 the relationship between the marginal rate of substitution and the ratio of the marginal utilities: $MRS = MU_1/MU_2$.

In the theory of the firm, we have a concept exactly analogous to marginal rate of substitution in the theory of the consumer, and we have a relationship just like $MRS = MU_1/MU_2$ in the theory of the consumer.

The *technical rate of substitution* of input 2 for input 1, formally written TRS_{x_1,x_2}, or TRS for short, is defined as

$$TRS_{x_1,x_2} = -\frac{\Delta x_2}{\Delta x_1},$$

where Δx_1 and Δx_2 are small (more precisely, infinitesimal) increments in inputs x_1 and x_2, one negative and the other positive, that leave the firm on the same isoquant. In other words, TRS is minus 1 times the slope of the isoquant. The intuition is this: If the firm uses a unit less of input 1, how much more of input 2 does it need to use in order to keep output constant; that is, to remain on the same isoquant? To put it another way, TRS is the value of a unit of input 1 in the production process, measured in terms of units of input 2 needed to replace it.

We can establish the relationship among TRS, MP_1, and MP_2 with an argument very similar to the one we made in Chapter 2 on the theory of the consumer. Imagine that we start at an input bundle (x_1, x_2) and we simultaneously reduce x_1 and increase x_2 in a way that leaves y unchanged. The increments are $\Delta x_1 < 0$ and $\Delta x_2 > 0$. Then output changes by $MP_1 \Delta x_1 < 0$ because of the reduction in input 1, and it simultaneously changes by $MP_2 \Delta x_2 > 0$ because of the increase in input 2. But we end up on the same isoquant, and the net effect is zero. This implies that

$$MP_1 \Delta x_1 + MP_2 \Delta x_2 = 0.$$

Therefore,

$$TRS = -\frac{\Delta x_2}{\Delta x_1} = \frac{MP_1}{MP_2} = \frac{\partial f(x_1, x_2)}{\partial x_1} \Big/ \frac{\partial f(x_1, x_2)}{\partial x_2}.$$

Now, let us reconsider the idea of convexity for an isoquant. Consider moving toward the right and down along a single isoquant. Convexity means that minus

1 times the slope of the isoquant, or the absolute value of the slope, is declining as we move to the right and down, or TRS declines as we move to the right and down. That is, as x_1, the quantity of input 1, gets greater and greater, the value of an extra unit of input 1 in the production process gets smaller and smaller. This seems a very plausible assumption for TRS, and another reason to view convexity for isoquants as a reasonable basic assumption.

Returns to Scale

The reader will recall that in Chapter 8, on the single-input/single-output model of production, we assumed that the production function $f(x)$ was either (1) concave, or more realistically, (2) at first convex and then concave. The intuition was that a concave production function, with a negative second derivative $f''(x)$, represents diminishing returns, and that a production function that starts convex and then becomes concave represents the more realistic real-world case of increasing returns when the firm is small, eventually becoming diminishing returns when the firm is large. We will now consider similar notions applied to the firm with two (or more) inputs.

For this purpose, it is conventional practice to consider what happens when all inputs are scaled up proportionately, rather than to consider what happens as each input is modified incrementally. Therefore, we proceed as follows. Assume that both inputs are scaled up by a constant $t > 1$. (Remember, we are talking about production in the long run, so there are no input quantities that are fixed and cannot be scaled up.) Then, if output changes by the same scale factor t, the production function is said to have the property of *constant returns to scale*. For instance, if the firm doubles all its inputs, or increases them by 100 percent, output should double – that is, rise by 100 percent. More formally, $f(x_1, x_2)$ is a *constant returns to scale* production function, if, for any $t > 1$ and any (x_1, x_2), $f(tx_1, tx_2) = tf(x_1, x_2)$.

If scaling up the inputs results in output increasing, but by less than the scale factor, the production function is said to have the property of *decreasing returns to scale*. For instance, the firm might double all its inputs and see its output rise by 50 percent as a result. More formally, $f(x_1, x_2)$ is a *decreasing returns to scale* production function, if, for any $t > 1$ and any (x_1, x_2), $f(tx_1, tx_2) < tf(x_1, x_2)$.

If scaling up the inputs results in output increasing, and by more than the scale factor, the production function is said to have the property of *increasing returns to scale*. For instance, the firm might double all its inputs and see its output rise by 150 percent as a result. More formally, $f(x_1, x_2)$ is an *increasing returns to scale* production function, if, for any $t > 1$ and any (x_1, x_2), $f(tx_1, tx_2) > tf(x_1, x_2)$.

When the isoquants for a constant returns to scale production function are graphed, they are "evenly spaced," in the sense that the $y = 2$ isoquant is twice as far from the origin as the $y = 1$ isoquant, the $y = 3$ isoquant is three times as

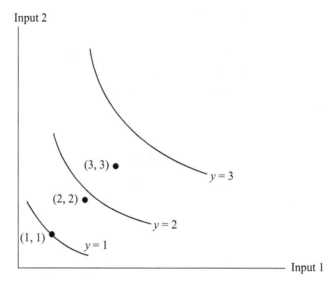

Fig. 9.2. Decreasing returns to scale.

far from the origin as the $y = 1$ isoquant, and so on. Figure 9.1 was drawn under the constant returns to scale assumption. Under increasing returns to scale, as one moves away from the origin, isoquants get closer and closer to each other, and under decreasing returns to scale, as one moves away from the origin, isoquants get farther and farther apart. Figure 9.2 illustrates decreasing returns to scale. Decreasing returns to scale is the scale assumption that corresponds to our Chapter 8 assumption of concavity for the production function $f(x)$.

In the Chapter 8 real-world case, the production function $f(x)$ starts convex and then becomes concave. The isoquant-spacing assumption that corresponds to this case is the following: when output is low, successive isoquants get closer and closer to each other, but when output is high, successive isoquants get farther and farther from each other. Loosely speaking, this is increasing returns to scale at the start, but becoming decreasing returns to scale at the end. Figure 9.3 shows the real-world case.

Marginal Products and TRS in the Constant Returns to Scale Case

A constant returns to scale production function $f(x_1, x_2)$ scales output proportionately when both the inputs are scaled up by a factor $t > 1$, so $f(tx_1, tx_2) = tf(x_1, x_2)$. Taking the partial derivative of the left side of this equation (that is, $f(tx_1, tx_2)$) with respect to x_1 (that is, differentiating with respect to x_1 while holding x_2 constant) gives

$$\frac{\partial f(tx_1, tx_2)}{\partial tx_1} \frac{d(tx_1)}{dx_1} = t\frac{\partial f(tx_1, tx_2)}{\partial tx_1} = tMP_1(tx_1, tx_2).$$

Input 2

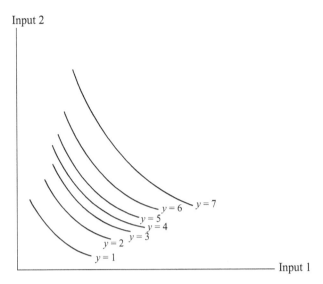

Input 1

Fig. 9.3. Returns to scale in the real-world case.

Taking the partial derivative of the right side of the equation (that is, $tf(x_1, x_2)$) with respect to x_1 gives

$$t\frac{\partial f(x_1, x_2)}{\partial x_1} = tMP_1(x_1, x_2).$$

Setting the partial derivative of the left-hand side equal to the partial derivative of the right-hand side, and canceling out the t's on the left and on the right, we get

$$MP_1(tx_1, tx_2) = MP_1(x_1, x_2).$$

We conclude that for a constant returns to scale production function, if both inputs are scaled up proportionately, the marginal products of the inputs do not change. Scaling (x_1, x_2) up or down is graphically equivalent to moving up or down a ray from the origin, in a graph with inputs 1 and 2 on the horizontal and vertical axes. Therefore, for a constant returns to scale production function, MP_1 and MP_2 are constant as the firm moves along rays from the origin, or, to put it another way, MP_1 and MP_2 remain constant as long as the input ratio x_2/x_1 remains constant.

Now, consider what happens to the technical rate of substitution as we vary x_1 and x_2, but keep the ratio x_2/x_1 fixed. Because

$$TRS = \frac{MP_1}{MP_2},$$

and because the marginal products don't change, TRS remains constant. In other words, for a constant returns to scale production function, if one scales up both inputs proportionately, the technical rate of substitution stays constant. In a graph with inputs 1 and 2 on the horizontal and vertical axes, if you move out a ray from the origin, the slopes of the isoquants crossing that ray are all the same.

9.3 Cost Minimization in the Long Run

We now turn to the topic of *cost minimization*. We continue to assume that the time horizon is long run, and that both inputs are freely variable. Cost minimization was not an issue in Chapter 8, in which we discussed profit maximization by a firm using only one input. This is because if a firm produces y with one input x, according to the production function $y = f(x)$, there is only one way to produce a given level of output y^0, and only one possible cost: use $x^0 = f^{-1}(y^0)$ and pay wx^0 for it. In the single-input case, it is a waste of time to search for a cheaper way to produce y^0.

Now, though, we are assuming that the firm is producing its output y, and it is using *two* inputs in quantities x_1 and x_2 to do so. The prices for the inputs are w_1 and w_2, respectively. The firm is, of course, constrained by its production function $y = f(x_1, x_2)$. But for any given level of output, say y^0, there may be infinitely many ways to produce that output; all the input combinations on the $y = y^0$ isoquant will do it. The firm wants to maximize its profits, but to maximize profits, it must minimize costs.

At the risk of belaboring the obvious, let us emphasize this point. The firm's profit equals its revenue less its cost, or, in our notation,

$$\pi = py - C(y) = py - (w_1 x_1 + w_2 x_2).$$

If, for a given y, the cost $C(y)$ is not at the minimum, then profit can obviously be increased by switching to a lower-cost method of producing the given y. In other words, cost minimization is a necessary condition for profit maximization.

Isocost Lines and the Condition for Cost Minimization

To facilitate the analysis of cost minimization, we use isocost lines. (Remember, "iso" means "the same" or "equal.") An *isocost line* is a set of input combinations (x_1, x_2), all with the same cost. For a given level of cost, say C^0, the isocost line is the graph of

$$w_1 x_1 + w_2 x_2 = C^0.$$

This equation may seem vaguely familiar to the reader, because it looks like the equation for the budget line in the theory of the consumer:

$$p_1 x_1 + p_2 x_2 = M.$$

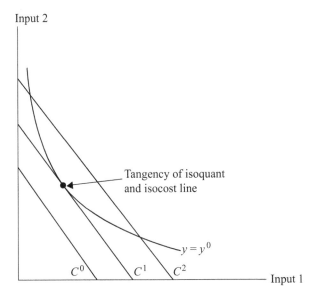

Fig. 9.4. Several isocost lines and one isoquant. Cost is minimized at the tangency point.

Of course, the consumer tries to get to the highest indifference curve, for a given budget line. The firm tries to get to the lowest isocost line, for a given isoquant.

Figure 9.4 shows several isoquants corresponding to cost levels C^0, C^1, and C^2. A lower isocost line in the figure corresponds to a lower level of cost, as w_1 and w_2 are both assumed to be positive. The slope of an isocost line is very much analogous to the slope of the consumer's budget line; it equals w_1/w_2 in absolute value. Note that Figure 9.4 includes one isoquant, which happens to be tangent to the C^1 isocost line. Figure 9.4 makes it clear that, in order to minimize the cost of producing y^0, the firm will try to find a point where the y^0 isoquant is tangent to an isocost line.

We noted earlier that cost minimization is a necessary condition for profit maximization. We now describe the tangency condition that must hold for cost minimization. Suppose the firm is producing y^0. Suppose the production function is differentiable, the isoquants are smooth and convex, and there is an isoquant/isocost line tangency. To produce y^0 at least cost, the firm must choose the input combination (x_1, x_2) at which the isoquant is tangent to an isocost line.

Because the slope of the isoquant is $-TRS$ and the slope of the isocost line is $-w_1/w_2$, we have the following basic cost-minimization condition:

$$TRS = \frac{w_1}{w_2}.$$

This condition should look familiar; it is exactly like the corresponding tangency condition in the theory of the consumer. The consumer tangency condition says that to get to the highest indifference curve subject to the budget constraint, the consumer must satisfy

$$MRS = \frac{p_1}{p_2}.$$

Now let us consider a variable output level y instead of a particular level y^0. The firm is facing input prices (w_1, w_2). To produce an arbitrary y at the least cost, the firm will solve for a pair of input levels, which we call x_1^* and x_2^*, that satisfy (1) the cost minimization tangency condition

$$TRS = \frac{w_1}{w_2}$$

and (2) the production function equation

$$y = f(x_1, x_2).$$

The desired input levels (x_1^*, x_2^*) now depend on the input prices (w_1, w_2) and on the output level y, and so we write them as $x_1^*(w_1, w_2, y)$ and $x_2^*(w_1, w_2, y)$. These two functions show how much of the two inputs the firm wants to hire, given the input prices, and given the level of output. These are called the *conditional factor demands* or *conditional input demands* for the firm. In a typical application of this kind of analysis, w_1 and w_2 are fixed, and the word "conditional" is used here because the amounts of the inputs that the firm demands depend on the level of output the firm will choose.

With the conditional input demands, we can define the firm's *long-run cost function* or *long-run cost curve*. This shows, for any level of output y, the least cost of producing y (assuming fixed input prices, and assuming efficient production techniques). The long-run cost function is

$$C(y) = w_1 x_1^*(w_1, w_2, y) + w_2 x_2^*(w_1, w_2, y).$$

The Relation between Long-Run Cost Curves and Returns to Scale

Loosely speaking, the returns of a technology and the costs of production are mirror images. That is, when returns are high, costs are low, and vice versa. Somewhat more precisely, when returns are increasing, costs are falling, and vice versa. As we will see next, this is what we find for constant, increasing, and decreasing returns to scale.

Suppose a firm's production function satisfies constant returns to scale. Let (x_1^*, x_2^*) be the cost-minimizing input combination that results in 1 unit of output. Then $C(1) = w_1 x_1^* + w_2 x_2^*$. Now, if the firm wants to produce an arbitrary y units of output, by constant returns to scale, it can do so by multiplying by y both the input quantities that gave 1 unit of output. Moreover, as we saw earlier, scaling up both the inputs in this fashion will leave MP_1, MP_2, and TRS unchanged.

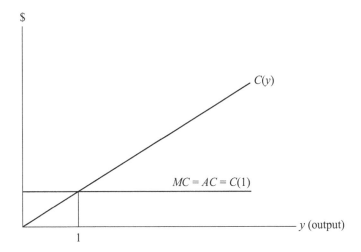

Fig. 9.5. Total cost $C(y)$ with constant returns to scale.

Therefore, because (x_1^*, x_2^*) was a point of tangency between an isoquant and an isocost line, (yx_1^*, yx_2^*) will also be a tangency point. Therefore, $C(y) = yC(1)$ is the least-cost way to produce y units of output. That is, for constant returns to scale, the long-run cost function is a very simple linear function that makes $C(y)$ directly proportional to output y.

We show this kind of linear cost function in Figure 9.5.

Remember that *average cost* is total cost divided by quantity, or $AC(y) = C(y)/y$. For our constant returns to scale case, average cost is constant. This is because $AC(y) = C(y)/y = yC(1)/y = C(1)$. Also recall that *marginal cost* is the derivative of the cost function, or, intuitively, the extra cost per additional unit of output. That is, $MC(y) = dC(y)/dy$. In the constant returns to scale case, $MC(y) = d(C(1)y)/dy = C(1) = AC(y)$. In short, with constant returns to scale, total cost is a linear function of y, and both average and marginal cost are constant, equal to each other, and equal to the cost of producing just 1 unit of output.

Next, we assume that the firm's production function satisfies increasing returns to scale. The cost of producing 1 unit of output is $C(1)$. If the firm wants to produce y units of output, it can scale up the input quantities by *less than* y, because if it scaled up by y, by the increasing returns to scale assumption, output would rise to more than y. Therefore, the cost of producing y will be less than $yC(1)$. In short, $C(y) < yC(1)$. This implies that the total cost curve is concave, as shown in Figure 9.6.

In Figure 9.6, we have included a line l_2 that is tangent to the total cost curve at a point P, as well as a line l_1 going from the origin through the point P. The slope of the tangent line is $dC(y)/dy$, or marginal cost, and the slope of the line from the origin is $C(y)/y$, or average cost. This is similar to what we did in Figure 8.3.

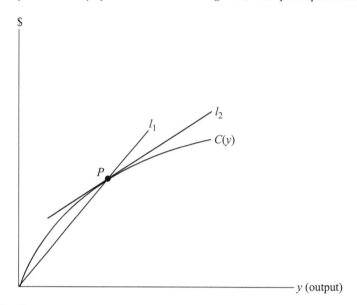

Fig. 9.6. Total cost $C(y)$ with increasing returns to scale. Average cost at the point P is the slope of l_1, and marginal cost is the slope of l_2.

It is clear from Figure 9.6 that at any point on the total cost curve, the slope of the tangent line, or marginal cost, is less than the slope of the line from the origin, or average cost. In short, for the increasing returns to scale case, $MC(y) < AC(y)$. Also, as y increases, both marginal cost and average cost are decreasing.

Now we assume that the firm's production function satisfies decreasing returns to scale. We continue to assume that the cost of producing 1 unit of output is $C(1)$. Now, if the firm wants to produce y units of output, it must scale up the input quantities by more than y. Therefore, the cost of producing y will be more than $yC(1)$. In short, $C(y) > yC(1)$. This implies that the total cost curve is convex, as shown in Figure 9.7.

In Figure 9.7, we have again included a line l_2 that is tangent to the total cost curve at a point P, as well as a line l_1 going from the origin through the point P. The slope of the tangent line is $dC(y)/dy$, or marginal cost, and the slope of the line from the origin is $C(y)/y$, or average cost. It is clear from Figure 9.7 that at any point on the total cost curve, the slope of the tangent line, or marginal cost, is greater than the slope of the line from the origin, or average cost. In short, for the decreasing returns to scale case, $MC(y) > AC(y)$. Also, as y increases, both marginal cost and average cost are increasing.

Finally, let us suppose, loosely speaking, that the production function satisfies increasing returns to scale at the beginning, changes to constant returns to scale, and then changes to decreasing returns to scale at the end. We say "loosely speaking" here because, as we have defined constant, increasing, and decreasing returns, the properties are universal, and not attached to particular scales of operation for the

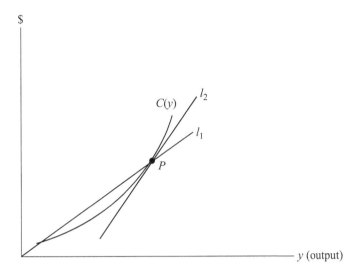

Fig. 9.7. Total cost $C(y)$ with decreasing returns to scale. Average cost at the point P is the slope of l_1, and marginal cost is the slope of l_2. ($C(y)$ position approximate.)

firm. In terms of isoquants, we are now assuming that the isoquants first get closer and closer together, and ultimately get farther and farther apart. Now the total cost curve is first concave, and then turns to convex, as in Figure 9.8. Note that this figure is just like Figure 8.3, on the single-input model.

The reader should refer to Figure 8.4 to recall the appearance of the U-shaped average and marginal cost curves in the real-world case for the single-input model. A similar figure applies here in the multi-input model. Both average and marginal costs first decline and then rise, and the marginal cost curve passes through the minimum of the average cost curve. When average cost is declining, marginal cost is below average cost, and when average cost is rising, marginal cost is above average cost.

9.4 Profit Maximization in the Long Run

Throughout this chapter, we have been assuming that the firm is competitive in the market for its inputs. That is, it takes the input prices w_1 and w_2 as given and fixed. It is too small to affect the input prices. We now also assume that our firm is competitive in the market for its output. That is, its choice of y does not affect the output price p. (We will return to a careful analysis of the competitive market assumption in a subsequent chapter.)

We now derive the conditions for profit maximization in the long run, as well as the firm's long-run supply curve. This section should look very familiar, because what we do here is very similar to what we already did in Chapter 8, the single-input model.

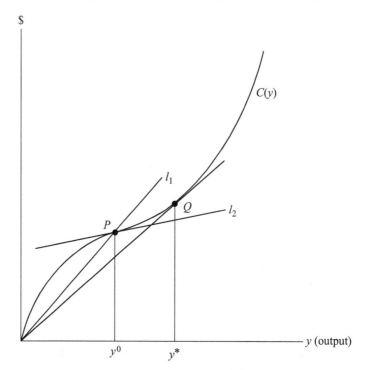

Fig. 9.8. Total cost $C(y)$ under increasing returns to scale followed by decreasing returns to scale. Average cost at P is the slope of l_1, and marginal cost is the slope of l_2.

In the long run, both (or all) inputs are free to vary. If the firm produces nothing, y, x_1, and x_2 are all zero, revenue is zero, total cost is zero, and profit is zero. Therefore, whenever the firm chooses a y to maximize its profit, it will consider only output quantities for which profit is nonnegative. Therefore,

$$\pi(y) = py - C(y) \geq 0.$$

Dividing both sides of the inequality by y leads to

$$p \geq \min AC(y).$$

That is, the firm will operate only if the market price equals or exceeds minimum average cost. In the long run, it will not be in business if being in business means losing money.

If the price p is high enough for the firm to operate without a loss, then it must decide how much to produce. Its profit is

$$\pi(y) = py - C(y).$$

The first-order condition for maximizing this function is

$$\frac{d\pi(y)}{dy} = p - \frac{dC(y)}{dy} = p - MC(y) = 0.$$

This gives

$$p = MC(y),$$

or price equals marginal cost.

The second-order condition for maximizing profit is

$$\frac{d^2\pi(y)}{dy^2} = \frac{d(p - MC(y))}{dy} \leq 0,$$

which gives

$$\frac{dMC(y)}{dy} \geq 0.$$

That is, at the profit-maximizing point, price equals marginal cost, and marginal cost is rising (or at least not falling).

We refer the reader to Figure 8.6 to view a graph illustrating the profit-maximizing choice in the real-world case of a firm with U-shaped average and marginal cost curves. That graph includes a horizontal line at a price p that is greater than the minimum of the average cost curve. The horizontal line intersects the marginal cost curve at two points; both points satisfy the first-order condition, but only one satisfies the second-order condition.

We also refer the reader to Figure 8.7 to view the graph of the profit-maximizing firm's supply curve in the real-world case.

In summary, in the typical competitive firm case, with U-shaped average and marginal cost curves, in the long run, the firm supplies nothing if $p < \min AC(y)$. But if $p \geq \min AC(y)$, the amount the firm supplies is given by the upward-sloping part of the marginal cost curve.

Returns to Scale and Long-Run Supply

We now analyze the firm's profit-maximization decision and its supply curve in the cases of constant, decreasing, and increasing returns to scale.

If the firm's production function is constant returns to scale, its total cost, average cost, and marginal cost curves are as illustrated in Figure 9.5. In particular, marginal cost and average cost are constant (that is, horizontal lines) at $C(1)$. For $p > C(1)$, the firm would want to supply an unlimited amount, and would have unlimited profit. For $p = C(1)$, the firm would supply any quantity; all would result in zero profit. For $p < C(1)$, the firm would supply nothing, and would have a profit of zero.

Next we assume an increasing returns to scale production function and the corresponding total cost curve, as in Figure 9.6. We can see from that figure that average cost (the slope of the ray l_1, from the origin through a point on $C(y)$) is always greater than marginal cost (the slope of the tangent l_2 to $C(y)$), and both

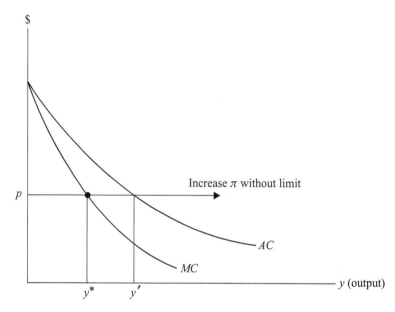

Fig. 9.9. Unbounded supply under increasing returns to scale.

average cost and marginal cost are declining as y increases. Figure 9.9 shows the average and marginal cost curves corresponding to this case. At the price/quantity combination (p, y^*) illustrated, the first-order condition $p = MC(y)$ is satisfied, but the second-order condition is not. In fact, that point is a profit minimum, rather than a profit maximum. Given the price p, if the firm increases its output to y', it will break even, and moving to the right of y' allows increasing profit without limit. In other words, given that average cost and marginal cost continue to decline, the firm wants to produce an infinite amount of its output and earn infinite profits. This, of course, would eventually result in the firm becoming so large that its choice of y would affect the price p. In other words, the assumption of increasing returns to scale, over all levels of output, is ultimately inconsistent with the assumption of competitive behavior.

Finally, we assume a decreasing returns to scale production function, and the corresponding total cost curve, as in Figure 9.7. In that figure, we can see that average cost is less than marginal cost, and both are increasing as y increases. Figure 9.10 shows the average and marginal cost curves corresponding to this case. Both curves are upward sloping, and the marginal cost curve lies above the average cost curve. Given a market price p, as shown, the firm will maximize profit by producing the y^* shown. The firm's profit will then be $\pi(y^*) = py^* - C(y^*) = py^* - AC(y^*)y^*$, or the area of the crosshatched rectangle. The marginal cost curve is also the firm's supply curve, at least for prices greater than or equal to the intercept of $MC(y)$ with the vertical axis.

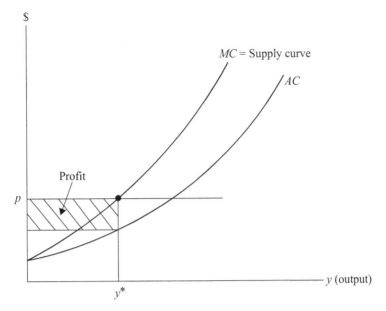

Fig. 9.10. The long-run supply with decreasing returns to scale.

9.5 A Solved Problem

The Problem

Consider the production function

$$y = f(x_1, x_2) = x_1^\alpha x_2^\beta,$$

where α and β are positive constants. Assume the input prices are w_1 and w_2. This production function is called a *Cobb-Douglas production function*, after the people who first studied it, Charles Cobb (1875–1949) and Paul Douglas (1892–1976). Cobb was a mathematician and economist; Douglas was an economist at the University of Chicago who became an important and influential Democratic senator from Illinois.

(a) Show that if $\alpha + \beta < 1$, the production function has the property of decreasing returns to scale. (We will say "the production function is decreasing returns to scale" for short.) Show that if $\alpha + \beta = 1$, the production function is constant returns to scale; and show that if $\alpha + \beta > 1$, the production function is increasing returns to scale.

(b) Find the marginal products MP_1 and MP_2, and the technical rate of substitution TRS.

(c) Now assume $w_1 = 1$ and $w_2 = 1$, and also assume $\alpha = 1$ and $\beta = 1$. Find the long-run cost function $C(y)$, the average cost function $AC(y)$, and the marginal cost function $MC(y)$.

The Solution

(a) Note that

$$f(tx_1, tx_2) = (tx_1)^\alpha (tx_2)^\beta = (t^{\alpha+\beta}) x_1^\alpha x_2^\beta,$$

and

$$tf(x_1, x_2) = t x_1^\alpha x_2^\beta.$$

A production function is decreasing returns to scale if for any $t > 1$, $f(tx_1, tx_2) < tf(x_1, x_2)$; it is constant returns to scale if for any $t > 1$, $f(tx_1, tx_2) = tf(x_1, x_2)$; and it is increasing returns to scale if for any $t > 1$, $f(tx_1, tx_2) > tf(x_1, x_2)$.

Therefore, the Cobb-Douglas production function is decreasing returns to scale if

$$(t^{\alpha+\beta}) x_1^\alpha x_2^\beta < t x_1^\alpha x_2^\beta \qquad \Leftrightarrow \qquad t^{\alpha+\beta} < t \qquad \Leftrightarrow \qquad \alpha + \beta < 1.$$

Similarly, the Cobb-Douglas production function is constant returns to scale if

$$(t^{\alpha+\beta}) x_1^\alpha x_2^\beta = t x_1^\alpha x_2^\beta \qquad \Leftrightarrow \qquad t^{\alpha+\beta} = t \qquad \Leftrightarrow \qquad \alpha + \beta = 1.$$

Finally, the Cobb-Douglas production function is increasing returns to scale if

$$(t^{\alpha+\beta}) x_1^\alpha x_2^\beta > t x_1^\alpha x_2^\beta \qquad \Leftrightarrow \qquad t^{\alpha+\beta} > t \qquad \Leftrightarrow \qquad \alpha + \beta > 1.$$

(b) To find MP_1, we take the partial derivative of $f(x_1, x_2)$ with respect to x_1. This gives

$$MP_1 = \frac{\partial x_1^\alpha x_2^\beta}{\partial x_1} = \alpha x_1^{\alpha-1} x_2^\beta.$$

MP_2 is found similarly:

$$MP_2 = \frac{\partial x_1^\alpha x_2^\beta}{\partial x_2} = \beta x_1^\alpha x_2^{\beta-1}.$$

The technical rate of substitution is MP_1 divided by MP_2, or

$$TRS = \frac{MP_1}{MP_2} = \frac{\alpha x_1^{\alpha-1} x_2^\beta}{\beta x_1^\alpha x_2^{\beta-1}} = \frac{\alpha x_2}{\beta x_1}.$$

(c) Now we are assuming $w_1 = w_2 = 1$, and we are also assuming $\alpha = \beta = 1$. These two assumptions will make things a lot easier. For cost minimization, in the general case, the firm finds input combinations where $TRS = w_1/w_2$. This gives

$$TRS = \frac{\alpha x_2}{\beta x_1} = \frac{x_2}{x_1} = \frac{w_1}{w_2} = 1.$$

Therefore, $x_2 = x_1$. Substituting back in the production function, we now get $y = x_1^\alpha x_2^\beta = x_1 x_2 = x_1^2$. Therefore, the cost-minimizing inputs are $x_1^* = y^{1/2}$ and $x_2^* = y^{1/2}$. The cost function is thus,

$$C(y) = w_1 x_1^* + w_2 x_2^* = y^{1/2} + y^{1/2} = 2y^{1/2}.$$

The average cost and marginal cost functions are

$$AC(y) = C(y)/y = \frac{2y^{1/2}}{y} = 2y^{-1/2},$$

$$MC(y) = \frac{dC(y)}{dy} = \frac{d(2y^{1/2})}{dy} = y^{-1/2}.$$

Exercises

1. Explain why the concepts of constant, increasing, and decreasing returns to scale make sense when applied to isoquants, but would not make sense in the theory of the consumer, if applied to indifference curves. That is, why does the spacing between successive isoquants make sense, whereas the spacing of successive indifference curves does not?

2. If the price of the output of a profit-maximizing firm rises, how will the firm's output change?

3. Suppose a firm's production function is $y = x_1^{1/4}x_2^{1/4}$. The prices of the inputs are $w_1 = 1$ and $w_2 = 2$.
   (a) Show that the long-run conditional factor demands are $x_1^*(y) = \sqrt{2}y^2$ and $x_2^*(y) = y^2/\sqrt{2}$.
   (b) Show that the long-run cost function is $C(y) = 2\sqrt{2}y^2$.
   (c) Show that the long-run supply curve for the firm is given by $y^*(p) = p/(4\sqrt{2})$.

4. A firm produces computers with two factors of production: labor L and capital K. Its production function is $y = LK/10$. Suppose the factor prices are $w_L = 10$ and $w_K = 100$.
   (a) Graph the isoquants for y equal to 1, 2, and 3. Does this technology show increasing, constant, or decreasing returns to scale? Why?
   (b) Derive the conditional factor demands.
   (c) Derive the long-run cost function $C(y)$.
   (d) If the firm wants to produce one computer, how many units of labor and how many units of capital should it use? How much will it cost? What if the firm wants to produce two computers?
   (e) Derive the firm's long-run average cost function $AC(y)$ and long-run marginal cost function $MC(y)$. Graph $AC(y)$ and $MC(y)$. What is the firm's long-run supply curve?

5. Let the firm's production function be given by $y = x_1 + x_2$. Suppose $w_1 = 2$ and $w_2 = 1$.
   (a) Derive the conditional factor demands and use them to find the long-run cost function for this firm.
   (b) For these factor prices, derive and graph the firm's long-run supply curve.
   (c) Suppose the price of the second input, w_2, rises to \$2 per unit. What is the long-run cost curve? Derive and graph the new supply curve.
   Hint: Because these isoquants are straight lines, cost minimization cannot require tangencies of isoquants and isocost lines.

6. Consider a production function that uses three inputs: $y = x_1^{1/5} x_2^{1/5} x_3^{1/5}$. Suppose the factor prices are $w_1 = w_2 = w_3 = 1$.

(a) What are the conditional factor demands $x_1^*(y)$, $x_2^*(y)$, and $x_3^*(y)$?

(b) Find the long-run cost function $C(y)$.

(c) Find the long-run supply curve $y^*(p)$.

Chapter 10

Theory of the Firm 3: The Short-Run, Multiple-Input Model

10.1 Introduction

In Chapter 8 we modeled a firm with one input and one output. In Chapter 9 we developed a more general model, with multiple inputs and one output. Both the Chapter 8 single-input/single-output and the Chapter 9 multiple-input/single-output models were long-run models, which means that the inputs were freely variable. If we assume a production function such as $y = f(x_1, x_2)$, long-run analysis means that both x_1 and x_2 can be varied by the firm. In the short run, however, some inputs cannot be varied, because the time horizon is too short. How short is "short run" and how long is "long run" in reality depends on the facts of the firm, so our economic analysis is necessarily a little vague about the time units. However, we can be exact about what we mean by a *short-run model*. A short-run theory of the firm model is one in which some of the input quantities are fixed.

In this chapter we develop our short-run model. If there are n inputs, x_1, $x_2, \ldots, x_n$, with input prices $w_1, w_2, \ldots, w_n$, *short run* means that some of the inputs are fixed at nonzero levels, whereas others are variable. If the production function is $y = f(x_1, x_2)$, with two inputs, *short run* means x_2 is fixed at a nonzero level, whereas x_1 is variable. One main implication should be immediately clear: In a short-run model, the cost function has a nonzero fixed part. When there are just two inputs, this is w_2 times the fixed quantity of input 2. When there are n inputs, this is the sum of the prices of the fixed inputs times the respective quantities of those inputs. Moreover, when there are just two inputs, one fixed and one variable, the short-run model will be much like the Chapter 8 model, but with a fixed cost element attached; if there are three or more inputs, with one or more fixed and two or more variable, the short-run model will be much like the Chapter 9 model, but with the fixed cost element attached.

163

10.2 The Production Function in the Short Run

In the short run, the firm does not have time to vary the level of one or more of its inputs. In the following discussion, we will generally assume that there are only two inputs, with x_1 variable but x_2 fixed, and a production function $y = f(x_1, x_2)$. We let $x_2^0 > 0$ represent the fixed level of the second input. The production function $f(x_1, x_2)$ is now constrained at $f(x_1, x_2^0)$. This constrained function is called a *short-run production function*.

Because $f(x_1, x_2^0)$ depends on only one variable (that is, x_1), the analysis of the short-run production function is almost exactly the same as the analysis of the single-input production function $f(x)$ of Chapter 8. The only differences arise when the variable input is zero: in the single-input model, if $x = 0$, then $y = 0$, and cost and profit are also zero; but in the two-input short-run model, if $x_1 = 0$, y may not be zero, cost is not zero (because $x_2^0 > 0$), and profit will probably not be zero. The short-run production function can be graphed, with x_1 on the horizontal axis and y on the vertical; the result will be similar to the graph of $f(x)$ in Figure 8.1, although it will not necessarily pass through the point $(0, 0)$.

As we did in Chapters 8 and 9, we can define average and marginal products for the variable input x_1 for the short-run production function. The average product of input 1 is y/x_1, and the marginal product is, roughly speaking, the extra output per extra unit of input 1. More formally, average product is

$$AP(x_1) = \frac{f(x_1, x_2^0)}{x_1}.$$

Marginal product is the derivative of the short-run production function $f(x_1, x_2^0)$ with respect to the variable x_1, or the slope of the short-run production function with the given x_2^0. More formally, marginal product is

$$MP(x_1) = \frac{\partial f(x_1, x_2^0)}{\partial x_1}.$$

If we need to show the underlying fixed level of input 2 in the expressions for average product and/or marginal product, we can add the term $|x_2^0$, which simply means "given $x_2 = x_2^0$." For average product, for example, we can write $AP(x_1|x_2^0)$.

As with the single-input model of Chapter 8, economists believe that the short run $MP(x_1)$ and $AP(x_1)$ curves for a "real-world" firm should be roughly parabolic – first increasing, and then decreasing, similar to the curves in Figure 8.8. That is, given a fixed x_2^0, marginal product of x_1 first rises, as the firm in a sense gets more productive; reaches a peak; and then declines, as the firm in a sense gets less productive. Average product does likewise, although it peaks after marginal product. Furthermore, where average product reaches its peak, marginal product passes through it.

10.3 Cost Minimization in the Short Run

Remember that the short run is a period of time so short that input 2 cannot be varied. Because it must pay for x_2^0, the firm has an inescapable cost of $w_2 x_2^0$. This is called the firm's *fixed cost*. Fixed cost is written

$$FC = w_2 x_2^0.$$

In the short run, the firm can vary x_1. Therefore, $w_1 x_1$ is the variable part of the firm's total cost. This is called the firm's *variable cost*, and it is written

$$VC(y).$$

We have written variable cost as an explicit function of y, which we did not do for FC. We did this for an obvious reason: variable cost varies with y, whereas fixed cost does not. To calculate the $VC(y)$ function, we first note that $VC(y) = w_1 x_1$. Next, we need to substitute a function of y in place of x_1.

To do this, we use the firm's *short-run demand function* for input 1. This is the amount of input 1 needed to produce a given quantity of y, subject to the constraint that input 2 is fixed at x_2^0. In the two-input model, with one input fixed in the short run, the short-run demand function is simply the inverse of the production function – with the constraint, of course, that input 2 is fixed at x_1^0. We write the inverse production function as

$$x_1(y) = f^{-1}(y).$$

If we need to show the underlying fixed level of input 2 in this expression, we can write $x_1(y) = f^{-1}(y|x_2^0)$.

Now we can show variable cost as an explicit function of y. It is simply

$$VC(y) = w_1 x_1(y) = w_1 f^{-1}(y).$$

The firm's *total cost* is the sum of its fixed cost and its variable cost, or

$$C^S(y) = FC + VC(y).$$

We have put a superscript S on the total cost function to emphasize that it is a short-run cost function, and that it is contingent on what is fixed in the short run, namely, x_2^0. If we need to be explicit about the level of the fixed input, we will write this as $C^S(y|x_2^0)$.

We will reserve the $C(y)$ notation, with no superscript, to represent long-run total cost. Note that FC and $VC(y)$ are defined only in the short run, and therefore, we do not bother to put S superscripts on them.

In Figure 10.1, we show an isoquant for a given level of output y^0. We show two isocost lines: one is the isocost line the firm could get to in the long run, when it could vary input 2 and escape its fixed cost $FC = w_2 x_2^0$. The other is the isocost line it must settle for in the short run, when it must use x_2^0 and cannot escape the

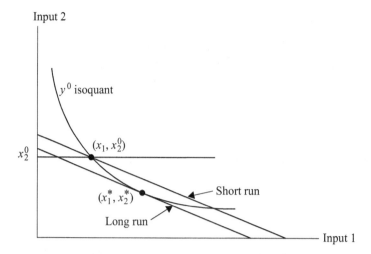

Fig. 10.1. Short-run cost minimization is at (x_1, x_2^0); long run is at (x_1^*, x_2^*).

fixed cost. The long-run cost-minimizing input combination is (x_1^*, x_2^*), but in the short run, the firm will simply use x_2^0 units of input 2 and whatever level of input 1 is sufficient to produce y^0 units of output when it is using x_2^0 units of input 2. That is, it will operate at the point (x_1, x_2^0) shown in the figure.

As we can plainly see from Figure 10.1, (x_1, x_2^0) is a more costly way to produce y^0 than (x_1^*, x_2^*). In other words, at (x_1, x_2^0) the firm is not "fully" minimizing costs. That is, for any given level of output, short-run total cost is greater than or equal to long-run total cost.

At (x_1, x_2^0), the firm is choosing a technologically efficient way to produce y^0, subject to the constraint that $x_2 = x_2^0$. Other than that, it is not doing anything clever when it decides on the x_1 that it will use. In other words, short-run cost minimization when there are only two inputs is a mindless process. Of course, if there are three or more inputs, and the third input is fixed in the short run, then the firm does have to make an intelligent choice of x_1 and x_2, along the lines we laid out in Chapter 9.

We can now rewrite the firm's short-run total cost function, based on the formulas discussed previously:

$$C^S(y) = FC + VC(y) = w_2 x_2^0 + w_1 x_1(y) = w_2 x_2^0 + w_1 f^{-1}(y).$$

In Figure 10.2, we show a short-run total cost curve, under the assumption that the marginal product of input 1 is first increasing, and then decreasing. Note that this figure is very similar to Figure 8.3, which illustrated the total cost curve in the real-world case for the single-input model. The notable difference is this: The short-run total cost curve starts out (when $y = 0$) at a positive intercept, namely, the fixed cost.

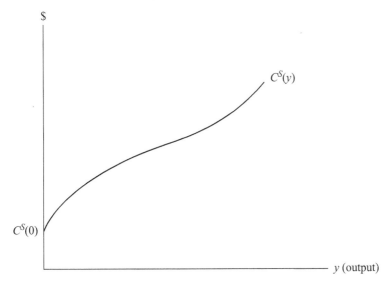

Fig. 10.2. The short-run total cost curve.

In Figure 10.3, we show marginal and average costs corresponding to Figure 10.2. This figure is, of course, similar to Figure 8.4. The idea of short-run marginal cost is similar to the idea of long-run marginal cost: just take the total cost function and differentiate it. However, it is important to note that short-run and long-run marginal costs are generally not equal, as the long-run cost function allows x_2 to freely vary. Therefore, we must distinguish between them. Just as we used a superscript S to identify short-run total cost ($C^S(y)$), we will use a superscript S to identify short-run marginal cost. That is, short-run marginal cost will be written $MC^S(y)$.

In the long-run analysis, there is only one concept of average cost: just take total cost and divide by y. In the short-run analysis, however, there are two relevant alternative notions of average cost, one that includes the firm's fixed cost, and the other that excludes it. The first is called *average total cost* (*ATC*), and the second is called *average variable cost* (*AVC*). They are formally defined as

$$ATC(y) = C^S(y)/y = (FC + VC(y))/y,$$

and

$$AVC(y) = VC(y)/y.$$

Because average total cost includes FC/y, whereas average variable cost does not, it is clear that $ATC(y) > AVC(y)$. Because we use the $ATC(y)$ and $AVC(y)$ terminology only in the context of short-run analysis, we will not bother to remind the reader that they are short-run concepts with the superscript S.

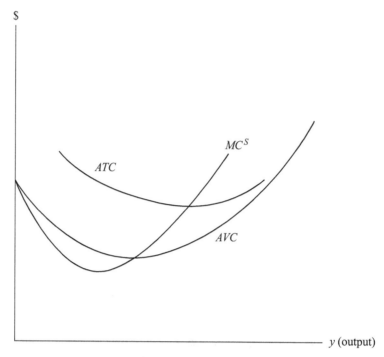

Fig. 10.3. Marginal, average variable, and average total cost curves in the short-run real-world case. (Position of *ATC* approximate.)

Figure 10.3 shows marginal cost, average variable cost, and average total cost curves in the case where the marginal product of input 1 is first increasing, and then decreasing. This is the "real-world" case for the short-run cost function.

We end this section by making some observations about long-run and short-run cost curves in real-world cases. We know that their shapes may be similar – first concave, and then convex. We also know that every short-run cost curve must lie on or above the long-run cost curve. This is so because no matter what the fixed x_2^0 might be, and no matter what y may be, the cost of producing y must be lower, or at least not higher, when x_2 is free to vary (that is, in the long run) than when it is fixed. The short-run total cost curve will just touch the long-run total cost curve if, for the given y, x_2^0 happens to precisely equal the long-run cost-minimizing level for input 2. Otherwise, the short-run total cost curve will be higher.

Figure 10.4 shows a long-run cost curve and two short-run cost curves in the real-world concave-then-convex case. One short-run cost curve, labeled $C^S(y|x_2^0)$, is based on x_2^0; the other, labeled $C^S(y|x_2^1)$, is based on a higher input 2 level, x_2^1. You can see that the long-run curve seems to lie just below the short-run curves, supporting them from below in a sense, or "enveloping" them. For this reason, the long-run cost curve is said to be the *envelope* of the short run curves. (Note that the long-run cost curve is the envelope of *all* the short-run curves, not just the two illustrated.) For each short-run curve, there is one y for which long-run

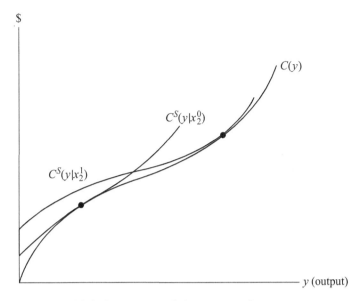

Fig. 10.4. Long-run and short-run total cost curves.

and short-run costs coincide; otherwise, the short-run curve lies above the long-run curve.

10.4 Profit Maximization in the Short Run

We are continuing to assume that x_2 is fixed at x_2^0. For any output level y, the firm chooses the technologically efficient x_1 that, when combined with x_2^0, produces y. In a previous section of this chapter, we constructed the short-run total cost curve $C^S(y)$, and in Figure 10.3, we graphed short-run marginal cost, average total cost, and average variable cost curves in the real-world firm case. Keep in mind that the $MC^S(y)$, $ATC(y)$, and $AVC(y)$ curves all depend on the underlying x_2^0.

We define short-run profit as

$$\pi^S(y) = py - C^S(y).$$

Because $C^S(y) = FC + VC(y)$, this implies

$$\pi^S(y) = py - FC - VC(y).$$

However, variable cost at $y = 0$ is zero; therefore, profit at $y = 0$ is $\pi^S(0) = -FC$. In other words, in the short run, if the firm elects to produce nothing, it loses money (in the amount FC). Therefore, in the short run, the firm will produce output even if it is losing money, provided the amount it is losing is less than FC. This implies that the firm is willing to produce as long as

$$\pi^S(y) = py - C^S(y) \geq -FC.$$

Rearranging gives $py \geq C^S(y) - FC = VC(y)$ and dividing both sides of the inequality by y leads to

$$p \geq \min AVC(y).$$

That is, in the short run, the firm is willing to lose money, but it is not willing to lose more than its fixed cost; this implies that it will operate only if the market price of its output is greater than or equal to the minimum of average variable cost.

Once the firm decides it is worthwhile to stay in business, it must choose the best y. Here is what it does. Its profit is

$$\pi^S(y) = py - C^S(y).$$

The first-order condition for maximizing this function is

$$\frac{d\pi^S(y)}{dy} = p - \frac{dC^S(y)}{dy} = p - MC^S(y) = 0.$$

This gives

$$p = MC^S(y),$$

or price equals short-run marginal cost. This condition looks just like the one derived in Chapter 8, the single-input model, and in Chapter 9, on the long-run multiple-input model. Of course, in the present context, the marginal cost function referred to is short-run marginal cost, contingent on x_2^0.

The second-order condition for maximizing profit is

$$\frac{d^2\pi^S(y)}{dy^2} = \frac{d(p - MC^S(y))}{dy} \leq 0,$$

which gives

$$\frac{dMC^S(y)}{dy} \geq 0.$$

In sum, at the profit-maximizing point, price equals short-run marginal cost, and short-run marginal cost is rising (or at least not falling). Again, this looks like the results we have already seen, except it is all short run, with input 2 fixed at x_2^0.

Figure 10.5 shows the short-run supply curve, and other relevant information, for the profit-maximizing firm. It is based on Figure 10.3. For $p < p_1$ in the figure, price is below the minimum of the average variable cost curve, and the firm shuts down (and loses FC). For a market price between p_1 and p_2, the firm stays open and covers some part of its fixed cost. However, its profit is negative or zero. (The firm's loss is FC if $p = p_1$, less than FC if $p_2 > p > p_1$, and 0 if $p = p_2$.) For $p > p_2$, the firm is making money; it is covering all of its costs, including fixed cost and more. It has money to spare. The firm's profit can be found graphically in a way similar to the way used in Figure 9.10.

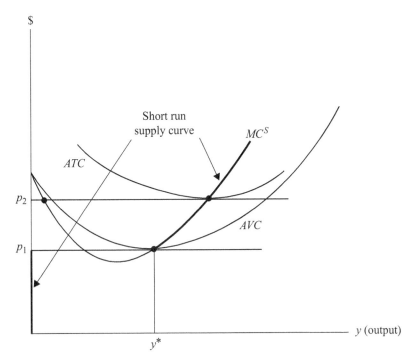

Fig. 10.5. The short-run supply curve of a competitive firm. When $p < \min AVC$, supply is zero. When $p = p_1 = \min AVC$, supply jumps to y^*. When $p > p_1 = \min AVC$, supply coincides with the MC^S curve. (Position of ATC approximate.)

We can describe the profit-maximizing firm's supply in the short run this way. The firm supplies nothing if the market price is below the minimum of average variable cost. However, when price is above that level, the firm's supply curve is the upward-sloping part of the $MC^S(y)$ curve. Given a market price of p, the firm maximizes profit by solving for the y^* where price equals short-run marginal cost, where short-run marginal cost is rising, and where price is greater than or equal to average variable cost.

10.5 A Solved Problem

The Problem

Consider the Cobb-Douglas production function

$$y = f(x_1, x_2) = x_1^{1/2} x_2^{1/2}.$$

Assume the input prices are $w_1 = 1$ and $w_2 = 2$. Assume the input 2 quantity is fixed in the short run at $x_2^0 = 9$. Assume the output price is $p = 2$.

(a) Find the short-run production function $f(x_1, x_2^0)$, the short-run average product function, and the short-run marginal product function.

(b) Find fixed cost FC, the variable cost function $VC(y)$, the average variable cost function $AVC(y)$, and the short-run total cost function $C^S(y)$.

(c) Find the short-run marginal cost MC^S. Find the the profit-maximizing output. Find the short-run profit level for the firm. Is the firm's profit positive or negative? Explain.

The Solution

(a) To get the short-run production function, we just substitute the constant $x_2^0 = 9$ for the variable x_2. This gives

$$f(x_1, x_2^0) = 3x_1^{1/2}.$$

To get the short-run average product, we divide $f(x_1, x_2^0)$ by x_1, or

$$AP(x_1) = \frac{3x_1^{1/2}}{x_1} = 3x_1^{-1/2}.$$

The short-run marginal product is found by differentiating the short-run production function, which gives

$$MP(x_1) = \frac{d(3x_1^{1/2})}{dx_1} = \frac{3}{2}x_1^{-1/2}.$$

(Note that we have written the derivative with d symbols instead of ∂ symbols.)

(b) Fixed cost is $FC = w_2 x_2^0 = 2 \times 9 = 18$. To find the variable cost function, we will need the inverse production function. Therefore, we invert the short-run production function $y = f(x_1, x_2^0) = 3x_1^{1/2}$. This gives $x_1(y) = y^2/9$. The variable cost function is now

$$VC(y) = w_1 x_1(y) = 1 \times \frac{y^2}{9} = \frac{y^2}{9}.$$

Average variable cost is $VC(y)/y$, which gives

$$AVC(y) = (y^2/9)/y = \frac{y}{9}.$$

The short-run total cost is

$$C^S(y) = FC + VC(y) = 18 + \frac{y^2}{9}.$$

(c) To get the short-run marginal cost, we differentiate the short-run cost function $C^S(y)$. This gives

$$MC^S = \frac{d(18 + y^2/9)}{dy} = \frac{2y}{9}.$$

Note that short-run marginal cost is an always-increasing function of y. To find the short-run profit-maximizing output y^*, we first set $MC^S(y) = 2y/9 = p = 2$ and solve. This gives $y^* = 9$. Next we check to see that price is greater than or equal to average variable cost. This gives $p = 2 \geq AVC(y^*) = y^*/9 = 9/9 = 1$, and it checks out. The profit for the firm is

$$\pi^S(y^*) = py^* - C^S(y^*) = 2 \times 9 - (18 + 9^2/9) = 18 - (18 + 9) = -9.$$

The firm's profit is negative, but it does not fold in the short run because if it produced nothing, its profit would be $\pi^S(0) = -FC = -18$.

Exercises

1. Let $f(x_1, x_2) = \left(243 + \frac{1}{3}(x_1 - 9)^3\right) x_2$.
   (a) Calculate $AP(x_1|1)$ and $MP(x_1|1)$. (This assumes that input 1 is the variable input and input 2 is fixed, as we assumed in most of this chapter, with $x_2^0 = 1$.)
   (b) Calculate $AP(x_2|x_1^0)$ and $MP(x_2|x_1^0)$. (This assumes that input 2 is the variable input and input 1 is fixed.)
   (c) Can you see from the comparison how these two inputs play very different roles in this technology?

2. Consider a profit-maximizing firm with a decreasing returns to scale production function $y(x_1, x_2)$ and input 2 fixed at x_2^0. Explain what happens to the conditional factor demand for input 1, x_1^*, and profit, π, in each of the following cases.
   (a) The price of input 1, w_1, rises.
   (b) The price of input 2, w_2, falls.
   (c) The price of the output, p, rises.

3. Recall the production function from Chapter 9, Exercise 3, $y = x_1^{1/4} x_2^{1/4}$. The prices of the inputs are $w_1 = 1$ and $w_2 = 2$. Assume that the amount of input 2 is fixed at one unit. The firm must, of course, pay for that one unit, but it cannot increase or decrease x_2.
   (a) Find the short-run cost function $C^S(y)$.
   (b) Show that the supply curve for the firm, given this constraint, is $y^*(p) = (\frac{p}{4})^{1/3}$.

4. Consider the production function $y = LK/10$, where L is labor and K is capital. (This is from Chapter 9, Exercise 4.) The factor prices are $w_L = 10$ and $w_K = 100$. Suppose the amount of capital, K, is fixed at 1 unit.
   (a) Derive the short-run cost function $C^S(y)$.
   (b) Derive and graph the average total cost function $ATC(y)$, the average variable cost function $AVC(y)$, and the short-run marginal cost function $MC^S(y)$. What is the firm's short-run supply curve? (For simplicity, assume $y > 0$.)

5. A baker bakes cakes. His short-run cost function is $C^S(y) = 100 + 10y - 2y^2 + y^3$, where y is the number of cakes.
   (a) Derive and graph his average total cost, average variable cost, and marginal cost curves.
   (b) What is his short-run supply curve?

6. Explain why a profit-maximizing firm might choose to produce output even though it is making negative profit by doing so.

Part III

Partial Equilibrium Analysis: Market Structure

Chapter 11

Perfectly Competitive Markets

11.1 Introduction

In this chapter, we put together consumers interested in buying a good and firms interested in selling the good. We start out by describing what we mean by perfect competition; this requires price-taking behavior by all parties, homogeneous goods, perfect information, and free entry and exit in the long run. We derive industry supply curves in the short run and in the long run. With consumers' actions aggregated into an industry demand curve, and firms' actions aggregated into an industry supply curve, we discuss excess demand and excess supply. Then we describe the competitive market equilibrium.

Next we turn to the welfare properties of the market equilibrium. We define *producer's surplus* for a single firm and *producers' surplus* for all the firms in the market. We will show how the competitive market equilibrium maximizes social surplus; that is, the sum of consumers' surplus and producers' surplus. Finally, we analyze the *deadweight loss*, or loss in social surplus, created by a per-unit tax on the good being sold in the market.

We use the idea of the market demand curve, developed in Chapter 4, and the idea of consumers' surplus, developed in Chapter 7. We also extend the welfare economics analysis of Chapter 7, but this time with an eye on both the consumers and the producers of the good.

11.2 Perfect Competition

As in Chapters 8 through 10, we are focusing on competitive firms. A firm is competitive if it takes prices as given; that is, beyond its control. A market is competitive if all the agents in that market (that is, all the buyers and all the sellers) take prices as given; that is, beyond their control.

The idea of competitive markets is fundamental in economic thinking, but it is of course an ideal, and the reality is often different. It is useful to study an ideal, though, even if the reality differs. For example, scientists analyze the motion of objects falling in a vacuum, even though true vacuums are rare on the surface of the earth. Where would Newton's laws be if he had to carefully incorporate in his equations the effects of atmospheric and other frictions? Let us try to justify the assumption of a competitive market by briefly describing the properties that result in competition. Perfectly competitive markets typically have the following features:

1. **Price-taking behavior**. Each firm is so small, compared with the total market, that whatever quantity it sells, it does not affect the market price. For instance, suppliers of commodities such as wheat, corn, heating oil, crude oil, gold, and silver are mostly so small that they do not influence world market prices. (However, decisions of Exxon-Mobil may affect oil prices, and the Hunt brothers of Texas once tried to corner the world market for silver.) The polar opposite of price-taking behavior is the behavior of a *monopolist*, a firm that is the one and only supplier of a good. For instance, a pharmaceutical firm producing a patented drug, for which there are few or no close substitutes, knows very well that it can sell many units if it charges a low price, and fewer units if it charges a higher price; it knows the downward-sloping demand curve it faces, and it finds the most profitable price/quantity combination, rather than taking the price as constant and solving for the most profitable quantity.

2. **Homogeneous goods**. The good that each firm produces is identical to the good that the other firms produce. For instance, the farmer producing number 2 corn, or winter wheat, is selling a product that is indistinguishable from that sold by thousands of other farmers. If what you produce is identical to what hundreds or thousands of other firms produce, you are unlikely to be able to sway the price; if you charge a penny more per bushel for your corn, you will not be able to sell any of it. On the other hand, the producer of Coca-Cola is selling a product that is somewhat different from Pepsi-Cola, RC Cola, or generic grocery-store cola. Therefore, the Coca-Cola Company can vary its price and still have plenty of sales. It will therefore search for the most profitable price/quantity combination, rather than taking its price as constant.

3. **Perfect information**. The standard economic model assumes that every buyer and every seller in the market has perfect information about all the relevant facts. All the buyers and all the sellers know the market price and the characteristics of the good being bought and sold. This assumption might be violated, for example, in labor markets, where workers might know things about their productivity that the firms that employ them do not know.

4. **Free entry and exit in the long run**. Recall that in Chapters 9 and 10 we made much of the distinction between the short run and the long run. For purposes of the theory of the firm, the short run is a period of time so short that a firm is unable to vary one of its inputs. The long run is a period of time long enough that all input levels can be freely varied by that firm. This implies, among other things, that short-run cost functions have a fixed term and a variable term, whereas long-run cost functions have no fixed term. It also implies that the long-run cost of producing zero units of output is zero, whereas the short-run cost of producing zero is positive.

   In this chapter, we introduce a different type of distinction between the short run and the long run, which is quite independent of the issue of whether a firm has time to vary the level of input 2. This distinction looks at the composition of the set of firms producing a good. We know that in reality, firms enter and exit industries, and that entering or exiting a business takes time. A feature of a perfectly competitive market is that, with enough time, entering and leaving a market are possible at a negligible cost. That is, in a competitive industry in which firms make positive profits, there are no barriers to entry to protect those profits. Similarly, in a competitive industry in which firms have losses year after year, firms shut down. For purposes of this chapter, when we are referring to the set of firms producing a good, the *short run* is a period of time so short that firms are unable to enter or leave the industry, and the *long run* is a period of time long enough that firms can freely enter or leave the industry.

For example, consider children setting up stands to sell cups of lemonade on a hot summer day in a nice residential neighborhood. With mom's help, they can put up a table on the sidewalk in 20 minutes, and they can bring out the lemonade and cups in 10 minutes. The short run is around 30 minutes; a couple of hours is a long run. Alternatively, consider power companies building nuclear generating facilities in the United States. Short run might be 10 years, and long run might be 50 years. Of course, as with the nuclear generating facilities, the time scale for entering or exiting the industry may be very much a consequence of various government policies.

In any case, in the long run, when there is sufficient time for competing firms to enter or exit an industry, it is more likely that firms in the industry will be competitive, and that they will have to take the price as given. Pharmaceuticals again provide an example: take the short run as a period of time during which a drug formula is protected by a patent, and the long run as a period of time longer than the patent duration. In the long run, producers of a particular drug formula will have generic competition, and firms producing the drug will be much more likely to have to accept the market price.

11.3 Market/Industry Supply

We begin by deriving the *short-run industry supply* curve. By "short run" in this chapter, we mean only that the number of firms is fixed; that is, there is insufficient time for firms to enter or leave the industry. We do not mean "short run" in the sense that a particular firm does not have time to vary one of its inputs – that is a separate issue. In fact, for the sake of simplicity, we will illustrate with average cost ($AC(y)$) and marginal cost ($MC(y)$) curves, rather than with (short-run) average variable cost ($AVC(y)$) and short-run marginal cost ($MC^S(y)$) curves from the last chapter.

How is industry supply determined? The answer is very easy in the short run, when the set of firms does not change. Simply add the separate supply curves of the various firms in the industry; for each price p, add up the desired amounts the various firms want to supply. In other words, add the supply curves horizontally. We will illustrate with some examples.

Example 1. Two firms with different cost curves. Figure 11.1 has three panels; the first is for firm 1, the second is for firm 2, and the third is for the market. We let y_1 and y_2 represent the output quantities of firms 1 and 2, respectively. In the firm 1

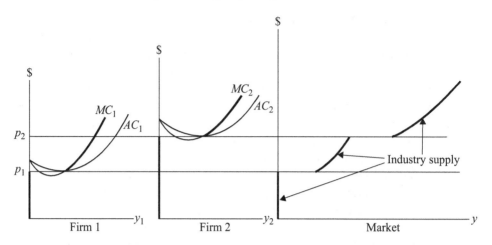

Fig. 11.1. Short-run industry supply with an industry of two firms.

panel, marginal cost (MC_1) and average cost (AC_1) curves are shown. A horizontal line at p_1 is drawn at the point at which marginal cost crosses the minimum of average cost. For prices below p_1, firm 1 wants to supply zero. For prices at or above p_1, it wants to supply the amounts indicated by the MC_1 curve. Firm 1's supply curve is shown in bold. The panel for firm 2 is similar, with a horizontal line at p_2 where firm 2's marginal cost curve crosses the minimum of average cost. In the market panel, the supply curves of the two firms have been added together horizontally, and the market supply is $y = y_1 + y_2$.

We see that there is a discontinuity of industry supply at the price p_1, and another one at the price p_2; these are the minima of the average cost curves of the two firms. That is, there are jumps in market supply y at each of these prices. If there are many similar firms, of course, the jump in market supply caused when one firm starts producing may be negligible.

Example 2. A large number of identical firms. Suppose the minimum of each firm's average cost curve is at p^*; p^* is the same for all firms. All the firms will supply nothing if the market price $p < p^*$. If $p \geq p^*$, each firm will go to its marginal cost curve to determine how much to supply. Let us assume there are 100 firms. The left-hand panel in Figure 11.2 shows the marginal cost (MC_i) and average cost (AC_i) curves for firm i. Firm i's supply curve is shown in bold. Because all the firms are the same, we will write $y_i(p) = y^*(p)$ for the ith firm's supply curve. The right-hand panel in the figure is the market supply curve. It is, of course, zero for $p < p^*$. For $p \geq p^*$, it is $y = \sum_{i=1}^{100} y_i(p) = 100y^*(p)$.

As we noted in Section 11.2, the short-run/long-run distinction in the theory of the firm is different from the short-run/long-run distinction in the theory of competitive markets. In the theory of the firm, short run means that one or more input levels is fixed; in the theory of competitive markets, short run means that

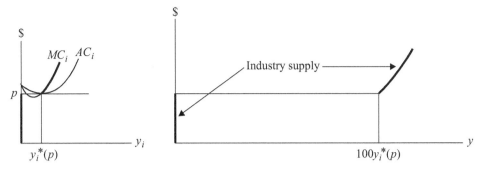

Fig. 11.2. The short-run industry supply (identical firms).

the number of firms in the market is fixed. If, however, the time frames were the same, so "short run" meant that for each firm some input levels were fixed *and* the number of firms in the market were fixed, then in Figures 11.1 and 11.2, we would simply replace AC_i with AVC_i, and MC_i with MC_i^S.

Deriving the long-run industry supply curve is slightly more complicated, because in the theory of competitive markets, "long run" means that the number of firms and the identity of firms in the industry are not fixed. In the competitive market in the long run, there is free entry and exit. When existing firms are making profits, other firms will enter the market; conversely, when existing firms are losing money, they will leave the market. Therefore, the number of firms in the market will vary – rising if incumbent firms are making profits, and falling if incumbent firms are incurring losses.

We now suppose that different firms, either in the industry or potentially in it, have different technologies and therefore different average and marginal cost curves. Every firm's average cost curve has a minimum, and those minima will generally vary among the firms. Let p^* represent the smallest of the average cost minima.

In the long run, there is free entry and exit by firms. Therefore, a firm will not be in the industry if the market price is below the minimum of its average cost curve; that is, if its profits are negative. Conversely, a firm will be in the industry if the market price is at or above the minimum of its average cost curve; that is, if its profits are greater than or equal to zero.

Now suppose, hypothetically, that the market price is below p^*. Then every firm that might potentially produce this good opts out of the business. Market supply is zero. Next, suppose the market price is exactly equal to p^*. Then the firm (or firms) whose minimum average cost equals p^* is in business, and producing the quantity that gives that average cost. This firm (or firms) has profits of zero. Finally, suppose the market price is $p > p^*$. Then the firm (or firms) whose minimum average cost equals p^* is in business, and making positive profits. Moreover, every firm with minimum average cost above p^* and *up to* p is also in business, and is making positive (or at worst zero) profits. Each one of the firms in the market will produce

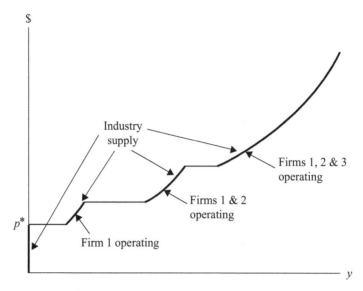

Fig. 11.3. Long-run industry supply with three potential firms with different cost curves.

that quantity y for which its marginal cost equals the price p. All this will give rise to a generally upward-sloping market supply curve. At the lowest price for which there is greater-than-zero supply, namely, p^*, only the firm (or firms) with minimum average cost equal to p^* is operating. As the price moves higher, the firm already in the market produces more of the output good. Then the price rises high enough for the next firm to enter the market, that is, the firm with the next-to-lowest minimum average cost. This produces a step in the supply function. Then another firm moves in, producing another step. If the firms are relatively small compared with the size of the market, these steps may be small; if the firms are relatively large, the steps are large. We show a market supply curve produced by this kind of reasoning in Figure 11.3.

The generally upward-sloping long-run market supply curve shown in Figure 11.3 looks the way it does because we assumed that the firms that are actually in the industry, and those that are potentially in the industry, have different average and marginal cost curves. Sometimes it is appropriate to assume otherwise. In particular, let us now consider the special case in which all firms in the industry, or potentially in the industry, have identical average and marginal cost curves. This means that they all have equal access to the same technologies, the same information, and so on. In the real world, many factors make firms different, including ownership of patents, copyrights and trademarks, different stores of knowledge and technical expertise, different locations, different managers, and different histories. We are now assuming away those differences.

In this case, all the firms in the industry, and all potential firms in the industry, have the same cost curves. The minimum average cost is the same for all, at, say,

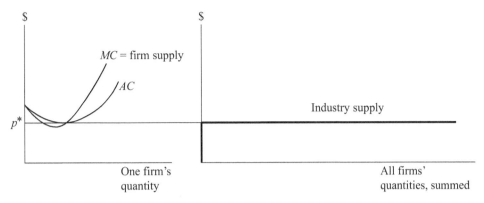

Fig. 11.4. Long-run industry supply when all the firms are identical.

p^*. At any market price $p < p^*$, every firm will choose, in the long run, to leave the industry. Market supply will be zero. At any market price $p > p^*$, every firm will have positive profits, and more and more firms will enter the industry, without limit. (Consider that if you owned one of the firms, you would be making X dollars in profit, and you would think to yourself: I shall open a second identical firm, and make $2X$, and then a third identical firm, and make $3X$, and so on.) Therefore, at any market price $p > p^*$, in the long run, market supply will be unlimited, or plus infinity. Finally, at the price p^*, market supply can be anything, depending on the number of firms choosing to operate (and earn zero profits). In short, in the case of a market with many identical firms, with minimum average cost for each firm equal to p^*, the market supply curve is a horizontal line at p^*.

Finally, in the long run, when the market price is p^*, each active firm in the industry will be producing where its marginal cost equals its average cost equals p^*. It will be making zero profits. (Zero profits does not mean zero returns to capital, so the zero-profit firm may be paying dividends to shareholders and interest to creditors.) The price for each unit of output will exactly equal the marginal cost of the unit (implying no profit at the margin, a consequence of profit maximization), and will also exactly equal the average cost of producing all the units the firm is producing (implying no profits overall). That is, the absence of barriers to entry in this long-run perfectly competitive market wipes out all positive economic profits. In Figure 11.4, we show the typical firm's average and marginal cost curves, as well as its supply curve, in the left panel. In the right panel, we show the market supply curve.

11.4 Equilibrium in a Competitive Market

A competitive market has buyers and sellers who are looking to buy or sell a good at the market price. The buyers are utility-maximizing consumers whose various demands for the good have been aggregated into a market demand curve, which we call $D(p)$. The sellers are profit-maximizing firms whose desired sales have been aggregated into a market supply curve, which we'll call $S(p)$. To put it another way, for a given price p, $D(p)$ represents the total amount that the various consumers want to buy, and $S(p)$ represents the total amount that the various firms want to sell.

If the aggregate demand is greater than the aggregate supply, or $D(p) > S(p)$, then some consumers will not be able to buy the quantities they planned to buy at the market price. They will be disappointed, frustrated, unhappy, and unable to purchase the good. This is called *excess demand*. In a market with excess demand, frustrated buyers will attempt to get what they want by bidding up the price, and sellers, seeing that there are unsatisfied buyers who could not get what they wanted, will likely raise their prices.

If the aggregate demand is less than the aggregate supply, or $D(p) < S(p)$, then some sellers will not be able to sell the quantities they planned to sell at the market price. They will be disappointed, frustrated, unhappy, and unable to get rid of the good. This is called *excess supply*. In a market with excess supply, frustrated sellers will attempt to sell what they have on hand by lowering the price, and buyers, seeing that there are unsatisfied sellers who could not sell what they wanted, will be likely to try to buy at a discounted price.

If the aggregate demand is equal to the aggregate supply, or $D(p) = S(p)$, then the number of units of the good that the various sellers want to sell is exactly equal to the number of units that the various buyers want to buy. Every party in the market can buy or sell the good, exactly as planned. We say that *the market clears*. There are no frustrated buyers or sellers, and no one has an obvious incentive to raise or lower the price. This is called a *market equilibrium*.

We can have a market equilibrium in the short run (with insufficient time for firms to enter or exit), or in the long run. Figure 11.5 shows a short-run equilibrium, with an upward-sloping market supply curve $S(p)$. Note that this figure does not include the steps that occur as different firms opt to start supplying positive quantities of the good. In the figure, there is equilibrium at price equal to p^* and market quantity (supplied and demanded) equal to y^*. At a lower price p_1, there is excess demand, and at a higher price p_2, there is excess supply.

Now, let us consider a competitive equilibrium in the long run, in that special case in which all firms in the industry, or potentially in the industry, have exactly the same average and marginal cost curves, with minimum average cost at p^*. As in Figure 11.4, the long-run industry supply curve is a horizontal line at p^*. The market equilibrium is shown in Figure 11.6. Note that if the market price were other than p^*, the market could not be in equilibrium. There would be excess demand for $p < p^*$, or excess supply for $p > p^*$. In these cases, either consumers want to buy more than firms are willing to supply, or firms end up with unsold units.

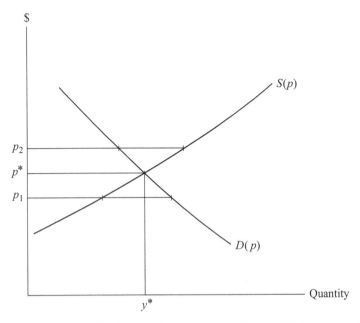

Fig. 11.5. Competitive equilibrium in the short run. The equilibrium price is p^*. The equilibrium quantity is y^*.

In a competitive industry in the long run, when all the firms are identical, the price of the good is entirely determined by technological considerations. Each firm is operating at the level at which average cost is minimized and equal to p^*, and each firm is making zero profits. The demand side determines only the number of units sold, and therefore the number of firms in the industry. (There is a small complication because, in reality, the number of firms should be an integer. But this is of minimal importance when the market equilibrium quantity is so large that there are many firms, and we will leave it to the interested reader to work out the details when there are only a few firms in equilibrium.)

11.5 Competitive Equilibrium and Social Surplus Maximization

Recall that in Chapter 7, we discussed the ideas of consumer's surplus and consumers' surplus. Note the locations of the apostrophes! One consumer's benefit from being able to buy a good at price p can be, under certain conditions, properly measured as the area under his demand curve and above the horizontal line at p. If the consumer is buying a single unit of the good, the surplus is very intuitive – it is equal to his (maximum) willingness to pay for the item, less what he actually pays. If he is buying many units, these increments can be added up, unit by unit, to the quantity he actually buys. This adding up of surplus amounts, unit by unit, implies that his consumer's surplus is the area under his demand curve and above p. We also found in Chapter 7 that under the assumption of quasilinear preferences, the

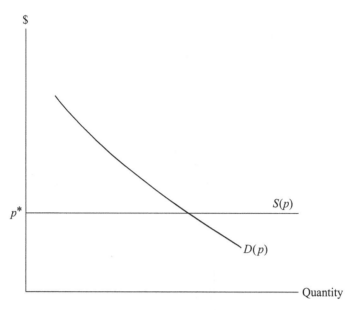

Fig. 11.6. Long-run competitive equilibrium, when all the firms are identical. The equilibrium price is p^*.

consumer's surpluses of various consumers can be calculated accurately, and can be aggregated accurately into consumers' surplus. Consumers' surplus can then be used to measure the aggregate net benefit, in dollars, to all the consumers in a market who are buying a good at price p. It is, roughly speaking, aggregate willingness to pay for all the units consumed, less the total amount actually paid. For the group of consumers in a market, consumers' surplus is measured by starting with the market demand curve, and calculating the area under the demand curve but above the horizontal line at the price p, from quantity zero to quantity $D(p)$, the market demand at price p.

There is a similar methodology for measuring the aggregate benefit to all the sellers of a good in a market, who are getting a market price p. The firms that produce the good measure their own benefits as profits, in dollars. Therefore, there is no conceptual difficulty in adding together the benefits of firm i and firm j, as there was when we wanted to add together the benefits of consumers i and j, who have noncomparable utility functions.

We will now define a measure of the benefit to a firm, or a group of firms, of being able to produce and sell a good at a market price p; that measure will be based on profit – almost. We say "almost" because we want a measure that can be seen on a graph with market supply and market demand curves. We know that the market supply curve is the horizontal sum of the supply curves of various firms, and we know that, for a single firm, the supply curve is just its marginal cost curve, above the minimum of its average cost curve. We want to use an area under a marginal cost curve when we figure a firm's costs, and therefore its profit, so that we can relate profit to the market supply curve.

The simple way to do this is to first note that for firm i producing output y_i, profit is

$$\pi_i = \text{Revenue} - \text{Cost} = py_i - C_i(y_i).$$

Next, note that the area under firm i's marginal cost curve is

$$\int_0^{y_i} MC_i(y)dy = C_i(y_i) - C_i(0),$$

where $C_i(0)$ is firm i's fixed cost. Therefore, firm i's profit is given by

$$\pi_i = py_i - \int_0^{y_i} MC_i(y)dy - C_i(0).$$

We define *producer's surplus* for firm i as

$$PS_i = py_i - \int_0^{y_i} MC_i(y)dy.$$

It follows that

$$\pi_i = PS_i - C_i(0) \qquad \text{or} \qquad PS_i = \pi_i + C_i(0).$$

What does producer's surplus mean graphically? Producer's surplus is revenue py_i, minus the area under the firm's marginal cost curve from zero to y_i. Revenue is the area under the horizontal line at height p, from zero to y_i. Producer's surplus is then the area below p but above marginal cost, from zero to y_i. This is the graphical measure we will use for finding firm i's benefit. Note that it equals firm i's profit plus a constant, the constant being firm i's fixed cost, that is, its cost at output level zero. Note also that if $C_i(0) = 0$, then producer's surplus is exactly the same as profit; this would be the case in what we have described as the long-run situation for a firm, the time horizon over which the firm can vary all its inputs, and set them all equal to zero when it is producing zero output.

Figure 11.7 shows producer's surplus for firm i in the special case in which the marginal cost curve $MC_i(y_i)$ is a straight line from the origin. The area of the crosshatched rectangle py_i^* is the firm's revenue, and the area under the marginal cost curve equals cost at y_i^* minus cost at zero. Producer's surplus is the area below the horizontal line at height p but above the marginal cost curve. It is equal to profit plus the constant $C_i(0)$, firm i's fixed cost.

In the real-world case of a U-shaped marginal cost curve, the supply curve for the firm is not exactly the marginal cost curve; it is zero up to the point at which average cost equals marginal cost, and then it coincides with marginal cost. (Look back at Figures 11.1 and 11.2.) This complicates the relationship between producer's

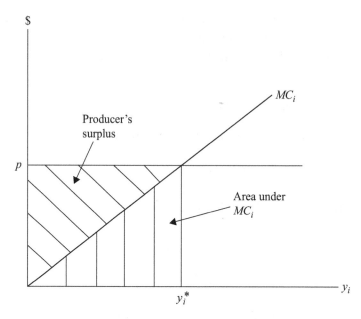

Fig. 11.7. Revenue, producer's surplus, and the area under the firm's supply curve, when marginal cost is a straight line from the origin.

surplus and profit slightly, but does not change it in a fundamental way. We will explore this complication in an exercise.

To go from *producer's surplus* to *producers' surplus*, we consider a market with various firms supplying the good, which sells at the market price p. The market supply curve $S(p)$ is constructed by horizontally adding the supply curves, that is, the marginal cost curves – of the various firms. For the given price p, we could figure each firm's producer's surplus separately, and then add them all together. This sum would then represent aggregate profit, plus the various $C_i(0)$ constants for the various firms. Or, equivalently, we can take the market supply curve, draw the horizontal line at height p going through it, and then take producers' surplus as the area below the horizontal line at height p but above the market supply curve.

In Figure 11.8, we provide two panels. Both are somewhat similar to Figure 11.5, in the sense that they show a downward-sloping market demand $D(p)$ curve and an upward-sloping market supply curve $S(p)$. In the left-hand panel, the market price is at p^*, the equilibrium price at which supply equals demand, and there are no frustrated buyers or sellers in the market. In this panel, the consumers' surplus area and the producers' surplus area are crosshatched, and are identified as CS and PS, respectively. In this market, the aggregate net benefit to the various consumers, who are able to buy the good they consume at price p^* but who are willing to pay more, is CS. The aggregate net benefit to the various firms, equal to aggregate producers' surplus – or, roughly speaking, aggregate profit – is PS. The sum of the two areas, therefore, represents total net benefit to society (except for the constants, the fixed costs) that results from the existence of this market for this good. This is called the *social surplus*.

The right-hand panel of Figure 11.8 shows what would happen in this market if all transactions had to be made at a price p^{**}, higher than the equilibrium price. (Imagine, for example, that the government passed a law that made it illegal to buy or sell the good at any price lower than p^{**}.) The number of units sold would then be $y^{**} < y^*$, the lesser of the amounts supplied and demanded at the nonequilibrium price. Some units might be produced but not sold. (This assumes that the law did not also force unwilling consumers to buy more units than they want at the high price p^{**}.) The right-hand panel also shows producers' surplus and consumers' surplus, given the new (nonequilibrium) situation. In fact, the area identified as producers' surplus in the right-hand panel may be an overestimate of the real producers' surplus: in this situation, it is possible that some of the units actually sold may have marginal costs higher than the height of $S(p)$ at y^{**}.

Note that the panels are based on identical $S(p)$ and $D(p)$ curves. A quick examination of the two panels should convince the reader that the total net benefit to society, or the social surplus, measured as the sum of consumers' surplus and producers' surplus, is greater in the competitive equilibrium (left-hand panel). To put this another way, the fact that the market is forced to operate at a nonequilibrium price p^{**} results in a loss to society. That loss is identified in the right-hand panel. Note that it is a triangular area below the demand curve and above the supply curve, from y^{**} to y^*. This triangular area is called the *deadweight loss triangle* or, for short, simply the *loss triangle*. This may underestimate the real loss because as mentioned earlier, the area identified as producers' surplus in the figure may be an overestimate of the real producers' surplus.

Figure 11.8 suggests an extremely important and remarkable result: The competitive market in which the price is allowed to find its equilibrium, and in which buyers and sellers engage in trade in order to individually maximize their utilities or profits, will result in a maximum net benefit to society as a whole. Markets in which the price is prevented from finding its natural equilibrium will show a deadweight loss. This reflects the position of free-market economists since the time of Adam Smith (1723–1790). The position is this: let the market operate, with each person seeking to maximize his or her own benefit, ignoring the welfare of others, and the outcome will actually be best for society. This beautiful and amazing result constitutes the basis for many recommendations made by market-oriented economists. Of course it depends on a number of assumptions, some of which have been explicit and some of which have been implicit. (Among our explicit assumptions are the assumptions of competitive behavior, and quasilinearity for consumers' utility functions. Among our implicit assumptions are the assumptions that all the buyers and sellers are knowledgeable and rational, and that there are no market failures of the types described in Chapters 17, 18, and 20 on externalities, public goods, and asymmetric information, respectively.)

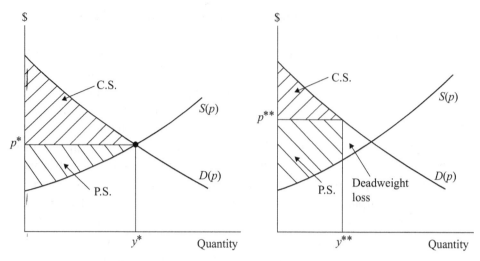

Fig. 11.8. On the left, the competitive equilibrium price and quantity, with consumers' surplus and producers' surplus. Social surplus is the sum of C.S. amd P.S. On the right, the price is too high, resulting in a deadweight loss.

We conclude this section with another intuition. If a consumer values a unit of a good at more than the market price p, he will benefit if he can consume another unit. If a producer can produce another unit at less than the market price p, he will profit if he can sell another unit. In a free competitive market, the equilibrium price adjusts so that all trades with possible gains – all the instances in which a producer can produce another unit of the good for an amount of money less than what some consumer is willing to pay – are carried out. At the final "marginal" trade, the willingness to pay is just p^*, and the marginal cost of the unit is p^*; the net benefit to society is zero for that last unit traded. All trades with positive net benefit have been made. In a market with a dictated nonequilibrium price, however, there are potential trades that would result in net gains to society but that can never take place.

11.6 The Deadweight Loss of a Per-Unit Tax

In our chapters on the theory of the consumer, we explored some of the effects of taxes on the consumer's behavior. Now we will explore how taxes affect a market equilibrium. We will use the consumers' surplus and producers' surplus measures, and we will see how per-unit taxes affect welfare.

Effects of a Per-Unit Tax in the Short Run

Suppose there is a market for a good, and a short-run equilibrium in that market. By short run we mean only that the set of firms in the industry is fixed; there is insufficient time for entry and exit. Assume that the government steps in and imposes a per-unit tax of t on that good.

Sometimes, when a government imposes a tax, the buyer is legally responsible for paying it; at other times, the seller is legally responsible. (Sometimes they have to split the tax and each pay half; this is the structure for Social Security and Medicare taxes in the United States.) If the buyer is legally responsible for the tax, the seller will sometimes act as the collection agent, collecting the tax and sending it on to the tax authorities. State sales taxes in the United States on items sold in local stores are legally structured this way. Sometimes the buyer is legally responsible for the tax, but the seller does not have to act as a collection agent. State sales taxes on items sold over the Internet are often set up this way. (In many states, residents who buy online from a vendor without a physical presence in the state, such as Amazon.com, are supposed to report their purchases and pay the taxes themselves directly to the state. Of course, almost nobody does.)

We will see later that the party who is legally responsible for the tax may or may not be the party who actually ends up paying it, even if the parties adhere strictly to the law. Who bears the burden of the tax will depend on the slopes of the demand and supply curves, or the elasticities of demand and supply. Most important, we will see that the introduction of a per-unit tax creates a deadweight loss.

We start with Figure 11.9, which shows an upward-sloping supply curve and a downward-sloping demand curve, as well as a no-tax market equilibrium. For simplicity of computation, we use linear supply and demand curves; supply is given by $S(p) = -\alpha_0 + \alpha_1 p$ and demand is given by $D(p) = \beta_0 - \beta_1 p$. The alphas and betas are all positive constants. The market equilibrium is the point E at which the supply and demand curves intersect; the market equilibrium price is $p^* = B$ and the market equilibrium quantity is y^*. The figure also shows consumers' surplus CS and producers' surplus PS. Social surplus is maximized, and there is no deadweight loss triangle. Note the vertical intercepts of the supply and demand curves. To find either one, set $S(p)$ or $D(p)$ equal to zero and solve for p. This gives α_0/α_1 as the intercept of the supply curve, and β_0/β_1 as the intercept of the demand curve.

Now, assume that the government imposes a per-unit tax t. Assume that the law specifies that the producers are legally liable for the tax. If the producers sell a unit of the good for a price p, they will actually end up with $p - t$, as they have to send t to the government. The result is that the market supply curve gets shifted; if p is the market price, the amount supplied will be $S(p) = -\alpha_0 + \alpha_1(p - t) = -\alpha_0 + \alpha_1 p - \alpha_1 t$. The new (posttax) supply curve has the same slope as the old one, as $dS(p)/dp$ is still equal to α_1. That is, the new supply curve is parallel to the old (pretax) supply curve. However, it is higher by the tax t, because to get firms to supply any particular quantity, one must pay them t more per unit than when there is no tax. (More formally, for the no-tax supply curve, the intercept on the vertical axis is α_0/α_1. For the with-tax supply curve, the intercept on the vertical axis, found by solving for p when $S(p) = 0$, is $\alpha_0/\alpha_1 + t$.)

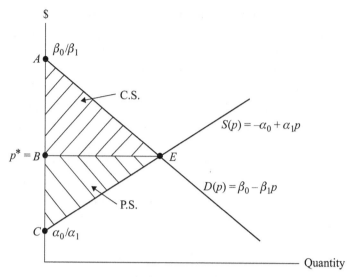

Fig. 11.9. The market equilibrium before the introduction of a per-unit tax, showing consumers' surplus and producers' surplus areas.

In Figure 11.10, we show what happens to the market when the per-unit tax is introduced. The new supply curve is shown, parallel to the original supply curve, but displaced upward by t. There is now a new consumers' surplus triangle, which is smaller than the original no-tax consumers' surplus triangle. There is a new producers' surplus triangle, also smaller than the original no-tax producers' surplus triangle. Therefore, the tax makes both consumers and producers worse off, even though legally this is a tax only on producers. However, there is a new benefit-to-society factor here, and that is government revenue from the tax. In dollar terms, it equals the area of the rectangle DFGH. All things considered, the net benefit to society is now given by the total of consumers' surplus, producers' surplus, and government revenue. However, this total is less than the social surplus when there is no tax, and is less by the deadweight loss triangle DEF.

Introducing the per-unit tax creates a deadweight loss, because it creates a gap between what the producers receive per unit $(p - t)$ and what the consumers pay per unit (p). Some consumers value extra units of the good at more than $p - t$ but less than p, and some producers could produce extra units of the good profitably at a cost more than $p - t$ but less than p. Unfortunately, there is no way for those parties to (legally) get together and make those mutually beneficial transactions. The result is much like the result shown in the right-hand panel of Figure 11.8, in which the government mandated a price above the market equilibrium price. Production and consumption stop at a point at which there would still be gains to society from producing and consuming more.

As we said previously, even though the tax is the legal responsibility of the producers, it is actually a burden on both producers and consumers. How much of

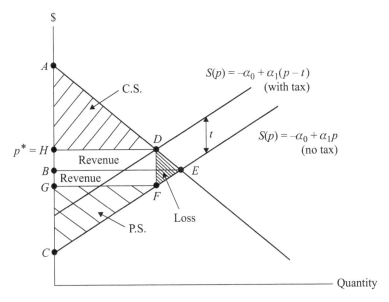

Fig. 11.10. The market equilibrium after the introduction of a per-unit tax, showing con-sumers' and producers' surplus area, government revenue, and the deadweight loss.

the tax burden actually falls on the producers and how much on the consumers will depend on the slopes (or elasticities) of the supply and demand curves. The general rule is that if the elasticity of supply is greater than the elasticity of demand, the demanders (i.e., consumers) will bear more of the burden, and vice versa. The less elastic side of the market gets stuck with more of the tax. We illustrate this result by looking at the long-run case of identical firms, in which the supply curve is horizontal – that is, infinitely elastic.

Long-Run Effects of a Per-Unit Tax, with Many Identical Firms

Let us go back to the long-run case with many identical firms. We assume that firms can freely enter and exit the industry and that all the firms in the industry, or potentially in the industry, have identical average and marginal cost curves. This means that they all have equal access to the same patents, the same technologies, the same information, the same management, and so on. In the long run, the industry supply curve is a horizontal line at a price equal to the minimum of the average cost curve that all the firms and potential firms share. The elasticity of supply is generally defined as a percentage change in quantity supplied divided by a percentage change in price. With a horizontal supply curve, the supply elasticity is plus infinity, as elastic as it can be. The intuition is that a tiny percentage increase in the price will result in an infinitely large percentage increase in the amount supplied.

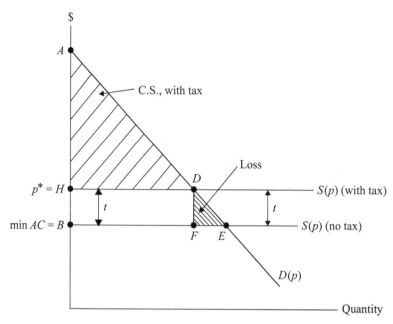

Fig. 11.11. Effects of a per unit-tax, in the long run, with many identical firms. All the tax, and the deadweight loss, falls on the consumers.

In Figure 11.11, we show what happens when a per-unit tax of t, a legal obligation of the producers, is introduced in a market with many identical firms in the long run. This figure is much like Figure 11.10, except that the no-tax supply curve is a horizontal line with a vertical intercept at min AC, the minimum of the firms' average cost curves. (See also Figure 11.4.) The supply curve with the per-unit tax, payable by firms, is another horizontal line, t dollars above the first.

In Figure 11.11, we see that when the supply curve is horizontal, that is, infinitely elastic – the introduction of a per-unit tax creates a deadweight loss triangle, as it did in the general case. What is new here is that even though the tax is theoretically paid by the firms that supply the good, in fact all the burden of the tax is borne by consumers. This is a consequence of the infinitely elastic supply curve.

11.7 A Solved Problem

The Problem

The market demand for good x is $x^D = a - bp$ and the market supply is $x^S = cp$, where $a > 0$, $b > 0$, and $c > 0$.

(a) Calculate the competitive equilibrium of this market (that is, the equilibrium price and quantity). Calculate the consumers' and the producers' surpluses.

(b) The government imposes a per-unit tax t on x, which must be paid by the sellers. Calculate the new competitive equilibrium and the government revenue.

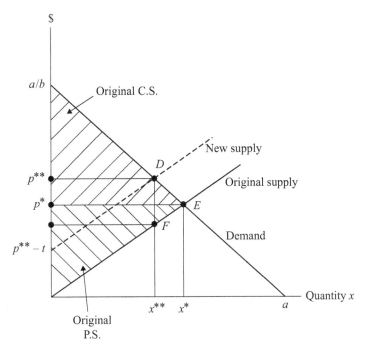

Fig. 11.12. The original market equilibrium, the new market equilibrium after the per-unit tax t is imposed, the original CS, the original PS, and the deadweight loss triangle DEF.

(c) Calculate the new consumers' and producers' surpluses.

(d) Is society better off or worse off after the tax? By how much?

The Solution

(a) To find the original competitive equilibrium, we set supply equal to demand, or $x^S = x^D$, or $cp = a - bp$. This gives the competitive equilibrium price

$$p^* = \frac{a}{b+c}.$$

We substitute back into either the supply function or the demand function to get the competitive equilibrium quantity

$$x^* = cp^* = \frac{ac}{b+c}.$$

To find consumers' surplus and producers' surplus, it is helpful to sketch a graph of the supply and demand curves; this is easy because they are straight lines. Our graph is Figure 11.12; we will use it for parts (a), (b), (c), and (d). Note that it is similar to Figures 11.9 and 11.10, although with slightly different notation.

In Figure 11.12, the original consumers' surplus is the area of the upper triangle, with positively sloped cross-hatching; producers' surplus is the area of the lower triangle, with negatively sloped cross-hatching. The area of a triangle is one half the base times the height, and we will now use the horizontal $x^* = ac/(b+c)$ as the triangle base.

The height of the consumers' surplus triangle is $a/b - p^* = a/b - a/(b + c)$. All this gives

$$CS = \frac{1}{2}\left(\frac{ac}{b+c}\right)\left(\frac{a}{b} - \frac{a}{b+c}\right) = \frac{1}{2}\left(\frac{ac}{b+c}\right)\left(\frac{ac}{b(b+c)}\right) = \frac{(ac)^2}{2b(b+c)^2}$$

for consumers' surplus. Similarly, producers' surplus is

$$PS = \frac{1}{2}\left(\frac{ac}{b+c}\right)\left(\frac{a}{b+c}\right) = \frac{a^2c}{2(b+c)^2}.$$

(b) With a per-unit tax of t payable by the sellers, we have to refigure the supply curve. Before the tax was imposed, the supply function was $x^S = cp$; because firms now have to pay t per unit off the top, they are netting $p - t$ for each unit they sell, rather than p. Therefore, the new supply function is $x^S = c(p - t)$. The new supply curve is the dashed line in Figure 11.12. Setting supply equal to demand now gives

$$c(p - t) = a - bp.$$

This gives the new competitive equilibrium price

$$p^{**} = \frac{a + ct}{b + c}.$$

We substitute back into either the supply function or the demand function to get the new competitive equilibrium quantity

$$x^{**} = c(p^{**} - t) = \frac{c(a + ct)}{(b + c)} - ct = \frac{ac - bct}{b + c}.$$

Figure 11.12 includes the new equilibrium price p^{**}, the new equilibrium price net of the tax $p^{**} - t$, and the new equilibrium quantity x^{**}. Note that the new price is greater than the old pretax price by an amount $\Delta p^{**} = (a + ct)/(b + c) - a/(b + c) = ct/(b + c)$. Consumers have to pay this new higher price, and are worse off. Producers are also worse off; they now receive $p^{**} - t = (a + ct)/(b + c) - t = (a - bt)/(b + c)$ per unit. Comparing this to the old p^* that they used to receive, producers are now getting $bt/(b + c)$ less per unit. Note that there is now a gap of t between the price p^{**} paid by consumers and the (net) amount $p^{**} - t$ received by producers. The revenue received by the government is

$$\text{Revenue} = tx^{**} = \frac{t(ac - bct)}{b + c}.$$

(c) To figure the new consumers' surplus, we again find the area of a triangle, one half the base times the height. The base of the new CS triangle is $x^{**} = (ac - bct)/(b + c)$. The height of the new CS triangle is $a/b - p^{**} = a/b - (a + ct)/(b + c)$. Therefore, the new consumers' surplus is

$$\text{New } CS = \frac{1}{2}\left(\frac{ac - bct}{b+c}\right)\left(\frac{a}{b} - \frac{a + ct}{b+c}\right)$$

$$= \frac{1}{2}\left(\frac{ac - bct}{b+c}\right)\left(\frac{ac - bct}{b(b+c)}\right) = \frac{(ac - bct)^2}{2b(b+c)^2}.$$

The new producers' surplus is the area of a triangle with base x^{**} and height $p^{**} - t$. This gives

$$\text{New } PS = \frac{1}{2}\left(\frac{ac - bct}{b + c}\right)\left(\frac{a + ct}{b + c} - t\right)$$

$$= \frac{1}{2}\left(\frac{ac - bct}{b + c}\right)\left(\frac{a - bt}{b + c}\right) = \frac{(a - bt)(ac - bct)}{2(b + c)^2}.$$

(d) We could take the original social welfare total of CS plus PS, and compare that to the new social welfare total, of the new CS plus the new PS plus government revenue. But that would require a lot of ugly algebra! Instead, let us look at Figure 11.12. Society is worse off by the area of the deadweight loss triangle DEF. To calculate the area of DEF, use the DE side as the base, and the difference $x^* - x^{**}$ as the height. The social loss produced by the tax is

$$\text{Welfare Loss} = \frac{1}{2}t(x^* - x^{**}) = \frac{1}{2}t\left(\frac{ac}{b + c} - \frac{ac - bct}{b + c}\right) = \frac{bct^2}{2(b + c)}.$$

Exercises

1. The short-run market for coffee can be described by an upward-sloping supply curve and a downward-sloping demand curve. Suppose this market is perfectly competitive. How are the equilibrium price and quantity exchanged affected by the following perturbations?

   (a) An increase in consumers' income (assume that coffee is a normal good)

   (b) An increase in the price of the factors of production

   (c) A technological improvement in the coffee industry

2. Suppose the best technology to produce a good is given by the production function $y = \sqrt{x_1 x_2}$. Let the input prices be $w_1 = 4$ and $w_2 = 1$. Assume that the number of firms in the industry can vary (this is long-run analysis), and that any firm can use this production function.

   (a) Show that the industry supply is infinitely elastic at $p = 4$.

   (b) If the market demand is given by $D(p) = 1,000,000 - 1,000p$, how many units of good y are exchanged in equilibrium?

3. Good h is produced in Asia. There are 10,000 firms producing good h according to the technology described by $h = K^{1/3}L^{2/3}$, where K is land and L is labor. The unit prices of land and labor are \$256 and \$1, respectively.

   (a) Derive the long-run marginal and average cost curves for each of these producers. What is the long-run market supply of good h?

   (b) This good is consumed mainly in the United States. Suppose the market demand is $h^D = 36,000/p$. Calculate the competitive equilibrium price, the amount of good h exchanged in the market, and each producer's output and profit.

   (c) Following a generalized campaign in the press and a few successful actions carried out by the DEA, the demand for good h shrinks to $h^D = 24,000/p$. Compute the new competitive market equilibrium for good h. Could we have a different number of producers in the market?

4. Suppose the wine industry is made up of many small identical firms. A representative firm's long-run cost function is $C(y_i) = \frac{99}{2} - \frac{1}{2}y_i^2 + y_i^3$ if $y_i > 0$, $C(y_i) = 0$ otherwise.
   (a) Derive the representative firm's market supply curve for wine.
   (b) If the market demand for wine is $y^D = 1,140 - 10p$, calculate the long-run competitive equilibrium of this industry (i.e., indicate the equilibrium price, the amount of good y exchanged in the market, the number of firms in the market, and each firm's output and profit).

5. Dakota is a firm that produces rocking horses. The market for rocking horses is perfectly competitive. Dakota's cost function is $C(y) = \frac{1}{2}y^2 + 40y + 2,450$. The market price of rocking horses is $p^* = 140$.
   (a) Write down Dakota's profit function $\pi(y)$.
   (b) What is the firm's optimal level of output y^*?
   (c) Calculate the firm's profits π^* at the optimal level of output.
   (d) What will happen to the number of firms in the rocking horse industry in the long run?

6. Now consider the market for rocking horses in the long run. Dakota's cost function is $C(y) = \frac{1}{2}y^2 + 40y + 2,450$.
   (a) What is Dakota's level of output in the long-run y^{**}?
   (b) What is the market price of rocking horses in the long-run p^{**}?
   (c) Show that the firm earns zero profits in the long run.
   (d) What will happen to the firm's profits if the government decides to impose a tax, $t = 5$, per rocking horse?

Chapter 12
Monopoly and Monopolistic Competition

12.1 Introduction

In the last chapter, we studied the behavior of competitive firms, that is, firms that take market prices as given and outside their control. Generally, such firms are small enough relative to their markets that their decisions have no effect on the market prices. Now we will study the polar opposite: the market in which only one firm supplies a particular good. This is called a *monopoly market* and the firm is a *monopoly firm* or *monopolist*. The word *monopoly* is from Greek, and means "one seller." In the first part of this chapter, we analyze the classical solution to the monopoly problem. Then we consider various price discrimination techniques that monopolies can employ to increase their profits. At the end of the chapter, we look at a special market structure, called *monopolistic competition*, in which there are many firms producing goods that are very similar, but not identical, such as different brands of laundry detergent.

There are various reasons that some markets are monopolies or near-monopolies. Sometimes there are technological reasons. For example, there may be very large startup costs. The classic example is the provision of a utility in an urban market via pipelines. If a firm is to sell water or natural gas in a city, it may need a network of underground pipes leading from source points to tens of thousands of residential and commercial customers. Having two or more firms installing such networks would be unnecessarily costly, and the first firm to get its pipes in the ground would have a tremendous advantage over later-arriving firms. This is the case of what is called a *natural monopoly*. The natural monopoly idea used to be applied to the provision of many utilities, including water, natural gas, electricity, and phone service. However, changes in law and in technology in the past forty years have taken telephone service off the list of natural monopolies. The natural monopolist was AT&T – "Ma Bell" in the United States. AT&T was broken up in legal actions between 1974 and 1984, and rapidly changing technology, culminating in the development of cellular phone systems, eventually undid the technological basis for that monopoly. Innovations in the provision of electricity have changed our view of the local electric company as a natural monopoly. Now, the firm that owns the wire network may be viewed as a natural monopolist, but there may be other different firms, nonmonopolists, that actually generate the power. The same may be true of natural gas. The firm that owns the pipeline may be a natural monopolist, but it may act simply as a delivery service between competitive gas producers and competitive gas customers.

Often monopolies exist because the government has granted them, and a firm has a monopoly in the provision of some good or service only because a state makes it very difficult – or illegal – for another firm to come in and compete. For example, the British East India Company originated with a charter granted by Queen Elizabeth I in 1600, giving that company a legal monopoly in the trade with India and China in various goods (including cotton, silk, tea, and opium). Patents, copyrights, and trademarks are legal monopolies granted by a state to an inventor (or writer, composer, performer, or artist), usually with a limited term. For instance, in the United States, a patent is granted by the U.S. Patent Office to a person or a firm, and gives its owner exclusive rights over an invention for a period of twenty years; other countries have similar patent laws. Copyrights last much longer and trademarks may last indefinitely.

In the formal analysis in the next section, we assume, as we did in our analysis of competitive markets, that there is one homogeneous good, and that all buyers and the seller have perfect information. However, we depart from our analysis of competitive markets by assuming that the seller does *not* take the price as given. We also assume that even if profits are positive, there are barriers to entry that serve to preserve the monopoly. A final note before proceeding with the monopoly model: A *monopoly* is a single *seller* of some good or service. A single *buyer* of a good or service is called a *monopsony*. As an example, suppose an isolated town has only one major employer – a large diamond mine located nearby. If the mine is the only (significant) buyer of labor services in the town, it is called a monopsony. In this chapter we will not analyze the theory of monopsonies, because that theory is formally quite similar to the theory of monopolies.

12.2 The Classical Solution to Monopoly

Let us now assume that there is a monopoly firm producing a good. We let y denote the quantity of the good. We assume in this section that the good is sold at a price p. (Later on we will analyze what happens when the monopolist sells the good to different people at different prices, or sells it to the same customer at different per-unit prices for different quantities. But for now there is one price in the market, which depends on the quantity y the monopolist decides to produce.) There is a downward-sloping demand curve for the good, written $y(p)$. The inverse demand curve is $p(y)$.

The monopoly firm wants to maximize its profit, just as a competitive firm wants to maximize its profit. The firm's revenue is $R(y) = p(y)y$. We assume that the monopolist has a long-run cost curve $C(y)$. The firm's profit is given by

$$\pi(y) = R(y) - C(y) = p(y)y - C(y).$$

The monopolist's problem is to choose y to maximize this function.

Before proceeding, let us consider how the monopolist's problem differs from the profit-maximization problem of the competitive firm. A competitive firm operates in a market. There is a market demand curve, but the competitive firm is small enough that its decisions have little or no impact on the market price. Therefore, its problem is to maximize

$$\pi(y) = R(y) - C(y) = py - C(y),$$

for a given p. That is, the competitive firm takes the price p as given and fixed, whereas the monopolist takes p as variable, and as a function of its own output y. In terms of the formal analysis, this is the crucial difference between the monopoly firm and the competitive firm.

From this point on, we assume that when the monopolist is choosing its profit-maximizing output, $p \geq AC(y)$, or price is greater than or equal to average cost. If this were not the case, the firm would be losing money, and would leave the market in the long run.

Now, let us turn to the profit-maximization conditions. The first-order condition for profit maximization says that the first derivative of profit with respect to y should be zero. The second-order condition says that the second derivative of profit with respect to y should be less than or equal to zero.

The first-order condition gives the following:

$$\frac{d\pi(y)}{dy} = \frac{dR(y)}{dy} - \frac{dC(y)}{dy} = 0$$

or

$$\frac{dR(y)}{dy} = \frac{dC(y)}{dy}$$

or

$$MR(y) = MC(y).$$

In short, marginal revenue equals marginal cost.

Now, let us focus on marginal revenue. Note that

$$MR(y) = \frac{dR(y)}{dy} = \frac{d}{dy}(p(y)y) = p(y) + \frac{dp(y)}{dy}y.$$

Because the demand curve is downward sloping, $\frac{dp(y)}{dy}$ is negative. Therefore, $MR(y) < p(y)$. That is, for any output level y, price is greater than marginal revenue. Because the profit-maximizing monopolist will set marginal revenue equal to marginal cost, the monopolist must end up charging a price that is greater than marginal cost.

Recall that in Chapter 4 we discussed the concept of price elasticity of demand. This is, roughly speaking, the percentage change in amount demanded divided by the percentage change in price. In that chapter, we used the symbol ϵ_{x_1,p_1} to represent the price elasticity of demand for good 1, with price p_1. We will use price elasticity of demand in this chapter also, but we will start with simplified notation, using ϵ to represent the price elasticity of demand for the good being sold by the monopolist.

Therefore, let the price elasticity of demand for the monopolist's product be

$$\epsilon = -\frac{dy/y}{dp(y)/p(y)}.$$

Inverting both sides and rearranging slightly gives

$$\frac{dp(y)}{dy}y = -\frac{p(y)}{\epsilon}.$$

Substituting this elasticity formula into the expression for marginal revenue gives the following:

$$MR(y) = p(y) + \frac{dp(y)}{dy}y = p(y) - \frac{p(y)}{\epsilon} = p(y)(1 - 1/\epsilon).$$

The result of all this is that the monopolist's first-order condition for profit maximization can be rewritten as follows, in terms of the elasticity of demand:

$$MR(y) = p(y)(1 - 1/\epsilon) = MC(y).$$

This implies

$$\frac{p(y)}{MC(y)} = \frac{1}{1 - 1/\epsilon}.$$

The competitive firm charges a price equal to marginal cost. As we observed earlier, however, the monopolist charges a price that is greater than marginal cost. We now know that the gap between the price and the marginal cost is $p(y)/\epsilon$. Because of this gap the monopoly market must be inefficient: there must be customers who would love to consume the gizmo that the monopolist is selling at the monopolist's marginal cost or above, but who will not buy it at the monopoly market price. The monopolist is setting the price too high (from the social point of view) and producing less than the (socially) optimal output, at which price equals marginal cost.

We can make a few more observations about the monopolist's first-order condition for profit maximization. In the preceding equations, both $p(y)$ and $MC(y)$ are positive numbers. Therefore, $(1 - 1/\epsilon)$ must be positive. It follows that $\epsilon > 1$. That is, the monopolist will always operate on the elastic part of the demand curve.

Let us now define a variable called *markup*. The intuition is this: A monopoly charges a price that exceeds the marginal cost of the good. The markup is the fractional (or percentage) amount by which price exceeds cost. For instance, if the markup is 0.5 (or 50 percent), the price exceeds marginal cost by 0.5 (or 50 percent). Formally, the markup is

$$\frac{p(y)}{MC(y)} - 1 = \frac{1}{1 - 1/\epsilon} - 1 = \frac{1}{\epsilon - 1}.$$

Therefore, the the markup increases as demand becomes less elastic. (Remember that $\epsilon > 1$.) If ϵ approaches 1, the markup approaches infinity. On the other hand, if ϵ approaches plus infinity (the competitive case), the markup approaches zero.

To this point, we have discussed only the first-order condition for profit maximization. We now turn briefly to the second-order condition. This condition says that at the profit-maximizing level of output, the second derivative of profit with respect to y must be less than or equal to zero. It follows that

$$\frac{d^2\pi(y)}{dy^2} = \frac{d^2R(y)}{dy^2} - \frac{d^2C(y)}{dy^2} \leq 0$$

or

$$\frac{dMR(y)}{dy} \leq \frac{dMC(y)}{dy}.$$

In short, the first-order condition for profit maximization says that marginal revenue must equal marginal cost. The second-order condition says that the slope of the marginal revenue curve must be less than or equal to the slope of the marginal cost curve.

Example. Let us assume that the inverse demand curve is given by $p(y) = 100 - y$. Then the monopolist's total revenue is $R(y) = p(y)y = (100 - y)y = 100y - y^2$. Differentiate to get marginal revenue: $MR(y) = 100 - 2y$. Assume the total cost function is $C(y) = y^2$. Differentiate to get marginal cost: $MC(y) = 2y$. Note that average cost $AC(y) = y^2/y = y$.

The first-order condition for profit maximization requires setting marginal revenue equal to marginal cost. This gives $100 - 2y = 2y$, or $y = 25$. Therefore, the monopolist knows it should sell 25 units. It then uses the inverse demand function again to determine the price to charge: $p(y) = 100 - y = 100 - 25 = 75$. Figure 12.1 shows the demand curve (graphically identical to the inverse demand curve), the marginal revenue curve, and the marginal cost curve for this example, as well as the profit-maximizing solution. The monopolist using this graph first finds the

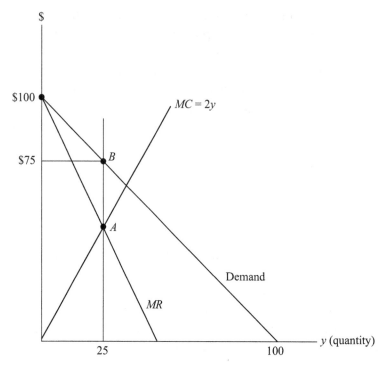

Fig. 12.1. The classical solution to the monopoly problem in a simple linear example.

point A, where $MR(y)$ and $MC(y)$ cross. This gives the profit-maximizing quantity $y = 25$. Then the monopolist reads up to the demand curve, point B, to get the profit-maximizing price $p(25) = 75$.

12.3 Deadweight Loss from Monopoly: Comparing Monopoly and Competition

We indicated earlier that the monopoly solution cannot be efficient because the monopoly firm is selling its product or service at a price greater than marginal cost. Therefore, there must be customers or potential customers who would like to buy additional units of the good at more than the additional cost of producing those units, but these potential transactions, which would be beneficial to some people and harmful to none, do not take place.

We now formalize this argument by examining consumers' surplus and producer's surplus in a monopoly market. (Recall the limitations on the possible use of the consumers' surplus concept described in Chapter 7.) We will show that the net benefit to society of the monopoly market, as represented by consumers' surplus plus producer's surplus, is not as great as it would be if the monopolist were acting like a competitive firm, that is, acting as a price taker. We will show this with the graph we used in the Example above. Consider Figure 12.2. This is based on the particular demand curve and marginal cost curve assumed in the preceding example, but the argument obviously generalizes.

In Figure 12.2, the monopolist finds the point A at which $MR(y) = MC(y)$. This determines the monopoly firm's profit-maximizing quantity, shown as "monopoly quantity" on the horizontal axis. To sell that quantity, the monopolist goes up to the demand curve, at point B, to find the optimal price, shown as "monopoly price" on the vertical axis. Aggregate dollar benefit to consumers can now be measured as the area under the demand curve and above the monopoly price. This is *consumers' surplus*, shown in the figure as the area with the upward-sloping cross-hatching. The benefit to the monopolist is the *producer's surplus*, which equals the producer's profit, if there are no fixed costs (as we have been assuming in this chapter), or profit displaced by $C(0)$ if there are fixed costs. In Figure 12.2, producer's surplus (i.e., profit) is the area under the horizontal line from the monopoly price and above the marginal cost curve. This is the area with the downward-sloping cross-hatching.

Point C in Figure 12.2 is where the demand curve and the marginal cost curve intersect. The horizontal coordinate of point C is labeled "competitive quantity" for reasons which will become clear. Note that in Figure 12.2 there are units of the good, to the right of the monopoly quantity, for which the height of the demand curve exceeds the height of the marginal cost curve. That is, for y greater than the monopoly quantity but less than the competitive quantity, $p(y) > MC(y)$. Now imagine, hypothetically, that the monopolist could get together with each of the potential customers who might like to buy one or more of those units and negotiate some price for each such unit, with the price being greater than $MC(y)$ and less than $p(y)$. All such transactions would make the buyers better off, and the monopolist better off, and would leave the buyers who were already buying at the monopoly price unaffected. The aggregate gain to society, if such hypothetical transactions were made, would be the area of the triangle ABC. Of course monopoly firms in the real world do not make these hypothetical transactions. That is, the area ABC represents the potential benefit to society that is unrealized in the presence of monopoly. It is called *deadweight loss due to the monopoly*.

What if the monopolist were somehow made to act as if it were a competitive firm? Suppose the firm is told that it must always charge a price p equal to marginal cost $MC(y)$. (This is, of course, the way a competitive firm acts, as profit maximization by a competitive firm implies $p = MC(y)$.) Suppose the firm continues to operate on the demand curve (that is, its price p equals $p(y)$). The result is that the firm ends up at the intersection of the demand curve and the $MC(y)$ curve, or at point C in Figure 12.2. There is a new consumers' surplus triangle (not shown in the figure), the floor of which goes through the point C. There is a new producer's surplus area (also not shown in the figure), whose ceiling goes through the point C. Total net benefit to society expands, and deadweight loss disappears.

This is the theoretical reason that economists are generally opposed to monopoly, and are generally inclined toward policies that promote competition. It is the basis

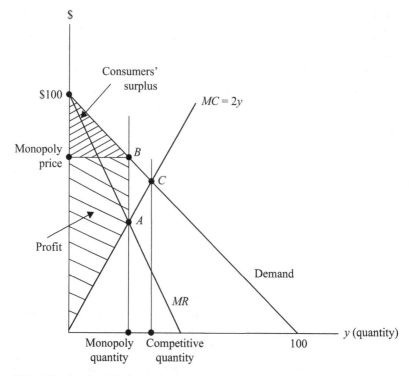

Fig. 12.2. The deadweight loss of a monopoly. The deadweight loss triangle is ABC.

for price-equals-marginal-cost regulation of natural monopolies. State-granted monopolies, such as patents, are more complicated; there is an economic rationale for granting such monopolies, namely, to encourage and promote innovation and invention. On the other hand, such monopolies create deadweight loss. Patents are granted for a period of time, currently twenty years in the United States. The first argument suggests that patent protection should last more than 5 days, but the second suggests it should last less than 500 years. Whether the lives of patents (and copyrights and trademarks) under the laws of the United States and other countries are too short or too long is an extremely interesting practical question, which we leave it to others to answer.

12.4 Price Discrimination

Sometimes a monopolist can increase its profits by charging different prices to different people, or different prices for different units sold to one person. This is known as *price discrimination*. A familiar version is the price discrimination practiced by airlines, which commonly charge business travelers much more than vacationing tourists for seats in the same section of the same plane.

Economists usually distinguish among three types of price discrimination. *Third-degree price discrimination*, which we will also call *common price discrimination*, means charging different customers different prices, but not different prices for different units sold to one customer. A customer is charged a price that depends on the pigeonhole that the monopolist has placed him into, but that is independent of the number of units he buys. *Second-degree price discrimination* means that the monopolist charges all its customers according to the same price schedule, but for any customer the price per unit depends on the number of units that customer is buying. *First-degree price discrimination*, which we will also call *perfect price discrimination*, means that the monopolist charges different prices to different people (that is, puts them in different pigeonholes), and charges individual people different per-unit prices, depending on the number of units the customer buys.

In this chapter, we limit our analysis to the first- and third-degree versions; that is, to common price discrimination and perfect price discrimination. Note that both these types of discrimination are possible only when the buyers of the monopolist's product or service cannot easily resell it among themselves. That is, suppose the monopoly firm is selling gizmos to you at $10 each, and to me at $20 each. If we all know about it, and if a gizmo is easy to transport and resell, I will go to you to buy some for a price between $10 and $20, and thereby undo the monopolist's discriminatory pricing scheme. The reader should think about the goods that are provided by discriminating monopolists in this light. Providers of electricity and natural gas may be able to price discriminate because it is difficult for customers to trade these things among themselves, but providers of heating oil, which can be easily trucked from place to place, may be less able to discriminate. Providers of airline trips are able to price discriminate because a ticket is issued to a *person*, and I cannot sell you my ticket to fly from New York to Los Angeles. Sellers of prescription pharmaceuticals are able to price discriminate because a prescription, like an airline ticket, is attached to a person, making it difficult for you to sell me Vicodin. Sellers of generic drugs such as ibuprofen, which can easily be bought and sold in large quantities by third parties, are much less able to price discriminate. (A five-minute investigation in a large drug store will reveal that the ibuprofen seller practices second-degree price discrimination, in the form of bulk discounts, but not first- or third-degree discrimination.)

Common or Third-Degree Price Discrimination

In this mild kind of price discrimination, the monopolist is able to partition the market for its product into a (typically small) number of distinct groups of buyers. For example, think of an airline selling tickets to business travelers and vacationers, or a publisher selling its academic journal to university libraries, professors, and (poor) students. We assume that the buying groups are separate in the sense that there is no possibility of buyers reselling the product between groups. (For instance, the vacationer cannot sell his airline ticket to a business traveler, and the student cannot sell her cheap journal subscription to the university library.) Because the customer groups are separate and the monopolist is charging different prices to customers in the different groups, there are distinct demand curves for the different customer groups.

We now turn to our formal model of simple price discrimination. We assume that there are two distinct groups of customers, and the monopolist discriminates between the two groups. (Analyzing three or more distinct buying groups is an easy and obvious extension of our model.) Customers in markets 1 and 2 may know that the monopolist is charging a different price in the *other* market, but they cannot do anything about it; they are stuck in the group they are in, and the product cannot be resold by customers from one market to the other.

As an aside, if you are interested in important policy debates related to this model, you can look into the issue of patent drug pricing in the United States versus pricing of the same drugs in Europe and Canada. Generally, pharmaceuticals are priced much higher in the United States than in the rest of the developed world, even when they are produced by U.S.-based companies. Many drug buyers in the United States wish they could buy their prescriptions elsewhere, but U.S. laws and regulations make doing so difficult.

We let y_1 and y_2 represent the quantities sold by the monopolist in markets 1 and 2, at prices p_1 and p_2, respectively. The total amount produced by the monopolist and sold in the two markets is $y = y_1 + y_2$. We let $p_1(y_1)$ and $p_2(y_2)$ represent the inverse demand curves in the two markets. The revenue functions in the two markets are $R_1(y_1)$ and $R_2(y_2)$. The product or service sold in market 1 is the same as that sold in market 2; therefore, the cost function for the monopolist just depends on its total output $y_1 + y_2$. That is, $C(y) = C(y_1 + y_2)$. The monopolist wants to choose the quantities y_1 and y_2 to maximize its profits. How should it do this? Its profit function can be written as follows:

$$\pi(y_1, y_2) = R_1(y_1) + R_2(y_2) - C(y_1 + y_2) = p_1(y_1)y_1 + p_2(y_2)y_2 - C(y_1 + y_2).$$

The first-order conditions for maximizing this function of two variables are that (1) the partial derivative of $\pi(y_1, y_2)$ with respect to y_1 must be zero, and (2) the partial derivative of $\pi(y_1, y_2)$ with respect to y_2 must be zero. Differentiating with respect to y_1 gives

$$\frac{\partial \pi}{\partial y_1} = \frac{dR_1(y_1)}{dy_1} - \frac{dC(y)}{dy}\frac{dy}{dy_1} = 0,$$

or

$$\frac{dR_1(y_1)}{dy_1} = \frac{dC(y)}{dy}.$$

Therefore, $MR_1(y_1) = MC(y)$. That is, *marginal revenue in market 1 must equal marginal cost.*

We now analyze the "marginal revenue equals marginal cost" result just as we did in Section 12.2, except that now we have to remember that there are two separate markets, and we are focusing on market 1 at the moment. Note that

$$MR_1(y_1) = \frac{dR_1(y_1)}{dy_1} = \frac{d}{dy_1}(p_1(y_1)y_1) = p_1(y_1) + \frac{dp_1(y_1)}{dy_1}y_1.$$

Let ϵ_1 represent the price elasticity of demand in market 1. By the same reasoning as in Section 12.2, we find that

$$MR_1(y_1) = p_1(y_1) + \frac{dp_1(y_1)}{dy_1}y_1 = p_1(y_1)(1 - 1/\epsilon_1).$$

Setting marginal revenue equal to marginal cost now gives

$$MR_1(y_1) = p_1(y_1)(1 - 1/\epsilon_1) = MC(y).$$

We have analyzed the first-order condition for profit maximization for market 1. Now let us turn to the first-order condition for market 2: the partial derivative of $\pi(y_1, y_2)$ with respect to y_2 must be zero. By the same reasoning used previously, this leads directly to

$$MR_2(y_2) = p_2(y_2)(1 - 1/\epsilon_2) = MC(y),$$

where ϵ_2 is the price elasticity of demand in market 2.

Putting our first-order conditions together gives

$$MR_1(y_1) = MR_2(y_2) = MC(y),$$

and

$$p_1(y_1)(1 - 1/\epsilon_1) = p_2(y_2)(1 - 1/\epsilon_2).$$

We are now ready to conclude our discussion of simple (third-degree) price discrimination. The monopolist that can price discriminate between two markets will end up selling quantities y_1 and y_2 such that $MR_1(y_1) = MR_2(y_2) = MC(y_1 + y_2)$. That is, marginal revenue in market 1 equals marginal revenue in market 2 equals marginal cost. By the same reasoning as in Section 12.2, the monopolist will operate in the elastic sections of the respective demand curves, that is, where $\epsilon_1, \epsilon_2 > 1$. By the previous price and elasticity formula, *the price will be lower in the market with demand that is more elastic.* For instance, if $\epsilon_1 = 3/2$, and $\epsilon_2 = 3$, then by the formula, p_1 will be twice p_2. The moral of all this is that if you are buying from a price-discriminating monopolist, it is better to be in the market with the higher price elasticity of demand. Be a flying vacationer rather than a business flyer!

Perfect or First-Degree Price Discrimination

Suppose a monopolist can charge different customers different prices, and charge different prices for different units going to the same customer. Moreover, suppose the monopolist knows exactly how much each customer is willing to pay for his first unit, his second, and so on. That is, the monopolist knows every customer's demand curve (or inverse demand curve). Suppose the customers cannot transfer units of the monopolist's product among themselves. Finally, assume (of course) that the monopolist wants to maximize profit. This is the most extreme price discrimination case, in which each incremental unit of the monopolist's product may be sold at a different price, a price that is the maximum that anyone would pay for the extra unit. This is perfect, or first-degree, price discrimination. Fortunately for consumers, perfect price discrimination is a theoretical construct. But here is how the theoretical construct works.

The monopolist knows all the customers, all their demand curves (or inverse demand curves), and every possible willingness to pay for additional units at every possible point. It therefore works its way down the market demand curve (more precisely, the inverse demand curve), and for each additional unit, it sells that unit to the person with the highest willingness to pay, given the number of units already sold to various buyers. Most important, the monopolist charges the customer the highest possible price for each additional unit. This price is exactly equal to the height of the inverse demand curve, given the number of units already sold. The profit-maximizing monopolist will continue to sell additional units (at different prices), as long as the price it is selling those units for exceeds $MC(y)$. However, once the monopolist reaches a price equal to $MC(y)$, it stops searching for additional sales.

Given that the perfect price-discriminating monopolist works its way down the inverse market demand curve, selling each incremental unit at a price given by the height of the curve, its revenue equals the area under the market (inverse) demand curve. That is, the revenue from selling y units is

$$R(y) = \int_0^y p(t)dt.$$

(Note that we are using a dummy variable t in the price function within the integral.)

The perfect price-discriminating monopolist's profit is now given by

$$\pi(y) = \int_0^y p(t)dt - C(y).$$

The first-order condition for profit maximization requires that the derivative of profit with respect to y equals zero. This gives:

$$\frac{d\pi(y)}{dy} = p(y) - \frac{dC(y)}{dy} = 0$$

or

$$p(y) = MC(y).$$

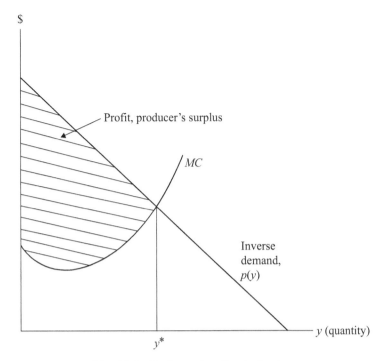

Fig. 12.3. Perfect price discrimination.

That is, price equals marginal cost. Remember, of course, that each unit produced by the perfect price-discriminating monopolist is being sold at a different price; the condition we have just derived is for the last, or marginal, unit.

The result of all this is shown is Figure 12.3. The figure shows an inverse demand curve $p(y)$. This is a straight-line demand curve, similar to the ones in Figures 12.1 and 12.2. The monopolist's marginal cost curve $MC(y)$ is also shown in Figure 12.3; this one is roughly parabolic, unlike the ones in Figures 12.1 and 12.2. (A marginal cost curve that first falls and then rises is more realistic than a straight-line marginal cost curve.) The monopolist is producing a quantity y^* where $p(y^*) = MC(y^*)$, and is charging the last customer this price for this unit. However, all the previous units were sold at higher prices to the various customers, with each incremental unit being sold at the highest possible price to its buyer. The monopolist's revenue equals the area under the inverse demand curve up to y^*, and its total cost equals the area under the marginal cost curve, up to that point (except possibly for any fixed cost $C(0)$). Profit is revenue minus cost, and is shown as the crosshatched area (except possibly for any fixed cost). This area is producer's surplus.

We conclude that: (1) There is no deadweight loss due to the operation of the perfect price-discriminating monopoly firm. The sum of consumers' surplus and producer's surplus is the same in this figure as it would be if the monopoly were acting as a competitive firm (that is, finding the output level at which price equals marginal cost, and selling to everybody at that price). In other words, a perfect price-discriminating monopoly market is efficient. This is the good news. The bad news is: (2) There is no consumers' surplus. The buyers get no net benefit in this monopoly; all the benefit flows to the monopoly firm. Therefore, although the outcome is efficient, it is grossly inequitable, with all the benefit flowing to the firm and none to the consumers.

We end this section with a final comment about the real world. It is hard to think of a real example of a perfect price-discriminating monopolist, because a typical monopolist firm simply does not know the amounts all its buyers would be willing to pay for additional units of its good or service. In fact, buyers are often careful to conceal how much they are willing to pay, as they do not want to be forced to pay extra for a product. Often buyers will actively conceal both their enthusiasm for the monopolist's product and their income or wealth – the depth of their pockets – and the typical firm has no good way to discover either of these ingredients in willingness to pay.

We are familiar, however, with one interesting case in which the monopolist firm goes to considerable lengths to discover the buyer's interest in the product, and to discover the buyer's income or wealth. This is the case of the Famous University (e.g., Harvard, Yale, Princeton, Brown) offering financial aid (that is, discounted tuition and fees) to prospective students. The university asks questions on application forms whose answers reveal how much the applicant wants to go to that university, and the university asks detailed questions on financial aid forms to discover how deep the applicant's (and his or her parents') pockets are.

Of course, universities are not profit-maximizing firms. Their price discrimination, although extensive, takes place only on the bottom part of the inverse demand curve; they do not actively try to extract the highest possible fees from students who are not on aid. However, this is a case in which the seller digs very deeply to find out how much the customer wants the product, and how much money the customer has available to pay for the product.

12.5 Monopolistic Competition

When economists use the term *monopolistic competition*, they are referring to a market in which there are many competing firms, producing products that are similar but not identical. Each particular product is produced by just one of the firms. The products produced by the firms are different, but just slightly; that is, they are close substitutes. Think of the market for laundry detergents, for example. Among the popular brands currently available in the United States are Tide, Gain, OxiClean, Method, All, and Cheer. Each is unique, possibly protected by patents, and certainly protected by trademarks. Therefore, each firm that produces one of these brands can be called a monopolist; it is the only firm producing that particular brand of detergent. However, the different brands of detergent are close substitutes, from the buyer's perspective. If a buyer usually uses Gain, but the price of Gain goes up slightly while the price of Tide goes down slightly, she will most likely switch. Therefore, the firm that sells Gain may be a monopoly, strictly speaking, but demand for its product is very sensitive to the price it charges, as well as to the prices charged by competing brands.

In Chapter 11 on competitive markets, we assumed that firms are price takers – they take prices for the goods they produce as given and outside their control. In the analysis of monopolistic competition, we drop that assumption. Rather, we assume, as we did in earlier parts of this chapter, that firms are aware of how their pricing decisions affect demand for their products. But now we also assume that, although the maker of one particular product or brand has a monopoly on that particular product or brand, other firms compete with very similar products or brands. We also assume that firms are free to enter or leave the market, and if the firms in the market are making profits, new firms will enter and try to sell similar new products.

The main formal difference between the model in this section and the models in prior sections of this chapter is that firm i's inverse demand curve does not depend only on y_i. It also depends on the total number of firms in the market n. We write $p_i(y_i, n)$ for firm i's inverse demand curve. As before, when y_i rises, $p_i(y_i, n)$ falls, and when y_i falls, $p_i(y_i, n)$ rises. That is, the inverse demand curve is downward sloping, for a given number of firms. We now also assume that as n rises, $p_i(y_i, n)$ falls, and as n falls, $p_i(y_i, n)$ rises. This means that to sell a given level of output, firm i must charge a lower price if the number of competing firms increases.

Firm i's problem is to choose its output y_i to maximize its profit $\pi_i(y_i, n)$. Of course, it controls only y_i; it has no control over n (short of the drastic step of leaving the business itself). Its profit is

$$\pi_i(y_i, n) = R_i(y_i, n) - C_i(y_i) = p_i(y_i, n)y_i - C_i(y_i).$$

The first-order condition for profit maximization says that the first derivative of profit with respect to y_i should be zero. This gives

$$MR_i(y_i, n) = MC_i(y_i),$$

or *marginal revenue for firm i equals marginal cost for firm i*.

So far, this is exactly like the classical analysis for monopoly. But now we turn to what is new. We can solve for the equilibrium number of firms in the market. We assumed free entry into the monopolistic competition market. This implies that if firms in the market are making profits, new firms will enter, driving up the number of firms n, and driving prices and output levels per firm down. An equilibrium will occur when profits disappear. Firm i's profit is zero when the price it is getting for its product equals average cost. This means that

$$p_i(y_i, n) = AC_i(y_i).$$

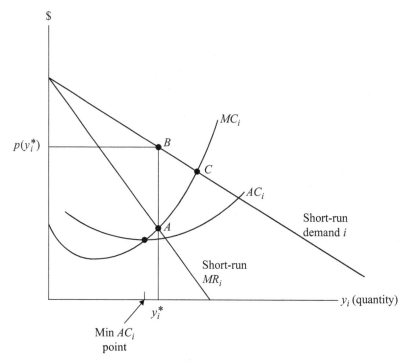

Fig. 12.4. Firm i in the short run, before competition has driven profit down to zero in the monopolistic competition market. Deadweight loss is the area of ABC.

We now have two equations describing the equilibrium under monopolistic competition. The first says that firm i's marginal revenue equals firm i's marginal cost. The second says that the number of firms in the market adjusts until p_i equals AC_i.

Figures 12.4 and 12.5 illustrate how monopolistic competition works.

Figure 12.4 revisits standard monopoly analysis. Recall that in Figures 12.1 and 12.2 we analyzed classical monopoly, but we used a special linear marginal cost function, $MC(y) = 2y$. Figure 12.4 is similar to Figures 12.1 and 12.2, except that it shows a standard U-shaped average cost curve and a standard marginal cost curve that falls at first and then rises, passing through the bottom of the average cost curve. $AC_i(y_i)$ and $MC_i(y_i)$ in Figure 12.4 represent average cost and marginal cost curves for a particular firm, firm i, in the group of monopolistic competitors. Figure 12.4 represents a short-run situation in which firm i has few competitors, lots of demand for its product, and substantial profit. The firm finds the point at which marginal revenue equals marginal cost (point A), it chooses the corresponding output y_i^*, and its profits are then substantial. Deadweight loss due to this monopoly is also substantial, equal to the area of the triangle ABC.

Figure 12.4 represents firm i's nicely profitable situation in the short run, before its competitors have entered the market and driven profits down to zero. As competitors enter, the inverse demand curve for i's product drops and flattens.

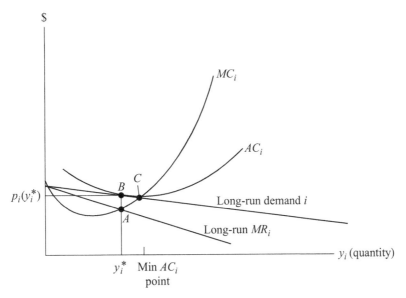

Fig. 12.5. A long-run equilibrium under monopolistic competition, with zero profit for firm i. Deadweight loss, the area of ABC, has shrunk.

Competitors continue entering (that is, n continues increasing) until i's profits are driven to zero, or $p_i(y_i, n) = AC_i(y_i)$. In the long run, firm i is making no profit, just like a firm in a competitive market in the long run. Figure 12.5 shows the long-run equilibrium.

Figure 12.5 is based on the same average cost and marginal cost curves as Figure 12.4. What has changed is that the demand and marginal revenue curves have shifted down and flattened. There is a new equilibrium y_i^* for firm i, which now lies to the left of the minimum of AC_i, and there is a new equilibrium price p_i^*, which equals average cost: $p_i^* = AC_i(y_i^*)$.

Notice how the long-run equilibrium in a monopolistic competition market has both competitive and monopolistic features. It is similar to an equilibrium in a competitive market in that the firms are making zero profits. It differs from a competitive equilibrium, however, in that the firms are not operating at the minima of their average cost curves. It is similar to an equilibrium for a monopoly in that there is a deadweight loss triangle. However, firm i has a much smaller deadweight loss triangle in the monopolistic competition equilibrium, Figure 12.5, than it does when it is a real monopolist, Figure 12.4. Finally, the regulatory implications of monopolistic competition are unclear. When firm i is a profitable monopoly, as in Figure 12.4, forcing it to act competitive (and produce and sell at a point at which price equals marginal cost) makes sense. However, when firm i is a monopolistic competition firm, as in Figure 12.5, there is not much latitude for the government to force it to do anything, as it is already making zero profit.

What, then, should the policy maker do about monopolistic competition? The answer is probably not much. However, consumers should be alert to the possibility that some of the firms in the market might want to force other firms out, to reduce competition, or that some of the firms in the market might want to create barriers to prevent other potential competitors from coming in. One can easily imagine a trade group – call it the U.S. Detergent Council – made up of the firms that make Tide, Gain, OxiClean, Method, All, and Cheer, getting together with their congressional allies to form a new government agency, say, the U.S. Administration of Cleanliness. The USAC could then prevent any other firms from selling detergent to U.S. consumers, without extremely time-consuming and expensive prior testing. This would enhance the profits of the firms already entrenched in the market – but it would be a dirty deal for the consumers.

12.6 A Solved Problem

The Problem

Esmeralda is a fortune-teller and can predict her clients' futures. The demand for future-telling sessions is given by $y^D = 20 - p$, where y is the number of client sessions, and p is the price per session. Her future-telling costs increase more than proportionally with each session (she gets horrible headaches after a while); her cost function is $C(y) = y^2$. She works in a theme park called Promised Land.

(a) Suppose Promised Land requires that she charge the same price per session, for all customers and all sessions. Assume she is the only fortune-teller who is allowed to operate in Promised Land. How many sessions does she sell? What price does she charge? What is her profit? What are the consumers' and producers' surpluses?

(b) Now, assume that Promised Land drops the uniform price requirement. Assume further that Esmeralda can not only tell the future but also read customers' minds, and see exactly how much each customer is willing to pay, at most, for each session. That is, she knows all their willingnesses to pay. What will she do now to maximize her profit? What prices will she charge? How many sessions will she sell? What profit will she make? What are the consumers' and producers' surpluses?

(c) Finally, assume that Promised Land decides to allow any and all fortune-tellers to come and operate in the park. The fortune-telling market becomes competitive. Assume that the supply curve in this competitive market is $y^S = p/2$, where p is the market price. Calculate the competitive equilibrium price and quantity. What are the consumers' and producers' surpluses? Compare these with corresponding values in parts (a) and (b). Note: Treat y as a continuous variable.

The Solution

(a) We first invert the demand function to get price as a function of quantity: $p(y) = 20 - y$. Esmeralda's revenue function is $R(y) = p(y)y = (20 - y)y = 20y - y^2$. We differentiate this to get marginal revenue: $MR(y) = 20 - 2y$. Because her cost function is $C(y) = y^2$, her marginal cost is $MC(y) = 2y$. The first-order condition for profit

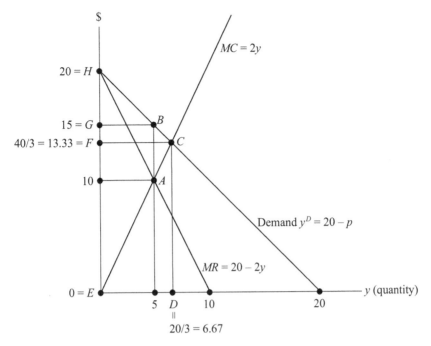

Fig. 12.6. Assuming Esmeralda charges a uniform price p, the profit-maximizing output is $y = 5$ and price is $p(y) = 15$.

maximization for a non–price-discriminating monopolist is $MR(y) = MC(y)$. This gives

$$MR(y) = 20 - 2y = 2y = MC(y).$$

The profit-maximizing number of sessions is therefore $y = 5$. If we substitute this into the inverse demand function, we get $p = 20 - y = 15$. Her profit is

$$\pi(y) = R(y) - C(y) = 20y - y^2 - y^2 = 100 - 25 - 25 = 50.$$

See Figure 12.6 for the demand function y^D, the $MR(y)$ function, and the $MC(y)$ function, all straight lines. (Note that Figure 12.6 is very similar to Figure 12.2.) Figure 12.6 also includes the profit-maximizing output $y = 5$ and price $p(y) = 15$, as well as capital letters identifying some crucial points. (Point A, for example, is where marginal cost crosses marginal revenue, point B is where a vertical line from $y = 5$ hits the demand curve, and point C is where marginal cost crosses the demand curve.)

Note that consumers' surplus, in the case of the monopolist charging one price, is the area under the demand curve but above a horizontal line at the monopoly price; this is the area of the triangle HBG in Figure 12.6, which is $1/2 \times 5 \times 5 = 12.5$. Producers' surplus is the area below the horizontal line at the monopoly price, but above the marginal cost curve; this is the area of the quadrilateral $GBAE$ in the figure. Alternatively, given that there are no fixed costs in this example, producers' surplus simply equals Esmeralda's profit. Therefore, producers' surplus is 50, and the sum of consumers' surplus and producers' surplus is 62.5. (See Figure 12.2 for another view of the same sort of thing, with cross-hatching.) Note that deadweight loss is the area of triangle ABC.

(b) If Esmeralda can read her customers' minds, and if she is allowed to charge different prices as she pleases, she charges each person the maximum that person would be willing to pay for that session, for each person, and for each session. She is now a perfect price-discriminating monopolist. This means that she works her way down the inverse demand curve, charging different prices for each session. She continues to do this, unit by unit, as long as it is profitable to do so. Once she hits the point at which willingness to pay equals marginal cost, she stops. To find that point, we set inverse demand equal to marginal cost, or $20 - y = 2y$, which gives $y = 20/3 = 6.67$. The price she charges for the *last unit* is $p = 20 - 20/3 = 40/3 = 13.33$.

Her profit is revenue minus cost. Revenue is slightly complicated, as she is charging a different price for each session. Given that the price for each session is the height of the inverse demand curve at that y, revenue is the area under the inverse demand curve from $y = 0$ to $y = 20/3$. That is, revenue is the area of the quadrilateral $HCDE$ in Figure 12.6. In the figure, we see that $HCDE$ is made up of a triangle HCF on top, plus a triangle FCE below the horizontal line at $p = 13.33$ but above the marginal cost curve, plus another triangle CDE below the marginal cost curve and to the left of a vertical line at $y = 6.67$. Using the usual rule for the area of a triangle, and adding together the areas of these three triangles, we get Esmeralda's revenue as a perfect price-discriminating monopolist:

$$R(y) = \left(\frac{1}{2} \times \frac{20}{3} \times \left(20 - \frac{40}{3}\right)\right) + \left(\frac{1}{2} \times \frac{20}{3} \times \frac{40}{3}\right) + \left(\frac{1}{2} \times \frac{20}{3} \times \frac{40}{3}\right) = 111.11.$$

We can find cost from the cost function: $C(20/3) = (20/3)^2 = 44.44$. Alternatively, we can find it as the area under the marginal cost curve; that is, the area of the triangle CDE in the figure, which gives

$$C(y) = \frac{1}{2} \times \frac{20}{3} \times \frac{40}{3} = 44.44.$$

Finally, Esmeralda's profit as a perfect price-discriminating monopolist equals revenue minus cost. In Figure 12.6, this is the area of the quadrilateral $HCDE$ minus the area of the triangle CDE, or the area of the large triangle HCE. This gives

$$\pi(y) = R(y) - C(y) = 111.11 - 44.44 = 66.67.$$

Note that for the perfect price-discriminating monopolist, consumers' surplus is zero, and producers' surplus equals 66.67, the entire area of the large triangle HCE.

(c) With a competitive fortune-telling market, and supply curve $y^S = p/2$, we calculate the equilibrium by setting supply equal to demand, or $y^S = y^D$, which gives $p/2 = 20 - p$. This gives a competitive equilibrium price of $p = 40/3$ and a competitive equilibrium quantity of $y = 20/3$. The inverse supply function is $p(y) = 2y$, identical to Esmeralda's marginal cost function in parts (a) and (b). Referring again to Figure

12.6, under the competitive outcome, consumers' surplus is the area under the demand curve but above $p = 40/3$, or the area of triangle HCF:

$$CS = \frac{1}{2} \times \frac{20}{3} \times \left(20 - \frac{40}{3}\right) = 22.22.$$

Producers' surplus is the area below the horizontal line at $p = 40/3$, but above the supply curve (which coincides with the original $MC(y)$ curve), or the area of triangle FCE:

$$PS = \frac{1}{2} \times \frac{20}{3} \times \frac{40}{3} = 44.44.$$

The sum of consumers' surplus and producers' surplus is now the area of the large triangle HCE:

$$CS + PS = \frac{1}{2} \times 20 \times \frac{20}{3} = 66.67.$$

We see that the sum of consumers' surplus and producers' surplus, or total social surplus, is the same 66.67 in the perfect price-discriminating monopolist case (part (b)), and in the competitive case (part (c)). In this sense, both the perfect price-discriminating monopolist case and the competitive case are better for society than the case of the monopolist charging one price (part (a)), where the total of consumers' surplus and producers' surplus was 62.5. In the competitive case, the consumers actually do benefit – consumers' surplus is 22.22. In the perfect price-discrimination case, however, the monopolist gets all the surplus and consumers get none.

Exercises $\frac{p}{MC} = \frac{1}{\varepsilon - 1}$

1. Suppose a monopolist with constant marginal costs practices third-degree price discrimination. Group A's elasticity of demand is ϵ_A and Group B's is ϵ_B, and $\epsilon_A > \epsilon_B$. Which group will face a higher price? Explain.

2. Vito Corleone's family is the only supplier of good h in the United States. The market inverse demand for good h has been estimated to be $p = 50 - \frac{h^D}{50}$. The costs of production and distribution are represented by $C(h) = 12h$. Calculate the monopolist's profit-maximizing level of output, the price at which it will be sold, and Corleone's profits.

3. Consider a third-degree price-discriminating monopolist. Suppose $p_1(y_1) = 100 - y_1$, $p_2(y_2) = 75 - \frac{1}{2}y_2$, and let the cost curve be $C(y) = y^2 = (y_1 + y_2)^2$. Show that the monopolist will produce $y_1 = 18.75$, $y_2 = 12.50$, and set prices $p_1 = 81.25$, $p_2 = 68.75$.

4. Horizon Telephone observes that there are two types of demand for telephone services: businesses and families. The businesses' demand curve is $x_B = 100 - p_B$, where x_B measures the hours of telephone services that businesses purchase per week and p_B is the price per hour charged to businesses. The families' demand curve is $x_F = 15 - \frac{p_F}{2}$,

where x_F and p_F represent hours and price, respectively. Horizon Telephone's cost function is $C(x) = x$, where $x = x_B + x_F$.

(a) Suppose Horizon Telephone can price discriminate between the two groups. Calculate the hours of telephone services that it sells to each group, the two prices, and total profits.

(b) Calculate the consumers' and producer's surplus under price discrimination.

(c) Suppose the government forbids price discrimination. Then, the total demand for telephone services is obtained from the horizontal sum of the demands from the two groups (businesses and families). Calculate the solution to the monopolist's problem and its profits.

(d) Now calculate the consumers' and producer's surplus if price discrimination is forbidden. Is society better off or worse off after this change is introduced?

5. Sue has a monopoly over the production of strawberry shortcake. Her cost function is $C(y) = y^2 + 10y$. The market demand curve for strawberry shortcake is $p(y) = 100 - \frac{1}{2}y$.

     (a) What is Sue's profit-maximizing level of output y^*?

     (b) What is the price p^* at this level of output?

     (c) Calculate her profit π^*.

     (d) Find the consumers' surplus at p^* and y^*.

[handwritten: $p(y) \, y = 100y - \frac{1}{2}y^2$]

[handwritten: $MR : 100 - y = 2y + 10$]

[handwritten: $y = 30 \quad p(30) = 8\xi-$]

6. Consider Sue, the strawberry shortcake monopolist from Question 5. Suppose the dictator decides to force Sue to price at marginal cost.

     (a) What is Sue's new profit-maximizing level of output y^{**}? Compare your answer to Q5(a).

     (b) What is the new price p^{**}? Compare your answer to Q5(b).

     (c) Calculate her profit π^{**}. Compare your answer to Q5(c).

     (d) Find the consumers' surplus at p^{**} and y^{**}. Compare your answer to Q5(d).

     (e) How does total welfare compare to the situation in Question 5?

Chapter 13

Duopoly

13.1 Introduction

In this chapter, we study market structures that lie between perfect competition and monopoly. As before we assume, at least in most of this chapter, that there is one homogeneous good that is the same no matter who makes it. We assume that everyone has perfect information about the good and its price. In our discussion of monopoly, we assumed that there were barriers to entry that preserved the monopolist's position. In this chapter, we also assume that there are barriers to entry that prevent other firms from entering the market. However, we now assume that there are already two (or more) firms in the market.

An *oligopoly* is a market with just a few firms. For instance, the market for cell phone service in our part of the United States is currently dominated by Verizon Wireless, AT&T, and Sprint, a total of three large companies. (There are also some smaller companies.) In this market, each of these large firms realizes that its own output and the output of each of its competitors will affect the market price. In contrast, in a competitive market (such as the markets for wheat, corn, or cattle), there are hundreds or thousands of firms supplying the good, and each firm can safely ignore the possible effect of its own output or each competitor's output on the price. In this chapter, we assume that each firm takes into account how its own output, and its competitors' outputs, affects the price, and through the price, its own profit.

Because one firm's output decision will affect the profits of the other firms, firms in an oligopoly are likely to act strategically. Two firms are acting *strategically* when each looks at what the other is doing, and thinks along these lines: "I have to make my production decisions contingent on what he does. If he sells 1,000 units, then to maximize my profits, I have to sell 1,100 units. And if I produce 1,100 units, does it make sense for him to produce 1,000 units?" The firms are reacting to each other. In a competitive market, in contrast, the firms do not react to each other; they react only to the market price, which they take as predetermined or fixed.

In this chapter, we assume that there are only two firms in the market. A market with just two firms is called a *duopoly*. Obviously, a duopoly is the simplest sort of oligopoly; many of the concepts and results that we will describe can be extended to the case of an oligopoly with more than two firms. Duopoly analysis by economists dates back to the nineteenth century. Some of the central concepts of duopoly analysis have to do with strategic behavior, and the analysis of strategic behavior is the heart of the twentieth-century discipline called *game theory*. Game theory builds on duopoly theory. We will turn to game theory in the next chapter.

There are two fundamentally different approaches to duopoly theory. The first assumes that duopolists compete with each other through their choices of *quantity*: each firm decides on the quantity it should produce and sell in the market, contingent on the other firm's quantity. The second assumes that duopolists compete with each other through their choices of *price*: each firm decides on the price it should charge, contingent on the price the other firm is charging. The first approach was taken by the French mathematician and economist Antoine Augustin Cournot (1801–1877), who wrote about duopoly in 1838. The second approach was developed by another French mathematician, Joseph Louis François Bertrand (1822–1900), in 1883.

We start in Section 13.2 by describing the basic Cournot duopoly model, and we develop that model in Sections 13.3 and 13.4. The crucial behavioral assumption of the Cournot model is that each firm assumes that the other firm's output is given and fixed, and maximizes its own profit based on that assumption. Other behavioral assumptions might be made about the two firms. One is the assumption made by the German economist Heinrich von Stackelberg (1905–1946). Stackelberg assumed, as did Cournot, that the firms make decisions about quantities. But he also assumed, unlike Cournot, that the two firms act differently; one of the duopolists acts as a *follower* (as in Cournot's model), taking the other firm's output as given and fixed, and choosing its own output based on that assumption, but the other duopolist acts as a *leader*, by anticipating that its rival will act as a follower, and choosing its own output based on that knowledge. We describe the Stackelberg model in Section 13.5. In Section 13.6, we describe the Bertrand model, in which the firms compete with each other through their choices of price, instead of competing, as in the Cournot (and Stackelberg) models, through the choices of quantity. We will see that there are two rather different versions of Bertrand's model, depending on whether the good produced by the two firms is exactly the same (the homogeneous good case), or somewhat different (the differentiated goods case, e.g., Coke and Pepsi).

13.2 Cournot Competition

Assume there are two firms in the market. Firm 1 produces y_1 units of the good; firm 2 produces y_2 units. The total amount produced is $y = y_1 + y_2$. We assume there is a downward-sloping inverse market demand curve $p(y) = p(y_1 + y_2)$. We assume firm i has a cost curve $C_i(y_i)$, for $i = 1, 2$. Firm 1 wants to maximize its profit π_1, given by

$$\pi_1(y_1, y_2) = p(y_1 + y_2)y_1 - C_1(y_1).$$

Similarly, firm 2 wants to maximize its profit π_2, given by

$$\pi_2(y_1, y_2) = p(y_1 + y_2)y_2 - C_2(y_2).$$

The basic Cournot assumption is this: When firm 1 chooses its output y_1 to maximize its profit, it takes firm 2's output y_2 as given and fixed; similarly, when firm 2 chooses its output y_2 to maximize its profit, it takes firm 1's output y_1 as given and fixed. Therefore, when firm 1 differentiates its profit function $\pi_1(y_1, y_2)$, it treats y_2 as a constant. This leads to the first-order condition

$$\frac{\partial \pi_1}{\partial y_1} = p(y) + \frac{dp(y)}{dy}y_1 - \frac{dC_1(y_1)}{dy_1} = 0.$$

Firm 1 can solve this equation for y_1 as a function of y_2. We write the result as

$$y_1 = r_1(y_2).$$

The function r_1 is called firm 1's *reaction function*. It shows, for any output level y_2 of firm 2, the quantity of the good that firm 1 should produce in order to maximize its profit.

Similarly, firm 2 maximizes its profit subject to the assumption that y_1 is a constant. This leads to

$$\frac{\partial \pi_2}{\partial y_2} = p(y) + \frac{dp(y)}{dy}y_2 - \frac{dC_2(y_2)}{dy_2} = 0.$$

Firm 2 can solve this equation for y_2 as a function of y_1, and we write the result as

$$y_2 = r_2(y_1).$$

The function r_2 is firm 2's reaction function. It shows, for any output level y_1 of firm 1, the quantity of the good that firm 2 should produce in order to maximize its profit.

If the two firms randomly choose their output levels y_1 and y_2, it is almost certain that neither would be maximizing its profits subject to what the other one is doing. Neither firm would be behaving in a clever way. The result would not make sense; it would be doubly stupid. And if firm 2 randomly chooses an output level y_2, and then firm 1 uses its reaction function r_1 to choose its output level y_1, the result would be half sensible – sensible on the part of firm 1, but stupid on the part of firm 2. However, suppose the reaction functions intersect at a point y_1^* and y_2^*, and suppose firm 1 chooses y_1^* and firm 2 chooses y_2^*. This outcome does make very good sense for both firms, because firm 1 is making the best choice it can, subject to what firm 2 has chosen, and firm 2 is making the best choice it can, subject to what firm 1 has chosen. A *Cournot equilibrium* in a duopoly model is a pair of output levels y_1^* and y_2^* that are consistent in this sense – each firm i is maximizing its profit at y_i^*, subject to what the other firm j has chosen, y_j^*. The Cournot equilibrium is Augustin Cournot's brilliant solution to the duopoly puzzle.

In short, a Cournot equilibrium is a consistent, self-sustaining, and self-reinforcing outcome in the duopoly model. We now turn to an example to show how the Cournot equilibrium can be found.

Example 1. Assume that the inverse demand curve is $p(y_1 + y_2) = 100 - y = 100 - y_1 - y_2$. Assume that the cost curves are $C_1(y_1) = 25y_1$ and $C_2(y_2) = 25y_2$. Marginal cost for either firm is a constant 25. To find firm 1's reaction function, we find the y_1 that maximizes $\pi_1(y_1, y_2)$, under the assumption that y_2 is constant. Firm 1's profit is

$$\pi_1(y_1, y_2) = (100 - y_1 - y_2)y_1 - 25y_1.$$

Differentiating with respect to y_1 while holding y_2 constant, and setting the result equal to zero, gives

$$\frac{\partial \pi_1}{\partial y_1} = 100 - 2y_1 - y_2 - 25 = 0.$$

Solving for y_1 as a function of y_2 gives firm 1's reaction function:

$$y_1 = r_1(y_2) = 37.5 - y_2/2.$$

Firm 2's profit $\pi_2(y_1, y_2)$ is

$$\pi_2(y_1, y_2) = (100 - y_1 - y_2)y_2 - 25y_2.$$

Differentiating with respect to y_2 while holding y_1 constant, and setting the result equal to zero, gives

$$\frac{\partial \pi_2}{\partial y_2} = 100 - 2y_2 - y_1 - 25 = 0.$$

Therefore, firm 2's reaction function is

$$y_2 = r_2(y_1) = 37.5 - y_1/2.$$

In Figure 13.1, we show the reaction functions and the Cournot equilibrium in Example 1. The Cournot equilibrium is the point at which the two reaction functions intersect. Solving the two reaction function equations simultaneously ($y_1 = 37.5 - y_2/2$ and $y_2 = 37.5 - y_1/2$) easily gives $(y_1^*, y_2^*) = (25, 25)$. At $(25, 25)$, each firm is maximizing its profit, given what the other firm is doing. The market price is $100 - 25 - 25 = 50$. The reader can easily check that profit levels for the firms are $(\pi_1, \pi_2) = (625, 625)$. The output levels are mutually consistent; neither firm has an incentive to change, given what the other firm is doing. The Cournot equilibrium $(25, 25)$ makes sense for firm 1, and simultaneously makes sense for firm 2.

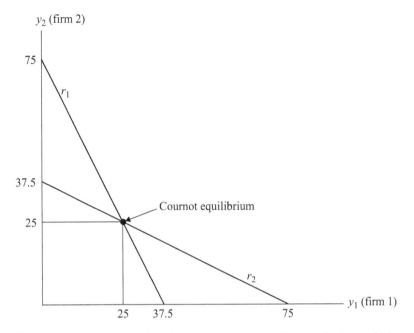

Fig. 13.1. The reaction functions and Cournot equilibrium in Example 1.

Comparison with Monopoly and Competition

We can use Example 1 to show how a Cournot equilibrium in a duopoly compares with a monopoly outcome and a competitive outcome. The general result is that in a duopoly (and, more generally, an oligopoly), total output and price lie somewhere between what they would be under competition or under monopoly.

In Example 1, remember that the Cournot equilibrium price is $50, and the total quantity is 50. How would we describe the competitive outcome? We would have the same demand curve, but price would be equal to marginal cost. That is, the competitive supply curve would be a horizontal line at $p = 25$. Combining this with the inverse demand curve $p = 100 - y$ gives a competitive equilibrium at $p_C = \$25$ and $y_C = 75$, where the C subscript means "competitive."

How would we describe the monopoly outcome? The monopolist would maximize profit by setting marginal revenue equal to marginal cost. In the example, $MR(y) = 100 - 2y$ and $MC(y) = 25$. Therefore, $100 - 2y = 25$, or $y = 37.5$. Putting this y in the equation for the inverse demand curve gives $p = 100 - y = 62.5$. In the monopoly solution, then, we have $p_M = \$62.5$ and $y_M = 37.5$, where the M subscript stands for "monopoly." We conclude that the Cournot equilibrium in a duopoly lies between the competitive outcome and the monopoly outcome, both for quantity and price.

What about efficiency? We will now investigate the social surplus created at the Cournot equilibrium in the duopoly. As you might expect, the duopoly social surplus

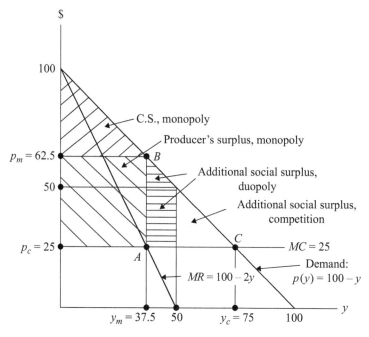

Fig. 13.2. Welfare analysis of the duopoly, based on Example 1. Social surplus is least for a monopoly, greater for a duopoly, and greatest for a competitive market.

lies between the social surplus in the monopoly market and the social surplus in the competitive market. In short, duopoly (and, more generally, oligopoly) creates some deadweight loss, but not as much as monopoly creates. We show this in Figure 13.2.

Figure 13.2 is based on Example 1. It shows total output y on the horizontal axis. The outermost line is the inverse demand curve $p(y) = 100 - y$. A monopolist in this market would find the corresponding marginal revenue curve $MR(y) = 100 - 2y$. This is the steeper downward-sloping line shown in the figure. A monopolist would set marginal revenue equal to marginal cost, point A in the figure, to get the quantity $y_M = 37.5$. He would then go up to the demand curve, to point B, and get the price $p_M = \$62.5$. Total social surplus under monopoly in this example would be consumers' surplus (the upward-sloping crosshatched triangle) plus producer's surplus (the downward-sloping crosshatched square).

If this market were a duopoly, the Cournot equilibrium total quantity would be 50 (shown on the horizontal axis), and the price would be $50 (shown on the vertical axis). In a transition from a monopoly to duopoly, consumers' surplus would grow and producers' surplus would shrink. However, the sum of the two welfare measures would definitely grow, by the area of the horizontally cross-hatched trapezoid in the figure.

Finally, if this were a competitive market, the equilibrium would require that price equal marginal cost (point C in the figure). In a transition from duopoly to competition, consumers' surplus would greatly expand and producers' surplus would disappear. However, social surplus would definitely grow, by the area of the non-cross-hatched triangle.

We conclude that the competitive outcome is best for society in the sense that it maximizes social surplus. The Cournot equilibrium in a duopoly is worse than the competitive outcome. The monopoly outcome is the worst of all.

13.3 More on Dynamics

We have been a bit vague about how our two firms get to the Cournot equilibrium. The sophisticated and modern game theory–oriented economist looks at Cournot's model and describes it as a *simultaneous move* game. This means that firms 1 and 2, with full knowledge of market demand and full knowledge of their own cost function and their rival's cost function, choose their output levels, one time only, and simultaneously. They end up with a pair of output levels (y_1, y_2). If the pair is a Cournot equilibrium, the outcome makes sense for both firms; it is doubly sensible. If it is not a Cournot equilibrium, the outcome fails to make sense for at least one of the firms, and possibly for both firms. If each firm is a rational profit maximizer and expects the other firm to also be a rational profit maximizer, they should end up at the Cournot equilibrium.

It may be useful to discuss some other possible dynamics in Cournot's model. These descriptions of dynamics necessarily go beyond the simple assumption of simultaneity. One possible dynamic has the firms taking turns reacting to each other. First, firm 1 reacts to firm 2's output; then firm 2 reacts to firm 1's output, and the process goes on until it (hopefully) gets to a Cournot equilibrium. To make this discussion more understandable, let us assume that there is a time dimension, and production and consumption are repeated time unit after time unit, say, day after day.

Let us assume, then, that firms 1 and 2 start at some initial output quantities, on day 0, say, (y_1^0, y_2^0). On the morning of day 1, firm 1 looks at firm 2's output, and calculates what it should produce, contingent on what firm 2 produced on day 0. That is, it goes to its reaction function, and calculates $y_1 = r_1(y_2^0)$. This gives (y_1^1, y_2^1) as the firm outputs on day 1, where $y_1^1 = r_1(y_2^0)$ and where $y_2^1 = y_2^0$.

On the morning of day 2, firm 2 looks at firm 1's output, and calculates what it should produce, contingent on what firm 1 produced on day 1. That is, it goes to its reaction function, and calculates $y_2 = r_2(y_1^1)$. This gives (y_1^2, y_2^2) as the firm outputs on day 2, where $y_1^2 = y_1^1$ and where $y_2^2 = r_2(y_1^1)$.

In other words, the two firms take turns reacting to each other. The process continues, day after day, until it (hopefully) converges to a point at which neither firm wants to make further modifications to its daily output. That point is a Cournot equilibrium. Of course, it is slightly odd to think that each firm will use its reaction

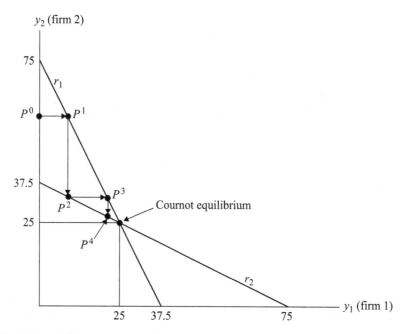

Fig. 13.3. A dynamic story about the Cournot equilibrium, based on Example 1.

function at each of its turns, because the reaction functions are based on the assumption that the rival's output is fixed, and that the rival is changing its planned output every other day. (A more rigorous treatment of this and other dynamic adjustment processes is beyond the scope of this book.)

Figure 13.3 illustrates this dynamic story. The process starts at some initial output levels $P^0 = (y_1^0, y_2^0)$, shown on the vertical axis in the figure. On day 1, the process moves to P^1; on day 2, it moves to P^2, and so on. As in the story of Genesis, on the seventh day they rest. In the figure, the process converges nicely to the Cournot equilibrium. However, this dynamic process would not converge if the reaction functions had the wrong slopes at the equilibrium. The reader is invited to relabel the reaction functions to see what happens if r_1 is less steep than r_2.

13.4 Collusion

Let us return to Example 1, and assume that our duopolists are at the Cournot equilibrium. Once again, to make this discussion more understandable, we assume that there is a time dimension, and production and consumption are repeated day after day. Because the two firms are at the Cournot equilibrium, they are producing and selling $y_1^* = y_2^* = 25$, day after day. Given those production levels, the market price is $p = 100 - 25 - 25 = 50$, day after day. Each firm has profits of $\pi_i = py_i^* - 25y_i^* = 625$, day after day.

Suppose that one day, the owners of the two firms meet for a game of golf. They have the following conversation: Firm 1 owner: "I'm maximizing my profits at $y_1^* = 25$. But this is based on your holding your output constant at $y_2^* = 25$. What if we both cut output a little bit? Could we make more money that way?" Firm 2 owner: "Well, if we each cut production by one unit, the market price would rise to \$52, as the price is given by $p = 100 - y_1 - y_2$. This means my revenue would change from \$50 × 25 to \$52 × 24. That's almost no change – it's a drop of \$2, to be exact." Firm 1 owner: "But your costs would drop by \$25. So your profit would shoot up." Firm 2 owner: "That's right. In short, if we both cut back output by one unit, your profit would rise by \$23, and mine would too!"

Then their caddy speaks up: "I'm an undercover federal agent. You are both under arrest for colluding and conspiring to fix prices in the market for the gizmos you are producing."

As the presence of our fictional caddy/federal agent suggests, it may be illegal for two duopolists, or, more generally, a group of firms in an oligopoly – to get together and make plans such as this. A *cartel* is a group of producers or firms that organize (or conspire) to raise the price of the good they are selling by restricting supply. Under the antitrust laws of the United States and other developed nations, cartels are usually, but not always, illegal. One of the most notorious (but outside the reach of law) cartels of recent history is the Organization of Petroleum Exporting Countries (OPEC). This is an organization of countries whose main purpose is to keep petroleum prices high by controlling production in member countries. Legal cartels in the United States include sports leagues, such as Major League Baseball and the National Football League.

What exactly would our two duopolists do if they took it upon themselves to maximize *joint* or *total profit*, rather than simply letting each firm maximize its own profit, conditional on the other firms's output? As our preceding discussion suggests, they might gain a lot if they both agree to reduce output.

Let $\pi(y_1 + y_2) = \pi_1(y_1, y_2) + \pi_2(y_1, y_2)$ represent total profit for the two firms combined. Then

$$\pi(y_1, y_2) = p(y_1 + y_2)(y_1 + y_2) - C_1(y_1) - C_2(y_2).$$

The first-order conditions for maximizing this function of two variables are:

$$\frac{\partial \pi}{\partial y_1} = p(y_1 + y_2) + \frac{\partial p(y_1 + y_2)}{\partial y_1}(y_1 + y_2) - \frac{dC_1(y_1)}{dy_1} = 0$$

and

$$\frac{\partial \pi}{\partial y_2} = p(y_1 + y_2) + \frac{\partial p(y_1 + y_2)}{\partial y_2}(y_1 + y_2) - \frac{dC_2(y_2)}{dy_2} = 0.$$

Both these conditions must hold for total profit to be maximized, at least for an interior maximum. (The first-order conditions for a maximum at a boundary are slightly different.)

In Example 2, we examine joint profit maximization for the simple duopoly introduced in Example 1.

Example 2. From Example 1, we have

$$\pi(y_1, y_2) = (100 - y_1 - y_2)(y_1 + y_2) - 25y_1 - 25y_2$$
$$= 100y_1 + 100y_2 - y_1^2 - y_2^2 - 2y_1y_2 - 25y_1 - 25y_2.$$

Taking partial derivatives with respect to y_1 and y_2, we get

$$\frac{\partial \pi}{\partial y_1} = 100 - 2y_1 - 2y_2 - 25 = 0$$

or

$$y_1 + y_2 = 37.5.$$

Similarly,

$$\frac{\partial \pi}{\partial y_2} = 100 - 2y_1 - 2y_2 - 25 = 0$$

or

$$y_1 + y_2 = 37.5.$$

The first-order conditions for joint profit maximization are identical, because the two firms have identical cost curves. We conclude that joint profit maximization requires $y_1 + y_2 = 37.5$. For example, each firm could produce $y_i = 37.5/2 = 18.75$. With these levels of output, $\pi_1(y_1, y_2) = \pi_2(y_1, y_2) = (100 - 37.5)18.75 - (25)18.75 = 703.125$. Each firm would be making \$703.125. This is considerably better than the \$625 profit for each firm at the Cournot equilibrium.

In Figure 13.4, we show the joint profit maximization points, the collusion outcomes, for this duopoly example. The bold line is the set of outcomes that maximize joint profits; that is, the set for which $y_1 + y_2 = 37.5$. Note that (18.75, 18.75) is one of many possibilities, but they all involve total output of 37.5 units. Finally, the reader should remember our Figure 13.2 comparison of monopoly, duopoly, and competition. In conjunction with that figure, we determined that a monopoly firm would produce 37.5 units. In Example 2 and Figure 13.4, the two duopolists together are producing a total of 37.5 units. We get the same answer because the duopolists in Example 2 are acting just like a monopolist.

Happily for consumers of their products, cartels and colluding duopolists are inherently unstable. Because a collusion agreement is not a Cournot equilibrium, each firm has an incentive to cheat on the agreement. For instance, to continue our

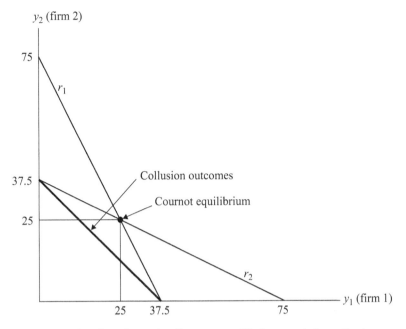

Fig. 13.4. The reaction functions, the Cournot equilibrium, and the collusion outcomes, all based on Example 2. The two duopolists have an incentive to collude.

numerical example, suppose the two duopolists have agreed to be at the joint profit maximizing point (18.75, 18.75). Some time later, the owner of firm 1 wakes up one morning, and says to himself, "The hell with that lawbreaking SOB. If he's going to produce 18.75 units per day, I shall greatly increase my own profits by using my reaction function to figure out what I should produce." The answer is

$$y_1 = r_1(y_2) = 37.5 - y_2/2 = 37.5 - 18.75/2 = 28.125.$$

As soon as the owner of firm 1 figures this out, he produces 28.125 units per day. This raises firm 1's profits from $703.125 per day to $\pi_1(y_1, y_2) = (100 - 28.125 - 18.75)28.125 - 25(28.125) = \$791$ per day, a gain of nearly $88. Shortly thereafter, the owner of Firm 2 realizes he has been duped, so firm 2 reacts to firm 1's output of $y_1 = 28.125$. Firm 2 switches to

$$y_2 = r_2(y_1) = 37.5 - y_1/2 = 37.5 - 28.125/2 = 23.44.$$

And so it goes. After a few rounds of this reacting and re-reacting, the duopoly may end up back at, or near, the Cournot equilibrium of (25, 25).

The point of this discussion is that duopolists – and, more generally, members of cartels – always have incentives to collude, to get together and plot against the public, to figure out how they might reduce output and increase their joint profits. However, having come to some kind of collusion agreement, the duopolists, or the cartel members, will be tempted to cheat. If they do start to cheat, they are likely to drift back toward a Cournot equilibrium. This, then, is the big dynamic: independent profit maximization leads toward the Cournot solution. Then joint profit maximization leads toward the collusion solution. Unless the firms can enforce their collusion agreements, cheating and independent profit maximization lead back toward the Cournot solution. So turns the world of duopoly, or the world of cartels. In the absence of collusion enforcement mechanisms, the likely prediction for a duopoly, or for a cartel, is instability.

$P = y_1 + y_2(y_1)$

13.5 Stackelberg Competition

We now turn to the duopoly model of the German economist Heinrich von Stackelberg. Stackelberg assumed that one of the duopoly firms acts as a Cournot duopolist. That is, it takes the other firm's output as given and fixed, and it chooses its own output based on that assumption. We call this firm the *follower*. Stackelberg assumed that the other firm anticipates this behavior, and maximizes its profit based on the assumption that its rival is a follower. We call this firm the *leader*.

Recall that in the analysis of the Cournot equilibrium, we formally assumed a simultaneous move structure. That is, we assumed the interaction between the two firms was one time only, and simultaneous. Our extensive informal discussion of dynamics involved stories about day-by-day interactions, reactions, and re-reactions, but that discussion was not necessary for the formal definition of the Cournot equilibrium.

To describe the Stackelberg model, we now formally assume that the interaction between the two firms is in two steps, sequentially. In the first step, the leader firm determines its planned output. In the second and final step, the follower firm determines its output. The firms then produce and sell their outputs, at a market price contingent on $y_1 + y_2$, and make their profits.

Here is how it works. We will let firm 1 be the leader firm; its output is y_1. Firm 2 is the follower firm; its output is y_2. The follower firm is the second firm to act. It knows what the leader firm is producing, because that was determined (and announced) at step one. The follower firm acts just like a firm in the Cournot analysis; it takes y_1 as given, and determines what maximizes its own profits given y_1. Therefore, it uses its reaction function to determine its output. That is, $y_2 = r_2(y_1)$.

But firm 1, the leader firm, knows how firm 2, the follower firm, behaves. That is, firm 1 anticipates that firm 2 will choose y_2 by using its reaction function formula. Therefore, firm 1 can use its knowledge of firm 2's behavior, and use the fact that it goes first and firm 2 goes second. It does this in a simple way: it just substitutes $r_2(y_1)$ for y_2 in its own profit function. This gets rid of the y_2 terms; firm 1's profit is now simply a function of y_1, and firm 1 simply chooses y_1 to maximize profits.

Formally, firm 1's profit is $\pi_1(y_1, y_2) = p(y_1 + y_2)y_1 - C_1(y_1)$. Substituting $r_2(y_1)$ for y_2 makes this a function of one variable only:

$$\pi_1(y_1) = p(y_1 + r_2(y_1))y_1 - C_1(y_1).$$

The first-order condition for profit maximization is to set the derivative of profit with respect to y_1 equal to zero. This gives

$$\frac{d\pi_1(y_1)}{dy_1} = p(y_1 + r_2(y_1)) + y_1 \frac{dp}{dy}\left(1 + \frac{dr_2(y_1)}{dy_1}\right) - MC_1(y_1) = 0.$$

Let us apply the result to Example 1. Recall that in that example, $p(y) = 100 - y = 100 - y_1 - y_2$, $C_1(y_1) = 25y_1$, and $r_2(y_1) = 37.5 - y_1/2$. Therefore, $\frac{dp}{dy} = -1$, and $\frac{dr_2(y_1)}{dy_1} = -1/2$. Plugging into the first-order condition then gives

$$(100 - y_1 - (37.5 - y_1/2)) - y_1(1 - 1/2) - 25 = 0. \qquad)_1 \text{ already maximized.}$$

This gives $y_1 = 37.5$. Putting this into the follower's reaction function gives

$$y_2 = r_2(y_1) = 37.5 - 37.5/2 = 18.75.$$

We know that a Stackelberg leader firm will never end up with a profit level lower than what it gets at the Cournot equilibrium. One option always available to the leader is to announce its Cournot output, to which the follower would respond with its own Cournot output. This would produce the Cournot profits for the two firms.

Figure 13.5 shows the Cournot equilibrium, the collusion outcomes, and the Stackelberg equilibrium for the numerical example we have been using throughout this chapter.

13.6 Bertrand Competition

We now turn to the model developed by the mathematician Joseph Louis François Bertrand. Whereas the Cournot model of duopoly assumes that each of the two firms decides on what *quantity* to produce, the Bertrand model assumes that each firm decides on what *price* to charge. As we shall see, this approach can lead to a very interesting but somewhat unrealistic model, with implications that are very different from the implications of the Cournot model, or it can lead to a model that is perhaps more realistic than Cournot's, but with implications similar to Cournot's. This difference arises because we can develop the Bertrand analysis in either of two ways:

(1) We can assume, as we assumed for the Cournot model, that the two firms are producing exactly the same good. That is, whether produced by firm 1 or firm 2, a unit of the good is a unit of the good, as far as the buyers are concerned. This is the property of *homogeneity*. Commodities such as electricity, oil, metals, or wheat are homogeneous; whether produced by firm 1 or firm 2, a gallon of fuel oil is a gallon of fuel oil. For a

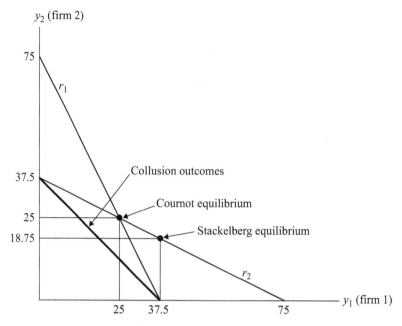

Fig. 13.5. The reaction functions, the Cournot equilibrium, the collusion outcomes, and the Stackelberg equilibrium, all based on Example 1.

homogeneous good being produced and sold by two firms, there can be only one price; if firm 1 tries to sell it at a slightly higher price than firm 2, its sales drop to zero.

(2) Alternatively, we can assume that the two firms produce goods that are similar but slightly different, or *differentiated*. Think of Coke and Pepsi, McDonald's and Burger King, Bud Light and Miller Lite, or Schick and Gillette. If the two firms produce goods that are differentiated, they can charge different prices, and in fact they commonly do so. Each is likely to claim that its good is both better *and* less expensive.

Homogeneous Goods Case

Let us now assume that firms 1 and 2 produce exactly the same good. For simplicity, we assume that the two firms have identical constant marginal cost functions. Let MC represent the marginal cost of producing a unit of the good, and let MC be the same for both firms and constant over all output levels. Let y_1 and y_2 represent the production levels of the two firms. We assume the firms set prices p_1 and p_2, and then sell their output to meet demand. Because the good is homogeneous, if firm i sets a lower price than firm j, then all the customers will buy from firm i. This implies that in any equilibrium at which both firms are operating, we must have $p_1 = p_2 = p$, where p is the (single) market price. If there is one price p, the market demand curve is given by a function $y = y(p)$. We assume that if both firms are charging the same price p, they will split the market demand equally— each will sell $y_1 = y_2 = y(p)/2$ units of the good.

This model cannot be solved using standard calculus techniques. This is because although the function $y(p)$ is well behaved, firm i's demand function $y_i(p_i)$ is not. It has a sharp discontinuity when p_i equals p_j. If $p_i < p_j$, demand for firm i is $y(p_i)$; if $p_i = p_j$, demand for firm i is $y(p_i)/2$; and if $p_i > p_j$, demand for firm i is zero.

Because we cannot use standard calculus techniques, we must reason along more abstract lines. Recall our definition of a Cournot equilibrium from Section 13.2. In a model in which the two duopolists are reacting to each other by setting quantities, a Cournot equilibrium is a pair of output levels y_1^* and y_2^* that are consistent, in the sense that each firm i is maximizing its profit at y_i^*, subject to what the other firm j has chosen, y_j^*. Let us now define an equilibrium in a similar way, but for the current model in which the two duopolists are reacting to each other by setting prices. A *Bertrand equilibrium* is a pair of prices p_1^* and p_2^* that are consistent, in the sense that each firm i is maximizing its profit with the choice of p_i^*, subject to what the other firm j has chosen, p_j^*.

What can we say about a Bertrand equilibrium in the homogeneous goods case? Let (p_1^*, p_2^*) represent the equilibrium prices and let (y_1^*, y_2^*) the corresponding equilibrium quantities. We can conclude the following:

(1) The firms must be charging the same price. That is, $p_1^* = p_2^* = p^*$. Suppose, to the contrary, that they are charging different prices, and without loss of generality, assume $p_1^* < p_2^*$. Then firm 1 is selling a positive quantity of the good, and firm 2 is selling nothing.

   (a) If $p_1^* < MC$, then firm 1 has negative profits and would be better off shutting down. Therefore, this cannot be an equilibrium.

   (b) If $p_1^* = MC$, firm 1 is making \$0 on each unit it produces and sells. It could increase its price somewhat, while keeping it below p_2^* and make positive amounts on all the units it sells. (It would sell fewer units, but it would make money on each one.) Therefore, this cannot be an equilibrium.

   (c) If $p_1^* > MC$, firm 1 is making positive profits on all the units it produces and sells. If this were the case, however, firm 2 would gain by entering the market with a price strictly between MC and p_1^*, taking all of firm 1's customers away. Therefore, this cannot be an equilibrium either.

   We have established that $p_1^* \neq p_2^*$ implies that we cannot have a Bertrand equilibrium. Therefore, at a Bertrand equilibrium, we must have $p_1^* = p_2^* = p^*$. Because we have assumed that demand is split equally between the two firms when their prices are the same, $y_1^* = y_2^* = y(p^*)/2$.

(2) Marginal cost cannot be less than price; that is, $MC < p^*$ cannot hold. Here is why. Suppose the inequality held. Assume for concreteness that $MC = 25$ and that $p_1^* = p_2^* = p^* = 26$. Then either firm, say, firm 1, could shave its price to $p_1 = 25.99$. By doing so, it would steal away all of firm 2's customers (half of the total market) and make almost a dollar profit on each of those sales, while giving up a penny's profit on each of the sales it already had (half of the total market). Its profits would obviously go

way up. This contradicts our assumption that firm 1 is choosing a price that maximizes its profit subject to what firm 2 has chosen.

(3) Marginal cost cannot be greater than price; that is, $MC > p^*$ cannot hold. With constant marginal costs, for either firm i, $MC > p^* = p_i^*$ would imply negative profits, and the firm would opt to go out of business, rather than sell y_i^* at a price of p^*.

(4) For both firms, marginal cost equals price; that is, $MC = p^* = p_1^* = p_2^*$. This obviously follows from (2) and (3).

We conclude that in a Bertrand equilibrium, in the homogeneous good case, under the assumptions we have made, firms 1 and 2 will charge the same price, and the price will be equal to marginal cost. But this means that the duopoly market, in the Bertrand model with a homogeneous good, looks just like a competitive market. In particular, there is no inefficiency (no loss of social surplus) in the duopoly market.

Differentiated Goods Case

Now we assume that firms 1 and 2 produce goods that are differentiated – similar, but not identical. (Think of Coke and Pepsi.) We continue to let y_1 and y_2 represent the outputs of the two firms, and p_1 and p_2 represent the prices. Because the goods are different, $p_i < p_j$ does not imply that firm j's sales will drop to zero, and the firms will not be forced to charge the same price in equilibrium.

Now the demand functions for each of the two firms depend on the two prices: $y_1 = y_1(p_1, p_2)$ and $y_2 = y_2(p_1, p_2)$. For firm i's demand function y_i, the partial derivative with respect to p_i is assumed to be negative (as i raises its price, demand for i's good falls), but the partial derivative with respect to p_j is positive (as i's competitor j raises its price, demand for i's good rises).

Firm 1's profit is

$$\pi_1(p_1, p_2) = p_1 y_1(p_1, p_2) - C_1(y_1(p_1, p_2)),$$

and firm 2's profit is

$$\pi_2(p_1, p_2) = p_2 y_2(p_1, p_2) - C_2(y_2(p_1, p_2))$$

We write these as functions of the two prices (p_1, p_2) because each firm chooses its own price, rather than its own quantity as in the Cournot model. Firm 1 chooses p_1 to maximize $\pi_1(p_1, p_2)$, taking p_2 as given and fixed; firm 2 chooses p_2 to maximize $\pi_2(p_1, p_2)$, taking p_1 as given and fixed.

Firm 1's first-order condition is

$$\frac{\partial \pi_1}{\partial p_1} = y_1(p_1, p_2) + \frac{\partial y_1(p_1, p_2)}{\partial p_1} p_1 - \frac{dC_1(y_1)}{dy_1} \frac{\partial y_1(p_1, p_2)}{\partial p_1} = 0.$$

We can write this more compactly as

$$\frac{\partial \pi_1}{\partial p_1} = y_1 + \frac{\partial y_1}{\partial p_1} p_1 - MC_1 \frac{\partial y_1}{\partial p_1} = 0.$$

Similarly, firm 2's first-order condition is

$$\frac{\partial \pi_2}{\partial p_2} = y_2 + \frac{\partial y_2}{\partial p_2} p_2 - MC_2 \frac{\partial y_2}{\partial p_2} = 0.$$

Recall that when we analyzed the Cournot model, we used the two firms' first-order conditions to derive reaction functions. We can do the same here, using firm i's first-order condition to find a reaction function that shows firm i's profit-maximizing price as a function of firm j's price: $p_i = r_i(p_j)$.

To find a Bertrand equilibrium, we look for a pair of prices p_1^* and p_2^* that are consistent in the sense that each firm i is maximizing its profit with the choice of p_i^*, subject to what the other firm j has chosen, p_j^*. We will again let y_1^* and y_2^* represent the corresponding equilibrium quantities. In the differentiated goods case, we use the first-order conditions for profit maximization (or the reaction functions) to find the equilibrium. We will illustrate with an example soon. Before we do, however, let us use firm 1's reaction function to show that in the differentiated goods Bertrand model (unlike the homogeneous good Bertrand model), at equilibrium, the price will be greater than marginal cost.

Here is why. At the equilibrium, firm 1's first-order condition must be satisfied, which gives

$$y_1^* + \frac{\partial y_1}{\partial p_1} p \qquad \cdots \frac{\partial y_1}{\partial p_1} = 0.$$

Rearranging gives

$$y_1^* = $$

But y_1^* is positive, $\frac{\partial y_1}{\partial p_1}$ is negative

That is, in the differentiated goods
than marginal cost for firm 1, a
goods case, a Bertrand equil
Cournot equilibrium discusse

Example 3. We again assume
and so $MC_1 = MC_2 = 25.$
2 are

y

(a) Assume firm 1 is a Stack
the Stackelberg equilibrium
equilibrium profit levels.

(b) What would happen if both firms be

Recall from Exa
the profit levels at th

$y_1 = $

the C

and

$$y_2(p_1, p_2) = 50 - p_2 + p_1/2.$$

Firm 1 wants to choose p_1 to maximize

$$\pi_1(p_1, p_2) = p_1\underbrace{(50 - p_1 + p_2/2)}_{y_1} - 25\underbrace{(50 - p_1 + p_2/2)}_{y_1},$$

taking p_2 as given. The first-order condition gives firm 1's reaction function,

$$p_1 = r_1(p_2) = 75/2 + p_2/4.$$

Similarly, firm 2 wants to choose p_2 to maximize

$$\pi_2(p_1, p_2) = p_2\underbrace{(50 - p_2 + p_1/2)}_{y_2} - 25\underbrace{(50 - p_2 + p_1/2)}_{y_2}.$$

The first-order condition leads to firm 2's reaction function,

$$p_2 = r_2(p_1) = 75/2 + p_1/4.$$

Solving the two reaction functions (or the two first-order conditions) simultaneously gives the Bertrand equilibrium prices of $p_1^* = 50$ and $p_2^* = 50$. The equilibrium quantities are $y_1^* = 25$ and $y_1^* = 25$. Equilibrium profit levels are easily calculated. For firm 1,

$$\pi(p_1^*, p_2^*) = p_1^* y_1^* - C_1(y_1^*) = 50 \times 25 - 25 \times 25 = 625,$$

and similarly for firm 2. Figure 13.6 shows the reaction functions and the equilibrium prices for Example 3.

13.7 A Solved Problem

The Problem

Recall the inverse demand function assumed in Example 1:

$$p(y_1 + y_2) = 100 - y_1 - y_2.$$

The cost functions in that example were $C_1(y_1) = 25y_1$ and $C_2(y_2) = 25y_2$. To find Cournot equilibrium, we used the reaction functions of firms 1 and 2:

$$r_1(y_2) = 37.5 - y_2/2, \qquad \text{and} \qquad y_2 = r_2(y_1) = 37.5 - y_1/2.$$

Example 1 that the Cournot equilibrium was $(y_1^*, y_2^*) = (25, 25)$, and Cournot equilibrium were $(\pi_1, \pi_2) = (625, 625)$.

Stackelberg leader, and firm 2 is a Stackelberg follower. Calculate price and quantities. In addition, find the Stackelberg

believed that they were Stackelberg leaders?

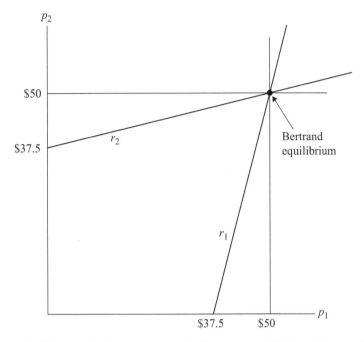

Fig. 13.6. The reaction functions and the Bertrand equilibrium in Example 3.

The Solution

(a) If firm 1 is a Stackelberg leader and firm 2 is a Stackelberg follower, firm 2 acts like a standard Cournot firm; it takes firm 1's output y_1 as given and fixed and chooses its own output in response. In other words, it chooses y_2 to maximize $\pi_2(y_1, y_2)$, under the assumption that y_1 is constant. This means that it derives and uses its reaction function $y_2 = r_2(y_1) = 37.5 - y_1/2$. Firm 1, on the other hand, knows that y_2 is not fixed; in fact, firm 1 knows exactly how firm 2 chooses y_2 based on y_1. In other words, firm 1 knows firm 2's reaction function and exploits that knowledge.

We can now write firm 1's profit function as

$$\pi_1(y_1, y_2) = p(y_1 + y_2)y_1 - C_1(y_1) = p(y_1 + r_2(y_1))y_1 - C_1(y_1)$$
$$= (100 - y_1 - r_2(y_1))y_1 - 25y_1.$$

The next step is to substitute for $r_2(y_1)$, using $r_2(y_1) = 37.5 - y_1/2$. After a little minor algebra and some rearranging, we get $\pi_1(y_1) = 37.5y_1 - y_1^2/2$. We differentiate this function, set the result equal to zero, and solve, which produces $y_1^* = 37.5$. The * denotes the Stackelberg equilibrium quantity for firm 1, the leader firm. Plugging y_1^* into firm 2's reaction function will allow us to solve for the follower firm's Stackelberg equilibrium quantity: $y_2^* = 37.5 - y_1^*/2 = 18.75$.

To find the Stackelberg equilibrium price, we insert y_1^* and y_2^* into the inverse demand function, which gives $p^* = 100 - 37.5 - 18.75 = 43.75$. Profit levels are given by $\pi_1^* = p^*y_1^* - 25y_1^* = (p^* - 25)y_1^* = (43.75 - 25)37.5 = 703.13$. Similarly, $\pi_2^* = (p^* - 25)y_2^* = (43.75 - 25)18.75 = 351.56$.

(b) If firm 1 is a Stackelberg leader, it knows firm 2's reaction function and takes advantage of it. In part (a), we found that this line of reasoning would lead firm 1 to choose $y_1^* = 37.5$. Let us now assume that firm 2 also acts as a Stackelberg leader. It figures out firm 1's reaction function $y_1 = r_1(y_2) = 37.5 - y_2/2$, plugs this into its own profit function $\pi_2 = (100 - r_1(y_2) - p_2)y_2 - C_2(y_2)$, and maximizes, which leads to $y_2^* = 37.5$. Now the market price would be $p^* = 100 - 37.5 - 37.5 = 25$ and the profit level for each firm is $\pi_i^* = (25 - 25)37.5 = 0$. In their quest for leadership, they end up with nothing.

This situation, however, is quite peculiar in that firm 1 believes firm 2 is choosing its output according to its reaction function, and firm 2 believes firm 1 is choosing its output according to its reaction function. But both beliefs are false. (We could call this situation a Stackelberg "disequilibrium.")

Exercises

1. The Corleone and Chung families are the only providers of good h in the United States. The market demand for good h is $h = 1{,}200 - 20p$. The costs of production for each of them are represented by the cost functions $C_1(h_1) = 10h_1$ and $C_2(h_2) = 20h_2$, respectively. Suppose both families must choose their output levels simultaneously.
   (a) Derive their reaction functions.
   (b) Calculate the Cournot equilibrium in this market. Indicate output levels, market price, and individual profits.

2. Consider the Corleone and Chung families from Question 1. Suppose the two families sign an agreement to restrict the amount of good h in the market. By doing this, market price and profits will increase. Suppose the agreement specifies that given the cost differential, Corleone will receive 3/5 of the total profits and Chung will receive 2/5.
   (a) Find the solution to this collusion problem. Indicate individual outputs, market price, total profits, and individual profits.
   (b) Does either family have an incentive to break the agreement? Who does, and why? **Hint**: Remember that the first-order conditions obtained from differentiation give an interior solution. If the first-order conditions do not yield a solution, try cases in which one of the firms produces zero.

3. MBI and Pear are the only two producers of computers. MBI started producing computers earlier than Pear. MBI's costs of production are given by $C_1(y_1) = y_1^2$. Pear's cost function is $C_2(y_2) = 5y_2$. The national demand for computers is $y = 10^6 - 10^5 p$.
   (a) Calculate the Stackelberg equilibrium in which MBI is the leader in this market. Indicate output levels, market price, and the profits of each firm.
   (b) Suppose that both firms enter this market at the same time. Calculate the Cournot equilibrium and compare it to the situation in part (a).

4. Reuben and Simeon are duopolists that produce jeans in a differentiated goods market. The market demand for Reuben's jeans is $y_1 = 80 - p_1 + \frac{1}{2}p_2$, whereas the market demand for Simeon's jeans is $y_2 = 160 - p_2 + \frac{1}{2}p_1$. Reuben's cost function is $C_1(y_1) = 80y_1$, whereas Simeon's cost function is $C_2(y_2) = 160y_2$.
   (a) Calculate the Bertrand equilibrium in this market. Indicate each firm's price, output level, and profits.
   (b) Find prices and output levels that would maximize joint profits, and calculate the maximum joint profits.

Cournot

Collusion

Bertrand

5. Laban and Jacob are sheep farmers in a differentiated goods market. The market demand for Laban's sheep wool is $y_1 = 34 - p_1 + \frac{1}{3}p_2$, whereas the market demand for Jacob's sheep wool is $y_2 = 40 - p_2 + \frac{1}{2}p_1$. Laban's cost function is $C_1(y_1) = 24y_1$, whereas Jacob's cost function is $C_2(y_2) = 20y_2$. They compete with each other through their choices of price.

    (a) Calculate the equilibrium in which Laban is the price leader in this market, and Jacob is the price follower. Indicate prices, output levels, and individual profits.

    (b) How do prices, output levels, and individual profits change if Jacob is the price leader in this market, and Laban is the price follower?

6. Compare the social welfare properties of the following models of duopoly behavior: simultaneous quantity setting (Cournot), quantity leadership (Stackelberg), simultaneous price setting (Bertrand, both homogeneous goods and differentiated goods cases), price leadership, and collusion. Which model results in the highest output? The lowest output? The highest price? The lowest price?

Chapter 14

Game Theory

14.1 Introduction

In the last chapter, we discussed duopoly markets in which two firms compete to sell a product. In such markets, the firms behave strategically; each firm must think about what the other firm is doing in order to decide what it should do itself. The theory of duopoly was originally developed in the nineteenth century, but it led to the theory of games in the twentieth century. The first major book in game theory, published in 1944, was *Theory of Games and Economic Behavior*, by John von Neumann (1903–1957) and Oskar Morgenstern (1902–1977). We will return to the contributions of Von Neumann and Morgenstern in Chapter 19, on uncertainty and expected utility.

A group of people (or teams, firms, armies, or countries) are in a *game* if their decision problems are interdependent, in the sense that the actions that all of them take influence the outcomes for everyone. *Game theory* is the study of games; it can also be called *interactive decision theory*. Many real-life interactions can be viewed as games. Obviously football, soccer, and baseball games are games. But so are the interactions of duopolists, the political campaigns between parties before an election, and the interactions of armed forces and countries. Even some interactions between animal or plant species in nature can be modeled as games. In fact, game theory has been used in many different fields in recent decades, including economics, political science, psychology, sociology, computer science, and biology.

This brief chapter is not meant to replace a formal course in game theory; it is only an introduction. The general emphasis is on how strategic behavior affects the interactions among rational players in a game. We provide some basic definitions, and we discuss a number of well-known simple examples. We start with a description of the *prisoners' dilemma* game, where we will introduce the idea of a *dominant strategy equilibrium*. We briefly discuss *repeated games* in the prisoners' dilemma context, as well as *tit-for-tat strategies*. Then we describe the *battle of the sexes* game, and introduce the concept of *Nash equilibrium*. We discuss the possibilities of there being multiple Nash equilibria, or no (pure strategy) Nash equilibria, and we discuss the idea of mixed strategy equilibria. We then present an *expanded battle of the sexes* game, and we see that in game theory, an expansion of choices may make players worse off instead of better off. At the end of the chapter, we describe *sequential move games*, and we briefly discuss *threats*.

14.2 The Prisoners' Dilemma, and the Idea of Dominant Strategy Equilibrium

The most well-known example in game theory is the *prisoners' dilemma*. It was developed around 1950 by Merrill M. Flood (1908–1991) and Melvin Dresher (1911–1992) of the RAND Corporation. It was so named by Albert W. Tucker (1905–1995), a Princeton University mathematics professor.

Consider the following. A crime is committed. The police arrive at the scene and arrest two suspects. Each suspect is taken to the police station for interrogation, and each is placed in separate cells. The cells are cold and nasty. The police interrogate them separately, and without any lawyers present. A police officer tells each one: "You can keep your mouth shut and refuse to testify. Or, you can confess and testify at trial."

We use some special and potentially confusing terminology to describe this choice. If a suspect refuses to testify, we say that he has chosen to *cooperate* with his fellow suspect. If a suspect confesses and testifies at trial, we say that he has chosen to *defect* from his fellow suspect. The reader will need to remember that to "cooperate" means to cooperate *with the other suspect*, not with the police, and also to remember that to "defect" means to defect *from the other suspect*.

The officer goes on: "If both of you refuse to testify, we will be able to convict you only on a minor charge, which will result in a sentence of six months in prison for each of you. If both of you confess and testify, you will each get five years in prison. If one of you refuses to testify (i.e., "cooperates") while the other confesses and testifies (i.e., "defects"), the one who testifies will go free, and the one who refuses to testify will get a full ten years in prison."

The officer concludes: "That's what we're offering you, you lowlife hooligan. Think it over. We'll be back tomorrow to hear what you have to say."

We now consider this question: given this information, how should a rational suspect behave? Should the suspects "cooperate" with each other (and tell the police nothing) or should they "defect" from each other (and confess)?

Table 14.1 shows the prisoners' dilemma game. In game theory, the people playing the game are called *players*, so we now refer to our suspects as players. Player 1 chooses the rows in the table, and player 2 chooses the columns. Each of them has two possible actions to choose: "Cooperate" or "Defect." Each of the four

Table 14.1. *The prisoners' dilemma*

		Player 2	
		Cooperate	Defect
Player 1	Cooperate	6 months, 6 months	10 years, None
	Defect	None, 10 years	5 years, 5 years

action combinations results in payoffs to each player, in the form of prison time to be served. The outcomes are shown as the vectors in the cells of Table 14.1. The first entry is always the outcome for player 1, and the second is always the outcome for player 2. For instance, if player 1 defects while player 2 cooperates (bottom row, left column of the table), prison time for player 1 is None, and prison time for player 2 is 10 years. Note that these outcomes are "bads" rather than "goods"; each player wants to *minimize* his outcome.

Each suspect wants to minimize his own jail time. But each must think about what the other suspect will do.

Let us now analyze the problem carefully. Here is how player 1 thinks about the game. He considers what player 2 might do. If player 2 cooperates, they are in the first column of the table. In this case, player 1 gets 6 months if he cooperates (first row), and no prison time if he defects (second row). Therefore, if player 2 cooperates, player 1 will defect. On the other hand, if player 2 defects, they are in the second column of the table. In this case, player 1 gets 10 years if he cooperates (first row), and 5 years if he defects (second row). Therefore if player 2 defects, player 1 will defect.

We now realize that whatever action player 2 chooses, player 1 will want to defect. We leave it to the reader to do the same type of analysis for player 2, whose payoffs are the second entries in each of the payoff vectors. When you do this, you will conclude that player 2 will want to defect, whatever action player 1 chooses.

In a game like this, actions that players might take are called *strategies*. A *dominant strategy* is a strategy that is optimal for a player, no matter what strategy the other player is choosing. In the prisoners' dilemma, the best thing for player 1 to do is to defect, no matter what player 2 might do. Therefore, "Defect" is a dominant strategy for player 1. Similarly, "Defect" is a dominant strategy for player 2. When each strategy in a pair of strategies is dominant for the player choosing it, the pair is called a *dominant strategy equilibrium* or a *solution in dominant strategies*. We now know that (Defect, Defect) is a dominant strategy equilibrium in the prisoners' dilemma. Rational players should choose dominant strategies if they exist; they clearly make sense, because a dominant strategy is the best for a player no matter what the other player is doing.

We conclude that the two suspects should both confess to the police, or defect from each other. Therefore, they will each end up with a prison sentence of 5 years. Between the two of them, the total will be 10 years of prison. But this outcome is very peculiar, because if they had both chosen to keep their mouths shut, or cooperate with each other, they would have ended up with prison sentences of only 6 months each, and a total of 1 year between the two of them.

In Chapter 11 on perfectly competitive markets, we introduced the reader to Adam Smith's free market philosophy – his invisible hand theory. In brief, this is the theory that if the market is allowed to operate freely, with each consumer seeking to maximize his own utility and each firm seeking to maximize its own profits, with each of the players in the grand market game ignoring the welfare of all the others and doing the best it can for itself, the outcome will actually be best for society. That is, self-interested consumers and firms in a competitive market will end up maximizing social surplus, the sum of consumers' and producers' surplus.

Now note the dramatically different conclusion in the prisoners' dilemma, however. In this game, in which we are focusing on the outcomes for the two suspects and ignoring the welfare of the police officers, the victims of the original crime, and the rest of society, the obvious and simple measure of social welfare for our two suspects is -1 times the sum of the two prison sentences. (We need the -1 because prison time is a "bad," not a "good.") Our preceding analysis, however, indicates that each player, pursuing his own self-interest, maximizing his own welfare by minimizing his years in prison, will choose "Defect." They will end up with a total of 10 years of prison between the two of them. If they had gotten together and determined what would be best for them, and if they had had some way to enforce their agreement, they would have decided on (Cooperate, Cooperate) instead. That would have resulted in a total of 1 year of prison between the two of them. However, (Cooperate, Cooperate) is not an equilibrium in the prisoners' dilemma, and even if they had agreed to keep silent before they were arrested by the police, they would likely have confessed anyway, because of the ever-present incentive to break such an agreement.

The moral of the story is important. In a game, because of the strategic interactions, pursuing individual self-interest may be inconsistent with maximizing social welfare. This matters in evaluating the performance of market institutions in these contexts. We saw in our analysis of duopoly in Chapter 13 that the Cournot equilibrium would not maximize the joint profits of the two duopolists. There are many other examples in which strategic interactions result in individual players' pursuit of private gains, producing a loss to the group of players. Famous examples include international arms races and overutilization of natural resources such as fisheries. In these examples, dominant strategies lead to socially undesirable outcomes. The prisoners' dilemma clearly illustrates the problem – the tension that may exist between self-interest and cooperation. These are two of the key forces in game theory and in reality.

14.3 Prisoners' Dilemma Complications: Experimental Evidence and Repeated Games

We have argued that (Defect, Defect) is a dominant strategy equilibrium in the prisoners' dilemma game. However, social scientists have performed experiments to see whether people actually choose the "defect" strategy. (These people are usually university students paid to be experimental subjects in a lab setting.) Often they do not; they choose "Cooperate" instead. There are many reasons why this might happen. Subjects may not understand the game, or they simply may not act in the "rational" way that game theorists say they should act. For instance, they might choose "Cooperate" because they believe cooperating is morally preferable to defecting, no matter what the payoffs are. Perhaps game theory is wrong in the sense that it does not correspond to how people actually behave. Another possibility is that the game theory model described previously is incomplete. Perhaps we have left something out. This possibility of incompleteness has led some game theorists to expand the model. One of the most important expansions is the idea of repeated games.

A one-shot game is a game that is played once. The players choose their strategies, there is an outcome, and there are payoffs, and that is that. A repeated game is played over and over. The players choose their strategies, there is an outcome, and there are payoffs. Then they do it again. And again. And perhaps again. A repeated game might repeat n times, where n is known beforehand, or it might repeat n times, where n is not known beforehand, or it might repeat an infinite number of times.

Now, suppose our prisoners' dilemma is a repeated game and the players do not know n, but think that n might be large. Then a player may choose "Cooperate," knowing it may cost him in the short run (the current game), but believing that if he chooses "Cooperate," the other player will be more likely to also choose "Cooperate" in future plays of the game. Similarly, if one player chooses "Defect" in the current game, he may fear that the other player will punish him by defecting in the future. Under certain conditions – if future payoffs matter enough – (Cooperate, Cooperate) is an equilibrium in the repeated prisoners' dilemma. The moral of the story is that we may see cooperation in situations such as the prisoners' dilemma, in which simple game theory indicates we should see defection, not because people are good-hearted or virtuous, but because of a dynamic social contract: "Let's cooperate with each other now and get good payoffs; for if we don't, in future periods we'll punish each other and get bad payoffs."

Players may also develop retaliatory repeated game strategies affecting their choices within a game, contingent on what has happened in prior periods in the game. One of the simplest is called "tit for tat." The *tit for tat* repeated game strategy works like this: In the first period of the game, the player chooses "Cooperate." In any subsequent period, the player looks at his opponent's action in the previous period of the game. If the opponent chose "Cooperate" in the previous period, then the player chooses "Cooperate" in the current period; if the opponent chose "Defect" in the previous period, then the player chooses "Defect" in the current period. In short, the player matches what his opponent did in the last period of the game. This kind of repeated game strategy might be described as "crazy" or "tough," but it might also be very effective. Under certain conditions, it can be shown that if player 1 plays tit for tat, there may be an equilibrium in which both players are choosing "Cooperate" most of the time. One lesson here is that it may sometimes be in the interest of people to have reputations as being crazy or tough in order to induce beneficial changes in the behavior of others.

The moral of this story is that game theory can sometimes improve its predictions in explaining real-world phenomena by expanding its models.

14.4 The Battle of the Sexes, and the Idea of Nash Equilibrium

Most games are not as simple to solve as the prisoners' dilemma. That is, in most strategic situations, players do not have dominant strategies. In general, what each player will want to do will depend on what the other players are doing. Consequently, each player's conjectures about the behavior of the other players are crucial for determining his own behavior. For example, remember the first duopoly game of the last chapter, and its solution, the Cournot equilibrium (y_1^*, y_2^*). (Here y_1^* is firm 1's output, and y_2^* is firm 2's.) It is obvious that the Cournot equilibrium is not a dominant strategy equilibrium. If firm 2 decided to flood the market with product and drive the price down to zero, for example, firm 1 would not choose y_1^*. Rather, firm 1 would produce zero and save its production costs. This shows that producing y_1^* is not a dominant strategy for firm 1. The same argument applies to firm 2.

We will now analyze a new game, the *battle of the sexes*. This was first studied by R. Duncan Luce (1925–) and Howard Raiffa (1924–), in their 1957 book *Games and Decisions: Introduction and Critical Survey*.

A young woman (player 1) and her boyfriend (player 2) are out on Saturday night, driving in their own cars, on their way to meet each other for an evening together. As this game was invented long before cell phones were around, they cannot communicate with each other. They had talked about two options previously: a football game and an opera performance. But neither one of them can recall which option they had decided on. They like each other very much, and both would hate to spend the evening without the other. The young woman likes opera much better than football, but her boyfriend likes football better than opera. If the woman ends up at the opera with her boyfriend, her payoff is 3. But her payoff is 0 if she ends

Table 14.2. *The battle of the sexes*

		2. Man	
		Football	Opera
1. Woman	Football	1, 3	0, 0
	Opera	0, 0	3, 1

up at the opera without him. If the woman ends up at the football game with her boyfriend, her payoff is 1. But her payoff is 0 if she ends up at the football game without him. Similarly for the young man, if he ends up at the football game with her, his payoff is 3; if he ends up at the opera with her, his payoff is 1; and if he ends up at either place without her, his payoff is 0.

Table 14.2 shows the game. The rows of the table are the woman's possible strategies, and the columns are the man's. In other words, the woman chooses the row, and the man chooses the column. Each vector in each cell of the table shows the payoffs to the two players. For instance, if both of them choose football, they are in the first row, first column cell of the table. The payoff to the woman is then 1, and the payoff to the man is 3. Note that these payoffs, unlike the payoffs in the prisoners' dilemma game, are "goods" rather than "bads"; each player want to maximize rather than minimize her/his outcome.

What predictions can we make about this game? First of all, note that there are no dominant strategies. For either player, "Football" is better if she/he expects the other to choose "Football," but "Opera" is better if she/he expects the other to choose "Opera."

The standard equilibrium concept in the battle of the sexes is the Nash equilibrium, named for the famous twentieth-century economist, mathematician, and game theorist John Nash (1928–). A *Nash equilibrium* is a pair of strategies, one for each player, such that player 1's strategy is the best for her given player 2's strategy, and such that player 2's strategy is the best for him given player 1's strategy. Each player's strategy is a best response to the other's.

The reader should note that a Cournot equilibrium in a duopoly model is a Nash equilibrium, and a Bertrand equilibrium in a duopoly model is also a Nash equilibrium in the corresponding duopoly game. Moreover, any dominant strategy equilibrium is a Nash equilibrium. For example, (Defect, Defect) in the prisoners' dilemma is also a Nash equilibrium. This is because a dominant strategy for a player is always a best response for that player; therefore, it is the best response when his opponent is playing his dominant strategy. But the reverse does not hold, and there will generally be Nash equilibria in a game that are not dominant strategy equilibria. Remember that there are no dominant strategies in our battle of the sexes, and therefore no dominant strategy equilibria. What about the existence of Nash equilibria in the battle of the sexes game?

There are two Nash equilibria in the battle of the sexes: (Football, Football) with payoffs (1,3), and (Opera, Opera) with payoffs (3,1). Here is why (Football, Football) is a Nash equilibrium. (The argument for (Opera, Opera) is entirely symmetric.) If player 1 expects player 2 to drive to the football game, that is what she will choose as well, because a payoff of 1 is greater than a payoff of 0. And if player 2 expects player 1 to drive to the football game, that is what he will choose as well, because a payoff of 3 is greater than a payoff of 0.

Each Nash equilibrium is a theory of how the game should be played, consistent with the assumed rationality of the players and the mutual knowledge of that rationality. It seems plausible to predict that the woman and her boyfriend will end up at a Nash equilibrium in this game, or at least that they *ought to* end up at a Nash equilibrium. It is certainly the case that at the planning stages of the game, when the players are talking to each other about going to a football game or going to the opera, they are only considering going to the same event together. That is, these rational players, in planning this game, would agree that the non-Nash outcomes are undesirable, and that the Nash equilibria, even though one is inferior to the other in each player's eyes, are reasonable in the sense that neither player would want to break an agreement to be at such an outcome.

14.5 Battle of the Sexes Complications: Multiple or No Nash Equilibria, and Mixed Strategies

From the battle of the sexes, we see that there may be multiple Nash equilibria. Therefore, the Nash equilibrium concept may have some predictive power – (Football, Football) and (Opera, Opera) seem more likely than (Football, Opera) and (Opera, Football) – but it may not point to a unique outcome.

Moreover, in this game, the players may end up at a non-Nash outcome by accident, if not by intent. That is, even though our young woman and her boyfriend know exactly what their preferences are, and are completely informed about Table 14.2 and the Nash equilibria in that table, they just do not remember which event they had planned to attend, and they have no cell phones with which to communicate. Therefore, they may end up apart, even though their feelings toward each other, and the power of Nash reasoning, say they should be together.

Things may get even trickier. There may be no equilibria of the kind we have been describing. Consider the following *strangely modified battle of the sexes*: Let the two players have the same payoffs as before when they are coordinated. That is, when they choose (Football, Football) and (Opera, Opera), the payoffs are (1, 3) and (3, 1), respectively. But when they are *miscoordinated*, and choose (Football, Opera) or (Opera, Football), they will not get payoffs of (0, 0). Rather, they will get the following: at (Football, Opera) the payoffs are (4, −4), and at (Opera, Football) the payoffs are (2, −2).

Table 14.3. *The strangely modified battle of the sexes*

		2. Man	
		Football	Opera
1. Woman	Football	1, 3	4, −4
	Opera	2, −2	3, 1

Here's a possible explanation for these rather strange payoffs. At the miscoordinated pairs of strategies, the totals of the payoffs to the young woman and her boyfriend are zero, as they were previously. The boyfriend's payoffs are simple to explain. He is happiest (payoff 3) when they are together at the football game, less happy (payoff 1) when they are together at the opera, even less happy (payoff −2) when he is alone at the football game, and miserable (payoff −4) when he is alone at the opera. It is more difficult to explain the young woman's preferences, perhaps because women are more complex. When she and her boyfriend are together, she is happier at the opera (payoff 3) than at the football game (payoff 1). However, if they are miscoordinated and she is at the football game by herself, she is happiest (payoff 4). This surprising payoff is because she feels that although she loves opera and her boyfriend, it would be really good for her to be forced to learn something about football, and for him to be forced to learn something about opera. If she is at the opera by herself, her payoff is 2, not as good as being at the opera with him (payoff 3), but better than being at the football game with him (payoff 1). Payoffs in the strangely modified battle of the sexes are shown in Table 14.3.

When we examine the table of payoffs in Table 14.3, we see the following. From the upper left cell, player 1 would want to move down to the lower left cell. From the lower left cell, player 2 would want to move right to the lower right cell. From the lower right cell, player 1 would want to move up to the upper right cell. From the upper right cell, player 2 would want to move left to the upper left cell. In short, at every pair of strategies, one of the players would be unhappy and would want to change his or her strategy. Therefore, at least based on our definition of Nash equilibrium to this point, there is no Nash equilibrium in this game.

In fact, our definition of Nash equilibrium up to now has assumed that a player can choose only a single strategy with certainty. Player 1, for instance, can choose either "Football" or "Opera." If she chooses "Football," she goes to the football game for sure. Going to the football game for sure is called a *pure strategy.* The games we have been discussing to this point allow only pure strategies. Player 1 can go to the opera, or she can go to the football game. That's it.

But there is another way to play games like this. Players might make random choices over pure strategies. For instance, player 1 might decide: "I'm going to flip a coin, and go to the football game if it's heads, and to the opera if it's tails." This means she decides: "I'll choose "Football" with probability 1/2, and I'll choose "Opera" with probability 1/2." This is an example of what is called a mixed strategy. More formally, if there are two pure strategies, say S_1 and S_2, a *mixed strategy* is a pair of probabilities, say p_1 and p_2, chosen by the player and summing to 1, with the player choosing S_1 with probability p_1 and choosing S_2 with probability p_2. (Note that any pure strategy is also a mixed strategy, but not vice versa. For example, the pure strategy S_1 is the same as the mixed strategy over S_1 and S_2 with $p_1 = 1$ and $p_2 = 0$.) A *pure-strategy Nash equilibrium* is a Nash equilibrium in which players use pure strategies. A *mixed-strategy Nash equilibrium* is a Nash equilibrium in which players use mixed strategies.

What we have shown with the strangely modified battle of the sexes is that there may be no pure strategy Nash equilibrium in a game. In a famous paper written in 1951, John Nash proved that under general conditions, any game with a finite number of pure strategies must have at least one mixed-strategy equilibrium. It follows that our strangely modified battle game must have a mixed-strategy Nash equilibrium, even though it does not have a pure-strategy equilibrium. In this chapter, however, we will not discuss how one might find the mixed-strategy equilibrium which we know, thanks to Nash, must exist.

In the rest of this chapter we will return to our focus on pure strategies and pure strategy equilibria.

14.6 The Expanded Battle of the Sexes, When More Choices Make Players Worse Off

In the decision problem for an individual consumer or firm, the expansion of the set of feasible actions has a clear effect – the decision maker cannot end up worse off than before, and will likely end up better off. Consider, for example, the basic consumer choice model. When the budget set expands, whether because of an increase in income with prices fixed, or because of a fall in prices with income fixed, the consumer will generally be better off, and will definitely not be worse off. In this section, we shall see that this basic property – expansion of the choice set is a good thing for the decision maker – may not hold in a strategic situation.

We now turn to an *expanded battle of the sexes* game. Here is the story. After the original battle of the sexes described previously (not the strangely modified version), some weeks pass. Our couple gets into a fight. They are mad at each other, but they are still together. Another Saturday rolls around, and it is time for another date. The old options of football and opera are still there, and our young woman and her boyfriend have exactly the same feelings they used to have about those options. But there is a new option available to them: the player can stay at home, and deliberately stand up her/his date. (We are assuming the two live separately, so if one stays at home, the other doesn't immediately observe it.) If

Table 14.4. *The expanded battle of the sexes*

		2. Man		
		Football	Opera	Stay Home
	Football	1, 3	0, 0	−1, 2
1. Woman	Opera	0, 0	3, 1	−1, 2
	Stay Home	2, −1	2, −1	0, 0

the woman stays at home and the boyfriend goes out, we will assume she gets a payoff of 2. (This is the satisfaction of hurting her boyfriend.) And we will assume the boyfriend gets a payoff of −1. (This is the pain from discovering he was deliberately stood up.) Similarly, if the boyfriend stays at home and she goes out, we assume he gets a payoff of 2 and she gets a payoff of −1. If they both stay at home, we assume a payoff of 0 to each.

Table 14.4 shows the table of payoff vectors. Note that the payoffs are exactly the same as they used to be for the four pairs of strategies in the original battle of the sexes, as shown in Table 14.2. What is new are the third row in Table 14.4, based on player 1 staying at home, and the third column, based on player 2 staying at home. Everything that player 1 and player 2 used to be able to do, they can still do. However, now they have more options. The table showing the possible payoff vectors is now 3 by 3 instead of 2 by 2; it has 9 cells instead of 4. Each of the new cells looks worse for both players than at least one of the old cells.

We have expanded the options available to the two players, but whatever was available to them in the past is still available. What are the effects of this expansion of choices?

First, it is easy to see that the old Nash equilibria, of the original battle of the sexes game, are no longer Nash equilibria in this new game. Take, for instance, the pair of strategies (Football, Football). Now, if the woman expects her boyfriend to drive to the football game, her best response is no longer to drive to the football game and meet him there, which would have given her a payoff of 1. Rather, she will stay at home, which will give her a payoff of 2. Similarly, the pair of strategies (Opera, Opera) is no longer a Nash equilibrium, as now the man (whose payoff is 1 at (Opera, Opera)) prefers to stay home, which will give him a payoff of 2.

In fact, the only Nash equilibrium in the expanded battle of the sexes is (Stay Home, Stay Home), which has payoffs of 0 for both players. Let us check this. If the woman expects her boyfriend to stay home, she looks at the third column of Table 14.4. She gets a payoff of −1 if she goes to the football game, a payoff of −1 if she goes to the opera, and a payoff of 0 if she stays home also. Her best response is therefore to stay home. The argument is symmetric for the man. If he thinks she is staying home, his best response is to stay home also. Therefore, (Stay

Home, Stay Home) is a Nash equilibrium. It is easy to see that any of the pairs of strategies in which one person goes out and the other person stays at home cannot be a Nash equilibrium. We leave it to the reader to check this.

The addition of a new strategy has had a major effect in the battle of the sexes. It has demoted the original pair of Nash equilibria – they are no longer Nash equilibria. It has created a new Nash equilibrium, which is now the only equilibrium in the game. Moreover, at the new Nash equilibrium, the payoff vector $(0, 0)$ is worse for both players than the original Nash equilibrium payoff vectors of $(1, 3)$ and $(3, 1)$. The expansion of choices has had the effect of making both players worse off at the Nash equilibria.

What produced this strange result? The addition of the new choice led to a very different strategic situation, which undermined the original Nash equilibria and paradoxically elevated a new, and worse, equilibrium.

14.7 Sequential Move Games

All the games we have presented so far are *simultaneous move games*. This means that (at least in theory) the two players choose their strategies at the same time, each one not knowing what the other is choosing. Then there is an outcome, and payoffs are made. (The repeated games we mentioned in Section 14.3 were sequences of simultaneous move games, with payoffs made at the end of each game in the sequence.)

However, there are other games in which time plays a crucial role, when one player moves first and is observed by the other player who moves second, after which payoffs are made. And there are games in which the players make a sequence of moves, alternating turns, with each player observing the other player's move at each step of the process, and with payoffs made at the end. These games are called *sequential move games* or *sequential games*. We discuss such games in this section.

In sequential move games, the conventional wisdom is that there is a first-mover advantage. It is better to move first, because a first move sets the tone for the rest of the game, and the first mover can create the kind of play that she or he wishes. In the game of tic-tac-toe, for instance, the first mover seems to have an advantage because he has nine squares available at his first move, whereas the second mover only has eight squares. (Studies indicate that there is a first-mover advantage in tic-tac-toe for players of average skill – who make errors – but not for expert players. A tic-tac-toe game between experts should result in a tie.) In chess, there is serious debate about whether white has a first-move advantage over black. There are studies that indicate white wins a slightly higher proportion of tournament games than black. Some chess experts claim that perfectly played games should result in a draw; others claim that perfectly played games should result in a win for white.

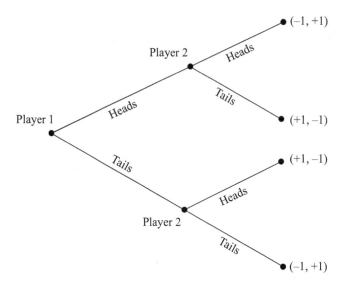

Fig. 14.1. The sequential version of matching pennies.

In the following examples, we show that, in theory, sequential games do not necessarily provide an advantage to the first mover. Whether there exists a first-mover or a second-mover advantage will depend on the specifics of the game.

We now consider a sequential version of what is called the *matching pennies* game. Generally, in a matching pennies game, two players each place a penny on the table. If the pennies match, meaning they are both heads or both tails, a dollar is paid by one of the players to the other player. If the pennies do not match (one is a head and the other a tail), the dollar transfer goes in the opposite direction. This can be a simultaneous move game (in which case it is like the ancient and familiar odds-and-evens game) or a sequential move game. We now consider the sequential move game.

Assume that player 1 moves first, and must put his penny on the table, either face up ("Heads") or face down ("Tails"). Player 2 observes this. Then she moves, and puts down her penny, either face up ("Heads") or face down ("Tails"). The rules of the game require that player 1 pay $1 to player 2 if the pennies match, and that player 2 pay $1 to player 1 if they do not match. Figure 14.1 shows the game in the form of a game tree.

A *game tree* is a diagram with connected nodes and branches. Time flows from left to right in the diagram. At the farthest left is a node, at which the first player to move (player 1 in this case) chooses a strategy. Each strategy is represented by a branch to the right. At the end of each of those branches are new nodes, at which the second player to move chooses her actions. The ultimate payoff vectors appear at the very end of the sequence of nodes and branches. In Figure 14.1, for example, the uppermost sequence of nodes and branches can be read as follows: Player 1 starts the game and chooses heads. Then player 2 goes and chooses heads. Then the game ends, with payoffs to players 1 and 2 of -1 and $+1$, respectively.

To solve a sequential game such as this, we apply a procedure called *backward induction*. This procedure assumes that at each decision node, each player will behave optimally, given his or her theory about how the players will behave at nodes further in the future. To solve the game with backward induction, we go to the last decision nodes in the game tree, the ones farthest in the future (and farthest to the right in the game tree). We determine the optimal action (or actions) for that player making the decision at that point in time. Having done so, we go backward in time (and to the left in the game tree) and determine the optimal action (or actions) at the previous set of decision nodes. We repeat this until we have gone all the way back in time (and all the way to the left in the game tree), and determined the optimal action at the first node of the game, for the first mover.

Let us do this in Figure 14.1. We go to the last decision nodes, the ones for player 2. At the upper node (which follows player 1's choice of "Heads"), if player 2 chooses "Heads," her payoff is $+1$. If she chooses "Tails," her payoff is -1. Therefore, she chooses "Heads." At the lower decision node (which follows player 1's choice of "Tails"), if player 2 chooses "Tails," her payoff is $+1$. If she chooses "Heads," her payoff is -1. Therefore, she chooses "Tails." We see at this stage that player 2 is always going to win the dollar. We now move to the left and decide what player 1 should do at the first decision node. The answer is that it does not matter; he can choose "Heads" or "Tails." The outcome is the same to him in either case. Either one of these leads to the payoff vector $(-1, +1)$. In short, in this game, player 2, the second mover, will win the dollar. This game has a clear second-mover advantage. This shows that whether there is a first-mover or a second-mover advantage in a game depends on the specifics of the game.

We complete the discussion of the sequential matching pennies game with an observation about the distinction between strategies and actions. In game theory, a strategy is a complete contingent plan of the actions that a player will play in a game. If it is a simultaneous move game, in which the actions all take place at one point in time, a strategy coincides with an action. In a sequential move game, a strategy does not necessarily coincide with an action because a player who moves later in the game can make his actions contingent on the history of actions before his. To be clear, in the sequential matching pennies game, player 1 has only two strategies, which coincide with his actions: "Heads" and "Tails." Player 2, however, has four strategies: "Always Heads: After Heads and After Tails, Play Heads," "Always Tails: After Heads and After Tails, Play Tails," "Matching: After Heads, Play Heads, and After Tails, Play Tails," and "Not Matching: After Heads, Play Tails, and After Tails, Play Heads." Therefore, there are two backward induction strategy solutions to this game: player 1 chooses "Heads" and then player 2 chooses "Matching," and player 1 chooses "Tails" and then player 2 chooses "Matching." This more careful analysis still leads to the conclusion that the second

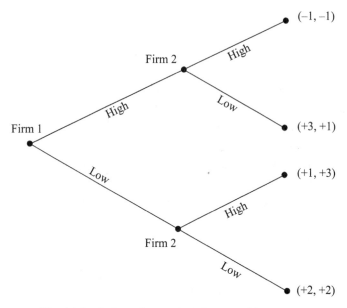

Fig. 14.2. A duopoly sequential competition game.

player in the game will match the action of the first player, and will win the dollar.

We now consider a slightly different game, which we will call a *duopoly sequential competition* game. The two players are now two firms in a duopoly market. Firm 1 moves first and can produce a "High" output or a "Low" output. After firm 2 observes firm 1's choice of output, it responds by also choosing either "High" or "Low." Assume that the payoffs to the firms, that is, profits, are $(\pi_1, \pi_2) = (-1, -1)$ if both firms choose "High," because the market is inundated with the product and the price falls below average cost. If both firms produce "Low," profits are $(\pi_1, \pi_2) = (2, 2)$. Finally, if one firm produces "High" and the other produces "Low," assume that the firm with the higher output ends up with profit of 3, while the firm with the low output has profit of 1. Figure 14.2 represents this game in a game tree.

Applying the backward induction procedure to this game, we go first to firm 2's decision nodes. If firm 1 has produced "High," firm 2 will produce "Low" because 1 is greater than −1. And if firm 1 has produced "Low," firm 2 will respond with "High" because 3 is greater than 2. Now we go back to firm 1's decision node. Firm 1 knows that firm 2 will do the opposite of what it has done. If firm 1 chooses "High," it will end up with a payoff of 3. If firm 1 chooses "Low," it will end up with a payoff of 1. Therefore, firm 1 will choose "High." Firm 2 will respond with "Low," and the ultimate profits will be $(\pi_1, \pi_2) = (3, 1)$.

As you can easily see, there is a first-mover advantage in this game. The game is completely symmetric in payoffs, and so, if the roles of firm 1 and 2 were reversed (with firm 2 moving first and firm 1 moving second), we would end up with a similar outcome, with the first mover choosing "High" and the second mover responding with "Low." With the roles reversed, the payoff vector would be $(\pi_1, \pi_2) = (1, 3)$. This game should remind the reader of the Stackelberg solution to the duopoly model.

14.8 Threats

We conclude this chapter by briefly discussing threats. A *threat* is an announcement made by a player at the beginning of a sequential move game, indicating that at some node, at some point in time, he will depart from what is rational in order to punish the other player. The sequential move game framework can help us to evaluate the credibility of threats. For instance, in the duopoly sequential competition game of the preceding section, firm 2 could try to change the outcome of (High, Low) by threatening firm 1 as follows: "No matter what you do, my plan is to produce 'High.' Therefore, if you decide to produce 'High,' we will actually end up with a payoff vector of $(-1, -1)$. I won't do what you think I ought to do. I will take us both down if you produce 'High.'"

Obviously, if firm 1 believes the threat, it should produce "Low," for which the payoff vector is $(1, 3)$. A payoff of $+1$ is much better than a payoff of -1. In a sequential move game like this, however, especially if it is played just one time, firm 1 probably should not believe firm 2's threat. The reason is this: If firm 2 made the threat before the game started, and if firm 1 ignored the threat at the first move, firm 2 would make itself better off when it moves by not carrying through on its threat. If it drops the threat, it ends up with $+1$. If it carries through on its threat, it ends up with -1. Therefore, threats like this seem less credible from the vantage point of the backward induction procedure.

Of course life may be more complicated if games are played over and over, or if people (or firms) play games with different partners and develop reputations that spread out to other players. If a game is played over and over between two players, an aggressive player may carry out threats in the initial games so his playing partner comes to believe that he will carry out his threats, no matter how self-destructive they may be. In this case, his partner becomes trained to give in to his threats. Or, if he plays with many different players who talk to one another, an aggressive player may want one player to see that he carries out his threats, so that word gets around.

Here is a final observation about some very large threats. For most of the second half of the twentieth century, there was a cold war with the United States on one side and the Soviet Union on the other. In this cold war, the two superpowers accumulated large stockpiles of nuclear weapons. (Those stockpiles of weapons still exist.) The superpowers threatened each other with those weapons. One reason the cold war never became a hot war was the two-way threat of *mutual assured destruction* (MAD), also called mutually assured destruction, *nuclear deterrence*, or *massive retaliation*. The idea of the MAD game was this. If one of the superpowers attacked the other, even in an indirect, nondevastating way, the superpower that had been

Table 14.5. *When is (A, A) a
dominant strategy equilibrium?
When is (B, B) a dominant strategy
equilibrium?*

		Player 2	
		A	B
Player 1	A	a, a	0, 0
	B	0, 0	1, 1

attacked would retaliate with a massive nuclear strike. For instance, if the Soviet Union invaded (Western) Europe, the United States would launch nuclear weapons against the Soviet Union. This retaliation would lead to a worldwide nuclear war, effectively destroying both superpowers.

The MAD game would have been played just one time. Our previous comments suggest that the Soviet Union's threats against the United States, and the United States' threats against the Soviet Union, may have all been hollow threats. Or maybe they weren't. Or maybe the threats were so huge that even if they were unbelievable, neither side could dare to test them.

14.9 A Solved Problem

The Problem

Consider the following coordination game. There are two players and two strategies available to each player: A and B. The payoffs in the first row (corresponding to player 1 choosing A) are (a, a) and $(0, 0)$. The payoffs in the second row (corresponding to player 1 choosing B) are $(0, 0)$ and $(1, 1)$.

(a) Draw the 2×2 payoff matrix.
(b) For what values of a is (A, A) a dominant strategy equilibrium?
(c) For what values of a is (B, B) a dominant strategy equilibrium?
(d) Can you find the Nash equilibria of the game as a function of the parameter a?

The Solution

(a) The payoff matrix is shown in Table 14.5.
(b) (A, A) can never be a dominant strategy equilibrium, no matter what a is. For (A, A) to be a dominant strategy equilibrium, A would have to be a dominant strategy for both players. However, if player 2 is playing B (right column), player 1 is better off with B (payoff 1) than with A (payoff 0). So no matter what a is, playing A cannot be a dominant strategy for player 1. (Similar comments apply to player 2.) Therefore, (A, A) cannot be a dominant strategy equilibrium.

(c) If $a \leq 0$, then B is a dominant strategy for player 1. If player 2 chooses A (left column), player 1 is at least as well off at B (payoff 0) as he is at a (payoff a); and if player 2 chooses B (right column), player 1 is better off at B (payoff 1) than at A (payoff 0). Similarly, B is a dominant strategy for player 2. If player 1 chooses A (top row), player 2 is at least as well off at B (payoff 0) as at A (payoff a); and if player 1 chooses B (bottom row), player 2 is better off at B (payoff 1) than at A (payoff 0). Because B is a dominant strategy for player 1, and B is a dominant strategy for player 2, (B, B) is a dominant strategy equilibrium. Because it is a dominant strategy equilibrium, it is also a Nash equilibrium.

(d) If $a \geq 0$, then (A, A) is a Nash equilibrium. At (A, A), both players compare the payoff a to the payoff 0, and because $a \geq 0$, (A, A) is a Nash equilibrium. But (B, B) is also a Nash equilibrium when $a \geq 0$. This is because no matter how big a might be, at (B, B), the payoff for both players is 1, and a deviation by either player 1 or player 2 (not both simultaneously) would reduce that player's payoff to 0. However, if $a < 0$, then (B, B) is the only Nash equilibrium.

Exercises

1. Consider the game of chicken with two players. If both players play "Macho," each of them gets a payoff of 0. If both players play "Chicken," each of them gets a payoff of 6. If one player plays "Macho" and the other plays "Chicken," the one who plays "Macho" gets a payoff of 7 and the one who plays "Chicken" gets a payoff of 2.
   (a) Draw the payoff matrix.
   (b) Does either player have a dominant strategy in this game?
   (c) Find the Nash equilibrium or equilibria.

2. Jack and Jill want a treehouse to play in. They have to decide simultaneously whether to build or not to build. Each individual who builds bears a cost of 3. They both have access to the treehouse once it is built. If only one of them builds the treehouse, they each derive a utility of 2. If both of them build the treehouse, they each derive a utility of 4 (presumably the treehouse is more elaborate because two heads are better than one). If the treehouse is not built, they each derive a utility of 0.
   (a) Draw the payoff matrix.
   (b) What is Jack's strategy? What is Jill's strategy? What is the Nash equilibrium or equilibria?
   (c) Does this game resemble the prisoner's dilemma, the battle of the sexes, or chicken? Explain.

3. Sam and Dan are twins who like playing tricks on each other. Sam is deciding whether to take Dan's blanket. Sam has a utility of 0 if he doesn't take Dan's blanket. If Sam takes Dan's blanket, there is a possibility of Dan retaliating by taking Sam's pillow, thereby earning Sam a utility of -5. If Dan doesn't retaliate, Sam gets a utility of 5. Dan has a utility of 10 if Sam doesn't take his blanket. If Sam takes his blanket, Dan's utility is -10. Dan's utility changes by X if he retaliates.
   (a) Draw the game tree.
   (b) For what values of X would we observe Sam taking Dan's blanket in the backward induction equilibrium?

4. Consider the following sequential strategic situation, called the centipede game. The game has 100 stages. Two players take turns making decisions, starting with player 1. At stage $t = 1, \ldots, 99$, player 1 (if the stage is odd) or player 2 (if it is even) chooses whether to "Terminate the game" or to "Continue the game." If the game is terminated at stage $t = 1, \ldots, 99$, the player terminating the game receives a payoff of t, while the other player receives a payoff of zero. Finally, at stage $t = 100$, player 2 chooses between action A with a payoff of 99 for each player, or action B with a payoff of zero for player 1 and a payoff of 100 for player 2.

    (a) Draw the game tree for this strategic situation (the name of the game will become apparent then).

    (b) What is the backward induction solution to this game?

5. Two players take turns choosing a number between 1 and 10, inclusive. The number is added to a running total. The player who takes the total to 100 (or greater) wins.

    (a) What is the backward induction solution to this game? Map out the complete strategy.

    (b) Is there a first-mover or a second-mover advantage in this game?

6. Consider a Bertrand duopoly with a homogeneous good, as in the first part of Section 13.6. Assume the market demand curve is $y = y_1 + y_2 = 1 - p$, where p is the relevant market price, y is the total amount demanded at that price, and y_1 and y_2 are the output levels for firms 1 and 2. Assume the firms' cost functions are $C(y_i) = \frac{1}{2} y_i$ for $i = 1, 2$. The rules of the pricing game are as follows. The firms must each simultaneously name a price in the interval $[0, 1]$. If the prices are different, the firm with the lower price sells all the units demanded at that price, while the other firm sells nothing. If they name the same price, the amount demanded at that price is split equally between the two firms. Show that there is a unique Nash equilibrium, and find the equilibrium price and quantities.

    Hint: Note that calculus cannot be used to solve this problem, because the firms' profit functions are not continuous in the price variables. For instance, $\pi_1(p_1, p_2)$ is not continuous at $p_1 = p_2 = p$.

Part IV

General Equilibrium Analysis

Chapter 15

An Exchange Economy

15.1 Introduction

What economists call a *pure exchange economy*, or more simply an *exchange economy*, is a model of an economy with no production. Goods have already been produced, found, inherited, or endowed, and the only issue is how they should be distributed and consumed. Even though this model abstracts from production decisions, it illustrates important questions about the efficiency or inefficiency of allocations of goods among consumers, and provides important answers to those questions.

In this chapter, we start with a very simple model of an exchange economy, and we will discuss *Pareto optimality* or *Pareto efficiency* for allocations of goods among consumers. Then we turn to the role of markets, and discuss *market* or *competitive equilibrium* allocations. Finally, we discuss the extremely important connections between markets and efficiency in an exchange economy. These connections between markets and efficiency are among the most important results in economic theory, and are appropriately called the *fundamental theorems of welfare economics*.

15.2 An Economy with Two Consumers and Two Goods

We will study the simplest possible exchange economy model, with only two consumers and two goods. A model of exchange cannot get much simpler, because if there were only one good or one person, there would be no reason for trade. However, even though our model is extremely simple, it captures all the important issues, and it generalizes easily.

Let us suppose that there are two consumers. In recognition of Daniel Defoe's early novel *Robinson Crusoe* (published in 1719), we call them Robinson and Friday. We abbreviate Robinson R; for Friday we use F. We assume there are only two consumption goods on their island, bread (good x) and rum (good y). In this model of exchange, we are abstracting from the fact that Robinson and Friday produce rum (or somehow have acquired a stock of it), and produce bread (by making flour, mixing, and baking). Therefore we assume that there are fixed totals of rum and bread available, and that the only issue is how to distribute those totals among the two consumers.

Here's how the distribution of the two goods works. The two consumers start with *initial endowments* of the goods; then they make trades. We let X represent the total quantity of good x, bread, that is available. We let Y represent the total quantity of good y, rum, that is available. In general, if we are talking about an arbitrary bundle of goods for Robinson, we show it as (x_R, y_R), where x_R is his quantity of bread and y_R is his quantity of rum. An arbitrary bundle of goods for Friday is (x_F, y_F).

Robinson has initial endowments of the two goods, as does Friday. We will use the "naught" superscript (that is, ^{0}) to indicate an initial quantity. Robinson's initial bundle of goods is (x_R^0, y_R^0). Friday's initial bundle of goods is (x_F^0, y_F^0). The quantities of the two goods in the initial bundles must be consistent with the assumed totals of bread and rum. That is,

$$X = x_R^0 + x_F^0 \qquad \text{and} \qquad Y = y_R^0 + y_F^0.$$

Moreover, if they start with their initial quantities and then trade, any bundles they end up with must also be consistent with the given totals. That is, if they end up at $((x_R, y_R), (x_F, y_F))$, it must be the case that

$$X = x_R + x_F \qquad \text{and} \qquad Y = y_R + y_F.$$

Robinson's preferences for bread and rum are represented by the utility function $u_R(x_R, y_R)$, and, similarly, Friday's preferences are represented by $u_F(x_F, y_F)$. That is, we assume that each consumer's utility depends only on his own consumption bundle. The utility functions u_R and u_F will generally be different, and unrelated to the initial bundles that Robinson and Friday happen to have. The facts that preferences are generally different, and initial bundles are also generally different, make mutually beneficial trade probable.

To show our simple exchange economy with a graph, we use a diagram first suggested (in 1881) by the great Anglo-Irish economist Francis Ysidro Edgeworth (1845–1926). (Actually, Edgeworth didn't really invent this diagram; the version we use today is due to the English economist Arthur Bowley (1869–1957).) This graph is called an *Edgeworth box diagram*. We show it in Figure 15.1. In the figure, the initial endowment is given by the point W. That is, W is the allocation of bread x and rum y giving Robinson the bundle (x_R^0, y_R^0) and giving Friday the bundle (x_F^0, y_F^0). There are two indifference curves shown in the figure: I_R belongs to Robinson, and I_F belongs to Friday. The small arrows attached to those indifference curves indicate the directions of increasing utility.

The novel feature of the Edgeworth box diagram, which makes it different from other diagrams we have used, is that it has *two origins*. The lower left origin is

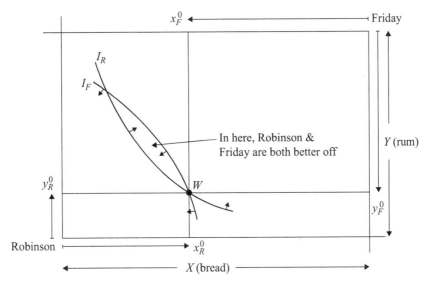

Fig. 15.1. The Edgeworth box diagram.

for Robinson; quantities for Robinson are measured from that origin. The upper right origin is for Friday; quantities for Friday are measured from that origin. Of course this is a little confusing at first, because in a sense Friday is upside down and backward! (This is why his indifference curve I_F seems to look wrong.) Once the reader is past this confusion, the advantages of the diagram become apparent.

First, we see that the quantities at the initial allocation W add up as they should; that is,

$$X = x_R^0 + x_F^0 \qquad \text{and} \qquad Y = y_R^0 + y_F^0.$$

Second, we see that any allocation of the given totals between Robinson and Friday could be represented by some point in the diagram. This is because if the totals in an arbitrary pair of bundles $((x_R, y_R), (x_F, y_F))$ add up to the given totals X and Y, that is, if

$$X = x_R + x_F \qquad \text{and} \qquad Y = y_R + y_F,$$

then the given allocation can be plotted as a single point in the box. (The interested reader should prove this is true by plotting such a point.) Third, the Edgeworth box diagram has the remarkable virtue that it easily shows four quantities, $((x_R^0, y_R^0), (x_F^0, y_F^0))$, in a two-dimensional picture.

15.3 Pareto Efficiency

In previous chapters, when we analyzed the welfare properties of competitive markets, monopoly, and duopoly, we looked at efficiency in terms of consumers' and producers' surplus. The sum of these two surpluses, or the social surplus, represents the total net benefit created in a market, to buyers and sellers, measured in money units such as dollars. Social surplus is a measure of the "size of the economic pie," created by the production and trade of some good. A market for a good is *inefficient* if there is a way to make that pie bigger (e.g., the standard monopoly case), and it is *efficient* if there is no way to make it bigger (e.g., the standard competitive case).

All this assumed that consumers' surplus is well defined, which in turn required some special assumptions about preferences. Note that this kind of analysis focused on one good under study, and ignored what might have been happening in other markets for other goods, for labor and savings, and so on. It was therefore what is called *partial equilibrium analysis*; models that study one good in this fashion are called *partial equilibrium models*.

We are now, however, looking at a simple model of exchange, without production. If we measure the size of the economic pie in terms of total quantities of bread and/or rum, the size cannot change because these total quantities are fixed. There is no money in the model (at least not yet), so it would not be easy to measure the size of the pie in money units. We might try to measure the economic pie in *utility* units, but we know that it would probably be wrong to try to add together Robinson's utility and Friday's utility. How, then, can we decide when an allocation of the fixed quantities of bread and rum between the two consumers is efficient (or when it is not)?

The solution to this problem was developed by the Italian economist Vilfredo Pareto (1848–1923), so we call the central concept *Pareto optimality* or *Pareto efficiency*. Here are some important definitions.

First, we need to be careful about which allocations of bread and rum are possible and which are not. We will say that a pair of bundles of goods, (x_R, y_R) and (x_F, y_F), is a *feasible allocation* if all the quantities are nonnegative and if

$$X = x_R + x_F \qquad \text{and} \qquad Y = y_R + y_F.$$

That is, a feasible allocation is one in which the goods going to Robinson and Friday add up to the given totals. In fact, the feasible allocations in the exchange model are simply the points in the Edgeworth box diagram, no more and no less.

Second, if A and B are two feasible allocations, we will say that A *Pareto dominates* B if both Robinson and Friday like A at least as well as B, and at least one likes it better. If A Pareto dominates B, we call a move by Robinson and Friday from B to A a *Pareto move*.

Third, a feasible allocation is *not Pareto optimal* if there is a different feasible allocation that both consumers like at least as well, and that is preferred by at least one of them. That is, a feasible allocation is not Pareto optimal if there is a Pareto move from it. Note that any Pareto move would get a unanimous vote of approval (possibly with an abstention).

Fourth, and finally, a feasible allocation is *Pareto optimal* or *Pareto efficient* if there is *no* feasible allocation that both consumers like at least as well, and that is preferred by at least one of them. That is, a feasible allocation is Pareto optimal if there is no Pareto move from it. The reader can see a nonoptimal feasible allocation in Figure 15.1 – the initial allocation W – and there are many points in the Edgeworth box diagram (the lens-shaped area to the northwest of W) that Pareto dominate W. (Of course W is not the only nonoptimal allocation in Figure 15.1.)

These Pareto-related definitions can easily be extended to exchange economies with any number of consumers and any number of goods, and can be extended, less easily, to any kind of economic model, including models with production as well as exchange. These definitions are not restricted to models of markets with just one good ("partial equilibrium models"). They are very general, and are useful in *general equilibrium models*, that is, models that consider supply and demand in all markets simultaneously.

Our pure exchange model, with two people and two goods, is a very simple example of a general equilibrium model.

Now think about a feasible allocation that is not Pareto optimal. It is obviously undesirable for society to be at that allocation, as there are other feasible allocations that are unambiguously better, in the sense that a move from the given nonoptimal allocation to the alternative would get unanimous consent. Obviously, if an economy is at a non-Pareto optimal point, it should move to something better. Note, however, that Pareto optimality has nothing to do with considerations of *distributional fairness* or *equity*. That is, a non-Pareto optimal allocation may be much more equal than a Pareto optimal one. In fact, allocating all the bread and rum to Robinson (for example) is Pareto optimal, as there is no Pareto move away from that totally lopsided and unfair allocation. Moreover, giving both Robinson and Friday exactly half the bread and half the rum, the allocation that is the most equal of all the feasible allocations, is probably not Pareto optimal.

With all this said, we now return to our Edgeworth box diagrams. They should make the mysteries of Pareto optimality and non-optimality clear.

Feasible Allocations and the Edgeworth Box

Suppose we have a bundle of goods (x_R, y_R) for Robinson and another bundle (x_F, y_F) for Friday. For the pair of bundles $((x_R, y_R), (x_F, y_F))$ to be a feasible allocation, the numbers must add up to the totals X and Y. Consider Figure 15.2. The two bundles are shown in it, but the quantities of bread (on the horizontal axis) and rum (on the vertical axis) do not add up to the total quantity of bread available, X (the width of the box), or the total quantity of rum available, Y (the height of the box). In other words, if you are interested in finding Pareto optimal allocations of bread and rum, don't even think about the pair of bundles (x_R, y_R) and (x_F, y_F) shown in Figure 15.2, because that pair of bundles *is just not possible*.

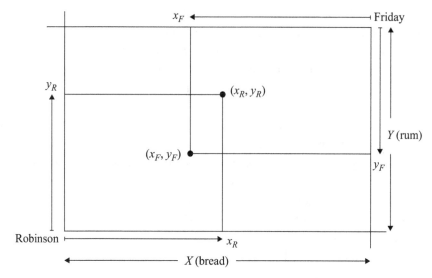

Fig. 15.2. This pair of bundles is not feasible. Therefore, it is not Pareto optimal.

In Figure 15.3, we show another pair of bundles of goods whose totals do not add up to X and Y. However, this time the totals fall short. We still consider this pair of bundles $((x_R, y_R), (x_F, y_F))$ *nonfeasible* and therefore non-Pareto optimal. (Some economists would pronounce $((x_R, y_R), (x_F, y_F))$ "feasible," because one could throw away some bread and some rum (the excesses of each good), starting at X and Y, and get to the lesser totals. But even if one takes this approach, $((x_R, y_R), (x_F, y_F))$ still would not be Pareto optimal, because it is Pareto dominated by another allocation formed by starting with $((x_R, y_R), (x_F, y_F))$, and then adding back half the excesses to each consumer's bundle.)

The moral of Figures 15.2 and 15.3 is that in the exchange economy model, an allocation of bread and rum must be feasible before one can decide whether it is Pareto optimal. To be feasible, it must be the case that

$$X = x_R + x_F \qquad \text{and} \qquad Y = y_R + y_F.$$

Tangencies of Indifference Curves and the Edgeworth Box

From this point on, we consider only feasible allocations. That is, we look only at pairs of bundles $((x_R, y_R), (x_F, y_F))$ that can be represented by single points in the Edgeworth box diagram. The point W in Figure 15.1 was such a feasible allocation. We will draw a fresh figure, Figure 15.4, with a similar point, labeled P. In the figure, the indifference curves I_R and I_F cross at the point $P = ((x_R, y_R), (x_F, y_F))$. The arrows on the indifference curves show the directions of increasing utility. The point P cannot be Pareto optimal, because a move to the interior of the lens-shaped area would make both consumers better off. (Moving to the other end of the lens,

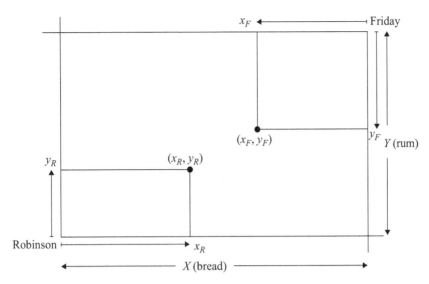

Fig. 15.3. This pair of bundles is not Pareto optimal either, because it is not feasible. Even if we were to expand our definition of feasibility to allow it, it still would not be Pareto optimal.

where I_R and I_F cross again, would leave both of them exactly as well off; moving to the edges of the lens would make one person better off and the other exactly as well off as at the highlighted point.)

We now have a tentative conclusion. If the indifference curves of the two consumers cross at a point in an Edgeworth box diagram, that point must be non-Pareto optimal, and there must be other points, other feasible allocations, that Pareto dominate it. Note, by the way, that if two indifference curves actually cross at a point in the box (rather than just touch each other), then that point must be in the interior of the box. That is, it must be the case that x_R, y_R, x_F, and $y_F > 0$.

If Robinson and Friday are at a point such as P in Figure 15.4, they can make trades that benefit one or both, and harm neither. That is, they can make Pareto moves. If they are free to trade, aware of the feasible allocations, and in touch with their preferences or utility functions, they will probably continue to trade until they can no longer make Pareto moves; that is, they will trade to a Pareto optimal allocation. Moreover, if the point at which they end up is in the interior of the Edgeworth box diagram, it cannot be a point at which Robinson's and Friday's indifference curves cross. Rather, assuming that the indifference curves are smooth and do not have kinks, the point at which they end up, when further Pareto moves are impossible, must be a tangency point.

In short, in the interior of the Edgeworth box diagram, the Pareto optimal points must be points of tangency between the indifference curves of Robinson and Friday. Figure 15.5 shows one such Pareto optimal point, identified as $Q = ((x_R, y_R), (x_F, y_F))$. Four arrows are drawn from Q. The one pointing

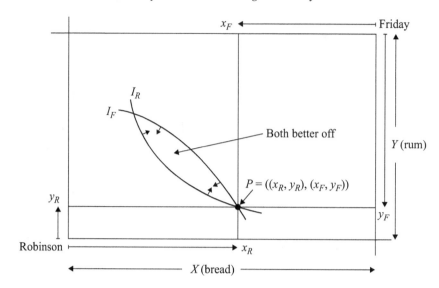

Fig. 15.4. A point in the Edgeworth box diagram that is not Pareto optimal.

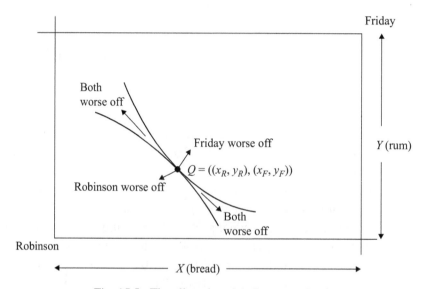

Fig. 15.5. The allocation Q is Pareto optimal.

northeast suggests a move that would make Robinson better off, but would make Friday worse off. The one pointing southwest suggests a move that would make Friday better off, but would make Robinson worse off. A move in the direction of each of the other arrows would make both consumers worse off. Therefore, there is no Pareto move away from Q, which means that Q must be Pareto optimal.

All this leads to a necessary condition for Pareto optimality for points in the interior of the Edgeworth box diagram. For such a point to be Pareto optimal, the

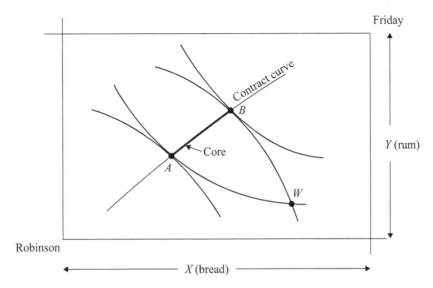

Fig. 15.6. The contract curve and the core.

slopes of the indifference curves of Robinson and Friday must be equal at the point. That is, Robinson's marginal rate of substitution of good y for good x must equal Friday's marginal rate of substitution of y for x. This gives

$$MRS^R = MRS^F,$$

which in turn gives

$$\frac{MU_x^R}{MU_y^R} = \frac{MU_x^F}{MU_y^F}.$$

Note that the R superscript is for Robinson and the F superscript is for Friday.

The set of Pareto optimal allocations in the Edgeworth box diagram is called the *contract curve*. The name is fitting, for these are the allocations that could potentially be outcomes of trading contracts. That is, Robinson and Friday would be likely to agree to a contract that would take them from the initial allocation W to the contract curve. Of course, where they end up on the contract curve depends on the location of the starting allocation W, and it may also depend on their bargaining abilities. If W gives most of the bread and most of the rum to Robinson, they will end up somewhere on the contract curve where Robinson still has most of the bread and most of the rum. In Figure 15.6, we show a contract curve. In the interior of the Edgeworth box diagram it is the set of tangency points. We show an initial allocation W that gives most of the bread to Robinson and most of the rum to Friday. In this exchange economy, Robinson and Friday will trade to the contract curve, but not to anywhere on the contract curve. They will want to make Pareto moves. This means that neither should end up worse off than they were at the initial allocation W. The part of the contract curve where neither is worse off than they were at W is between allocations A and B. This is called the *core*.

Most economists believe that Pareto moves are unambiguously good, and that Pareto optimality is desirable, as any non-Pareto optimal point is unambiguously inferior to some Pareto optimal one. Most economists who look at the Edgeworth box diagram agree that it would be a good thing to end up on the contract curve. There is, of course, disagreement about distribution, so we do not claim that the Pareto optimal point A is better than (or worse than) the Pareto optimal point B. But we do agree that it would be a good thing to end up at *some* Pareto optimal point—at some point on the contract curve. We have suggested that in the exchange economy model, our two traders, starting at some initial allocation W, can simply trade, or barter, to get to the contract curve. Is there another way to get there? The answer is "Yes," through *market trade*.

15.4 Competitive or Walrasian Equilibrium

We now model a *competitive market* in our simple two-person, two-good Robinson/Friday economy. This theory was first developed by the French economist Leon Walras (1834–1910). The market equilibrium idea we describe is called a *competitive equilibrium* or a *Walrasian equilibrium*. The connections between market equilibria and Pareto optimality were rigorously analyzed in the 1950s, especially by the American economists Kenneth Arrow (1921–) and Lionel McKenzie (1919–) and the French economist Gerard Debreu (1921–2004).

Here is the story of Walrasian equilibrium. Imagine that an auctioneer lands on the island with Robinson and Friday. The auctioneer has no bread and no rum, nor does he have any desire to consume any. His sole function is to create a market in which people can trade the two goods. He does this by calling out prices for the two goods. He starts by announcing p_x, the per-unit bread price, and p_y, the per-unit rum price. He announces that he will buy or sell any quantities of bread and/or rum, at those prices. He asks Robinson and Friday, "What do you want to do at those prices?"

In our model of a competitive market economy, we assume that Robinson and Friday take those prices as given and fixed, unaffected by their actions. (This is obviously a little unrealistic when we are talking about just two consumers, but the model is meant to be extended to cases in which there are many consumers, when the assumption of competitive behavior becomes plausible.) Robinson and Friday hear the Walrasian auctioneer announce a pair of prices (p_x, p_y), and they understand that they should tell him what bundle they want to consume, based on those prices.

Our traders have no money in the bank or in their pockets; they have only their initial bundles. Robinson and Friday hear the announced prices and know the bundles they start with. If Robinson starts with 10 loaves of bread, and decides he wants to consume 12 loaves, he will go to the auctioneer and swap some of his rum for the extra 2 loaves of bread. What exactly is his budget constraint? We could figure it in terms of such a swap; it would then be "value of bread acquired = value of rum given up," or

$$(x_R - x_R^0)p_x = (y_R^0 - y_R)p_y.$$

With a little rearranging, this gives

$$p_x x_R + p_y y_R = p_x x_R^0 + p_y y_R^0.$$

Alternatively, we could derive Robinson's budget constraint by realizing that in a world in which consumers do not have money income, what substitutes for income in the budget constraint is the value of the bundle the consumer starts out with. Robinson's budget constraint should then say "value of his desired consumption bundle = value of the bundle he starts with," which also gives

$$p_x x_R + p_y y_R = p_x x_R^0 + p_y y_R^0.$$

Recall that the Walrasian auctioneer has called out some prices, and asked Robinson and Friday, "What do you want to do at these prices?" Robinson, of course, wants to maximize his utility, or get to the highest indifference curve, subject to his budget constraint. That is, he wants to maximize

$$u_R(x_R, y_R)$$

subject to the constraint

$$p_x x_R + p_y y_R = p_x x_R^0 + p_y y_R^0.$$

Think of the budget line implied by this budget constraint. The absolute value of the slope of the budget line is p_x/p_y, and the budget line must go through the initial bundle (x_R^0, y_R^0). All this leads Robinson to conclude that he wants to consume some bundle; call it A_R for now. Robinson tells the auctioneer that based on the announced prices, he wants to consume A_R.

Friday goes through the same exercise, and he ends up telling the auctioneer that he wants to consume B_F.

In Figure 15.7 we plot the results. There is one budget line going through the initial allocation W. We do not have two separate lines, one for Robinson and the other for Friday. This is because, first, either trader's line must go through W, which represents both their initial bundles, and second, because the auctioneer called out only one set of prices, there is only one possible price ratio p_x/p_y and only one possible slope. In the figure, we show the bundle A_R that Robinson would like to consume, and the bundle B_F that Friday would like to consume.

Now it is time for the Walrasian auctioneer to act. He asks himself, "Is it possible for Robinson to consume A_R and for Friday to consume B_F?" The reader should immediately see the answer: "No," because (A_R, B_F) is not a feasible allocation.

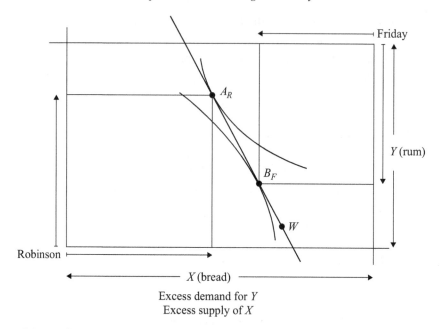

Fig. 15.7. At these prices, there is excess supply of good x and excess demand of good y. The Walrasian auctioneer should announce new prices with a lower relative price for x, p_x/p_y.

The totals do not add up to X and Y. In particular, the amount of bread that the two want to consume is less than the amount X that is available, and the amount of rum that the two want to consume is greater than the amount Y that is available. Therefore, (A_R, B_F) is just not possible.

The Walrasian auctioneer sees this. He says to himself, "The (p_x, p_y) I announced must be changed. There is excess supply of bread and excess demand for rum. I must lower the relative price of bread p_x/p_y." He then tells Robinson and Friday that there will be no trading at the previously announced prices. Instead, he announces a new pair of prices, for which p_x/p_y is a little lower than the first pair of prices. (For instance, if the original (p_x, p_y) was (2, 1), he announces new prices (1.75, 1).) He tells Robinson and Friday to forget about the bundles they wanted to consume at the previous pair of prices. Instead, they should now tell him what bundles they want to consume at his newly announced prices. Robinson and Friday then figure out what bundles they want to consume at the new prices, and duly report back to the auctioneer.

The auctioneer, Robinson, and Friday continue this price-to-desired-consumption-bundles-to-price process until, finally, they end up with a pair of prices and desired consumption bundles that work. That is, the process continues until Robinson and Friday tell the Walrasian auctioneer that based on his latest price combination (p_x^*, p_y^*), they want to consume certain bundles A_R^* and B_F^*, and those bundles are consistent with the given totals of bread and rum; they are a feasible allocation, a single point in the Edgeworth box diagram. That is, at the pair of bundles A_R^* and B_F^*, for each of the goods, total demand = total supply.

Once this end has been reached, the Walrasian auctioneer makes his final announcement to Robinson and Friday: "We're finally there. Make the trades at the (p_x^*, p_y^*) prices, either through me as an intermediary or directly between yourselves. Then consume and enjoy!"

(We have been somewhat casual about the nature of the dynamic price adjustment process. Analysis of convergence for the process is beyond our scope.)

The process we described above is called a *Walrasian auctioneering process* or *Walrasian process* or *tatonnement process*. (The word "tatonnement" is French for "groping.") The end result is called a *competitive equilibrium* or *Walrasian equilibrium*. The pair of prices at which it ends up, p_x^* and p_y^*, are called the *competitive equilibrium prices*. The Walrasian process produces the equilibrium prices and a pair of consumption bundles A_R^* and B_F^*, such that A_R^* maximizes Robinson's utility subject to his budget constraint with the equilibrium prices, B_F^* maximizes Friday's utility subject to his budget constraint with the equilibrium prices, and (A_R^*, B_F^*) is a *feasible allocation*; that is, the desired total consumption of each good equals the total supply of that good. The allocation (A_R^*, B_F^*) is called a *competitive equilibrium allocation*.

Figure 15.8 shows a competitive equilibrium. Note the crucial difference between Figure 15.7 and Figure 15.8: In Figure 15.7 the desired consumption bundles are two distinct points in the Edgeworth box, which means they are not a feasible allocation; there is excess supply of bread and excess demand for rum. This suggests the relative price of bread p_x/p_y, should fall. That is, the budget line should get flatter. Figure 15.8 has a flatter budget line, and in that figure the desired consumption bundles do coincide in the Edgeworth box. They constitute a feasible allocation. Supply equals demand for each good.

Note two extremely important facts about (A_R^*, B_F^*) in Figure 15.8. First, the competitive equilibrium allocation is a tangency point for the two indifference curves shown. That means it is on the contract curve. It is Pareto optimal. Second, a look at Figures 15.6 and 15.8 together should convince you that the competitive equilibrium allocation is in the core.

15.5 The Two Fundamental Theorems of Welfare Economics

The relationships between free markets and efficiency, and between market incentives and national wealth, have been written about since the time of Adam Smith (1723–1790), who published *The Wealth of Nations* in 1776. Smith's arguments were neither formal nor mathematical; the formal and mathematical analysis was developed in the late nineteenth and mid twentieth centuries. We now call the two basic results that relate Pareto optimality and competitive markets the first and second fundamental theorems of welfare economics. Figure 15.8 illustrates

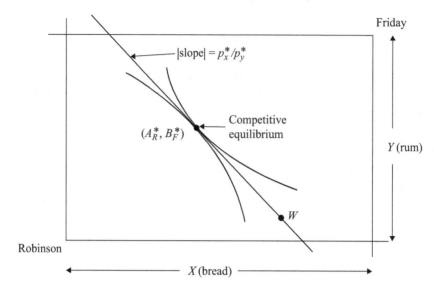

Fig. 15.8. The Walrasian or competitive equilibrium.

the first fundamental theorem in our simple pure exchange model, with only two people and two goods. The figure shows that a competitive equilibrium allocation is Pareto optimal. That result easily extends to exchange models with any number of people and any number of goods, as well as to economic models with production as well as exchange. The result requires only a few assumptions; in particular, we must assume that there are markets and market prices for all the goods, that all the agents are competitive price takers, and that any individual's utility depends only on his or her own consumption bundle, and not on the consumption bundles of other individuals. (Similarly, if there are firms, we must assume that they are all competitive price takers, and that any firm's production function depends only on that firm's inputs and outputs.) We now state the first fundamental theorem, for a general exchange economy.

First Fundamental Theorem of Welfare Economics

Suppose that there are markets and market prices for all the goods, that all the people are competitive price takers, and that each person's utility depends only on her own bundle of goods. Then any competitive equilibrium allocation is Pareto optimal. In fact, any competitive equilibrium allocation is in the core.

This is an extremely important result, because it suggests that a society that relies on competitive markets will achieve Pareto optimality. It is a remarkable result because, although there are many competitive allocations, most allocations in an exchange model are actually *not* Pareto optimal. The reader should look back at Figure 15.6 and think about throwing a dart at that Edgeworth box diagram, hoping to hit the contract curve. What are the odds you will hit it? At least in theory the odds are zero, because a line has zero area. Therefore, ending up at a Pareto optimal allocation is not easy, and the fact that the market mechanism does it is impressive. Moreover, the market mechanism is cheap (it requires only a Walrasian auctioneer, in theory, or perhaps something such as eBay, in reality). It does not require that some central power learn everybody's utility function (which would be terribly intrusive and dangerous) and then make distributional decisions; it requires only publicly known prices that move in response to excess supply or demand. In short, the competitive market mechanism is relatively cheap, relatively unobtrusive, relatively benign, and remarkably effective. This is what the first fundamental theorem of welfare economics helps us understand.

However, one important shortcoming of the first fundamental theorem is that the location of the competitive equilibrium allocation is highly dependent on the location of the initial allocation. In other words, if we start at an initial allocation that gives Robinson most of the bread and rum, we will end up at a competitive equilibrium allocation that gives Robinson most of the bread and rum. Or, more generally, if a society has a very unequal distribution of talents and abilities and initial quantities of various goods, it will end up with a competitive equilibrium that, while Pareto optimal, is very unequal. What can be done? This is where the second fundamental theorem comes in.

The second fundamental theorem of welfare economics uses all the assumptions of the first theorem, and adds an additional one, convexity. In particular, at least for the exchange version of the second fundamental theorem, we will assume that the traders have convex indifference curves. (This is, in fact, how we drew the indifference curves in Figures 15.4 through 15.8.) Here is what the theorem says. Suppose the initial allocation in society is very skewed, very unfair, and therefore a competitive equilibrium based on it would be very unfair. Suppose that people in society have decided that there is a different, perhaps much fairer Pareto optimal allocation, that they want to get to. However, they want to use the market mechanism mostly to get to that desired Pareto optimal point; they do not want a dictator announcing what bundle of goods each and every person should consume. Is there a slightly modified market mechanism that will get society from the initial allocation to the target Pareto optimal one? The answer is "Yes."

Figure 15.9 illustrates the theorem. The initial allocation W gives all the bread and most of the rum to Robinson. Given this initial allocation, the Walrasian mechanism we described earlier, if left alone, will produce a competitive equilibrium that gives most of the bread and most of the rum to Robinson. This allocation is labeled *Laissez-faire* in the figure. This is the outcome of the unshackled free market. ("Laissez-faire" is French for "let do"; that is, let the market do its thing.) But it is very unfair; it leaves Friday a pauper. A more equitable goal would be the Pareto optimal allocation labeled *Target*. Can the market, with a relatively small fix, be used to get society to Target?

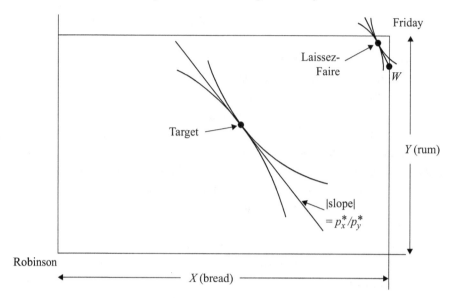

Fig. 15.9. A very unfair laissez-faire competitive equilibrium, and a more equitable, and Pareto optimal, target.

Referring now to Figure 15.9, this is how the market mechanism is modified to get the economy to Target, the Pareto optimal allocation that is more equitable than what the market would produce by itself. Because Target is Pareto optimal, and is in the interior of the Edgeworth box diagram, it must be a tangency point of the two traders' indifference curves. (The argument is more complicated if Target is not an interior point.) Because it is a tangency point, we can draw a tangent line like the one in Figure 15.9. From the slope of the tangent line, we can figure out what price ratio p_x^*/p_y^* we are going to need. One of the prices could be arbitrarily set to 1, and then the required price ratio would give the other price. (A good whose price is set equal to 1 is called a *numeraire* good.) This gives the required pair of prices (p_x^*, p_y^*).

Now, the government must step in and introduce some *lump-sum taxes and transfers*. These are imposed on Robinson and Friday. They are "lump sum" because they are independent of the quantities of goods the parties want to consume. A tax (money taken from a person) will be represented by a negative number; a transfer (or subsidy) will be represented by a positive number. Let T_R be Robinson's tax or transfer, and let T_F be Friday's. The government is not creating or destroying wealth, so we require that

$$T_R + T_F = 0.$$

Whatever the government taxes away from one party will be quickly sent to the other party. The government now sends Robinson a message: "Put T_R onto the right-hand side of your budget constraint, and assume prices (p_x^*, p_y^*) for the two goods. If T_R is a negative number, too bad for you. You've lost some money; send it to us. If it's a positive number, good for you. You've gained some money; we'll be wiring it to you today." The government sends Friday a similar message about T_F. The budget constraints of Robinson and Friday now become

$$p_x^* x_R + p_y^* y_R = p_x^* x_R^0 + p_y^* y_R^0 + T_R$$

and

$$p_x^* x_F + p_y^* y_F = p_x^* x_F^0 + p_y^* y_F^0 + T_F.$$

Robinson and Friday now choose their desired consumption bundles, based on these budget constraints. If the government sets the taxes and transfers at the right level, Robinson and Friday will end up at the desired Pareto optimal point, the point Target.

In short, by properly setting lump-sum taxes and transfers, society can get from any initial allocation, no matter how inequitable, to a more desirable Pareto optimal allocation without abandoning the use of the market mechanism. The second fundamental theorem of welfare economics says all this is possible. Here is a more formal statement.

Second Fundamental Theorem of Welfare Economics

Suppose that there are markets for all the goods, that all the people are competitive price takers, and that each person's utility depends only on his or her own bundle of goods. Suppose further that the traders have convex indifference curves. Let Target be any Pareto optimal allocation.

Then there are competitive equilibrium prices for the goods, and a list of lump-sum taxes and transfers for the people, which sum to zero, such that when the budget constraints based on these prices are modified with these taxes and transfers, Target is the resulting competitive equilibrium allocation.

Loosely speaking, the first fundamental theorem of welfare economics says that any competitive equilibrium is Pareto optimal, and the second says that any Pareto optimal point is a competitive equilibrium, given the appropriate modification of the traders' budget constraints. The second theorem needs an additional assumption (convexity), and relies heavily on the budget constraint modifications. However, the existence of the second theorem allows all economists to agree, more or less, "We like the market mechanism; it gets us Pareto optimality." Conservative economists tend to say, "The market's great, don't touch it; let's go to the Pareto optimal outcome it gives us." Liberal economists tend to say, "The market's great, but the initial allocation is terrible; let's use some taxes and transfers to fix the inequities, and then let's go to the Pareto optimal outcome it gives us."

This debate is one of the things that makes life interesting for economists, and for many others.

15.6 A Solved Problem

The Problem

Consider a pure exchange economy with two consumers, 1 and 2, and two goods, x and y. Consumer 1's initial endowment is $w_1 = (1, 0)$; that is, 1 unit of good x and 0 units of good y. Consumer 2's initial endowment is $w_2 = (0, 1)$; that is, 0 units of good x and 1 unit of good y. Let $W = (w_1, w_2)$ represent the initial allocation. Consumer i's utility function (for $i = 1, 2$) is $u_i(x_i, y_i) = x_i y_i$, where (x_i, y_i) represents i's consumption bundle.

(a) Show this economy (with some indifference curves and the initial endowments) in an Edgeworth box diagram.

(b) Write down the equations that describe the Pareto efficient allocations. Identify them in the Edgeworth box. Is the initial endowment point Pareto efficient? Why or why not?

(c) Calculate the competitive equilibrium of this pure exchange economy. You should indicate final consumption bundles for each agent, and the equilibrium prices p_x^* and p_y^*. (Remember that you can normalize the price of one good to be 1.)

(d) For any pair of prices (p_x, p_y), consumers 1 and 2 can figure their desired consumption levels and the net amounts of good x and good y that they want to buy or sell. For example, consumer 1's net demand for good x will be $x_1 - 1$. (This is a negative number, meaning that he will want to sell some of his initial 1 unit of x.) Similarly, consumer 2's net demand for good x will be $x_2 - 0$. Adding over both consumers gives the total net demand for good x, or the *excess demand for x* measured in units of x. (This might be positive or negative. If it is negative, there is excess supply of good x.) Multiplying by p_x would give the excess demand for x measured in dollars.

Assume that (p_x, p_y) is any pair of positive prices. (Note that this is *any* pair of prices, not just the competitive equilibrium prices.) Show that the sum of excess demand for good x in dollars and excess demand for good y in dollars must be zero.

This kind of result was first formally established by Leon Walras, and is therefore called *Walras' law*. Walras' law can be put this way: the sum of market excess demands, over all markets, measured in currency, must be zero.

The Solution

(a) We will not draw the Edgeworth box diagram; it is very similar to Figure 15.8. However, we will describe the diagram. Please sketch the diagram as you read this, if you have not already drawn it. The Edgeworth box diagram is a square, one unit on each side. Consumer 1's origin is the lower left-hand corner; consumer 2's origin is the upper right-hand corner. The initial point W is the lower right-hand corner of the box. Indifference curves are generally symmetric hyperbolas, symmetric around the diagonal of the box that goes from consumer 1's origin to consumer 2's origin, that is, from lower left to upper right. However, the indifference curves that go through the initial point W are "degenerate" hyperbolas; this means that for consumer 1, for instance, the indifference curve through his initial bundle $(1, 0)$ is given by $x_1 y_1 = 0$; graphically, this is his horizontal axis plus his vertical axis.

(b) The Pareto optimal points in this example are points of tangency between indifference curves of the two consumers. Tangency requires that consumer 1's marginal rate of substitution equal consumer 2's marginal rate of substitution. Consumer i's marginal rate of substitution is

$$MRS^i = \frac{MU_x^i}{MU_y^i} = \frac{y_i}{x_i}.$$

Setting the two consumers' marginal rates of substitution equal, and then substituting $1 - x_1$ for x_2 and $1 - y_1$ for y_2, gives

$$\frac{y_1}{x_1} = \frac{y_2}{x_2} = \frac{1 - y_1}{1 - x_1}.$$

This leads directly to

$$x_1 = y_1.$$

Therefore, the set of Pareto optimal points, that is, the contract curve, is simply the upward-sloping diagonal of the box diagram, from consumer 1's origin to consumer 2's origin. The initial point W is obviously not efficient; it is not on the contract curve. In fact, any move from W into the interior of the Edgeworth box diagram would make both consumers better off.

(c) At a competitive equilibrium in the interior of an Edgeworth box diagram, the price ratio p_x^*/p_y^*, consumer 1's marginal rate of substitution, and consumer 2's marginal rate of substitution must all be equal. On the contract curve, where $MRS^1 = MRS^2$, we found that $x_1 = y_1$ must hold. Because $MRS^1 = y_1/x_1$, $MRS^1 = 1/1 = 1$ on the contract curve. Therefore, $p_x^*/p_y^* = 1$ at the competitive equilibrium. We are free to set the price for one of the goods (the numeraire good) equal to 1. Let us make good y the numeraire good. Then $p_y^* = 1$, and because $p_x^*/p_y^* = 1$, $p_x^* = 1$ also.

To find the exact location of the competitive equilibrium allocation, we note that the competitive equilibrium budget line must have slope $p_x^*/p_y^* = 1$ in absolute value, and must start at the initial allocation W, which is the lower right-hand corner of the box. Therefore, the competitive equilibrium budget line is the diagonal of the box going from the lower right corner to the upper left corner. The competitive equilibrium will be at the intersection of the competitive equilibrium budget line and the contract curve, which we already noted was the lower left to upper right diagonal. It follows that the competitive equilibrium allocation is the exact center of the box.

Consumer 1's competitive equilibrium bundle is therefore $(1/2, 1/2)$. Consumer 2's competitive equilibrium bundle is also $(1/2, 1/2)$.

(d) Let (p_x, p_y) be any pair of positive prices, and let (x_1, y_1) and (x_2, y_2) be the corresponding desired consumption bundles of the two consumers. (The assumption of positive prices guarantees that no one wants to consume an infinite amount of x or y.) We will let $\$ED(x)$ represent the excess demand for x, measured in dollars, and similarly $\$ED(y)$ will represent excess demand for y, measured in dollars. Note that

$ED(x) = p_x(x_1 - 1) + p_x(x_2 - 0)$. The sum of excess demands, for goods x and y is

$$ED(x) + ED(y) = p_x(x_1 - 1) + p_x(x_2 - 0) + p_y(y_1 - 0) + p_y(y_2 - 1)$$

$$= (p_x x_1 + p_y y_1 - p_x) + (p_x x_2 + p_y y_2 - p_y).$$

But consumer 1's budget constraint says

$$p_x x_1 + p_y y_1 = p_x \times 1 + p_y \times 0 = p_x,$$

so the terms in the first set of parentheses sum to zero. Similarly, by consumer 2's budget constraint, the terms in the second set of parentheses sum to zero. Therefore,

$$ED(x) + ED(y) = 0,$$

which is Walras' law.

Exercises

1. There are two goods in the world, tiramisu (x) and espresso (y). Michael and Angelo both consider tiramisu and espresso to be complements; each will consume a slice of tiramisu only if it is accompanied with a cup of espresso, and vice versa. Michael has five slices of tiramisu and a cup of espresso. Angelo has a slice of tiramisu and five cups of espresso.

   (a) Draw an Edgeworth box for this exchange economy. Label it carefully. Mark the original endowment point W.

   (b) Draw Michael's and Angelo's indifference curves passing through the endowment point.

   (c) Can you suggest a Pareto improvement over the original endowment? Mark the new allocation W'. How many slices of tiramisu and cups of espresso will each of them consume at the new allocation?

2. Ginger has a pound of sausages ($x_g = 1$) and no potatoes ($y_g = 0$), and Fred has a pound of potatoes ($y_f = 1$) and no sausages ($x_f = 0$). Assume Ginger has the utility function $u_g = x_g^\alpha y_g^{1-\alpha}$, Fred has the same utility function, $u_f = x_f^\alpha y_f^{1-\alpha}$, and the parameter $0 < \alpha < 1$ is the same for Ginger and Fred. (You may remember that these are called Cobb-Douglas utility functions.)

   (a) Show that the contract curve is the diagonal of the Edgeworth box.

   (b) Show that at the competitive equilibrium,

   $$\frac{p_x}{p_y} = \frac{\alpha}{1 - \alpha}.$$

3. Consider an exchange economy with two goods, x and y, and two consumers, Rin and Tin. Rin's utility function is $u_r = x_r y_r$ and his endowment is $\omega_r = (2, 2)$. Tin's utility function is $u_t = x_t y_t^2$ and his endowment is $\omega_t = (3, 3)$. Duncan suggests that there might be a competitive equilibrium at $(x_r', y_r') = (4, 1)$, $(x_t', y_t') = (1, 4)$, with prices $p_x = p_y = 1$.

   (a) Does Duncan's suggested equilibrium allocation have the right totals of the two goods x and y? Explain.

(b) Is Duncan's suggested equilibrium allocation a Pareto improvement over the endowment? Explain.

(c) Write down Rin's budget constraint given these prices. Solve for Rin's optimal consumption bundle, (x_r^*, y_r^*).

(d) Write down Tin's budget constraint given these prices. Solve for Tin's optimal consumption bundle, (x_t^*, y_t^*).

(e) Is Duncan right that these bundles and these prices make a competitive equilibrium? Explain.

4. Consider Rin and Tin from Question 3. We shall now solve this general equilibrium model. We are free to set one of the prices equal to 1. We will let good x be the numeraire good; that is, we will set $p_x = 1$, and we will solve for the appropriate p_y.

(a) Write down Rin's budget constraint. Solve for Rin's optimal consumption bundle, (x_r^*, y_r^*), with x_r^* and y_r^* figured as functions of p_y.

(b) Write down Tin's budget constraint. Solve for Tin's optimal consumption bundle, (x_t^*, y_t^*), x_t^* and y_t^* figured as functions of p_y.

(c) Write down the market-clearing (i.e., total demand = total supply) condition for x. Using your answers from (a) and (b), rewrite the market-clearing condition as a function of p_y, and solve for p_y.

(d) Plug p_y back into your answers from (a) and (b) to find the competitive equilibrium.

5. There are two goods in the world, milk (x) and honey (y), and two consumers, Milne and Shepard. Milne's utility function is $u_m = x_m y_m^3$ and his endowment is $\omega_m = (4, 4)$. Shepard's utility function is $u_s = x_s y_s$ and his endowment is $\omega_s = (0, 0)$. We will again let $p_x = 1$, and we will let p_y vary.

(a) Is the original endowment Pareto optimal? Explain.

Suppose the dictator sets Milne's lump-sum tax at $T_m = -4$, and Shepard's lump-sum transfer at $T_s = 4$.

(b) Write down Milne's new budget constraint. Solve for Milne's optimal consumption bundle, (x_m^*, y_m^*), with x_m^* and y_m^* figured as functions of p_y.

(c) Write down Shepard's new budget constraint. Solve for Shepard's optimal consumption bundle, (x_s^*, y_s^*), with x_s^* and y_s^* figured as functions of p_y.

(d) Solve for the competitive equilibrium; that is, the market-clearing (x_m^*, y_m^*) and (x_s^*, y_s^*), and the equilibrium p_y.

(e) Prove that the new equilibrium allocation is Pareto optimal.

6. "To achieve an efficient allocation, lump-sum taxes on consumers' endowments and per unit taxes on the prices of goods are equivalent." Do you agree with this assertion? Explain, using the welfare theorems in your arguments.

Handwritten annotations (Question 5):

$M \quad \dfrac{Y_m}{3 X_m} = \dfrac{Y_s}{X_s} = \dfrac{4 - Y_m}{4 - X_m}$

$\dfrac{Y_m}{3 X_m} = \dfrac{1}{P_y} \qquad 3 X_m = P_y Y_m$

$P_x X_m + P_y Y = 4 P_y$

$X_m = P_y$

$X_s + P_y Y_s = 4$

$\dfrac{Y_s}{X_s} = \dfrac{1}{P_y}$

$X_s = 2.$

$(P_y, 3)$

$(2, 3)$

$\begin{cases} X_m^* + X_s^* = 4 \\ Y_m^* + Y_s^* = 4 \end{cases}$

$X_m^* = 2$

$P_y = 2$

Chapter 16

A Production Economy

16.1 Introduction

In the last chapter, we analyzed a model of a pure exchange economy. Although there were only two people, Robinson Crusoe and Friday, and only two goods, bread and rum, our model was a general equilibrium model. That is, it was a model that took everything into account simultaneously: Robinson's preferences for bread and for rum, as well as Friday's, and Robinson's initial endowments of bread and rum, as well as Friday's. To keep that model simple, there were only two people and two goods, and there was no production. The quantities of the two goods were taken as given and fixed.

We now turn to another general equilibrium model, in which everything is taken into account simultaneously. However, in this model we analyze production. To keep this model easy, we assume that there is only one person in the economy, who functions both as a producer and as a consumer. We call that one person Robinson Crusoe. (The reader interested in literature may remember that in Defoe's novel, Robinson was alone on the island for many years before Friday arrived. Our production model can be viewed as an economic analysis of work and consumption on the island, before Friday's arrival.)

In our analysis of the pure exchange economy, we discussed Pareto optimality (or Pareto efficiency) and related concepts, and we analyzed market equilibria. We showed the crucial connections between Pareto optimality and the market, connections that are expressed in the first and second fundamental theorems of welfare economics. Recall that the first theorem says, roughly speaking, that a market equilibrium is Pareto optimal. The second says, roughly speaking, that any Pareto optimal allocation can be achieved with the market mechanism.

In this chapter, we describe the production economy and identify the Pareto optimal production outcomes in that economy. We discuss market equilibria in the production economy. We end the chapter with production versions of the first and second fundamental theorems of welfare economics, which provide the connections between the market mechanism and efficiency in production.

16.2 A Robinson Crusoe Production Economy

Robinson Crusoe is now alone on the island; Friday has not yet arrived. Robinson spends his days working and resting. We let l represent the time he spends working per day (or per week, month, or other time unit). This is his *labor*. Time spent resting we call *leisure*, written L. As there are only 24 hours in the day, labor and leisure time are connected: $l + L = 24$. (You may recall this kind of analysis of a consumer's consumption/leisure choice from Chapter 5.)

We assume for now that when Robinson works, he produces bread. We use x to represent a quantity of bread (per day). Near the end of this chapter we will complicate matters by introducing the other good, rum, represented by y. But for now, we assume Robinson is producing only bread.

As a consumer, Robinson has preferences for the two things he enjoys, leisure and bread. We assume for simplicity that he cares about the time he spends working, l, but only insofar as it limits the time he spends resting, as $l = 24 - L$. (Recall that this is what we assumed in Chapter 5.) Robinson's preferences regarding leisure and bread might be represented by a utility function $v(L, x)$. The indifference curves for this utility function are downward sloping, with the usual convexity. However, our analysis of Robinson's behavior as a consumer *and producer* will be much easier if we get rid of leisure L in the utility function, and replace it with labor l. Of course, leisure is a *good* (Robinson prefers more of it), and labor is a *bad* (Robinson prefers less of it, because it limits his leisure).

Let $u(l, x)$ represent Robinson's utility from labor and bread. For the utility function $u(l, x)$, the marginal utility of bread, $MU_x = \partial u(l, x)/\partial x$, is positive, and the marginal utility of labor, $MU_l = \partial u(l, x)/\partial l$, is negative. Robinson prefers more bread and less work. Because of this, the indifference curves for the utility function $u(l, x)$ will be upward sloping and convex, instead of downward sloping and convex as with the indifference curves for $v(L, x)$.

Figure 16.1 shows two indifference curve graphs; the top one is for the $v(L, x)$ utility function, and has standard downward-sloping indifference curves; the bottom one is for the $u(l, x)$ utility function, and has upward-sloping indifference curves.

Now let us consider Robinson as a *producer* of bread. He has a production function $x = f(l)$. This shows what is technologically feasible for him – how many loaves of bread he can produce (at best) for a given number of hours of labor. If we graph the production function, we get a picture of the best levels of output (bread) Robinson can achieve for given levels of input (labor). These are the points on the production function itself. Such points are called *technologically efficient*.

The production function is graphed in Figure 16.2. Points below the graph of the production function are *feasible, but technologically inefficient*. These points are

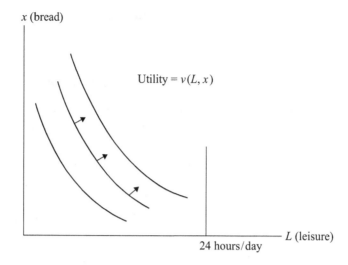

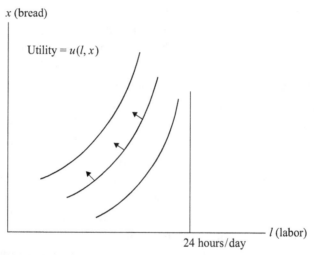

Fig. 16.1. Robinson as a consumer. Indifference curves in a leisure/bread graph (top) and in a labor/bread graph (bottom). Arrows show directions of increasing utility.

possible combinations of labor and bread, but not the best Robinson could do; that is, with the same amounts of labor, he could produce more bread. Points above the graph of the production function are *nonfeasible*; they are simply impossible given Robinson's technology for producing bread.

16.3 Pareto Efficiency

Recall the definitions of Pareto optimality and related concepts that we discussed in the last chapter. First, to be optimal or efficient, an alternative must be feasible. Second, it must be the case that nothing Pareto dominates it. When there are two or more people in the economy, and A and B are two feasible alternatives, we say

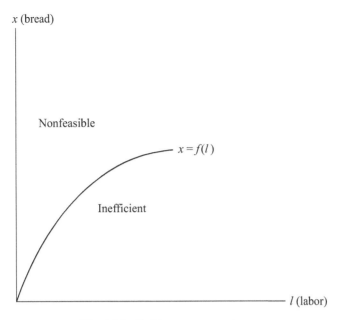

Fig. 16.2. Robinson as a producer.

that *A Pareto dominates B* if everybody likes *A* at least as well as *B*, and at least one person likes it better.

When there is just one person, Robinson, *A Pareto dominates B* if both are feasible and Robinson likes *A* better. An alternative is *Pareto optimal* or *Pareto efficient* if it is feasible and there are no other feasible alternatives that Robinson likes better. In short, in a one-person economy, the Pareto optimal or efficient outcomes are simply the feasible outcomes that Robinson likes best. Figure 16.3 shows the (unique) efficient alternative in this simple economy. It is simply the point on the production function that maximizes Robinson's utility. This is the point at which the production function curve is tangent to the highest indifference curve, the point (l^*, x^*) in Figure 16.3.

Figure 16.3 reveals the conditions that must hold for an interior $(l^*, x^* > 0)$ Pareto optimal point in this simple economy.

First, (l^*, x^*) must be technologically efficient. It must be on the production function – not below it, which would make it feasible but inefficient, and not above it, which would make it impossible, or nonfeasible. It must satisfy the equation

$$x = f(l).$$

Second, it must be a tangency point between the production function and an indifference curve. Very loosely speaking, the slope of an indifference curve is the marginal rate of substitution of bread for labor. We say "very loosely speaking" because in this model, labor l is a *bad* rather than a *good*; this means that the marginal rate of substitution will not have the usual sign.

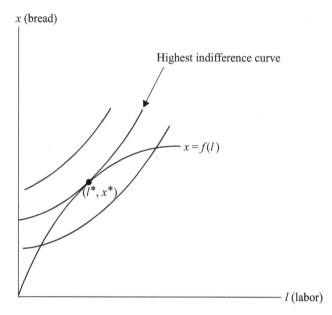

Fig. 16.3. The Pareto efficient production/consumption point.

Remember that when we are looking at two *goods*, the marginal rate of substitution of the second good for the first good is the amount of the second good we would have to give the consumer to compensate for his consuming one less unit of the first good. Under our definition of *MRS* in Chapter 2, for two goods x_1 and x_2, $MRS_{x_1,x_2} = MU_1/MU_2$, which is positive. But because labor is a bad, the marginal rate of substitution of bread for labor, or $MRS_{l,x} = MU_l/MU_x$, is negative. That is, to compensate Robinson for working one hour less, we would have to give him a negative quantity of bread.

In Figure 16.3, Robinson's indifference curves are positively sloped. The slope of an indifference curve at any given point equals -1 times the *MRS* at that point, or

$$\text{Indifference curve slope} = -MRS_{l,x} = -\frac{MU_l}{MU_x} > 0.$$

The slope of the production function is

$$MP(l) = \frac{df(l)}{dl} > 0.$$

Therefore, the optimal point (l^*, x^*) must satisfy the equation

$$-MRS_{l,x} = MP(l).$$

If there were a social welfare optimizer in heaven overseeing this simple Robinson Crusoe production economy, we now know what she would like to do. She would want to bring about the allocation (l^*, x^*) that maximizes Robinson's utility, subject to his technological constraint. She would like to solve the preceding two equations. Could she do this with the market mechanism?

16.4 Walrasian or Competitive Equilibrium

We will now bring the market to Robinson. Of course, this seems artificial and bizarre, something only crazy economists would want to do, as Robinson can get along fine without prices, profit maximization, budget constraints, and so on. We do it anyway, however, because we want to model how the market works, and our particular story is odd only because we chose to develop the simplest possible production model, with just one person, who is simultaneously the producer and consumer of everything.

We assume there is a market for bread and a market for labor. Robinson, as a worker, sells his labor in the labor market. Robinson, as a consumer, buys his bread in the bread market. Robinson, as an entrepreneur, is 100 percent owner of a bread-producing firm, called Robby's Natural Breadworks, or "Robby's" for short. Robby's buys labor on the labor market (from Robinson, of course); it sells bread on the bread market (to Robinson, of course), and if it has profits, those profits go to its owner, namely, Robinson. We also assume that the markets for bread and labor are *competitive*; that is, we assume that the parties all take prices as given and fixed.

We let p_x be the price (per loaf) of bread, and we let w be the price (per hour) of labor. The reader may recall from the last chapter that because only relative prices matter in a general equilibrium model, one of the prices can be set equal to 1. The good whose price is set at 1 is called the *numeraire*. To simplify our Robinson production model slightly, we now make bread the numeraire good. That is, we set $p_x = 1$. Later on, when we introduce a second good, we will go back to using p_x for the price of bread, and we will then make labor the numeraire good.

Let us now discuss what our players want to do in this market economy.

The Firm

Robby's Natural Breadworks wants to maximize profit. Its revenue is $p_x x = 1x = x$, where x is the amount of bread it supplies on the market (per day or per unit time). Its cost is wl, where w is the wage and l is the number of hours of labor it is buying on the labor market (per day or per unit time.) Its profit is $\pi_R = x - wl$. It wants to maximize profit given its production technology; that is, its production function $x = f(L)$. Any profit that Robby's makes is immediately paid to its owner, Robinson.

In Figure 16.4, we show the profit maximization problem of the firm, and how that problem is solved. The vertical axis is now "x or \$" instead of just "x." This

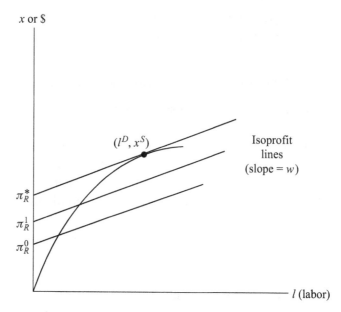

Fig. 16.4. The firm maximizes profit at (l^D, x^S), at which point profit equals π_R^*.

is because we are assuming x is a numeraire good, with price equal to 1. The figure includes the production function $x = f(l)$, and it also includes something new: isoprofit lines. An *isoprofit line* is a locus of input–output combinations in the figure that all produce the same level of profit. (Recall that "iso" means "the same," as in "isoquant" in the theory of the firm.) The equation for an isoprofit line is

$$x - wl = \pi_R = \text{a constant.}$$

We can rewrite this as

$$x = wl + \pi_R.$$

We can easily see from the latter equation that the slope of an isoprofit line is w, and the intercept of the isoprofit line on the vertical (bread) axis is the constant π_R. In the figure, the higher isoprofit lines correspond to higher profit levels.

Robby's wants to get to the highest isoprofit line in Figure 16.4. The solution to the profit-maximization problem is shown in the figure as (l^D, x^S). l^D is Robby's demand for labor, and x^S is Robby's supply of bread. (Both are per day or per unit time.) At the desired point (l^D, x^S), the production function is tangent to an isoprofit line. That is, their slopes are equal, and therefore

$$w = \frac{df(l)}{dl} = MP(l).$$

Robby's profit level at (l^D, x^S) is $x^S - wl^D = \pi_R^*$. Here π_R^* represents Robby's *maximum profit level.*

The Consumer

Now, let us turn to Robinson. He wants to maximize his utility subject to his budget constraint. His utility function is $u(l, x)$. His budget constraint says that what he wants to spend, $1x = x$, must be less than or equal to his income. We assume that he always wants more bread, and so he will spend all his income. His total income is the sum of his earnings as a worker and his income as owner of Robby's. In short, Robinson wants to solve the following problem:

$$\max u(l, x) \qquad \text{subject to} \qquad x = wl + \pi_R.$$

To solve this utility-maximization problem, Robinson looks for a tangency between one of his indifference curves and his budget line. Because the slope of an indifference curve is $-MRS_{l,x}$ and because the slope of the budget line is w, the tangency condition is

$$-MRS_{l,x} = w.$$

To connect Robinson the consumer with Robby's the firm, we replace the general term π_R in Robinson's budget constraint with the maximum profit level of Robby's, namely, $\pi_R^* = x^S - wl^D$. This gives Robinson the budget constraint

$$x = wl + \pi_R^*.$$

In Figure 16.5 we show the production function $x = f(l)$, and Robby's profit-maximizing point (l^D, x^S), as well as Robinson's budget line and one of his indifference curves tangent to his budget line. His budget line, based on his budget constraint $x = wl + \pi_R^*$, is exactly the same line as Robby's maximum profit isoprofit line $x - wl = \pi_R^*$. The optimal point in the figure for Robinson, the tangency point, is the point (l^S, x^D). In short, Robinson wants to supply l^S hours of labor (per day or per unit time unit), and he wants to consume x^D loaves of bread (per day or per unit time).

The reader who looks at Figure 16.5 for a moment should see a giant problem: the numbers don't add up. The amount of labor demanded by Robby's the firm exceeds the amount of labor supplied by Robinson the worker. That is, there is excess demand for labor. The amount of bread supplied by Robby's the firm exceeds the amount demanded by Robinson the consumer. That is, there is excess supply of bread. In a real economy, excess demand for labor should make the wage rate rise, and excess supply of bread should make the price of bread fall. In our model, in which bread is the numeraire good, the price of bread is fixed at $1 per unit, but the wage rate w should rise. Therefore, the isoprofit lines in Figure 16.4 and the budget line in Figure 16.5 should all get steeper. (Their slopes equal w, which should increase.) The slopes of those lines should all change until there is neither excess demand for nor excess supply of either labor or bread.

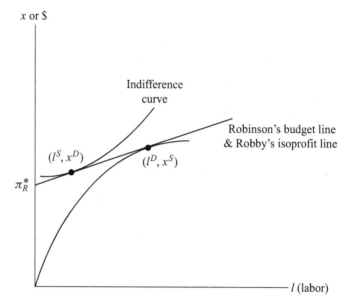

Fig. 16.5. Robinson the consumer maximizes utility at (l^S, x^D), whereas Robby's the firm wants to maximize profit at (l^D, x^S).

Let us now define a *Walrasian* or *competitive equilibrium* in our simple production economy. This is a list of prices, w for labor and $p_x = 1$ for bread, an input-output vector for the firm (l^D, x^S), and a labor-supply and consumption vector (l^S, x^D) for the consumer, such that:

1. Given the prices, the firm maximizes profits at (l^D, x^S). That is, (l^D, x^S) solves the following problem:

$$\max \pi_R = x - wl \qquad \text{subject to} \qquad x = f(l).$$

2. Given the prices, and given his budget constraint, the consumer maximizes utility at (l^S, x^D). That is, (l^S, x^D) solves the following problem:

$$\max u(l, x) \qquad \text{subject to} \qquad x = wl + \pi_R^*,$$

where π_R^* represents the firm's maximum profit level.

3. There is no excess demand and no excess supply, of labor or bread:

$$l^D = l^S \qquad \text{and} \qquad x^D = x^S.$$

Figure 16.5 shows a nonequilibrium situation; it fails point 3 in the definition of a competitive equilibrium. In Figure 16.6, we modify the budget line of Figure 16.5. We make it steeper (that is, we increase its slope w), so that the point chosen by Robby's the firm (l^D, x^S) and the point chosen by Robinson the consumer (l^S, x^D) just *coincide*. In Figure 16.6, there is neither excess demand for nor excess supply of either labor or bread. In short, Figure 16.6 shows a competitive equilibrium.

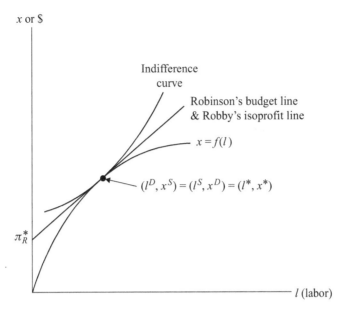

x or $

Indifference
curve

Robinson's budget line
& Robby's isoprofit line

$x = f(l)$

$(l^D, x^S) = (l^S, x^D) = (l^*, x^*)$

π_R^*

l (labor)

Fig. 16.6. A Walrasian or competitive equilibrium at $(l^D, x^S) = (l^S, x^D) = (l^*, x^*)$.

As the reader can plainly see in the figure, the competitive equilibrium point $(l^*, x^*) = (l^D, x^S) = (l^S, x^D)$ is Pareto optimal. In fact, in this simple economy, there is only one Pareto optimal point and only one competitive equilibrium point, and they are the same point.

16.5 When There Are Two Goods, Bread and Rum

Before turning to the production versions of the two fundamental theorems of welfare economics, we complicate our Robinson Crusoe model slightly by putting another consumption good into the picture. We now assume that Robby's adds a second good to its (short) line of products, namely rum, and changes its name to Robby's Natural Bread and Rum Works. (It is still Robby's for short.) As before, l is a quantity of labor, x is a quantity of bread, and now y is a quantity of rum. We now have three prices: the wage rate w, the price of bread p_x and the price of rum p_y. In the previous sections of this chapter we let bread be the numeraire; that is, we assumed $p_x = 1$ for simplicity. In this section, we let labor be the numeraire; that is, we will set $w = 1$, and let p_x and p_y vary. As before, we have one consumer/worker, namely, Robinson.

The Firm

As before, Robby's wants to maximize profit. Its revenue is now $p_x x + p_y y$, and its cost is $wl = l$. (All the units, as usual, are per day or per unit time.) Its profit is

$\pi_R = p_x x + p_y y - l$. It wants to maximize profit given its production technology. Any profit that Robby's makes is immediately paid to its owner, Robinson.

Describing Robby's production technology is slightly tricky, because we now have one input and two outputs. The familiar picture of a production isoquant from Chapter 9 is based on two inputs and one output, and Figures 16.2 through 16.6 in this chapter are based on one input and one output. The alert reader may remember that we discussed a one input, two output model in Section 8.4. But here is a direct and easy way to think about this problem.

Suppose Robby's has two sheds; one is for baking and the other is for brewing. Robinson the worker spends part of each day in the baking shed, and part of each day in the brewing shed. Each of these activities has a production function similar to the one pictured in Figures 16.2 through 16.6; the functions are concave, meaning that these activities are both decreasing returns to scale activities. Now let us fix Robinson's total daily work hours at some number, such as $l^0 = 8$ hours per day. Quantities that are contingent on the assumed l^0 will be called *provisional*.

Let us think about the possible maximum combinations of bread and rum that Robinson the worker might produce, given that he is around for only 8 hours. That is, if he produced 0 loaves of bread, what is the most rum he could produce? If he produced 1 loaf of bread, what is the most rum he could produce? And so on. The answers to these questions would give a locus of points in a graph with bread x on one axis and rum y on the other axis. The usual convention is to put x on the horizontal axis and y on the vertical axis of such a graph. This locus of points is called Robby's *production frontier*. Now the question is: What is the curvature of Robby's production frontier? The reader should be able to convince himself or herself that if the separate production functions for bread and rum are concave, then the production frontier will also be *concave*. Note that the production frontier, as we have defined it, depends on the given input level (that is, $l^0 = 8$); that is, it is provisional, and a different input level would give a different provisional production frontier.

Figure 16.7 is a graph with bread x on the horizontal axis and rum y on the vertical axis. The figure includes Robby's provisional production frontier, a concave curve. Robby's would never want to be below the production frontier, because below it the company could make more bread and more rum for the given labor total of 8 hours per day. Points below the frontier are technologically inefficient. Robby's cannot get above the frontier with the given labor total; points above the frontier are nonfeasible.

Now, let us consider Robby's provisional profit-maximizing problem. At this point we are analyzing only Robby's choice of two variables, x and y, for a given level of the third variable l^0. Robby's wants to maximize its profit $\pi_R = p_x x + p_y y - l$, but for a given $l = l^0$, maximizing profit is the same as maximizing revenue $p_x x + p_y y$. In Figure 16.7 we have plotted two isoprofit lines. On each of these lines revenue, and therefore profit, is constant. They are straight lines with

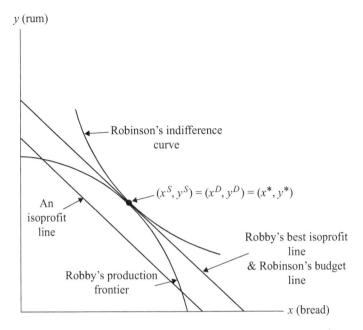

Fig. 16.7. With two goods, bread and rum, and for a given amount of labor l^0, the provisional Walrasian or competitive equilibrium is at $(x^S, y^S) = (x^D, y^D) = (x^*, y^*)$.

slope p_x/p_y. The lower one is identified as "an isoprofit line," and the higher one is identified as "Robby's best isoprofit line." Robby's wants to maximize profit, so it wants to get to the highest isoprofit line it can, subject to its production frontier. Given the prices p_x and p_y, and given the l^0 value of 8 hours per day we started with, (x^S, y^S) represents the amounts of bread and rum that Robby's wants to supply in the market.

We will let π_R^* represent Robby's profit level at the best-of-all isoprofit line. Note that

$$\pi_R^* = p_x x^S + p_y y^S - l^0.$$

Also note the equation for the best isoprofit line is

$$p_x x + p_y y = p_x x^S + p_y y^S.$$

The Consumer

Now, let us turn back to Robinson the consumer. He wants to maximize his utility subject to his budget constraint. His utility function is $u(l^0, x, y)$. (Remember, we are holding l constant at l^0, so this utility maximization will be provisional.) His budget constraint says that what he wants to spend, $p_x x + p_y y$, must be less than or equal to his income. We will assume that he always wants more bread and rum, so he will spend all his income. His total income is the sum of his earnings as a worker and his income as owner of Robby's. In short, Robinson wants to maximize $u(l^0, x, y)$, subject to

$$p_x x + p_y y = l^0 + \pi_R.$$

To solve this provisional utility maximization problem, Robinson looks for a tangency between one of his indifference curves and his budget line.

To connect Robinson the consumer with Robby's the firm, we replace the general term π_R in Robinson's budget constraint with the maximum profit level of Robby's, namely, $\pi_R^* = p_x x^S + p_y y^S - l^0$. This gives Robinson the budget constraint

$$p_x x + p_y y = l^0 + \pi_R^* = l^0 + p_x x^S + p_y y^S - l^0 = p_x x^S + p_y y^S.$$

But this is precisely the same equation as the equation for Robby's best isoprofit line.

Therefore, Robinson's budget line, and Robby's best isoprofit line, are one and the same line, the straight line tangent to the production frontier in Figure 16.7. We call Robinson's utility-maximizing consumption bundle (x^D, y^D). At this consumption bundle, one of his indifference curves must be tangent to his budget line. We use the D superscripts because the bundle (x^D, y^D) represents Robinson's provisional levels of demand for bread and rum in the market.

We now see that, contingent on l^0, there is a supply bundle (x_S, y_S) that Robby's intends to supply to the market, and there is a demand bundle (x_D, y_D) that Robinson wants to buy in the market. If these bundles are different, then supply and demand for bread are inconsistent, and there must be excess demand for one of the goods and excess supply of the other good. (This would be a two-output analogy to what we saw in Figure 16.5, the one-output model.) With excess demand in one market and excess supply in the other market, p_x/p_y must change. The price ratio would continue to change until there is no excess demand and no excess supply.

When there is no excess supply and no excess demand, the supply and demand bundles coincide. That is, $(x_S, y_S) = (x_D, y_D) = (x^*, y^*)$. This is what we show in Figure 16.7. In that figure we show what must hold in a provisional Walrasian or competitive equilibrium when there are two goods. The reader can plainly see in the figure that, contingent on the assumed l^0, the competitive equilibrium point (x^*, y^*) is Pareto optimal. It is the best Robinson can do, given l^0, and given the available production technology. In fact, in this economy, as in the one-input, one-output version of the Robinson Crusoe model discussed in previous sections of this chapter, there is only one Pareto optimal point and only one competitive equilibrium point, and they are the same point.

Up to this point in this section we assumed a fixed amount of labor l^0, so the quantities of bread and rum were all provisional. We conclude by briefly sketching how to solve for the equilibrium quantity of labor. This would allow us to transform *provisional equilibria* into *genuine equilibria*. Here is how the argument goes, in rough terms:

In the previous paragraphs, based on a given l^0, we derived a provisional competitive equilibrium (x^*, y^*). Now, imagine doing this analysis over and over, with different labor quantities. For each l we start with, we derive a competitive equilibrium consumption bundle, which we now write $(x^*(l), y^*(l))$, to show that it depends on l. Robinson's utility function becomes a function of l alone; that is,

$$u(l, x, y) = u(l, x^*(l), y^*(l)) = u(l).$$

Robinson's utility function has been reduced to a function of just one variable. Under the assumptions we have made in this chapter, $u(l)$ is a concave function and has a unique maximum. Let l^* be the labor quantity that maximizes $u(l)$. The triple $(l^*, x^*(l^*), y^*(l^*))$ is the absolute best combination of work and consumption for Robinson. It is the unique Pareto optimal consumption bundle of work, bread, and rum.

What about prices and the competitive equilibrium? We continue to assume that labor is the numeraire good, so $w = 1$. To find the price ratio p_x/p_y, we look at the slope of the production frontier, based on l^*, where that production frontier is tangent to an indifference curve, also based on l^*. This is similar to our discussion at Figure 16.7. Multiplying that slope by -1 gives p_x/p_y. Finally, to connect the price of labor ($w = 1$) and the separate prices for bread and rum (p_x, p_y), we set -1 times Robinson's marginal rate of substitution of bread for labor, evaluated at point the $(l^*, x^*(l^*), y^*(l^*))$, equal to the price ratio $w/p_x = 1/p_x$. This allows us to find p_x, and then to find p_y. Once we have all three prices, $(w = 1, p_x, p_y)$ for labor, bread, and rum, respectively, we show that Robinson is maximizing his utility subject to his budget constraint at $(l^*, x^*(l^*), y^*(l^*))$, *and* that Robby's is maximizing its profit at the same point.

In conclusion, we start by finding the l^* that maximizes Robinson's utility, and the corresponding amounts of bread and wine $(x^*(l^*), y^*(l^*))$. These constitute the unique Pareto optimal combination of labor, bread, and rum. Then we find the right prices $(w = 1, p_x, p_y)$. With these prices, $(l^*, x^*(l^*), y^*(l^*))$ is the unique competitive equilibrium combination of labor, bread, and rum. It is a genuine equilibrium, not a provisional equilibrium. And in this economy, the competitive equilibrium vector of labor, bread, and rum, and the Pareto optimum, are one and the same point.

16.6 The Two Welfare Theorems Revisited

The reader may recall the two fundamental theorems of welfare economics from Chapter 15 on the exchange economy model. The first fundamental theorem said that a competitive equilibrium allocation in an exchange economy is Pareto optimal. The second fundamental theorem said that if indifference curves are convex, then any Pareto optimal allocation can be achieved by the market, provided the market is modified with taxes and transfers. Figures 16.6 and 16.7 indicate that something similar must be true in the production model, as in those figures, the competitive equilibrium is Pareto optimal (theorem 1), and the (unique) Pareto optimal point is a competitive equilibrium (theorem 2).

In this section, we carefully state the two welfare theorems for economies with production. We state these theorems for models that are more general than the one-firm, one-consumer, one-input, one(or two)-output model we have been examining.

Now let us assume that there are any number of consumers and any number of firms. The firms are owned by the consumers; each consumer has shares in the various firms. For example, Robinson may own 3 shares out of 100 (or 3 percent) of firm 1, 20 shares out 200 (or 10 percent) of firm 2, and so on.

We assume that the consumers own various inputs (such as`labor l) that they sell on input markets to the firms. We assume that each firm uses various inputs to produce some output (such as bread x), which it sells to consumers on a market for that product. All the markets are competitive, which means that all agents, consumers, and firms take prices as given. We assume that each consumer's utility depends only on his own bundle of goods, and that each firm's output depends only on the inputs it is using. For the second fundamental theorem, we also assume that all the consumers' indifference curves are convex, and that the firms' production technologies are also convex. (For a firm that uses only one input, such as Robby's Natural Breadworks, this means the production function is concave, as in Figure 16.2. That is, it satisfies the assumption of diminishing returns to scale.)

In this more general production economy model, a Walrasian or competitive equilibrium is a list of prices for inputs and outputs; a set of planned input-output vectors, one for each firm; and a set of planned consumption bundles (including intended supplies of inputs such as l), one for each consumer, such that:

1. Given the list of prices, each firm is maximizing profits at its planned input-output vector. The firm distributes those profits to its shareholders, according to their ownership percentages.
2. Given the list of prices, and given the profits received from the firms in which it owns shares, each consumer is maximizing utility subject to his budget constraint, at the planned consumption bundle.
3. At these prices, total supply equals total demand for every good.

In the more general production economy model, Pareto optimality is defined in much the same way as it is in the pure exchange model. That is, we first define what is feasible. This depends on the initial allocation of all the goods to the consumers, including the various goods that are used as inputs by the firms. It also depends on the production technologies of the firms. Then, if A and B are both feasible, we say that A Pareto dominates B if everyone likes A at least as well as B, and at least one person likes it better. Finally, a feasible allocation is *Pareto optimal* or *efficient* if there is nothing feasible that Pareto dominates it.

As an aside, it is interesting to note that the concept of Pareto optimality in a general equilibrium model of an economy with firms and consumers ultimately looks only at the welfare of the consumers. It does not look at the welfare, or the profit levels, of the firms. Those profits flow back to the owners of the firms, and those owners are consumers. The reader may recall that partial equilibrium analysis, done in a market for a single good, adds together consumers' surplus and producers' surplus, which seems to imply that society should place some weight on the welfare (i.e., profitability) of firms. But general equilibrium analysis treats firms as producers of goods rather than money. Certainly they produce profits, and they should be profit maximizers, but those profits flow right back to the owners/consumers. In general equilibrium analysis, the ultimate purpose of firms, their reason for being, is to expand the set of things that are feasible so that consumers can achieve higher utility levels.

We now turn to the two fundamental theorems of welfare economics for an economy with production and consumption, with any number of firms, consumers, and goods. We are making all the assumptions as listed previously, and we are repeating only the crucial assumptions.

First Fundamental Theorem of Welfare Economics

Suppose there are markets and market prices for all the inputs and outputs; that is, all the goods. Then any competitive equilibrium is Pareto optimal.

Second Fundamental Theorem of Welfare Economics

Suppose there are markets and market prices for all the inputs and outputs, that is, all the goods. Suppose further that all the consumers have convex indifference curves, and that all the firms have convex technologies. Suppose there is a Pareto optimal allocation that is society's target. Then there is a vector of lump-sum taxes and transfers in the numeraire good, which sum to zero, such that when budget constraints are modified with these taxes and transfers, the target is the resulting competitive equilibrium allocation.

As with the first and second fundamental theorems of welfare economics in the pure exchange model of the last chapter, the moral is simple: society should aim for Pareto optimality. In a competitive economy with producers and consumers, the market mechanism gives us Pareto optimality. That is the first fundamental theorem. If the untouched competitive equilibrium is very unfair – if it makes some people very rich and many people very poor – don't throw the baby out with the bath water. The market mechanism can be modified in a relatively minor way – by appropriate taxes and transfers – so that the modified competitive equilibrium is any Pareto optimal allocation we might want. That is the second fundamental theorem.

16.7 A Solved Problem

The Problem

Robby's production function for transforming labor l into bread x is given by $x = 12\sqrt{l}$. Robinson Crusoe's utility function for labor and bread is $u(l, x) = x - l^2/9$. Robinson Crusoe owns Robby's, and both Robinson the consumer and Robby's the firm are price takers.

(a) Show that at the Pareto efficient allocation Robinson works 9 hours per day.
(b) Find the market equilibrium allocation, and explain why it is Pareto efficient.
(c) Find the equilibrium market prices and the equilibrium profit level for Robby's.

The Solution

(a.1) Here is a direct, brute force approach. In order to find the efficient outcome, we substitute the production function $x = 12\sqrt{l}$ into the utility function, making utility a function of only one variable, l:

$$u(l) = x - l^2/9 = 12\sqrt{l} - l^2/9.$$

Next we differentiate with respect to l and set the result equal to zero:

$$(12l^{-1/2})/2 - 2l/9 = 0.$$

Rearranging terms gives $l^{3/2} = 27$, and therefore $l^* = 9$. Substituting this into the production function then gives $x^* = 36$.

(a.2) Here is a less direct, but more intuitive, graphical story. Consider Figure 16.8, which is really Figure 16.3 with some new labels. We are looking for the utility-maximizing point (l^*, x^*), where an indifference curve and the production function are tangent. The tangency condition says the absolute value of the marginal rate of substitution of bread for labor, or $-MRS_{l,x}$, should equal the marginal product of labor in the production of bread, or $MP(l)$. This gives

$$-MRS_{l,x} = -\frac{MU_l}{MU_x} = 2l/9 = MP(l) = (12l^{-1/2})/2.$$

A little rearranging gives $l^{3/2} = 27$, which leads to $l^* = 9$. Substituting into the production function gives $x^* = 36$.

(b) In this simple economy, for any pair of prices (x, p_x) there will be one and only one line representing both Robinson's budget line and Robby's highest isoprofit line. (See Figure 16.5.) Given this line, Robinson the consumer will want a point (l^S, x^D), and Robby's the firm will want a point (l^D, x^S). To have a competitive equilibrium, with supply and demand equal in both markets, (l^S, x^D) and (l^D, x^S) must coincide. (See Figure 16.6.)

   Therefore, our market equilibrium must be at the point $(l^*, x^*) = (9, 36)$ in Figure 16.8. But this is the Pareto efficient point. (And, of course, the first fundamental theorem of welfare economics says the competitive equilibrium must be Pareto optimal.)

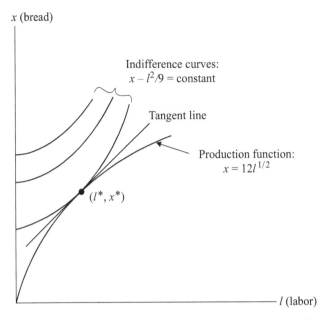

x (bread)

Indifference curves:
$x - l^2/9 = $ constant

Tangent line

Production function:
$x = 12l^{1/2}$

(l^*, x^*)

l (labor)

Fig. 16.8. The Pareto efficient production/consumption point (l^*, x^*).

(c) Let us set the price of bread equal to 1, so bread is the numeraire good. The slope of Robinson's budget line and the slope of Robby's isoprofit line equals the price ration $w/p_x = w/1 = w$. However, at the market equilibrium, the budget line, the isoprofit line, and the tangent line to the production function are all the same. The slope of the tangent line to the production function at (l^*, x^*) is

$$MP(l^*) = (12l^{*-1/2})/2 = 6 \times 9^{-1/2} = 2.$$

Therefore, the equilibrium wage is $w = 2$.

Robby's equilibrium profit is $\pi_R = 1 \times 36 - 2 \times 9 = 18$. Robby's sends this profit to its shareholder Robinson, whose budget constraint now says

$$x = 2l + 18.$$

At $(l^S, x^D) = (l^*, x^*) = (9, 36)$, Robinson's income is $2 \times 9 = 18$ from his wages as a worker, plus 18 from his ownership of Robby's, for a total of 36, all of which he spends on 36 loaves of bread.

Exercises

1. Robinson's technology for producing coconuts (x) is represented by $x = \sqrt{l}$, where l is labor, in hours per day. His preferences for coconuts and labor are given by the utility function $u(l, x) = x - l/2$. Assume Robinson is the only consumer of coconuts, and the owner of the only firm that produces coconuts. Suppose the price of coconuts is set at 1.

   (a) Calculate the Pareto efficient allocation of this simple production economy.
   (b) Derive the competitive equilibrium of this economy. Find Robinson's consumption of coconuts, his labor supply, the market wage rate, and the firm's profits.

2. Consider Robinson from Question 1. Suppose his technology for producing coconuts (x) changes to $x = l^{2/3}$. His utility function remains the same: $u(l, x) = x - l/2$.

    (a) Calculate the new Pareto efficient allocation.

    (b) Derive the competitive equilibrium of this economy. Find Robinson's consumption of coconuts, his labor supply, the market wage rate, and the firm's profits.

3. Remy produces omelettes (x) according to the technology $x = \sqrt{l} + 1$. He derives the following utility from his consumption of omelettes (x) and his labor (l): $u(l, x) = x - 2l^2$. Remy is the only consumer and producer of omelettes in his household.

    (a) Show that Remy consumes 1.5 omelettes at the Pareto efficient allocation.

    (b) Suppose the price of omelettes is set at 1. Find the market equilibrium allocation and wage rate.

4. Wendy's technology for studying chapters of economics (x) and chapters of mathematics (y) is given by $x = \sqrt{l_x}$ and $y = \sqrt{l_y}$, respectively, where l_x and l_y are hours per day spent studying economics and mathematics, respectively. Her utility function is $u(l_x, l_y, x, y) = xy - \sqrt{l_x + l_y}$. Suppose that Wendy has decided to study for a total of four hours per day.

    (a) How many hours should she spend on economics? How many hours on mathematics?

    (b) How many chapters of each subject does she study?

    (c) Calculate her utility.

    (d) How does her utility change if she decides to double the number of hours she studies?

5. Robinson has expanded his production to coconuts (x) and mangos (y). His inverse production function is represented by $l = x^2 + y^2 + 3xy$, where l is labor, in hours per day. His utility function is $u(l, x, y) = 3xy/2 + x + y - l/2$. Suppose the market wage rate w is set at 1.

    (a) Solve Robinson's profit maximization problem. Derive his supply of coconuts and mangos, $x^S(p_x, p_y)$ and $y^S(p_x, p_y)$.

    (b) Solve Robinson's utility maximization problem. Derive his demand for coconuts and mangos, x^D and y^D, and find his labor supply, l_S.

    (c) Find the price of coconuts and mangos, p_x and p_y.

6. Consider an economy where Robinson is the sole producer and the sole consumer of three goods, x, y, and z. Given prices p_x, p_y, and p_z, the wage w, and his inverse production function $l(x, y, z)$, write down his profit maximization problem and his utility maximization problem.

Part V

Market Failure

Chapter 17

Externalities

17.1 Introduction

The last two chapters focused on the connections between the market mechanism and Pareto optimality. We showed that in exchange and in production, the free market leads to efficiency, and that any efficient situation can be achieved via a slightly modified market mechanism. These important results relied on some equally important assumptions. One assumption was that all the parties in the economy must act competitively; they must all assume that prices are given and fixed, beyond their control. We know that when the assumption of competitive behavior breaks down, as with monopoly, duopoly, or oligopoly, the market does *not* lead to efficiency. The behavior of a monopolist, or, more generally, the noncompetitive behavior of any player in a market, leads to what is called *market failure*.

In this chapter, we examine another very important kind of market failure, the kind produced by *externalities*.

When we analyzed trade between two people, we assumed that person i's utility depended only on his bundle of goods, and not on person j's. When we analyzed production by firms, we assumed that firm i's costs and output depended only on its inputs, and not on the inputs or outputs of firm j. When we analyzed the interactions between firms and consumers, we assumed that a consumer buying a firm's output cared only about how much he consumed, and the price he paid. If the consumer was selling labor to the firm, he cared only about the quantity he was selling, and the price he received. The consumer did not care about what quantities of its output the firm might be selling to others, or what quantities of its inputs it might be buying from others.

In other words, in past chapters we assumed that the players in the market economy – the consumers and the firms – affected each other only through market trade and the prices paid for inputs and outputs in various markets. Person j's consumption of food might have an effect on person i, but that would be an "indirect" effect via the prices; j's food consumption might result in food prices being somewhat higher than they would have been, thereby affecting i. However, such indirect effects would be entirely incorporated in the market prices.

However, the world is full of examples in which the actions of consumers directly affect other consumers, in ways not captured by market prices; in which the actions of firms directly affect other firms, in ways not captured by prices; and in which the actions of firms and consumers directly interact, in ways not captured by prices. These interactions are called *externalities*. As we will see, they lead to inefficiency in markets. Externalities create very important market failures.

In this chapter we analyze externalities. We start with some examples. Then we carefully describe how the market fails when externalities are present, and we describe various possible remedies for the market failures created by externalities. The classical remedies for such market failures include Pigouvian taxes and subsidies and Coasian legal remedies involving property rights. More modern remedies involve markets for pollution rights, including cap and trade markets.

[handwritten: e.g. A firm produce a good, and in doing so, it emits waste products into the surrounding area. The individuals living close to firm are adversely affected by emissions]

17.2 Examples of Externalities

Externalities can be small or large, trivial or extremely important, and negative or positive. Here are some examples.

1. *Hip-hop music.* Your neighbor buys hip-hop music and plays it on his stereo speakers. He downloads it for $1 per song. He plays it too loud, and each song he buys causes you $2 worth of misery. The result: his consumption of hip-hop has a direct effect on you, imposing a cost of $2 per unit on you. However, that cost is not captured in the market price of $1. As a result, he consumes too much hip-hop, and the market outcome is inefficient. *[handwritten: negative]*

2. *Flowers in your neighbor's garden.* Your neighbor has a flower garden that you can see from your window. She buys tulip bulbs that produce beautiful blooms. She pays $3 per bulb, but each bulb also gives you $1 worth of enjoyment. The result: her consumption of tulip bulbs has a direct positive effect on you, creating a benefit to you of $1 per unit. That benefit is not reflected in your neighbor's calculations. As a result, she buys too few bulbs, and the market outcome is inefficient. *[handwritten: positive]*

3. *Harley-Davidson motorcycles with aftermarket pipes.* Harley-Davidson motorcycles, particularly the ones modified with "aftermarket" exhausts, can be heard by people within a half-mile radius. Their exhaust pipes produce a low-pitched, rumbling, thundering sound. The Harley owners love that sound, but the rest of us may not. Assume that such a bike costs its owner $0.25 per mile to own, maintain, and fuel. But assume that each mile of riding irritates 25 people who live, work, or play within earshot of the Harley, and assume that these neighbors, on average, would say that the noise of the bike causes them $0.01 worth of irritation. The result: the Harley rider rides too much. He rides to the point at which his extra benefit from another mile equals what it costs him, namely, *[handwritten: negative]*

$0.25, but he does not take into account the $0.25 worth of irritation imposed on the neighbors. The market is inefficient.

4. *Food consumption by people you care about.* People you care about do not have enough money to buy all the food they would like to eat. It pains you to see them hungry. The result: their consumption of food is inefficient. They consume to the point at which another dollar's worth of food produces a marginal benefit to them of $1. But another dollar's worth of food that they might consume would also produce a benefit to you, say, $0.50 worth. They are consuming too little food, and the market is inefficient.

   Note that this externality problem is probably not a problem at all if the people you care about live in your house and you can easily share. The more distant they are, however, the more difficult the problem.

5. *Mountaintop removal mining in Appalachia.* In West Virginia, Kentucky, and other Appalachian states in the eastern United States, mining companies are mining coal by blasting the summits and summit ridges off of mountains to expose the coal seams lying below. This is a less costly process than underground mining, but it may have unfortunate results. Although mountaintop mining firms are required to do some reclamation of the land after the coal is removed, the reclamation can only be partial. The mined areas are extensively deforested and the topography permanently altered. The soil and rock that was blasted off the coal seams may end up in valleys and streams below. Some watersheds may be polluted. Toxins and dust from blasting and removal of the overburden may have adverse health effects on nearby residents. In short, there may be various negative effects on local people and firms, as well as wider adverse environmental effects.

   In making their production decisions, the mountaintop mining firms consider the price of coal, the usual labor and materials costs of their operations, and the costs of required reclamation. However, they may not count the costs of adverse health effects on the residents, or the costs of stream pollution, or the possible costs of permanent alteration of the terrain. Therefore, they may produce too much coal, and their market decisions may be inefficient.

6. *Fossil fuels and global warming.* When we use fuel oil to heat our houses, gasoline to fuel our cars, or coal to generate our electricity, we release CO_2 into the atmosphere. CO_2 is a greenhouse gas, and many experts believe it contributes to global warming. The ultimate effects of global warming are uncertain, but the effects might be large and negative. The consumer is deciding how big a car to drive, and how many miles to drive it. The consumer looks at the price of gasoline and consumes to the point at which the marginal benefit per gallon of gasoline equals the price. However, the consumer does not take into account the cost imposed on others, possibly 50 or 100 years in the future, created by the CO_2 produced by a gallon of gasoline. Therefore, he uses too much gasoline, and his market decision is inefficient.

The list could go on and on. It is obvious that there are many externalities in the global economy, some questionable and some very clear, some minor and some extremely important. In the next section we carefully analyze one externality situation.

17.3 The Oil Refiner and the Fish Farm

Suppose we have an oil (petroleum) refinery located on a river. The oil refinery is an industrial process plant that transforms crude oil into refined products, such as gasoline, heating oil, diesel fuel, and liquefied petroleum gas. By accident or by design, it sometimes dumps its wastes in the river, which flows down to a bay in the ocean. A fish farm is located in the bay. The fish farm is adversely affected by the oil refiner's water pollution. More oil produces more pollution, and more pollution increases the fish farmer's costs.

We will let o and f represent quantities of oil refined and fish produced by the two firms, respectively. They are competitive in the markets in which they sell their outputs and buy their inputs. We assume that the refiner's output is measured in barrels of crude oil converted into refined products. The price for refining a barrel of crude oil is p_o; the price for a unit of fish is p_f. The oil refiner's cost function is $C_o(o)$, and the fish farmer's cost function is $C_f(f, o)$. The fish farmer's cost function depends both on its own level of output f, and on the oil refiner's level of production o. The externality in this example is the fact that o shows up in C_f.

When they maximize profits, the firms set price equal to marginal cost. We assume that both firms have positive and increasing marginal costs, as usual. We let $MC_o(o)$ represent the oil refiner's marginal cost function, and we let $MC_f(f, o)$ represent the fish farmer's marginal cost function. Profit maximization by the oil refiner will lead it to its market-based level of output, which we will call o^M. Similarly, profit maximization by the fish farm will lead it to its market-based level of output f^M.

We turn to the oil refiner first. His economic problem is straightforward. (The actual oil refining process is complex.) He solves the following equation to find o^M:

$$p_o = \frac{dC_o(o)}{do} = MC_o(o).$$

Now consider the fish farmer. His problem is slightly less straightforward. His profit-maximization condition is

$$p_f = \frac{\partial C_f(f, o)}{\partial f} = MC_f(f, o).$$

The fish farmer has no control over o, even though it appears in his cost function. He will take it as given, as it is outside his control.

On the other hand, he does know that the oil refinery upstream hurts him at his fish farm. The damage shows up in his cost function $C_f(f, o)$. Obviously, if he produces more fish, his costs increase:

$$MC_f(f, o) = \frac{\partial C_f(f, o)}{\partial f}$$

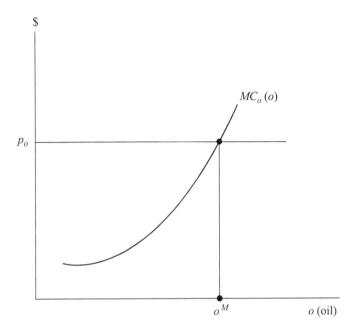

Fig. 17.1. The market level of oil refining. The oil refines chooses o^M to maximize its profit.

is positive and increasing. However, if the refinery processes more oil, it also costs the fish farmer more: *cost*

$$\frac{\partial C_f(f, o)}{\partial o}$$

is also positive. The term $\frac{\partial C_f(f,o)}{\partial o}$ is called the *marginal external cost* imposed by the oil refiner on the fish farmer, or *MEC* for short. But the fish farmer cannot do much about *MEC*, at least not by himself.

In Figure 17.1, we show the oil refiner's profit maximization problem. The firm faces a market price p_o, and has a marginal cost curve $MC_o(o)$. It maximizes profit at o^M, where price equals marginal cost.

Here is how the market equilibrium for oil refining and fish production is determined. The oil refiner finds o^M by setting price equal to marginal cost, or by using Figure 17.1. Then the fish farmer incorporates o^M in his price-equals-marginal-cost equation; that is, he solves

Therefore. $$p_f = MC_f(f, o^M).$$

This gives f^M. We now have o^M and f^M, with both firms maximizing profits, and everything looks fine. If the first fundamental theorem of welfare economics applied here, the market outcome would be Pareto optimal.

However, it turns out that it is not optimal. Everyone calculated everything properly, *except that MEC was ignored.* No one took into account the fact that more oil refined means higher costs for the fish farmer.

To carefully show the market failure, we must first define optimality in this small model. Then we must show that the competitive market outcome (o^M, f^M) is not optimal.

What, then, does optimality mean in this model with two firms? Each firm is interested in only one thing: its profit. Let π_o be the oil refiner's profit, and let π_f be the fish farmer's profit. If there were some alternative to the market equilibrium that increased the profit of both firms, (o^M, f^M) would not be Pareto optimal. Because cash could be easily transferred from one firm to another, a necessary condition for optimality is that joint or total profit, $\pi_o + \pi_f$, must be maximized. In this model, $\pi_o + \pi_f$ is the size of the "economic pie" created by the activities of the two firms combined.

To find the Pareto efficient solution in this simple economy, then, we need only to solve the joint profit maximization problem.

Therefore, let us assume that the two firms are combined, or merged, into an oil refining/fish farming conglomerate. The merged firm refines oil upstream on the river and produces fish at the fish farm downstream in the bay. However, merging the two firms into one *internalizes the externality.* That is, a profit-maximizing manager of a merged oil refining/fish farming firm would not ignore the marginal external cost imposed by his oil refining activity on his own fish production activity. The merged firm is interested in maximizing total profit from its two activities, $\pi(o, f) = \pi_o + \pi_f$. The cost functions for the two activities remain as they were, but now the oil refining/fish farming firm wants to maximize

$$\pi(o, f) = p_o o + p_f f - C_o(o) - C_f(f, o).$$

There are two first-order conditions for maximizing the function $\pi(o, f)$.

The first requires that the partial derivative of $\pi(o, f)$ with respect to o must equal zero:

$$\frac{\partial \pi}{\partial o} = p_o - \frac{dC_o(o)}{do} - \frac{\partial C_f(f, o)}{\partial o} = 0,$$

or

$$p_o = \frac{dC_o(o)}{do} + \frac{\partial C_f(f, o)}{\partial o} = MC_o(o) + MEC.$$

The second requires that the partial derivative of $\pi(o, f)$ with respect to f must equal zero:

$$\frac{\partial \pi}{\partial f} = p_f - \frac{\partial C_f(f, o)}{\partial f} = 0,$$

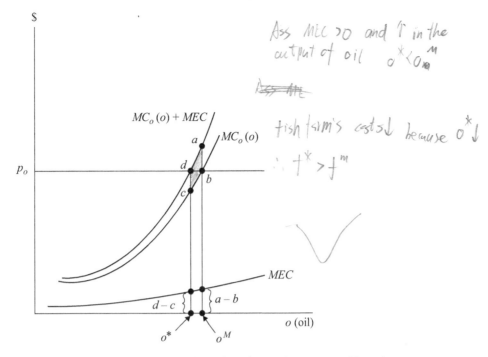

Handwritten annotations:
Ass $MEC > 0$ and $\uparrow$ in the output of oil $\quad o^* < o_{\bullet}^M$

fish farm's costs↓ because o^*↓

$\therefore \ f^* > f^m$

Fig. 17.2. The efficient amount of oil to refine is less than the market amount. Note that $d - c$ equals the height of *MEC* at o^*, and $a - b$ equals the height of the *MEC* curve at o^M. (Scale differs from Figure 17.1.)

or

$$p_f = \frac{\partial C_f(f, o)}{\partial f} = MC_f(f, o).$$

We will let (o^*, f^*) represent the solution to the two first-order condition equations. That is, (o^*, f^*) is the Pareto optimal combination of production levels for oil and fish. How does the market combination (o^M, f^M) compare to the Pareto optimal (joint profit-maximizing) combination (o^*, f^*)? They are different, because the pair of equations that produced (o^M, f^M) is different from the pair of equations that produced (o^*, f^*). Because (o^M, f^M) and (o^*, f^*) are different, the market outcome was not optimal.

The difference was in the equation for determining the oil refinery quantity o. The market equation was $p_o = MC_o(o)$. This equation ignores *MEC*. But the joint-profit maximizing equation is $p_o = MC_o(o) + MEC$. This equation takes *MEC* into account. For efficiency, we must have price equals marginal cost plus marginal external cost.

In Figure 17.2, we provide a graph that we can use to find o^*. In the figure, we have a marginal cost function $MC_o(o)$, as in Figure 17.1. We also have a horizontal line at the oil refining price p_o. We now add another curve, a positive (and upward-sloping) *MEC* curve. (To find o^* in the figure, we need $f = f^*$. This is because the exact position of the *MEC* curve depends on f.) We also show the sum of the marginal cost and marginal external cost curves. We see in the figure that the optimal quantity of oil to refine o^* must be less than the market amount o^M.

In short, the competitive market is inefficient, or non-Pareto optimal, when oil refining creates an externality that adversely affects fish production. This is a market failure, created by the oil refining/fish farming externality. Too much of the externality-causing good is produced, because under the market the negative effect of that good on the other firm, namely, *MEC*, is ignored. For optimality to hold, external effects must not be ignored.

What can be done about situations such as this? A free-market zealot might say, "The government should do nothing. Never touch the market. Socialists, keep your hands off! The market knows what it is doing!" As we have seen, though, the analysis suggests that this is wrong. On the other hand, an environmental zealot might say, "The government should crack down on those polluting sons of b–s. Activities that create water pollution and harm fish farms should be shut down." This would also be wrong, however, because the optimal amount of oil to refine (with accompanying pollution) is not zero. (And we are aware that, in reality, fish farms also pollute.) In the next section of this chapter, we discuss solutions to the externality problem.

17.4 Classical Solutions to the Externality Problem: Pigou and Coase

We have seen that market decisions about production may be nonoptimal or inefficient when there are external effects; that is, when one producer's production decisions have direct effects on another producer's costs. There are several possible solutions to externality-generated market failures, which will be outlined here and in the next two sections.

Pigouvian Taxes and Subsidies

The problem we saw in the last section came about because the oil refiner did not have to pay the external cost it imposed on the fish farmer. One possible solution is to tax the oil refiner. The tax would be collected by the government. Ideally, the tax would be tightly linked to the cost imposed by the oil refiner on the fish farmer.

Such taxes were advocated in 1920 by the great English economist Arthur Pigou (1877–1959), in his book *The Economics of Welfare*. Therefore, we call them *Pigouvian taxes*. If an externality is positive instead of negative, efficiency might require that the government pay a subsidy to the firm creating the externality, to increase its output of the good with the beneficial externality. Such a subsidy is called a *Pigouvian subsidy*.

A Pigouvian tax can be defined *at the margin*, or *in total*. For our oil refiner/fish farmer example, the Pigouvian tax at the margin, which we will call $t(o)$, is set equal to

$$t(o) = MEC = \frac{\partial C_f(f^*, o)}{\partial o}.$$

When deciding how much oil to refine, the oil refiner now reasons that an extra unit of oil refined costs him his marginal cost $MC_o(o)$, plus $t(o) = MEC$. This means that he uses the $MC_o(o) + MEC$ curve in Figure 17.2, finding the point at which it crosses the horizontal line at p_o. This leads him to the choice of o^*, the optimal output for the refinery.

The *in total* version of the Pigouvian tax, which we will call $T(o)$, is simply the integral of the marginal Pigouvian tax, from a base point o^0 to whatever refinery output o the firm chooses, all contingent on the efficient fish output f^*. (A note about notation: We apologize for o^0!) That is, it is the area under the MEC curve from o^0 to o. If the base point $o^0 = 0$, then the oil refiner must pay a total tax of $T(o)$, based on every unit of oil refined, with

$$T(o) = C_f(f^*, o) - C_f(f^*, 0),$$

the total extra cost imposed on the fish farmer by the presence of the oil refiner.

The marginal version and the total version of the Pigouvian tax are really two versions of the same thing. The only notable difference between them is that the base point for calculating the tax is explicit in our definition of the total tax, whereas it is unstated in our definition of the marginal tax.

Finally, the base point for calculating the total version of the Pigouvian tax need not be zero. The government may decide that the oil refiner was there first, and ought to be allowed to produce some output $o^0 > 0$ tax-free. As long as o^0 is set less than or equal to o^*, imposing the total version of the Pigouvian tax on the oil refiner, that is, setting

$$T(o) = C_f(f^*, o^*) - C_f(f^*, o^0),$$

will still induce that firm to choose o^*.

Coasian Property Rights

It might be argued that the oil refiner is really not the "bad guy" in our story. It is just unfortunate that the fish farmer is located in the bay that the oil refiner's river flows into. If it were not for that accident of location, there would be no externality. (The same kind of comment would apply to our hip-hop music story, and to our Harley exhaust noise story.) Often, people (and firms) solve the problem of a bad location by moving. The fish farmer could move to a different bay; if you live next to a hip-hop music fan and you like Beethoven, you could move to a different apartment. Moving is expensive, though, and for some externalities (for instance, global warming) it is impossible. In the text that follows, we assume that moving away from the externality is prohibitively expensive, or impossible.

An English-born American economist, Ronald Coase (1910–), in a 1960 article titled "The Problem of Social Cost," took the position that externality problems are more the result of unlucky location than the result of bad behavior by bad guys. Coase argued that economists are too quick to advocate taxes, including Pigouvian taxes, to fix various problems, including externality problems. He argued that externality-based market failure is not a consequence of nasty firms dumping their costs on innocent firms. Rather, this kind of market failure is a consequence of ill-defined property rights. That is, the trouble between our oil refiner and our fish farmer, who happen to be neighbors connected by a river, is a consequence of the absence of clear legal rights to clean water in the river, or clear legal rights to dump waste in the river. (Of course, Coase wrote before the enactment of clean water legislation in the United States, but laws such as the 1972 Clean Water Act in the United States do not provide the legal structure that Coase had in mind anyway.)

Here is the Coase solution to our market failure: Courts should create legal rules to deal with interactions such as the one between the oil refiner and the fish farmer. (In fact, in Anglo-American law there are areas of law, such as nuisance law, that lay out rights of parties in somewhat similar situations.) The legal rules should make perfectly clear whether the oil refiner has the right to dump waste in the river, or whether the fish farmer has the right to waste-free water. The legal rules should specify how a party whose rights are violated can take legal action against the violator, and what remedies a court hearing such a case can use. Standard remedies include imposing money damages, or granting an injunction – a legal order to cease the violation. Hopefully, the legal process should be quick, effective, and inexpensive. (Coase is aware that these are properties that legal action may or may not have.)

Let us now assume that courts give fish farmers clear rights to unpolluted waters, and let us assume that courts use money damages (rather than injunctions) as remedies. Suppose the oil refiner is producing o^M and the fish farmer is producing f^M. The fish farmer goes to court (assumed to be quick, easy, and cheap). He makes his case. The court rules in his favor, and grants money damages. Under the law, damages are set equal to the costs imposed on the fish farmer by the actions of the oil refiner. The court calculates damages accurately, and rules that the oil refiner must pay the fish farmer $C_f(f^M, o^M) - C_f(f^M, 0)$.

Now, suppose that all the output variables and costs are per year, and will repeat over and over again as long as the parties do not change their behavior. By the beginning of the next year, the oil refiner figures out what the legal system is going to do to him. He wises up, knowing that if he continues to produce o^M he will be assessed money damages just like total Pigouvian taxes, year after year, even though no Internal Revenue Service agents or other tax collectors are involved in this process. He then decides to stop producing o^M, and instead to produce o^*, the efficient output. And the fish farmer ends up producing f^*, and collecting money damages every year from the oil refiner.

But the Coasian story does not stop there. Let us now assume that the law allocates the initial rights in the opposite way. That is, courts lay out legal rules that say firms have clear and unambiguous rights to dump waste in rivers. Let us now also assume that the firm managers can meet, negotiate, and enter into contracts with each other, and do so at minimal cost. Here is what happens. The oil refiner starts out producing o^M. The fish farmer is aware of the pollution and the external costs imposed on him. He goes to the oil refiner and says, "I know you have a legal right to put waste in the river. However, I will pay you if you reduce your output somewhat, from o^M to o^*. If you do this, and if I produce f^*, my costs will drop by $C_f(f^*, o^M) - C_f(f^*, o^*)$. Your profit from the oil refining operation will drop when you reduce output from o^M to o^*. However, if you look at this graph I drew [at this point he pulls out Figure 17.2, which he tore out of this book], your reduction in profit is the area of triangle *bcd*. I will reimburse you that amount *plus* one half the area of triangle *abd*. What do you say?" The oil refiner responds, "Yes, I have had courses in economics and calculus at MIT, and I see that your proposed contract would make my firm more profitable when your payment is added to my operating profit from oil refining." They sign the contract, and from that point onward, they produce (o^*, f^*) per year, with the fish farmer paying the contracted amount to the oil refiner each year.

In short, Coase argues that the oil refiner/fish farmer externality problem can be remedied through the use of legal principles, rather than through the imposition of taxes. The law should grant clear rights to either one side or the other. If using the law is quick, easy, and cheap, and if it is easy and cheap to negotiate mutually beneficial contracts, then for purposes of efficiency it does not matter whether the fish farmer is granted the right to clean water, or the oil refinery is granted the right to dump its waste into the river. Of course, which party is granted the right does affect the profitability of the two parties.

Coase does not claim that the assumptions we have made about quick and low-cost legal structures, and cheap and easy negotiation of contracts, necessarily hold in reality. He takes the position that if there are high costs or frictions on one side or the other, courts should take those costs or frictions into consideration when they make their initial decisions about which side should be granted rights.

The Coase argument is now summed up in what is called the *Coase Theorem*. Applied to our oil refiner/fish farmer example, it says this:

1. Suppose the law grants a clear right to fish farmers to recover money damages from firms that pollute their water. Suppose further that the courts are quick, accurate, and cheap to use. Then the two firms will end up at the efficient output levels (o^*, f^*), and the oil refiner will pay damages to the fish farmer for the external costs imposed on him.

2. Moreover, suppose the law grants a clear right to oil refiners to dump waste in the river. Suppose further that making and enforcing contracts between the parties is cheap, quick, and easy. Then the two firms will end up at the efficient output levels (o^*, f^*), with the fish farmer making periodic contractual payments to the oil refiner in exchange for the reduction in his refinery output from o^M to o^*.

17.5 Modern Solutions for the Externality Problem: Markets for Pollution Rights

Let us complicate our oil refiner/fish farmer example slightly. Instead of just putting oil in the fish farmer's cost and marginal cost functions, let us call the amount of pollution or waste produced by the oil refiner x. The oil refining firm processes o units of oil, and simultaneously produces x units of pollution as an unintentional byproduct. Its cost function is now $C_o(o, x)$, with $\partial C_o(o, x)/\partial o > 0$. The amount of pollution x might or might not be proportional to o. In fact, we assume that there will be various different (costly) techniques to reduce pollution x, for a given amount of oil refined o. We assume that x is easy to observe and measure. Turning to the fish farmer, we replace o with x in its cost and marginal cost functions. Its cost function is now $C_f(f, x)$.

If the oil refiner and the fish farmer maximize profits in the usual fashion, they end up at the usual place, (o^M, f^M), with a corresponding pollution level x^M.

Now, we assume that the government sets up a market for pollution rights. This sounds odd, because no sane person wants to buy pollution. Here is what we mean:

1. The government decides on some benchmark level of pollution. We will call this benchmark level x^0. The idea is that the government will allow at most x^0 units of pollution (per unit time). Government officials must decide on how high (or low) to set x^0. To do so, they do an optimality analysis similar to what we did earlier to find (o^*, f^*), and they figure out the corresponding pollution level x^*. The government officials decide that the oil refining firm must be allowed to produce at least x^* units of pollution (per unit time), for otherwise (o^*, f^*) is unattainable. Therefore, they set the benchmark level at some $x^0 \geq x^*$.

2. They create *pollution permits*. A pollution permit allows its owner to produce one unit of pollution per unit time. A firm that produces a quantity of pollution without an equal number of permits is shut down.

3. They distribute the permits. The obvious way to distribute them would be to give them all to the oil refiner. This is not the only way, however; they could also be given to the fish farmer, or split between the two firms, or given to poor people, or kept by the government.

4. Finally, the government sets up a market for pollution permits (or allows someone else to set up such a market). On the market, firms that want permits can buy them, and firms or people or governments that have permits can sell them. We assume that the participants in this newly created pollution permit market act competitively.

The presence of this market solves the externality problem, because the externality gets incorporated in the pollution permit price. Here are some partial explanations of this important result.

Suppose all the permits are granted to the fish farmer. The oil refiner needs permits (creating a source of demand in the permit market), and the fish farmer has permits he does not need (creating a source of supply). The fish farmer sells x^* of his permits on the market; the oil refiner buys them. The market price is *MEC* at (o^*, f^*). (This outcome is somewhat similar to Coase's first scenario.) Or suppose x^* permits are granted to the oil refiner, and $x^0 - x^*$ are granted to the fish farmer. Then no sales take place on the market. Or suppose all the permits are granted to the oil refiner, and $x^0 > x^*$. Then the fish farmer buys $x^0 - x^*$ permits on the market from the oil refiner. (This outcome is similar in flavor to but much more plausible than Coase's second scenario.) Or suppose all the permits are granted to the government (which can sell them on the market). Then the oil refiner buys x^* permits, and the fish farmer buys the remaining $x^0 - x^*$. (This outcome is somewhat similar to the outcome of the Pigouvian tax, paid on all units of oil refined, from zero.)

In short, we see that a market for pollution permits is another reasonable solution to market failure due to externalities. The permit market solves the externality problem because the externality gets incorporated in the price of the permit, and is therefore not ignored.

17.6 Modern Solutions for the Externality Problem: Cap and Trade

A pollution permit market can also be used to achieve a slightly different efficiency goal. We now turn to what is called a *cap and trade* system. A cap and trade market is a version of a pollution rights market, similar to what was described in the last section, but redesigned for use in an economy with multiple polluting firms. The purpose of cap and trade is to create market coordination of pollution abatement activities by multiple polluters. Market coordination of pollution abatement will result in an efficient distribution of pollution abatement activities, or what we might call an efficient distribution of pollution origination (so called because this is about which of the oil refining firms originate which amounts of pollution).

To explain cap and trade, we now assume that there are many oil refining firms on the river. Each oil refiner refines oil and produces pollution simultaneously; producer i produces (o_i, x_i). Their cost functions are different, and their pollution reduction techniques are different. Some firms are able to cut pollution output cheaply when their oil refining output is high, some when it is low, some always, some never. The fish farmer's cost function depends on the total pollution in the river, the sum of the x_i's, which we call x.

We let (o_i^M, x_i^M) represent firm i's output of oil refined and pollution produced, under a market or laissez-faire policy. As usual, we let f^M represent the fish farmer's output in the market equilibrium. Of course, the market outcome is not efficient or Pareto optimal. We let (o_i^*, x_i^*) represent efficient levels of oil refined and pollution produced by firm i, f^* represent the efficient output of fish, and $x^* = x_1^* + x_2^* + \dots$ the efficient total pollution level.

Now the government steps in to set up a cap and trade market. The government may not know the pollution reduction techniques of the different firms; it may not know the cost functions of the different firms. However, we assume the government can easily observe each firm's pollution output x_i. Here is how cap and trade works:

1. The government first decides on some benchmark level of total pollution from all the oil refiners. We call this benchmark level x^0. We assume now that the government chooses the efficient pollution level as its benchmark, so that $x^0 = x^*$. The government creates $x^0 = x^*$ permits. (The model could be generalized to allow more permits than the efficient total pollution level, similar to what we did in the last section. However, it is simpler this way.) A firm needs one permit for each unit of pollution that it produces. Any firm operating without the required number of permits is shut down.

2. The government allocates those permits to the polluting oil refining firms. Because the government does not have detailed information about all the firms, the number of permits allocated to firm i may not equal x_i^*. Let a_i represent the number of permits allocated to firm i. The government *gives* a_i permits to firm i; it does not sell them to firm i. We will assume for simplicity that the government allocates all x^* permits to the oil refiners. (The model could be easily generalized to allow the government to retain some of its permits for itself, or to allocate some permits to other parties.)

3. The government sets up a market for pollution permits (or allows someone else to set up such a market). On the market, firms that need permits can buy them. That is, if a firm wants to produce x_i units of pollution, and $x_i > a_i$, then the firm can buy the additional permits it needs. On the other hand, if a firm wants to produce x_i units of pollution, and $x_i < a_i$, then it was allocated more permits than it needs, and it can sell the extra permits on the market. (Similarly, in a more general model, if the government has allocated itself some permits it could sell those on the market, as could other parties who were allocated permits.)

What is the result? First, if the government set its benchmark correctly and created x^* permits in total, then the total output of pollution will be efficient, as will the fish farmer's output f^*. Second, and more important, pollution will be mitigated in an efficient way. Here is an intuitive argument for this result.

Once again, we must decide what we mean by efficiency or Pareto optimality in this model. Because we are considering only the group of oil refining firms, the optimal set of production and pollution decisions is the one that maximizes total profit of all these firms. Thus, we consider a conglomerate firm made up of all the oil refiners. As a group, they have been allocated x^* permits in total. As a group, they do not pay for permits. (They certainly pay each other for permits, but the total net amount paid, when summed over all the oil refining firms, is zero.) Let n

be the number of oil refiners. Aggregate profit for all n firms is given by:

$$\pi = p_o(o_1 + o_2 + \cdots + o_n) - C_1(o_1, x_1) - C_2(o_2, x_2) - \ldots - C_n(o_n, x_n).$$

This is maximized subject to the constraint that

$$x_1 + x_2 + \ldots + x_n = x^*.$$

A necessary condition for maximizing π subject to this constraint is that for every pair of firms i and j,

$$\frac{\partial C_i(o_i, x_i)}{\partial x_i} = \frac{\partial C_j(o_j, x_j)}{\partial x_j}.$$

On the left-hand side of the equation is firm i's marginal cost of pollution (which is negative). This equals -1 times its marginal cost of pollution abatement (which is positive). A similar comment applies for firm j on the right-hand side of the equation.

This equation now has a nice intuitive interpretation. It says that holding o_i and o_j constant, efficiency requires that the marginal cost of pollution abatement at firm i must equal the marginal cost of pollution abatement at firm j.

This is an intuitively clear efficiency condition. Suppose, to the contrary, that these marginal costs were different. For instance, suppose it costs firm i \$100 to reduce pollution by 1 unit, holding o_i constant, whereas it costs firm j \$50 to do the same thing, holding o_j constant. This could not be efficient because the manager of the conglomerate firm that includes i and j could instruct i to allow 1 more unit of pollution (saving \$100) and simultaneously instruct firm j to cut 1 unit of pollution (at a cost of \$50). The net result would be the same total amount of oil refined, the same total amount of pollution, but \$50 more in profit.

Finally, we need to explain why the existence of the cap and trade market implies that

$$\frac{\partial C_i(o_i, x_i)}{\partial x_i} = \frac{\partial C_j(o_j, x_j)}{\partial x_j}$$

must hold for every pair of firms. As we indicated above, abbreviating marginal cost with MC, the equation says:

Firm i's MC of pollution abatement $=$ Firm j's MC of pollution abatement.

The reason is this: A competitive market price for pollution permits has been established in the cap and trade market. Call it p_x. With the cap and trade market in place, the independent oil refining firms all buy and sell pollution permits on that market. If $p_x > i$'s MC of pollution abatement, firm i can sell a permit on the market and spend its money on abating its pollution by 1 unit. It would increase its profit that way, by the difference between p_x and its MC of pollution abatement. Similarly, if $p_x < i$'s MC of pollution abatement, firm i can increase its profit by buying a pollution permit and saving the cost of abating a unit of pollution. Therefore, for it to be maximizing its profit, firm i must end up at a point where p_x equals its MC of pollution abatement.

However, this must be true for all the oil refining firms. That is, $p_x = -\partial C_i(o_i, x_i)/\partial x_i$ for all i. Therefore, for all firms i and j,

$$\frac{\partial C_i(o_i, x_i)}{\partial x_i} = \frac{\partial C_j(o_j, x_j)}{\partial x_j}$$

must hold, which is our condition for efficiency.

In sum, a cap and trade market establishes a price for a unit of pollution. All the oil refiners face that price. They all adjust their oil refining and pollution abatement activities so the marginal cost of pollution abatement at all the firms equals the market price for a unit of pollution. This guarantees that they end up at a place at which the marginal cost of pollution abatement is the same for every one of the firms; this is the condition that must hold for efficiency.

Before ending this chapter, we should comment on the politics of cap and trade. If the government were to allocate all the pollution permits to itself, and none to the oil refiners, the government would end up selling the permits to the firms and efficiency would still hold. This would be analogous to a Pigouvian-style tax on pollution, on all units produced, with the tax rate set equal to the permit price. However, the oil refiners have a strong preference for having the permits allocated to the oil refiners, rather than to the government or others. This way their only loss, in the aggregate, is the difference between profit at x^M and profit at x^*. Moreover, cap and trade might make it more difficult for new competitors to enter the oil refining business. In short, polluting firms are happiest with no regulation at all. They would be less happy with cap and trade. They would be least happy with pollution taxes.

17.7 A Solved Problem

The Problem

Assume that there are two firms producing steel; firm 1's output is s_1 and firm 2's is s_2. Assume there is no fish farm. Assume that the market price for steel is $p_s = 1$. There is a negative externality because of pollution: Firm 1's operation causes firm 2's costs to rise. Assume that firm 1's cost function is $C_1(s_1) = s_1^2$ and that firm 2's cost function is $C_2(s_1, s_2) = (s_2 + 0.75s_1)^2$. In short, firm 1 is not affected by firm 2, but firm 2 is adversely affected by firm 1.

(a) Remember that in the short run, firms can have negative profits, but that in the long run, their profits must be nonnegative. Find the market equilibrium (s_1^M, s_2^M) in the short run.

(b) Show that the short-run equilibrium from part (a) is not efficient.

(c) Describe the market equilibrium in the long run.

(d) Assume that the negative externality works both ways; that is, assume $C_1(s_1, s_2) = (s_1 + 0.75s_2)^2$ *and* $C_2(s_1, s_2) = (s_2 + 0.75s_1)^2$. Find the market equilibrium, and show that it is not efficient.

The Solution

(a) Firm 1 maximizes profit by setting price equal to marginal cost. Marginal cost for firm 1 is $MC_1 = 2s_1$. Price equals marginal cost gives

$$1 = 2s_1 \quad \text{or} \quad s_1^M = 0.5.$$

Firm 1's profit is

$$\pi_1 = p_s s_1^M - C_1(s_1^M) = 0.5 - (0.5)^2 = 0.25.$$

Firm 2 maximizes profit by setting price equal to marginal cost also, but s_1 will appear in its marginal cost function. Firm 2 cannot do anything about s_1, so it assumes s_1 is constant. Marginal cost for firm 2 is $MC_2 = 2(s_2 + 0.75s_1)$. Price equals marginal cost for firm 2 gives

$$1 = 2(s_2 + 0.75s_1) \quad \text{or} \quad s_2 = 0.5 - 0.75s_1.$$

Plugging in $s_1^M = 0.5$ now gives

$$s_2^M = 0.5 - 0.75 \times 0.5 = 0.125.$$

Firm 2's profit is

$$\pi_2 = p_s s_2^M - C_2(s_1^M, s_2^M) = 0.125 - (0.125 + 0.75 \times 0.5)^2$$
$$= 0.125 - 0.25 = -0.125.$$

Firm 2 is losing money, which is possible in the short run but not in the long run.

(b) To show that the outcome above is not efficient, we only have to show that there is an alternative arrangement which would result in higher total profits for firms 1 and 2. With the (s_1^M, s_2^M) we've just calculated,

$$\pi_1 + \pi_2 = +0.25 - 0.125 = 0.125.$$

Here is an alternative that produces higher total profits. Shut down firm 1; that is, force $s_1 = 0$. Then $\pi_1 = 0$. Then firm 2 sets price equal to marginal cost, based on $s_1 = 0$; this gives $s_2 = 0.5$. Firm 2's profit is now

$$\pi_2 = 0.5 - (0.5)^2 = 0.25 > 0.125.$$

(c) In the long run, firm 2 will exit the market, as its profit is negative in the short run. With firm 2 gone, firm 1 sets $s_1 = 0.5$ and has profit of $\pi_1 = 0.125$. The externality problem disappears in the long run, as firm 2 has exited the market.

(d) Now we are assuming the externality works both ways, and so firm 1's cost function incorporates the externality just like firm 2's. That is,

$$C_1(s_1, s_2) = (s_1 + 0.75s_2)^2.$$

The profit maximization condition for firm 1 is

$$1 = 2(s_1 + 0.75s_2) \qquad \text{or} \qquad s_1 = 0.5 - 0.75s_2.$$

For firm 2, the profit maximization condition is

$$1 = 2(s_2 + 0.75s_1) \qquad \text{or} \qquad s_2 = 0.5 - 0.75s_1.$$

Solving the two profit maximization conditions simultaneously (and writing them in fractional instead of decimal form) gives

$$s_1^M = s_2^M = 2/7.$$

Profit levels are

$$\pi_1 = \pi_2 = 2/7 - (2/7 + 3/4 \times 2/7)^2 = 1/28.$$

Total profits of both firms together are

$$\pi_1 + \pi_2 = 2 \times 1/28 = 0.071.$$

The outcome is inefficient; total profits would increase if one of the firms were forced to produce zero. For example, shut down firm 1; that is, force $s_1 = 0$. Firm 2 sets price equal to marginal cost; this gives

$$s_2 = 0.5$$

and

$$\pi_2 = 0.5 - (0.5)^2 = 0.25,$$

as in part (b) above. Firm 1's negative (short-run) profit is now

$$\pi_1 = 0 - (0 + 0.75 \times 0.5)^2 = -0.141.$$

The sum of firm 1's (short-run) profit and firm 2's profit is now

$$\pi_1 + \pi_2 = -0.141 + 0.25 = 0.109 \; > \; 0.071.$$

Exercises

1. Moe has two puppies, and he is the sole caretaker of the puppies. Moe also has two housemates, Larry and Curly. Larry likes playing with the puppies, whereas Curly dislike the mess the puppies make. The three housemates' utilities from the puppies are $u_m(x) = x^2 - 2x + 2$, $u_l(x) = x^2$, and $u_c(x) = -x^2 - 1$, respectively, where x is the number of puppies.

   (a) Calculate Moe's, Larry's, and Curly's utilities from the two puppies.

   (b) Suppose Moe is considering getting a third puppy. How would each of the housemates' utility change?

   (c) What number of puppies would maximize the total utility of the three housemates?

2. Sam and Gam are neighbors. Sam maintains a beautiful garden. His production function is $p = 2h$ and his utility function is $u_s(p, h) = 50p - p^2 - 28h$, where p is the number

of plants in the garden and h is the number of hours spent gardening per week. The plants cost nothing, but they require time. Gam enjoys his neighbor's garden but does not help; his utility is given by $u_g(p) = \frac{1}{4}p^2 + 3p$.

(a) What is the equilibrium number of plants in Sam's garden? How many hours per week does he spend gardening?

(b) Calculate Sam's and Gam's utilities.

(c) What is the Pareto optimal number of plants in Sam's garden?

3. Eleven people with identical preferences live in an apartment building. Each of them likes blasting his or her music, but complains about everyone else's music. They all play music at different times during the day, so at any point in time at most one person is playing music. Each individual's utility function is represented by $u_i(m, x) = 8m - 2m^2 - \frac{3}{10}x$, where m is the number of hours per day that that individual is blasting his or her music, and x is the total number of hours per day that others are blasting their music.

(a) If each individual is unaware of the impact of his or her music on the other tenants, how many hours per day does each person blast music? What is the total number of hours per day during which somebody's music is blasting?

(b) Calculate each individual's utility.

(c) Suppose the tenants get together and recognize the negative impact of each of their actions on the other tenants. They collectively agree to limit the number of hours of music-blasting in order to maximize everyone's utility. They decide to limit everybody's music playing to m^* hours per day. What is m^*?

4. Flo is a farmer and grows flowers on her farm, which is located right next to Beatrice's property. Beatrice is a beekeeper. Each of Beatrice's beehives pollinates an acre of Flo's flowers. Flo's cost function is $C_f(f) = 5\left(f - \frac{1}{3}b\right)^2$, and Beatrice's cost function is $C_b(b) = 10\left(b - \frac{1}{2}f\right)^2$, where f is the number of acres of flowers, and b is the number of beehives. Each acre of flowers yields \$50 worth of flowers, and each beehive yields \$100 worth of honey.

(a) Suppose Flo maximizes her profits, taking the number of beehives as given. Likewise, Beatrice maximizes her profits, taking the number of acres of flowers as given. How many acres of flowers and how many beehives will there be? Calculate each of their profits.

(b) If Flo and Beatrice jointly maximize profits, how many acres of flowers and how many beehives will there be? Calculate each of their profits.

(c) What sort of transfer would be necessary for both Flo and Beatrice to agree to jointly maximize their profits?

5. Clyde produces chemicals. His cost function is $C_c(c) = 5c^2 + 100c$, where c is the number of liters of chemicals produced. The market price for a liter of a chemical is $p_c = 700$. Bonnie is a baker. She is adversely affected by the noxious fumes emitted by Clyde's production of chemicals. Her cost function is $C_b(b) = \frac{1}{2}b^2 - 140b + bc$, where b is the number of baked goods produced. The market price for a baked good is $p_b = 10$.

(a) How many liters of chemicals and how many baked goods will be produced in the market equilibrium?

(**b**) Suppose Clyde and Bonnie were to jointly maximize profits. How many liters of chemicals and how many baked goods will be produced?

(**c**) Compare the competitive market outcome from (a) and the joint profit maximization outcome from (b). Which outcome is Pareto optimal? Why?

(**d**) One of the solutions to the externality problem is Pigouvian taxes. In this example, who pays the tax? How does the Pigouvian tax solve the externality problem?

(**e**) Another solution is Coasian property rights. Suppose Clyde has the legal right to emit noxious fumes. How can they arrive at the Pareto optimal outcome?

6. There are two factories emitting air pollutants in Pollutopia. The government decides to crack down on pollution and cap total pollution at 30 units. Each factory is issued 15 permits; one permit allows the emission of one unit of pollution. A factory may consume more or fewer permits than originally issued by buying from or selling to the other factory. The two factories' cost of pollution abatement are $C_1(x_1) = 60x_1^2$ and $C_2(x_2) = x_2^3$, respectively, where x_i is the number of units of pollution produced by factory i. How many permits does each factory end up with in equilibrium?

Chapter 18

Public Goods

18.1 Introduction

In the last chapter we looked at market failures created by externalities. A good creates a consumption-based external effect, or an externality, when person i's consumption of it has a direct effect – an effect that is not reflected in the market price – on someone else, person j. When externalities are present, the market fails to give us efficiency or Pareto optimality. This is because person i, considering only the market prices he must pay for it, fails to account for the cost (or the benefit) imposed on person j by i's consumption of the good.

In this chapter, we look at market failures created by public goods. A *public good* is a good that is *nonexclusive in use*. That is, if it is there and available for use by one consumer, then it is there and available for use by all consumers. In a sense, these are goods that create super-externalities. For example, a judicial system is a public good. If the laws, courts, and police are in place to protect person i, they are there to protect person j as well. (Obviously a public good may be valued differently by the different people; i might be a shopper, happy to have the police around to protect her, and j might be a thief!)

A nonpublic good is sometimes called a *private good*. A pair of socks is a private good. If i is wearing a pair of socks, then j is not wearing that pair of socks. But if i has that judicial system, then j has it also. We know that markets should provide efficient or Pareto optimal quantities of things such as socks. However, as we will see, markets provide inefficient quantities of public goods. The presence of public goods creates another important type of market failure.

In this chapter, we first provide some examples of public goods. Next we describe a simple model of public goods. The model makes it clear why private market provision of a public good is inefficient. That is, it makes clear why public goods result in market failure. Then we turn to the *Samuelson optimality condition*, the condition that must hold for the quantity of a public good to be Pareto optimal or efficient. After that we discuss the *free rider* problem – the problem of consumer i's taking advantage of consumer j's decision to produce some of the public good, which, since it is available for i to use, causes i to take a free ride on j's good citizenship. In the same section, we discuss provision of the public good through voluntary contributions. Finally, we close the chapter with some possible solutions to the problem of efficient provision of public goods. The solutions include *Wicksell/Lindahl taxes* and *demand-revealing taxes*.

18.2 Examples of Public Goods

Public goods create externalities on steroids. If person i is consuming the public good, then it is available for consumption by everyone. We have already mentioned one example, a judicial system. Here are some other examples:

1. *National defense.* For the people in one country, national defense is a public good. If the armed forces are protecting i from the threat of attack by dangerous outsiders, then they are also protecting j from that attack. Of course, if i lives in one country and j lives in another, national defense in i's country may not be viewed as a public good by j. In short, national defense is an excellent example of a public good in the sense that it is truly nonexclusive in use, but one must be careful about the identity of the group that is using it.

2. *Lighting on a city street.* City streets are often brightly lit at night to deter crime. If i and j live on the street and the street is lit up for i, then it is lit up for j as well. The light is clearly nonexclusive in use. Of course, i may like the light, and j may dislike it.

3. *Fire departments.* If a city has a fire department to fight fires, it will almost surely try as hard to put out a fire on i's property as on j's property. It would be impractical to provide firefighting services to one person in the city without providing the same services to others.

4. *Broadcast television.* In days gone by, television was broadcast from towers, and anyone within range of the broadcast signal could set up an antenna to capture that signal and watch programs on a TV. If the signal was in the air for i, it was also in the air for j. (This is still how television is delivered to a fraction of its audience in the United States.) Television stations in the United States did not charge for delivery of the signal to watchers; their revenue came from the sale of advertisements.

   Broadcast television is interesting because it shows how public goods might be transformed into private goods by excluding potential users. In Great Britain, BBC television has historically charged a television license fee that households with a TV must pay. Therefore, if i and j are British BBC watchers, and if the signal is in the air for i, it is also in the air for j (nonexclusivity in use). However, if either i or j watches TV without having paid the licensing fee, he or she is fined (producing exclusivity in use).

   Moreover, broadcast television in the United States has now been largely replaced by cable television, or other methods of delivery of television signal via paid subscriber services. If you are a cable TV subscriber, there is nothing public about the delivery of your TV service to your house; you pay a monthly fee if you want the service, and if you stop paying, your service is shut off. Satellite television is carried on a signal broadcast from a satellite; everybody in your area gets the signal, but you must pay a monthly fee to get a box to unscramble it.

5. *Public parks, public libraries, and public monuments.* If the Grand Canyon National Park is there for i, it is also there for j. If the New York Public Library is there for one New Yorker, it is there for all; if the Eiffel Tower is available for your viewing pleasure, it is available for all of us. Note, however, that things such as parks, libraries, and monuments may have the potential of privatization if access can be restricted. Public parks and libraries might charge for access, for example. Of course, there are many private parks (such as Disney World), and many private libraries.

6. *Public education and public health.* In modern countries, an educated population is considered generally beneficial – a good thing for society as a whole. Therefore, education is commonly provided by the government – at least education through secondary school. A similar comment can be made about medical care. Note, however, that education and medical care were historically provided privately, and both could be privatized now. Education and medical services can be restricted and made contingent on fees, as college students in the United States know. Both education and medical care are what we might call *quasi-public goods*, goods whose provision is largely public and nonexclusive, but is not necessarily so.

7. *Scientific and technological knowledge.* Knowledge in the public domain is an exceptionally important type of public good, and it is really public in the sense that if the laws of physics and chemistry (for example) are available and known to i, they are also available and known to j. The significant exception to nonexclusivity of use of knowledge is created by patent law, which privatizes some knowledge for a period of time. (For example, the use of the formula for a patent drug is exclusive to the owner of the patent, but only for the limited life of the patent.)

In the next section of this chapter, we describe a simple model of public goods. This model makes it clear why private market provision of a public good is inefficient.

18.3 A Simple Model of an Economy with a Public Good

We assume that there are only two goods – a public good and a private good. The quantity of the public good is x. Think of this as a composite of things that are nonexclusive in use, such as public parks, highways, schools, courts, and armed forces. Rather than defining units of the public good and discussing a production function for that good, we will measure it by expenditure in dollars. Thus, one unit of the public good is one dollar spent on this composite of parks, and so on. That is, the price of the public good is $1 per unit.

We assume that whatever quantity of the public good is available, is available to all. Therefore, x will enter every consumer's utility function, although different consumers will value it differently. Generally, the consumers like the public good, but some may be indifferent to it and some may actually dislike it.

The private good is also a composite, but of things that are exclusive in use, such as food, clothing, housing, and so on. It is private in the sense that person i's consumption of that good benefits person i alone. We will let y_i represent person i's consumption of the private good. Person i's private good consumption enters i's utility function, but no other utility function. We will measure the private good in dollar units also, so the price of the private good is also \$1 per unit.

Production in this simple model involves transforming a private good into a public good, or vice versa. We will assume for simplicity that a unit of private good can be transformed by firms into a unit of public good, or vice versa. This means that an additional unit of either the public good or the private good costs \$1 to produce; that is, both marginal costs equal \$1. The firms doing the transforming are competitive and make zero profits.

We will assume that there are n people. Person i's income is M_i and his utility function is $u_i(x, y_i)$. To make our analysis simpler, we will assume that our consumers' utility functions satisfy the special property of *quasilinearity*. The reader may recall this assumption was made in the context of the discussion of consumers' surplus, back in Chapter 7. We say our consumers have *quasilinear preferences* if their utility functions can be written as

$$u_i(x, y_i) = v_i(x) + y_i.$$

Under the assumption of quasilinearity, every person's private good consumption y_i enters his utility function as a simple additive term. The function $v_i(x)$ is called i's *benefit from the public good*, and its derivative is his *marginal benefit from the public good*, abbreviated $MB_i(x)$. We assume that $v_i(x)$ is an increasing and concave function.

Let us turn to consumer i's budget. We will assume for now that person i buys his consumption of the public good; that is, he pays for it himself just as he pays for his consumption of the private good. Of course, this assumption is a little strange, because if i is buying x units of the public good, that public good is then available to everybody. Nonetheless, we make the assumption, because it is important to see what happens when public goods are privately provided by the market. Because we are assuming that both goods are measured in dollar units, if person i is buying x units of the public good, and if he is consuming y_i units of private good, then his budget constraint is

$$x + y_i = M_i.$$

In short, we are now assuming that person i solves the following problem:

$$\max u_i(x, y_i) = v_i(x) + y_i \qquad \text{subject to} \qquad x + y_i = M_i.$$

Consumer i's indifference curves are convex under our assumptions about the $v_i(x)$ functions. To maximize his utility subject to his budget constraint, our consumer finds the point on his budget line at which the marginal rate of substitution

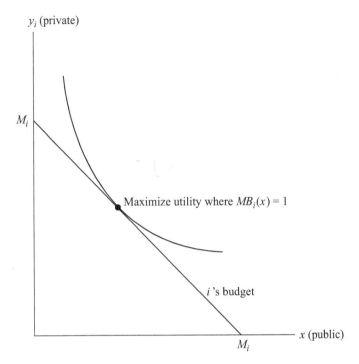

Fig. 18.1. How consumer i maximizes his utility when he is buying both the public good x and his own private good y_i. He chooses x where his marginal benefit from the public good equals 1.

of the private good for the public good equals the price ratio, which is 1 given our definitions of the units. That is,

$$MRS_{x,y_i} = \frac{dv_i(x)/dx}{dy_i/dy_i} = \frac{v_i'(x)}{1} = MB_i(x) = 1.$$

The assumption of quasilinearity implies that the marginal rate of substitution of the private good for the public good equals the marginal benefit of the public good, which depends only on x. This makes our public good analysis relatively simple.

Figure 18.1 shows how a consumer chooses his utility-maximizing bundle if he is buying quantities of both the public good and the private good. The figure ignores possible complications created by other consumers' having already bought and provided some public good. We will face those complications shortly.

We will now let (x_i^M, y_i^M) represent the market quantities of the public good and the private good that consumer i buys when he maximizes his utility subject to his budget constraint, as described earlier. The subscript i on the quantity x needs some explanation, as x is the *public* good. We simply mean that x_i^M is the quantity of the public good that i buys and pays for. The superscript M stands for market. We let $x^M = x_1^M + x_2^M + \cdots + x_n^M$ represent the total amount of public good, bought by all the consumers, when each consumer is paying the full cost of each unit of public good he or she is buying.

A *market equilibrium*, or *private market equilibrium*, or *private market outcome*, is what results when the various consumers do what we have described previously. That is, $(x^M, y_1^M, y_2^M, \ldots, y_n^M)$ is a market equilibrium. We will let $(x^*, y_i^*, y_2^*, \ldots, y_n^*)$, represent an efficient combination of public and private goods.

We claim that the market equilibrium cannot be efficient. To explain why, let us assume that there are only two consumers, with identical tastes and identical income levels. Our argument is illustrated in Figure 18.2. The figure shows consumer 1's budget line, and two indifference curves, which could belong to either consumer, as we have assumed they have the same tastes. Assume that consumer 1 goes through the previous exercise, decides that (x_1^M, y_1^M) maximizes his utility subject to his budget constraint, and buys those quantities. Note that (x_1^M, y_1^M) is a tangency point of consumer 1's budget line with an indifference curve, and that x_1^M is the quantity of the public good for which consumer 1's marginal benefit equals 1. $MB_1 = 1$

Now consumer 2 steps up, and thinks about what to do. He sees that consumer 1 has already bought and paid for x_1^M units of the public good, which are available for him to use because x is public. In other words, consumer 2 is getting x_1^M units of the public good free of charge, thanks to consumer 1. If he wanted to, he could buy an additional amount of the public good, call it x_2^M, but he would have to pay \$1 per unit for any additional amount. His budget constraint, therefore, is not a standard straight line with slope -1. If he spent all his money M_2 on private consumption, he could still consume up to x_1^M units of the public good, because it is there thanks to consumer 1. So the first part of his budget line is a horizontal line, starting at M_2 on the vertical axis, and extending out to x_1^M. The second part of his budget line starts at the point (x_1^M, M_2) and extends toward the right. On this part, the budget line is a straight line with slope -1, because if he wants to consume more public good than x_1^M, he has to consume less private good, and the tradeoff is a unit of private good per additional unit of public good.

Consumer 2's budget line is shown in Figure 18.2 as the dashed line, with a horizontal section at the top, and then a straight line section with slope -1. Now, let us consider this question: How much additional public good does consumer 2 want to buy? If he wants to be at some point on the downward-sloping part of his budget line, he must look for a point of tangency between an indifference curve and the budget line, which means that he looks for a point at which $MB_2(x) = 1$. However, we assumed that consumer 2's utility function was the same as consumer 1's. Therefore, the marginal benefit functions are the same: $MB_2(x) = MB_1(x)$. Therefore, if $MB_1(x) = 1$ at x_1^M, $MB_2(x)$ also equals 1 at x_1^M.

In short, consumer 2 is happy with $x = x_1^M$, and he wants to add nothing to it; that is, he chooses $x_2^M = 0$. Note that Figure 18.2 shows an indifference curve for consumer 2 touching the downward-sloping part of consumer 2's budget line, at the point (x_1^M, M_2). (Saying that consumer 2's indifference curve is tangent

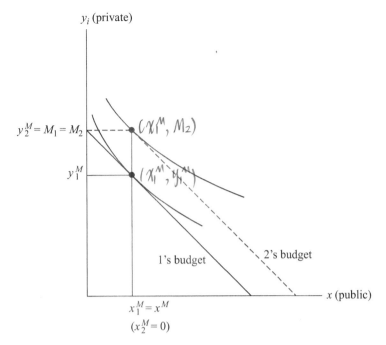

Fig. 18.2. There are two consumers with identical preferences and incomes. Consumer 1 moves first, and buys some of the public good. Consumer 2 moves second, takes advantage of consumer 1's having bought x_1^M, and buys no additional public good.

to the budget line at the point (x_1^M, M_2) would be slightly inaccurate, because the budget line has a kink at that point, making its slope undefined. However, (x_1^M, M_2) is clearly the point that maximizes consumer 2's utility subject to his budget constraint.)

We now have the private market equilibrium. Consumer 1 purchases (x_1^M, y_1^M), as shown in Figure 18.2; consumer 2 purchases $(x_2^M = 0, y_2^M = M_2)$ and consumes (x_1^M, y_2^M), as shown in the figure. The total amount of the public good produced and consumed by the two consumers is $x^M = x_1^M + x_2^M = x_1^M$, also shown in the figure.

Let us consider the market equilibrium further. Consumer 1's marginal benefit from the public good at his consumption point (x^M, y_1^M) is 1. Consumer 2's marginal benefit from the public good at his consumption point (x^M, y_2^M) is also 1. Adding the two marginal benefits together, we have

$$MB_1(x^M) + MB_2(x^M) = 2.$$

This cannot be efficient (that is, Pareto optimal) because the sum of the marginal benefits is 2, whereas the cost of an additional unit of the public good is only 1. The consumers could easily rearrange things so that both would be better off. For instance, each consumer could contribute $0.50 to pay for one additional unit of x. The result would be a change in consumer 1's utility; it would go up by 1.0 because of the increase in x and simultaneously fall by 0.5 because of the decrease in private good consumption. The net change in u_1 would be $1.0 - 0.5 = 0.5$. u_2 the same Similarly, consumer 2's utility would rise by 1.0 because of the increase in x and simultaneously fall by 0.5 because of his decrease in private good consumption. The net change in u_2 would be $1.0 - 0.5 = 0.5$. Because we have shown a way to make both consumers better off, (x^M, y_1^M, y_2^M) is not Pareto optimal.

18.4 The Samuelson Optimality Condition

Let us formalize the optimality ideas we used at the end of the last section. Suppose again that there are n people with quasilinear preferences in our public good economy. As a group, they are choosing $(x, y_1, y_2, \ldots, y_n)$ subject to the constraint that the total cost of $(x, y_1, y_2, \ldots, y_n)$ must not exceed the total amount of money they start with, $M_1 + M_2 + \cdots + M_n$. Under the quasilinearity assumption, $u_i(x, y_i) = v_i(x) + y_i$. Because the term y_i appears in every consumer's utility function, for every consumer, an extra dollar is equivalent to an extra unit of the private good, and equivalent to an extra unit of utility.

Therefore, we can legitimately add together the utilities of the n consumers, much as we added together the utilities (or willingnesses to pay) of n consumers when we discussed consumers' surplus. It follows that $(x, y_1, y_2, \ldots, y_n)$ is Pareto optimal if (and only if) it maximizes

$$u_1(x, y_1) + u_2(x, y_2) + \cdots + u_n(x, y_n)$$
$$= v_1(x) + y_1 + v_2(x) + y_2 + \cdots + v_n(x) + y_n$$

subject to society's overall budget constraint,

$$x + y_1 + y_2 + \cdots + y_n \leq M_1 + M_2 + \cdots + M_n.$$

We can clearly replace the less-than-or-equal-to sign in the constraint with an equal sign. Therefore, Pareto optimality requires that society maximize

$$v_1(x) + v_2(x) + \cdots + v_n(x) + y_1 + y_2 + \cdots + y_n$$

subject to

$$y_1 + y_2 + \cdots + y_n = -x + M_1 + M_2 + \cdots + M_n.$$

Noting that $M_1 + M_2 + \cdots + M_n$ is a constant and can therefore be ignored in the maximization problem, and substituting from the constraint, we conclude that the condition for Pareto optimality in our public good model is that

$$v_1(x) + v_2(x) + \cdots + v_n(x) - x$$

must be maximized. The function $v_1(x) + v_2(x) + \cdots + v_n(x) - x$ has a simple and intuitive interpretation. It is the total benefit of the public good, to all consumers in the economy, net of its cost. We call it the *total net benefit from the public good*. In our public good model, optimality means maximization of total net benefit from the public good.

We conclude with an efficiency condition called the *Samuelson optimality condition*, after the great twentieth-century American economist Paul Samuelson (1915–2009). Maximizing the total net benefit function gives the following necessary condition:

$$v_1'(x) + v_2'(x) + \cdots + v_n'(x) = 1,$$

or

$$MB_1(x) + MB_2(x) + \cdots + MB_n(x) = 1.$$

In words, *the sum of the marginal benefits from the public good must equal the marginal cost*. This is the Samuelson optimality condition.

To understand the intuition of the Samuelson condition, think of this example. Suppose there are 100 people, and suppose an extra unit of the public good costs $1. Suppose every person would get a 2-cent benefit from another unit of the public good. Then more of the public good should be produced, because the cost of another unit is only $1, but the total benefit to society from another unit is $2.

Our market equilibrium of the last section failed the Samuelson optimality condition. That is why it was not efficient.

To wrap up this section, let us think about the intuitive contrast between the market provision of a private good and the market provision of a public good. Whether he is buying a private good or a public good on the market, a consumer will buy it up to the point at which the marginal benefit *to him* from the good equals its price, $1 in our model. If the good is private, this makes sense, because the consumer doing the buying is the only one getting that benefit; from a social perspective, the benefit of that last unit just equals $1. But if our consumer is buying another unit of the public good, it creates a marginal benefit for him *and for others as well*. Therefore, from the social perspective, that last unit of the public good purchased by one consumer results in an aggregate benefit that far exceeds its cost. This means that if a public good is bought on a private market like a private good, the market equilibrium quantity of the good will be too low.

18.5 The Free Rider Problem and Voluntary Contribution Mechanisms

In Section 18.3 we presented an example to show that the standard market mechanism results in a nonoptimal or inefficient amount of public good. In our example, we had two identical consumers. Consumer 1 went first and bought x_1^M units of the public good. Consumer 2 went second, and he bought no public good at all.

He saw that consumer 1 had already bought x_1^M, which was there for consumer 2 to enjoy because the good is public. In other words, consumer 2 took a free ride on consumer 1's prior purchase of the public good. This was an example of a widespread problem called the *free rider problem.*

The equilibrium we described in that section was slightly special because it obviously depended on which consumer moved first. In this section we tell a somewhat different story about the provision of the public good, a story that is slightly more general, and more in line with the game-theoretic Nash equilibrium concept. However, the new story has the same moral as the old: the provision of public goods creates free riders, resulting in nonoptimality or inefficiency.

This is the story of a voluntary contribution mechanism to supply the public good. We again assume that there are two consumers with quasilinear preferences. We now allow that their $v_i(x)$ functions and their income levels M_1 and M_2 might be different. We assume, as before, that the public good and the private good can be transformed into each other at a rate of 1 to 1, and that the price of a unit of public good or a unit of private good is $1.

The consumers buy and consume the private good as before. Now, however, instead of going to the market and buying units of the public good, they are brought together in a room, and they are asked by a kind intermediary named Mr. Rational Fundraiser to make a voluntary contribution of money, to be used to purchase the public good. Let x_1 represent consumer 1's voluntary contribution, and let x_2 represent consumer 2's voluntary contribution. Mr. Fundraiser will take $x_1 + x_2$ to the market and buy $x = x_1 + x_2$ units of the public good, to be used by consumers 1 and 2.

Mr. Fundraiser tells them, "I want you to be virtuous, but I know you are rational. Therefore, when you decide on your contribution x_i, choose it in anticipation of x_j, and choose it in a way that maximizes your utility subject to what you think x_j will be."

An equilibrium of the voluntary contribution mechanism is a pair of contributions (x_1, x_2) such that each consumer is maximizing his or her utility, given what the other is doing. That is, given what i anticipates j will do, x_i maximizes $v_i(x_i + x_j) + y_i$ subject to i's budget constraint $x_i + y_i = M_i$. This is now a game, similar to the games we discussed in Chapter 14 (also similar to the duopoly analysis of Chapter 13), and we will be looking for Nash equilibria of the game.

Now let us focus on consumer 1. He chooses x_1 to maximize his utility $u_1(x, y_1) = v_1(x_1 + x_2) + y_1$, subject to his budget constraint $x_1 + y_1 = M_1$, and in anticipation of some contribution x_2 by consumer 2. He can easily solve this maximization problem, by substituting x_1 from the budget constraint into the function he is maximizing. In addition, he can ignore M_1, which is a constant. This means that he wants to maximize $v_1(x_1 + x_2) - x_1$. He treats x_2 as a constant, differentiates, and sets the derivative equal to zero. This gives

$$v_1'(x_1 + x_2) = 1.$$

Consumer 1 uses this equation to solve for his x_1, contingent on the x_2 anticipated from consumer 2.

Now we move on to consumer 2. He goes through a process very much like the one we described for consumer 1. He ends up with an analogous equation, $v_2'(x_1 + x_2) = 1$. He uses this equation to solve for his x_2, contingent on the x_1 anticipated from consumer 1.

Let us define an *equilibrium of the voluntary contribution mechanism*. We say that (x^e, x_1^e, x_2^e) is an equilibrium if x^e is the sum of x_1^e and x_2^e; if x_1^e is the x_1 that maximizes $v_1(x_1 + x_2^e) - x_1$; and if x_2^e is the x_2 that maximizes $v_2(x_1^e + x_2) - x_2$. We now see that (x^e, x_1^e, x_2^e) is an equilibrium if and only if the following hold:

1. $x^e = x_1^e + x_2^e$.
2. $v_1'(x_1^e + x_2^e) = 1$.
3. $v_2'(x_1^e + x_2^e) = 1$.

In the special case in which the marginal benefit functions are the same, so $v_1'(x_1 + x_2) = v_2'(x_1 + x_2) = v'(x_1 + x_2)$, it is easy to find all the voluntary contribution mechanism equilibria (of which there are many). First, find the x^e for which $v'(x^e) = 1$. Then let x_1^e and x_2^e be any pair of contributions that sum to x^e. They are all voluntary contribution mechanism equilibria.

But whether it is the special case or the more general case, we can be sure of one thing: an equilibrium of this mechanism is not Pareto optimal. It obviously fails the Samuelson optimality condition, because

$$v_1'(x_1^e + x_2^e) + v_2'(x_1^e + x_2^e) = 1 + 1 = 2 > 1.$$

This

Voluntary contributions as we have described them result in too little of the public good. Each consumer i is taking a free ride on the anticipated contribution of the other consumer j, although perhaps not as big a free ride as consumer 2 took on consumer 1's public good purchase in Section 18.3.

the situation *...*
consumer 2 in last

18.6 How to Get Efficiency in Economies with Public Goods

We have seen that public goods may create market failure. A private market does not produce enough of the public good, nor does a system of voluntary contributions, if consumers are acting rationally. Here are some possible solutions to the problem of market failure resulting from public goods.

Command Policies

If the government has enough information, and if it is interested in Pareto optimality, it can calculate the optimal quantity of the public good x^*, and then arbitrarily impose taxes on the various consumers, adding up to x^*, to pay for it. This may

sometimes be possible; however, it will not work if the government lacks information about the marginal benefit functions (or, more generally, about the individuals'
marginal rates of substitution of the private good for the public good). It will not
work if the government imposes the taxes in some objectionable, offensive, unfair,
or discriminatory way. It will not work if the government simply does not care
about efficiency. Moreover, command policies may be bad simply because intelligent people do not like to be told, "Uncle Sam (or Uncle Vladimir) has decided that
our society needs x^* units of armed forces (or scientific research or public schools
or street lights), so you need to pay us \$10,000 (or 10,000 rubles)."

Wicksell/Lindahl Taxes and the Lindahl Equilibrium

The government might set up a lovely taxation scheme for financing the public good,
one that was developed early in the twentieth century by Swedish economists Knut
Wicksell (1851–1926) and Erik Lindahl (1891–1960).

One of Wicksell's important contributions to economics was to develop the
principle of *just taxes*. As long as there have been taxes, people have grappled with
the issues of who should pay, and how much they should pay. Loosely speaking,
there are three main schools of thought: (1) The first school believes that taxes
should be calculated as a more-or-less flat percentage of income (or wealth).
Making taxes proportional to income (or wealth) seems fair and simple. This
position dates at least to the time of the Old Testament and tithing. (2) The second
school believes that taxes should be based on the payer's ability to pay. This implies
progressive taxes, with the wealthy paying a higher proportion of their income than
the poor. This is the position of utilitarians, who believe that the marginal utility
of income declines as income increases. Therefore, if two taxpayers are to make
the same sacrifice in utility when they pay their taxes, the rich man must pay a
higher proportion of his income than the poor man. (3) The third school believes in
taxation according to benefit. According to this principle, it is unjust to tax Ms. i to
pay for something that she does not care about and may not want. It is just to make
Mr. j pay a high tax for what is very useful, beneficial, or profitable to him. This
is the position that Wicksell took: the taxes a person has to pay should be based on
the benefit he or she receives from the public good.

We now turn to a system of taxation to finance the public good based on
Wicksell's principle of taxation according to benefit. More precisely, we will use
the principle of *taxation according to marginal benefit*. We return to our model
with n consumers, and we continue to assume quasilinear preferences. Person i's
utility function is $u_i(x, y_i) = v_i(x) + y_i$. The government collects taxes and uses
what it collects to pay for the public good.

We assume that the government initially decides on a list of tax shares, one for
each consumer. Consumer i's *tax share*, written t_i, is the fraction of the total cost
of the public good that will be placed on i. The government's revenue must equal

what it spends on the public good; so we require that

$$t_1 + t_2 + \cdots + t_n = 1.$$

We assume that the government sends each consumer i the following message:
"Dear Mr./Ms. i: We are going to provide the public good. We will tax everybody
to pay the cost. Your tax share, that is, your share of the total cost, is going to be
t_i. In other words, if we end up providing x units of the public good, at a cost of
x dollars, you will be billed $t_i x$. Please tell us: Given this policy, how much of the
public good do you want us to provide?"

Mr. i gets the message, sits, and thinks. He can think about this in an honest
and straightforward way, or a devious and not-so-straightforward way. We will
get to the not-so straightforward way later; here is his honest and straightforward
line of thought. He wants to maximize his utility subject to his budget constraint.
Suppose the government produces the quantity that he tells them to. Call it x. His
utility is $v_i(x) + y_i$ and his budget constraint is now $t_i x + y_i = M_i$, given what the
government has told him about how he will be taxed. Using his budget constraint, he
substitutes for y_i in his utility function and he drops the M_i from his maximization
problem because it is a constant. Therefore, he wants to maximize $v_i(x) - t_i x$. He
takes the derivative of this function and sets it equal to zero, which gives

$$v_i'(x) = MB_i(x) = t_i.$$

He solves this equation for x; we will call the solution $x_i(t_i)$ because it is the
public good output that Mr. i wants, and it is contingent on the tax share that the
government assigned him.

He now responds to the government, and tells them the quantity he wants, $x_i(t_i)$.
(He reports only the number, not the whole function.)

At this point, the government has a list of desired amounts of the public good,
one for each person. They will most likely differ.

If they do differ, the government sends out a new set of messages. In the transition
from the old set of messages to the new set of messages, the government raises the
tax shares of people who wanted a lot of the public good, and lowers the tax shares
of people who wanted very little of it. The new messages say:

"Dear Mr./Ms. i: Please disregard our last message. We have assigned you a new
tax share. Use the new tax share, shown on this message, to recalculate the level of
public good that you want. Then please tell us, once again, how much of the public
good you think we should provide."

This process goes on until everyone agrees on the quantity of the public good
that should be produced. The result is called a *Lindahl equilibrium*. This is a set
of tax shares $(t_1, t_2, \ldots, t_n)$, and a quantity of the public good x^e, such that every
consumer, when told his or her tax share is t_i, reports back a desired public good

quantity $x_i(t_i)$, and they all agree:

$$x_1(t_1) = x_2(t_2) = \ldots = x_n(t_n) = x^e.$$

The Wicksell/Lindahl scheme we have described has two virtues. First, it bases a person's tax on his or her marginal benefit. If i gets a lot of utility from the marginal unit of the public good, his tax share is going to be high; if not, it is going to be low. Second, at least as we have described it so far, with everybody reporting honestly, it results in an efficient or Pareto optimal level of output for the public good. Here is why. Each i calculated his desired quantity based on the equation $MB_i(x) = t_i$, and they all got their desired quantities, because the definition of the Lindahl equilibrium requires that the desired quantities of the public good all agree. Therefore,

$$MB_1(x^e) + MB_2(x^e) + \cdots + MB_n(x^e) = t_1 + t_2 + \cdots + t_n = 1.$$

Therefore, x^e satisfies the Samuelson optimality condition.

In Figure 18.3, we show how a Lindahl equilibrium looks in a graph when there are only two people. This graph is slightly different from what we are used to. The horizontal axis shows both t_1 and t_2. This axis is a line segment 1 unit long. A point on the line shows t_1 and t_2; we measure t_1 as the distance from the left end of the line segment to the given point, and t_2 as the distance from the right end of the line segment to the given point. The graph has two vertical axes, one at the left end of the horizontal line segment, and one at the right end. Both vertical axes show quantities of the public good. Consumer 1's desired quantity of the public good $x_1(t_1)$ can be be read off the left vertical axis, and consumer 2's desired quantity $x_2(t_2)$ can be be read off the right. Note, however, that the height of any point represents a quantity of the public good, whether read off the left or the right vertical axis. As t_i increases for either consumer, that consumer wants to see less of the public good produced, so there are two downward-sloping curves in the figure, representing the functions $x_i(t_i)$ for $i = 1, 2$. These can be interpreted as public good demand curves, contingent on tax shares. Consumer 1's curve looks downward sloping as it should, but consumer 2's curve may confuse the reader because it looks upward sloping. The explanation is that t_2 is measured from the right origin, so t_2 increases as you move left in the figure. The public good demand curves may be asymptotic to their respective axes, because a consumer whose tax share is zero may want an infinite amount of the public good. Note also that the height of the point at which i's demand curve reaches j's vertical axis shows the amount of the public good that i wants when $t_i = 1$, which is analogous to i's having to buy it (and pay 100 percent of the cost) on the private market.

The Lindahl equilibrium in Figure 18.3 is found by looking for the point at which the two public good demand curves cross. For the tax shares (t_1, t_2) at that

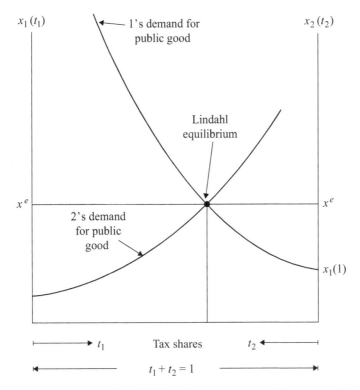

$x_1(t_1)$ ← 1's demand for public good $x_2(t_2)$

Lindahl equilibrium

x^e 2's demand for public good x^e

$x_1(1)$

→ t_1 Tax shares t_2 ←

← $t_1 + t_2 = 1$ →

Fig. 18.3. A Lindahl equilibrium in an economy with two people.

point, the two demands are the same. The height of the crossing point is the Lindahl equilibrium public good output. This is the efficient public good output.

We will conclude this discussion by turning to the fatal flaw in the Wicksell/ Lindahl scheme. When we were describing Mr. i's thought process after he was asked by the government to reveal his desired quantity of the public good, we said that there was a straightforward way for him to think about the question, and a not-so-straightforward way. We then gave the straightforward line of thought. We now turn to the devious line of thought.

We can see this vividly in Figure 18.3, so we now assume that there are just two people. Suppose consumer 1 is a straight-arrow Boy Scout type who never lies. Suppose consumer 2 is not. Consumer 2 is willing to stretch the truth a little bit. When the government asks him how much public good he wants it to produce, contingent on any t_2, he says, "Public good? I don't care much for it. If you're going to tax me for the lousy stuff ($t_2 > 0$), my answer is always zero. If it's free to me ($t_2 = 0$), then produce whatever amount the straight-arrow wants, I don't care." In Figure 18.3, this makes consumer 2's demand curve for the public good a horizontal line at zero, for all $0 < t_2$, with a (discontinuous) jump up when $t_2 = 0$. The new Lindahl equilibrium quantity is at $x^e = x_1(1)$, which is inefficient. This is exactly the outcome we saw under the private market provision of the public good, with 1 moving first. The free rider problem strikes again, and with a vengeance.

Demand-Revealing Taxes

In the 1960s and 1970s, various American economists, including Edward H. Clarke (1939–) and Theodore Groves (1942–), devised an ingenious scheme to provide the public good and to tax people to pay for it. This scheme was designed (1) to guarantee that the Pareto optimal quantity of the public good would be produced, (2) to raise enough money to pay for that quantity, and (3) to not create incentives for taxpayers to lie about their demands for the public good.

In the demand-revealing mechanism, or demand-revealing tax scheme, each consumer sends a message to the government. The message is his or her public good benefit function, $v_i(x)$. Of course, if i's message is false (like consumer 2's message in our previous discussion of the Wicksell/Lindahl scheme), the government will be tripped up and the mechanism will fail. The virtue of the demand-revealing scheme, however, is that the consumers will have no incentives to reply with false messages. Therefore, they will all reveal their true demands, or, more precisely, their true $v_i(x)$ functions.

When the government gets all the $v_i(x)$ functions, it proceeds with the exercise of maximizing total net benefit from the public good. It solves the Samuelson optimality condition and obtains x^*. Then it sends out tax bills. The tax bills are carefully crafted so that consumers do not have any incentives to lie about their $v_i(x)$ functions. The bills have two parts: a main part, which we will describe below, and a secondary part. We will say only this about the secondary part: it is designed to ensure that enough money is collected, and it creates no incentives for consumers to lie.

The main part of the tax bill says that consumer i must pay a dollar amount T_i which equals the total cost x^e, minus the sum over everyone *except* i of the benefit $v_j(x^e)$. That is,

$$T_i = x^e - \sum_{j \neq i} v_j(x^e).$$

It is not difficult to prove (although we will not do so here) that with this tax assessment, i has nothing to gain by lying to the government about his $v_i(x)$ function. Moreover, i gains nothing from lying, whether the other people are telling the truth or not. In other words, telling the truth is a dominant strategy for the demand-revealing mechanism.

Therefore, the scheme truly is *demand revealing*, or *incentive compatible* – it causes people to honestly reveal their benefit functions. It results in the optimal output of the public good, because the government uses the (true) $v_i(x)$ functions along with the Samuelson optimality condition to find x^e.

In short, the demand-revealing tax scheme is a clever mechanism for financing the public good. It should cause people to be truthful about their demands for, or benefits from, the public good, and it should result in Pareto optimality.

We conclude this section with a numerical example. For the sake of simplicity, the example is discrete – either the public good is provided or not – so there are no real $v_i(x)$ functions, and there certainly are no derivatives of functions. The public good is a bridge. The government either builds it ($x = 1$) at a cost of $1000, or does not build it ($x = 0$) at a cost of $0. There are five people. If the bridge is not built, they get no benefit from it. If it is built, each person gets a different amount of benefit, as follows:

$$v_1(1) = 0, \ v_2(1) = 500, \ v_3(1) = 100, \ v_4(1) = 200, \ \text{and} \ v_5(1) = 300.$$

With this discrete example, we cannot use the Samuelson optimality condition, but we can easily see that the way to maximize total net benefit from the public good is to build the bridge. (With the bridge, the total net benefit is $0 + 500 + 100 + 200 + 300 - 1000 = 100$; without the bridge, the total net benefit is 0.)

Now, recall how the demand-revealing scheme works. The government asks each person for his or her $v_i(1)$. ($v_i(0)$, or the value to i of no bridge, is obviously 0 for everybody, which the government knows.) Each i knows exactly how T_i will be calculated, and that the T_is will be

$$T_1 = -100, \ T_2 = 400, \ T_3 = 0, \ T_4 = 100, \ \text{and} \ T_5 = 200,$$

providing all report their true $v_i(1)$s. Now, we ask: Is the mechanism demand revealing? Or does someone have an incentive to lie?

The reader should choose one of these five people at random and think about the following. Person i's net benefit when the bridge is built is $v_i(1) - T_i$. If i exaggerated the value of the bridge, would that change the government's decision to build it? Would it change his tax T_i? Would he gain by exaggerating the value? If i said the bridge was worth less to him than it truly was, the government's decision might or might not change. If the government's decision does not change, would i's tax T_i change? Would i gain from the lie? If the government's decision does change, and the bridge was not built, would i gain from the lie?

The reader is encouraged to do this mental exercise. If you do, you will quickly realize that no one can gain by reporting a false value for the bridge. That is the remarkable virtue of the demand-revealing tax scheme.

Unfortunately, the demand-revealing scheme is too complex to be useful in most situations. There are related mechanisms used in the provision of *private goods* (particularly what are called *second-price auctions*) that are very important in some modern business applications. In a second-price auction, or *Vickrey auction*, named after Canadian economist William Vickrey (1914–1996), an object is put up for bids at an auction. It is sold to the highest bidder, but at the price bid by the second-highest bidder. Like the demand-revealing tax scheme we have discussed, the second-price auction is incentive compatible – it causes the auction bidders to reveal their true valuations. And it is much simpler, and therefore much more usable, than the demand-revealing scheme. In short, the demand-revealing scheme is a cousin of the second-price auction, but it is the unpopular cousin.

18.7 A Solved Problem

The Problem

There are three people who consume public and private goods. As usual, the public good is x, and y_i represents person i's consumption of the private good. The prices of both the public good and the private good are $1 per unit. The initial endowments of the private good are $(M_1, M_2, M_3) = (10, 10, 10)$. The three people have the following utility functions:

$$u_1(x, y_1) = \ln x + y_1.$$

$$u_2(x, y_2) = 2 \ln x + y_2.$$

$$u_3(x, y_3) = 3 \ln x + y_3.$$

(a) Assume that the public good is purchased, privately and that person 3 is the first to go to the market and buy the public good. Assume he does not act strategically; he ignores persons 1 and 2 when he buys x, and thinks only of his own utility maximization problem. What is the outcome? How much of the public good does person 3 buy? How much do persons 1 and 2 buy?

(b) Use the Samuelson optimality condition to find the Pareto optimal quantity of the public good x^*.

(c) Describe the Lindahl equilibrium.

(d) Show how any of the three people could gain by misrepresenting his or her preferences to the government.

The Solution

(a) Person 3 maximizes $u_3(x, y_3) = 3 \ln x + y_3$, subject to his budget constraint $x + y_3 = 10$. Using the budget constraint to substitute for y_3, and ignoring the constant in the function being maximized, gives

$$u_3(x) = 3 \ln x - x.$$

Differentiating and setting the result equal to zero gives

$$x = 3.$$

Person 3 buys 3 units of x with his own money; but the public good is public and available for all. Now, persons 1 and 2 have to decide whether or not to buy any additional amounts of it. The marginal benefit function for person 1 is $MB_1(x) = 1/x$. At $x = 3$, the marginal benefit to person 1 of the public good is $1/3$. But the price is $1, so person 1 buys no additional public good. The same argument holds for person 2.

The market result is therefore $(x_1^M, x_2^M, x_3^M) = (0, 0, 3)$. Three units of the public good are purchased, all by person 3; persons 1 and 2 are free riders.

(b) The Samuelson optimality condition says that the sum of the marginal benefits from the public good must equal the marginal cost. In our example, the marginal benefit functions are $MB_1(x) = 1/x$, $MB_2(x) = 2/x$, and $MB_3(x) = 3/x$. Therefore, the optimality condition says

$$\frac{1}{x} + \frac{2}{x} + \frac{3}{x} = 1.$$

This gives $x^* = 6$.

(c) Assuming that no one is misrepresenting his or her preferences, at the Lindahl equilibrium, person i's tax share t_i ends up equal to his marginal benefit from the public good. That is, $MB_i(x) = t_i$. Also, assuming that the everybody is honest, at the Lindahl equilibrium, the public good quantity is efficient, $x^* = 6$. Using the marginal benefit functions given earlier, and setting $x = 6$, gives $t_1 = 1/6$, $t_2 = 2/6$, and $t_3 = 3/6$. With these tax shares, each person wants the government to provide 6 units of the public good. Person 1 pays $t_1 x = 1$; person 2 pays $t_2 x = 2$; and person 3 pays $t_3 x = 3$. The government collects taxes totaling 6 units of the private good, and produces the 6 units of the public good that everybody wants.

(d) Suppose person 1 claims that he always gets zero marginal benefit from the public good; for any $t_1 > 0$, he wants $x = 0$. But continue to assume that persons 2 and 3 report honestly. The government then finds a Lindahl equilibrium at which the tax shares are $(t_1, t_2, t_3) = (0, 2/5, 3/5)$, and it produces 5 units of the public good. Person 1's tax bill is now zero. Person 1's utility is now

$$u_1(x, y_1) = \ln 5 + y_1 = \ln 5 + 10 = 11.61.$$

When he was honest in part (c) above, his utility was

$$u_1(x, y_1) = \ln 6 + y_1 = \ln 6 + 10 - t_1 x = \ln 6 + 10 - 1 = 10.79 < 11.61.$$

Therefore, it pays for person 1 to lie.

Exercises

1. Fabio and Paolo are housemates. They are thinking of buying a TV that costs $300. Each of them would receive a $200 benefit from having the TV. If neither of them pays, the TV is not purchased. There are a couple of ways they could make the purchase. They could simultaneously chip in $150 each, and buy the TV. Or, one housemate could pay $300 upfront, in the hope that his housemate would reimburse him $150. However, the housemates are irresponsible jerks, and in fact never reimburse each other.

(a) What two conditions must hold for the TV to be considered a public good?

(b) Draw the payoff matrix, and find all Nash equilibria.

   Now suppose the World Cup is approaching, and they will each receive a $400 benefit from having the TV.

(c) Draw the new payoff matrix, and find all Nash equilibria.

2. Consider Fabio and Paolo again. Now assume each consumes two goods, movie streaming and beer. Assume for now that they watch their movies separately. They have identical utility functions: $u_i = \sqrt{x_i y_i}$, where x_i is the amount of movie streaming for person i and y_i the amount of beer consumed by person i. A unit of either good costs $1. Fabio has an income of $10 a week, and Paolo has an income of $20 a week.

   (a) How much money does Fabio spend on movie streaming and on beer? How about Paolo? Calculate each of their utility levels.

   After a month, Fabio and Paolo realize that they could share a movie streaming account instead of having two separate accounts, and watch their movies together, instead of separately. Movie streaming is now a public good, instead of a private good; their utility functions are now $u_i = \sqrt{xy_i}$, for $i = f, p$, and $x = x_f + x_p$. The price of movie streaming is still $1 per unit.

   (b) Suppose Fabio and Paolo agree to maintain their allocation from part (a). Calculate each of their utility levels and compare them to their utility levels in part (a).

   (c) Is the allocation from part (a) Pareto optimal?

   (d) Show that Pareto optimality requires that Fabio spend all his income on beer and that Paolo spend $10 on beer and $10 on movie streaming.

3. Three little pigs are looking to buy a house of stone. Their utility functions are as follows: $u_1 = (3 + H)y_1$, $u_2 = (2 + H)y_2$, and $u_3 = (1 + H)y_3$, respectively, where $H = 1$ if they buy a stone house and $H = 0$ otherwise, and y is the amount of money spent on private consumption. They have each saved up M_1, M_2, and M_3, respectively.

   (a) What is the maximum amount each pig is willing to contribute toward buying a stone house?

   (b) Suppose $M_1 = \$2,800$, $M_2 = \$1,800$, and $M_3 = \$1,000$. There is a house of stone on sale for $1,800. Do the pigs buy it?

4. There are 1,000 people in the village of Fasching. The villagers enjoy only two goods, festivals and food. Festivals are a public good, whereas food is a private good. The villagers have identical preferences for the two goods, denoted by $u_i = \sqrt{x}/5 + y_i$, where x is euros spent on festivals and y_i is euros spent on food.

   (a) Calculate the marginal rate of substitution of food for festivals, MRS_{x,y_i}.

   (b) What is the Pareto optimal amount of money spent on festivals?

5. Consider the voluntary contributions mechanism in the free rider section. Suppose that $u_1(x, y_1) = \sqrt{x} + y_1$ and $u_2(x, y_2) = 2\sqrt{x} + y_2$. Show that agent 2 will never free ride on agent 1. Can you interpret that?

6. The mayor of Keukenhof would like to build a new public park, if he can raise enough taxes to cover the cost, which is 1,000 euros. There are four families in the town. Each family's benefit from a public park is as follows: $v_1 = 100$, $v_2 = 200$, $v_3 = 300$, and $v_4 = 400$. The mayor wants to use the demand-revealing tax mechanism described in Section 18.6.

   (a) If each family reports its true benefit, v_i, how much will each family have to pay, T_i?

   (b) Suppose family 4 misreports its benefit as 500, whereas the other families report their true benefits. Does the park get built? If so, how much does family 4 have to pay? Is family 4's net benefit different from its net benefit in part (a)?

(c) Suppose family 4 misreports its benefit as 300, whereas the other families report their true benefits. Does the park get built? If so, how much does family 4 have to pay? Is family 4's net benefit different from its net benefit in part (a)?

(d) Show that the Samuelson optimality condition is satisfied.

Chapter 19

Uncertainty and Expected Utility

19.1 Introduction and Examples

In most of this book, we have assumed *perfect information*. That is, we have assumed that every buyer and every seller of every good and service in the market has complete information about all the relevant facts. All the buyers and all the sellers know the market prices, and they all know the characteristics of the things being bought and sold. This is a reasonable assumption in the markets for many goods, whose characteristics are easily observed. But it is often unreasonable. The following are some examples of things we buy and sell, or consume and pay for, whose properties or qualities may be quite uncertain. The buyers and sellers, or consumers and providers of these things, face substantial *uncertainty* or *randomness*.

1. *Used cars*. When you buy a used car, you are very unsure about its condition. You may bring it to an independent mechanic to check it over, and you may check it out on CarFax, but you can never be sure that the previous owner changed the oil any time in the last 25,000 miles. In other words, you might be lucky and get a beautifully maintained car with no mechanical problems, or you might get a lemon.
2. *New cars*. Of course you cannot be 100 percent sure about a new car either. Even if you are a thoughtful and careful consumer and you buy a Toyota Prius, you may have mechanical problems, perhaps even the much dreaded problem (in 2010, and probably exaggerated) of unintended acceleration.
3. *College/university*. You chose a university for an undergraduate degree. Your university is very expensive. When you choose which university (or universities) to apply to, how much do you know about it (or them)? Do you know what your major will be? Do you know what you might learn in your classes? Do you know how many professors are interesting and informative, and how many are deadly dull and uninterested in teaching? Do you know what a blessing or what a curse your classmates and roommates might be?

4. *Dangerous activities.* You travel between home and school by car, or by train, or by plane. Each mode of travel creates some very small risk of a fatal accident. Do you know what the odds are? And if you do know, how does this knowledge enter into your utility maximization calculation and your decision process?

5. *Life insurance and annuities.* You fear you may die too young, and you want to buy a life insurance policy to protect your spouse and children in the event of your premature death. What kind of policy should you buy, and how much insurance should you have? Alternatively, you think you may live too long, and you may run out of savings before you go. You do not want to be a burden to your children. You have heard that you can buy insurance against this possibility also. Should you buy an annuity, and how big an annuity should you get?

6. *Investments.* You have some money that you are going to either invest in bank certificates of deposit (with minimal risk and also minimal reward), or in shares of stock (with considerable risk but greater rewards). What should you do?

7. *Gambling.* You can play a game in a casino or buy a state lottery ticket. The game or the state lottery requires that you put in $1, and in exchange, you have a certain chance of winning nothing, a chance of winning $50, a chance of winning $1,000, and a chance of winning $1 million. If you know the odds for each outcome, what do you do?

We could go on and on. The point is that many of the things we buy, or invest in, or receive from our governments, friends, and relatives have a good measure of uncertainty attached to them. Also, many things that we do increase the uncertainty in our lives, whereas other things reduce it. Sometimes we pay money to buy risk; at other times we pay money to avoid risk. The modeling we have done so far has ignored all this. We will now turn to modeling that explicitly addresses uncertainty.

In the next two sections of this chapter we lay out the basic model of consumer behavior under uncertainty, developed by John von Neumann and Oskar Morgenstern. This model gives a utility function that can be used to analyze uncertainty. Then we will turn to some examples, which show how the von Neumann–Morgenstern utility function approach can be applied to consumers who want to reduce or avoid risk, and to consumers who like risk and want to increase it. The examples also show how people can trade risk in ways that make everybody better off.

19.2 Von Neumann–Morgenstern Expected Utility: Preliminaries

In the initial chapters of this book, we modeled consumer choice, in what is called the *standard consumer choice model.* In the standard model, the consumer chooses among bundles of goods, which have known quantities of various goods in them. The consumer knows what the goods are and how much (or how little) she likes them. There is nothing random or uncertain about such a bundle. The consumer is choosing among certain alternatives. We assume that the consumer has complete and transitive preferences over these alternatives. We also assume monotonicity and convexity, to ensure that the indifference curves have the usual shape. Then we define the consumer's utility function. The utility function is based on, and perfectly represents, the consumer's preferences.

Utility functions in the standard consumer choice model are ordinal utility functions. For such functions, only relative values matter; saying $u_i(X) = 15$, $u_i(Y) = 10$, and $u(Z) = 5$ only means that consumer i prefers X to Y to Z. There is no intrinsic meaning to the utility numbers, and if the function u_i represents i's preferences, then any order-preserving transformation of u_i works just as well to represent i's preferences. For instance, if u_i is always positive, then $v_i = \sqrt{u_i}$ works just as well to represent i's preferences as u_i does.

We now develop a model of consumer choice over alternatives that are *random* or *uncertain*. Based on our model of choice over uncertain alternatives, we will develop a new type of utility function. This new utility function will no longer be purely ordinal; it will have some properties that make it similar to (but certainly not identical to) the cardinal utility functions of nineteenth-century utilitarian economists. Most important, it will provide a basis for the rigorous analysis of choice under uncertainty.

To proceed, we need to introduce a few concepts and terms from probability and statistics. These concepts and terms may be familiar to you if you have taken any kind of statistics or econometrics course.

For this purpose, we start by considering a simple kind of gamble or game, with two possible outcomes. (In this chapter, we will use the word "game" in the usual vernacular fashion; this is actually simpler than a "game" in the sense of Chapter 14, as it involves only one decision maker.) The possible outcomes in this game are dollar (or money) prizes; one is X dollars and the other is Y dollars. These are the only possible outcomes, so the person playing this game must end up with either X or Y. Each outcome will happen with a given likelihood, or *probability*. We will write p_x and p_y for the probabilities. (Note that in this chapter, symbols such as p_x and p_i will represent the probabilities of outcome X or X_i, not the price of good X or good i, as in earlier chapters.)

Because X and Y are the only possible outcomes in this game, the probabilities must sum to 1; that is, $p_x + p_y = 1$. A sensible person looking at this will want to know the (weighted) average outcome if she plays the game. That weighted average outcome is called the *expected value* or *expectation* of the game. We write E for expected value. The weighted average outcome, the expected value, is $E = p_x X + p_y Y$. For example, if $X = \$5$ and if $Y = \$10$, and if $p_1 = 0.9$ and $p_2 = 0.1$, then $E = \$5.50$. However, if $p_1 = 0.1$ and $p_2 = 0.9$, then $E = \$9.50$. (The moral of this chapter so far: if you play this gamble, know the odds!)

The idea of expected value is easily generalized to the case of n outcomes. Consider a game with n outcomes, $(X_1, X_2, \ldots, X_n)$, all of which are dollar prizes. Each outcome X_i occurs with a given probability p_i. We call this a *lottery*, written L. (A state-sponsored lottery such as Powerball is a special example of what we call a lottery, although the state-sponsored version may try to conceal the bad odds. The simple two-outcome gamble discussed previously is a lottery. Other more complex lotteries are discussed later.) The expected value or expectation of the lottery with n outcomes is given by

$$E(L) = p_1 X_1 + p_2 X_2 + \cdots + p_n X_n.$$

A lottery may have outcomes that are other lotteries. For example, a coin is tossed. If it is heads, the game is over and you win \$10. If it is tails, it is tossed again. If it is heads on the second toss, you win \$10. If it is tails on the second toss, you lose \$40. (Would you buy this game?)

Let us now consider how we can calculate the expected value of a lottery on lotteries. We again assume that the ultimate prizes are amounts of money, in dollars. We illustrate with another example. Let L be a *compound lottery* whose possible outcomes are other lotteries L_1, L_2, and L_3. Assume that the probabilities of these outcomes are $(p_1, p_2, p_3) = (1/3, 1/3, 1/3)$. (A note about notation: p_{12}, for example, is the probability of outcome X_2, given that lottery L_1 was the outcome at the first stage of the compound lottery.)

Suppose the L_is are as follows: L_1 pays $X_1 = \$0$ and $X_2 = \$50$ with probabilities $(p_{11}, p_{12}) = (1, 0)$; L_2 pays $X_1 = \$0$ and $X_2 = \$50$ with probabilities $(p_{21}, p_{22}) = (1/2, 1/2)$; and L_3 pays $X_1 = \$0$ and $X_2 = \$50$ with probabilities $(p_{31}, p_{32}) = (1/3, 2/3)$. How is $E(L)$ calculated? The expected value of the compound lottery is the *expectation of the expectations*. That is,

$$E(L) = p_1 E(L_1) + p_2 E(L_2) + p_3 E(L_3)$$
$$= \frac{1}{3}(0) + \frac{1}{3}\left(\frac{1}{2} \times 50\right) + \frac{1}{3}\left(\frac{2}{3} \times 50\right) \approx 19.44.$$

More generally, suppose there are n different ultimate outcomes, indexed by i, and m different possible outcomes of compound lottery L, each one itself a lottery, indexed by j. Assume that lottery L_j has the ultimate prizes (for instance, amounts of money) as its outcomes, and let p_{ji} be the probability of outcome X_i from lottery L_j. Then the expected value of the compound lottery is again the expectation of the expectations, or

$$E(L) = \sum_{j=1}^{m} p_j E(L_j) = \sum_{j=1}^{m} p_j \sum_{i=1}^{n} p_{ji} X_i$$
$$= \sum_{j=1}^{m}\sum_{i=1}^{n} p_j p_{ji} X_i = \sum_{i=1}^{n}\left(\sum_{j=1}^{m} p_j p_{ji}\right) X_i.$$

The term in the far right summation, within the parentheses, is the ultimate probability of getting prize X_i, after the two stages of the compound lottery have played out.

19.3 Von Neumann–Morgenstern Expected Utility: Assumptions and Conclusion

We are now ready to describe the model of consumer behavior under uncertainty. This model was first developed by John von Neumann (1903–1957) and Oskar Morgenstern (1902–1977) in their 1944 book *Theory of Games and Economic Behavior*. Von Neumann was a Hungarian-American genius, a mathematician who made major contributions to mathematics, nuclear physics, nuclear weapons, game theory, and other fields. Morgenstern was a noted German-born Austrian-American economist.

We assume that the consumer is considering some set of alternatives. The alternatives include certain things, such as bundles of goods, amounts of money, and so on. For now we will continue to use notation such as X_1 and X_2 for the certain outcomes. In addition to these certain outcomes, there are risky alternatives. We will use notation like X, Y, and Z for arbitrary alternatives, both certain and risky. A risky alternative is a lottery that attaches probabilities to all its outcomes. When we want to emphasize the fact that something is a lottery, we will use notation such as L, L_1, and L_2. The consumer has complete and transitive preferences over all the alternatives.

If the possible outcomes of a lottery are the certain outcomes, and if we assume a finite number n of them, a risky alternative is simply a lottery over $(X_1, X_2, \ldots, X_n)$. That is, it is just a list of probabilities, summing to 1, over all the certain outcomes. (If there are infinitely many certain outcomes, the model requires more complex mathematical description. For the purposes of exposition, we will stick to the easier finite n story.)

Any certain outcome can also be viewed as a (degenerate) lottery, because getting X_1 for certain is the same as having a lottery with $p_1 = 1$ and $p_2 = p_3 = \ldots = p_n = 0$.

Risky alternatives also include lotteries whose outcomes are other risky alternatives (that is, lotteries over lotteries), or some of whose outcomes are certain and some risky. (Many gambles in the real world are just like this. For example, you might buy a state lottery ticket for \$1 with three possible outcomes: you win \$0 with probability 0.95, you win \$10 with probability 0.04, or you win a lottery ticket in a different lottery with probability 0.01.)

Von Neumann–Morgenstern utility theory is based on the following five assumptions:

1. *Completeness and transitivity*. The consumer's preferences over all the alternatives, certain and uncertain, are complete and transitive.
2. *Continuity*. Suppose that the consumer prefers X over Y over Z. That is, Y is somewhere between X and Z in the consumer's preference ranking. Then there must exist a probability p_x, with $0 < p_x < 1$, such that the consumer is indifferent between the middle alternative Y, and a lottery with the best alternative X with probability p_x and the worst alternative Z with probability $1 - p_x$.

3. *Independence.* Suppose the consumer is indifferent between alternatives X and Y, and suppose that Z is any alternative. Consider two lotteries. One has outcomes X and Z, and the other has outcomes Y and Z. Suppose both these lotteries assign the same probability to the "indifferent" alternative (that is, X or Y), and therefore the same probability to the "other" alternative Z. Then the consumer must be indifferent between these two lotteries.

4. *Unequal probabilities.* Suppose the consumer prefers X to Y. Consider two lotteries; both have only X and Y as possible outcomes. Suppose the two lotteries attach different probabilities to the two outcomes. Then the consumer prefers the lottery that assigns a higher probability to her preferred outcome X.

5. *Compound lotteries (complexity).* A consumer is given a choice between two lotteries. Lottery L_1 is a straightforward lottery that provides the certain outcomes $(X_1, X_2, \ldots, X_n)$ with probabilities $(p_1, p_2, \ldots, p_n)$. Lottery L_2 is a lottery whose outcomes are other lotteries. However, after the intermediate lotteries play out, it ultimately ends up with the same certain outcomes, and with the same probabilities $(p_1, p_2, \ldots, p_n)$. (These probabilities are calculated using formulas similar to the probability expression in our earlier equation for the expected value of a compound lottery.) Then the consumer is indifferent between L_1 and L_2.

Before proceeding to the Von Neumann–Morgenstern result, we should make a few comments about these assumptions.

Assumption 1, completeness and transitivity, is an obvious extension of the assumptions we made in the standard consumer theory model. Assumption 2, continuity, seems obvious and intuitive. However, we shall see that this assumption causes the von Neumann–Morgenstern utility function to be more than ordinal, although not quite cardinal. Assumption 3, independence, seems very intuitive, and assumption 4, unequal probabilities, seems as if it has to be true. Surely a consumer should prefer the gamble that gives him better odds of the preferred prize. Assumption 5, compound lotteries, is very plausible for a "rational" consumer who should focus on the ultimate probabilities of the ultimate outcomes. But some consumers may like or dislike intervening lotteries (even though in our model they take no time and cost nothing to run). Some theorists have investigated what happens to the von Neumann–Morgenstern model without some of these assumptions.

Now we can turn to the remarkable theorem.

Von Neumann–Morgenstern Expected Utility Theorem

Suppose consumer i faces a set of alternatives, certain and uncertain. Suppose her preferences satisfy assumptions 1 through 5. Then there exists a utility function u_i such that:

1. *It represents the consumer's preferences.* That is, the function assigns utility numbers to all the alternatives, and for any pair of alternatives X and Y, $u_i(X) > u_i(Y)$ if and only if consumer i prefers X to Y, and $u_i(X) = u_i(Y)$ if and only if consumer i is indifferent between them.

2. *It satisfies the expected utility property.* Let L be any risky alternative, that is, any lottery. Suppose its outcomes are $X, Y, \ldots, Z$. These may be certain outcomes, or other lotteries. (Note that there may be any number of such outcomes, although for simplicity we assume a finite number.) Suppose the corresponding probabilities are $p_x, p_y, \ldots, p_z$. Then the *utility of the risky alternative L is the expectation of the utilities of its possible outcomes.* That is,

$$u_i(L) = p_x u_i(X) + p_y u_i(Y) + \cdots + p_z u_i(Z).$$

19.4 Von Neumann–Morgenstern Expected Utility: Examples

We now turn to some examples of Von Neumann–Morgenstern utility functions. In this section, when we write $u(X)$ or $u_i(X)$ or $u_j(x)$ we are referring to such functions.

1. **An example showing that Von Neumann–Morgenstern utility is not ordinal.** Suppose that consumer i prefers X to Y to Z. Suppose her utilities from X and Z are $u_i(X) = 15$ and $u_i(Z) = 5$. If her preferences were ordinal, the utility she assigns Y could be any number greater than 5 and less than 15. However, the continuity assumption ties down her $u_i(Y)$. Here is why.

   Given that assumption, she can be asked the following question: "Consider a lottery L that gives you alternative X (your favorite) with probability p_x and alternative Z (your least favorite) with probability $1 - p_x$. What probability p_x would make you indifferent between L and your middle alternative Y?" She must answer the question with a single number p_x. Then her utility from Y must equal her utility from L, which, in turn, must equal the expectation of the utilities of the outcomes of L. This gives

$$u_i(Y) = u_i(L) = p_x u_i(X) + (1 - p_x)u_i(Z) = p_x 15 + (1 - p_x)5 = 5 + 10 p_x.$$

Once she says what p_x is, her utility from Y is uniquely defined.

   Let us assume she answers the question, "My $p_x = 0.4$." Then her utility from Y must be 9. For her, the fact that $u_i(X) = 15$, $u_i(Y) = 9$, and $u_i(Z) = 5$ means more than "I like X best, Y second best, and Z least." It also reveals something about her attitude toward uncertainty. Moreover, the utility function generated in this fashion is not preserved by an order-preserving transformation of u_i.

   For example, if $u_i(X) = 15$, $u_i(Y) = 9$, and $u_i(Z) = 5$, and if we let $v_i = \sqrt{u_i}$, then $v_i(X) = 3.87$, $v_i(Y) = 3.00$, and $v_i(Z) = 2.24$. Now the utility of the lottery L would be

$$v_i(L) = p_x v_i(X) + (1 - p_x)v_i(Z) = p_x 3.87 + (1 - p_x)2.24 = 2.24 + 1.63 p_x.$$

Setting $p_x = 0.4$ then gives

$$v_i(L) = 2.89 \neq 3 = v_i(Y).$$

In other words, if we were to transform u_i into v_i in this fashion, consumer i would no longer be indifferent between L with $p_x = 0.4$ and Y; the transformation would destroy this property of her preferences.

The upshot of this is that a von Neumann–Morgenstern utility function, like a purely ordinal utility function, allows utility levels for two alternatives to be set arbitrarily. That is, for some pair X and Y, where consumer i prefers X to Y, utility levels can be set in any way, as long as $u_i(X) > u_i(Y)$. Once these two levels are selected, however, all other utility levels are tied down, and are not subject to arbitrary order-preserving transformations. This is the sense in which von Neumann–Morgenstern utility is more than ordinal, and is sometimes called, somewhat carelessly, a *cardinal utility* measure.

2. **A risk-averse consumer.** For a *risk-averse* consumer, risk is a bad thing, something to pay to avoid. We now assume the certain outcomes are amounts of money. Let x represent dollars for consumer i. Assume that her utility function is $u_i(x) = 10\sqrt{x}$. For this utility function, $u_i(\$0) = 0$ and $u_i(\$100) = 100$. This means that we have chosen our two arbitrary utility levels in a way that makes i's utility function go through two convenient points: $(0, 0)$ and $(100, 100)$. In Figure 19.1, we have graphed this utility function, with amounts of money x on the horizontal axis and i's utility $u_i(x)$ on the vertical axis. The graph of the utility function is a parabola, passing through $(0, 0)$ and $(100, 100)$, and "opening to the right." It is a concave function, meaning that its slope $du_i(x)/dx$ decreases as x increases. The derivative $du_i(x)/dx$ is i's marginal utility of money (or marginal utility of income), so this individual has a declining marginal utility of income.

We assume that consumer i starts out with $50 for sure. This gives her utility, $u_i(\$50) = 10\sqrt{50} = 70.71$.

Now, let us introduce some risk. Suppose she discovers that she might suffer a loss of $25, because of a possible auto accident, a theft, or some other random event. We assume the probability of having no loss is $1/2$, and the probability of a $25 loss is $1/2$. The expected loss is thus $12.50.

How much would she be willing to pay to insure against this loss? Suppose she pays P for an insurance policy that fully reimburses her if she suffers a loss. Then she has traded a random situation, which we will call lottery L, for a certain amount of money, equal to what she started with minus the insurance premium, or $50 − P$.

The lottery L is what she has with no insurance; it is $50 − $25 = $25 with probability $1/2$, and $50 with probability $1/2$. Her maximum willingness to pay for the insurance policy is the P that would make her indifferent between having no insurance and having insurance:

$$u_i(L) = u_i(50 - P), \text{ or}$$

$$(1/2) \cdot u_i(25) + (1/2) \cdot u_i(50) = 10\sqrt{50 - P}, \text{ or}$$

$$(1/2) \cdot 10\sqrt{25} + (1/2) \cdot 10\sqrt{50} = 10\sqrt{50 - P}.$$

Solving for P gives $13.57.

All this is illustrated in Figure 19.1. In the figure, the utility outcomes of L are shown on the vertical axis; these are $u_i(25) = 50$ and $u_i(50) = 70.71$. The utility level of L is exactly halfway between these points, because the probabilities of the two outcomes are

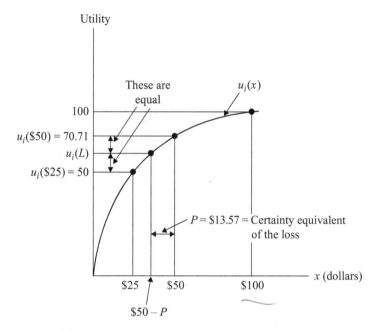

Fig. 19.1. The risk-averse consumer who starts with $50 and faces a $25 loss with probability $1/2$. She has a lottery L, which leaves her with $25 with probability $1/2$, and $50 with probability $1/2$. The utility levels from these two outcomes are shown on the vertical axis, as is $u_i(L)$, which must be midway between them because of the assumed probabilities. The certainty equivalent of the loss is P; the expectation of the loss is $12.50. The concavity of the $u_i(x)$ function implies that $P > \$12.50$.

1/2 and 1/2. The fact that $u_i(L)$ is halfway between $u_i(25)$ and $u_i(50)$ forces P in the figure to be more than $1/2 \times (\$50 - \$25) = \$12.50$.

We have found that our risk-averse consumer is willing to pay as much as $13.57 to ensure against a random loss with expectation $12.50. The random loss, to her, is the equivalent of a certain loss of $13.57, so she is willing to pay up to that amount to get rid of it. The $13.57 is called consumer i's *certainty equivalent of the loss*. It is significantly greater than the expected value of the loss because she is risk-averse.

3. **A risk-loving consumer.** For some consumers, risk is a good thing, something to pay extra for, rather than a bad thing to be avoided. A consumer who seeks risk instead of avoiding it is called a *risk-loving* consumer, or a *risk lover* for short. Here is an example. Again, we assume that the certain outcomes are amounts of money, measured in dollars. We assume that consumer j's utility function is $u_j(x) = x^2/100$. This utility function, like risk-averse consumer i's in the last example, goes through the points $(0, 0)$ and $(100, 100)$. The utility function is shown in Figure 19.2. Like consumer i's utility function, $u_j(x)$ is a parabola, but this one "opens upward," instead of "opening to the right." Therefore, it is a convex function, and consumer j's marginal utility of money $du_j(x)/dx$ is increasing rather than decreasing.

In the preceding example, we assumed that consumer i started with $50 in certain money, but faced a random loss of $25, with probability $1/2$. We calculated how much she would pay, at most, to get rid of the risk.

We will change the story a little bit for our risk lover j. The change may make it slightly easier to see the certainty equivalent in our figure. We now assume that consumer j starts out with a very risky position. In fact, we assume that she starts with this L: $0 with probability $1/2$, and $100 with probability $1/2$. The expectation of L is

$$E(L) = (1/2) \cdot \$0 + (1/2) \cdot \$100 = \$50.$$

Now j is approached by someone who wants to trade her cash for L. How much cash would she require? We now let P represent the minimum amount she would need to be paid for L. How can we find P? If she trades away L, all she has is P, a certain amount of money. The utility of this alternative to her is $u_j(P) = P^2/100$. If she keeps L, her utility is

$$u_j(L) = (1/2) \cdot u_j(0) + (1/2) \cdot u_j(100) = (1/2) \cdot 0 + (1/2) \cdot 100 = 50. \quad \textit{Because P is} \dots$$

If P is the minimum amount she would accept in exchange for her lottery L, she must be indifferent between accepting the sure-thing P and holding onto the random L:

$$u_j(P) = u_j(L), \text{ or}$$

$$P^2/100 = 50.$$

Solving this equation gives $P = \$70.71$. This amount is *consumer j's certainty equivalent of the lottery L.* This risk lover, who owns a risky L with expectation $50, would need to be paid at least $70.71 to part with it.

All this is illustrated in Figure 19.2. Note that in the figure, the utility outcomes of L are shown on the vertical axis; these are $u_j(\$0) = 0$ and $u_j(\$100) = 100$. The utility level of L is at 50, exactly halfway between these points, because the probabilities of the two outcomes are $1/2$ and $1/2$. The fact that $u_j(L)$ is halfway between $u_j(\$0)$ and $u_j(\$100)$ forces P in the figure to be more than half of $E(L) = \$50$.

4. **A risk-neutral consumer.** A consumer is called *risk-neutral* if she neither avoids risk nor seeks it. This means that her utility function does not curve downward (as in the risk-averse case), or upward (as in the risk-loving case). If consumer k is risk neutral, the graph of her utility function is an upward-sloping straight line. The simplest version of such a utility function is $u_k(x) = x$. A risk-neutral consumer values a lottery at its expected value. For instance, the possible loss that our risk-averse consumer was contemplating, $0 with probability $1/2$ and $25 with probability $1/2$, would be viewed as equivalent to a certain loss of $12.50 by the risk-neutral consumer.

Let us conclude this discussion by illustrating an extremely important point. There are, in reality, all sorts of people and all sorts of firms with all sorts of attitudes toward risk. If two parties with different attitudes toward risk get together, they can often make great gains by trading risk. For example, suppose our risk-loving consumer j has $70.71 in her pocket, but has no lottery. Suppose she meets

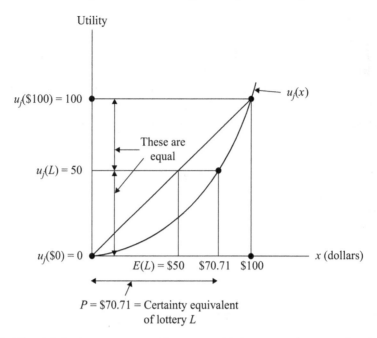

Fig. 19.2. The risk-loving consumer, who starts with lottery L that gives her $100 with probability $1/2$, and $0 with probability $1/2$. The utility of the lottery is 50, and the certainty equivalent is $P = \$70.71$. The convexity of the $u_i(x)$ function implies $P > E(L) = \$50$.

risk-neutral k, who runs a casino. Risk-neutral k can make up games and sell them to people who want them. Here is what k does – she offers a gamble to consumer j: "You pay me $69.95, and I will flip a coin. If it's heads, you win $100. If it's tails, you get nothing." Consumer j will accept this gamble because she loves risk, and her maximum willingness to pay is $70.71. She ends up slightly better off than she was with $70.71 in her pocket. Consumer k is now much better off. We can measure k's gain in utility units, or in expected dollars, as her utility function is $u_k(x) = x$. Let us measure in dollars. Her revenue is $69.95, and her expected cost is $50. Therefore, her expected profit is $19.95.

   In short, both parties are better off after the exchange, especially risk-neutral k, who has made almost $20. We will leave it to the reader to show that our risk-averse consumer i could trade her chance of a $25 loss, either to our risk lover j or our risk neutral k, in a swap that makes both parties better off.

19.5 A Solved Problem

The Problem

Suppose consumer i has utility function $u_i(x) = \sqrt{x}$. There are two financial assets; both cost $100. Consumer i is going to buy one of these. They will both pay off after a short time. Asset 1 pays $103 with certainty. Asset 2 pays $110 with probability 0.95, and $0 with probability 0.05. Which asset does she buy?

Consumer j has utility function $u_j(x) = x^2$. Which asset would she buy?

The Solution

Consumer i's utility from $A_1 = \$103$ is

$$u_i(103) = \sqrt{103} = 10.149.$$

Her expected utility from A_2 is

$$u_i(A_2) = 0.95u_i(110) + 0.05u_i(0) = 0.95\sqrt{110} + 0.05\sqrt{0} = 9.964.$$

Therefore, consumer i buys the sure thing, A_1.

Consumer j's utility from $A_1 = \$103$ is

$$u_j(103) = 103^2 = 10,609.$$

Her expected utility from A_2 is

$$u_j(A_2) = 0.95u_j(110) + 0.05u_j(0) = 0.95 \times 110^2 + 0.05 \times 0^2 = 11,495.$$

Therefore, consumer j buys the risky thing, A_2.

Exercises

1. The risk-averse consumer of Section 19.4 meets up with the risk-neutral consumer of that section. Describe a simple trade that they can make that makes both better off.

2. George is on a game show. He has equal probabilities of winning \$5, \$50, and \$500. His utility function is $u_g(x) = \frac{1}{2}x^2$, where x is the dollar amount he wins.
   (a) Calculate the expected value of the lottery.
   (b) Calculate George's expected utility from the lottery.
   (c) Calculate his certainty equivalent of the lottery. Explain what it means.
   (d) Is George risk averse, risk neutral, or risk loving? How can you tell?

3. Jack and Jill go up a hill to fetch a pail of water. There is a 25 percent chance that Jack will trip and fall, a 25 percent chance that Jill will trip and fall, a 25 percent chance that both will trip and fall, and a 25 percent chance that neither will trip and fall. If neither trips and falls, the pail will contain 6 gallons of water. If one of them trips and falls, the pail will contain 2 gallons of water. If both of them trip and fall, the pail will contain no water. Jack's utility from fetching a pail of water is $u_a(w) = w^2$, and Jill's utility is $u_i(w) = 2w$, where w is gallons of water in the pail.
   (a) How many gallons of water do you expect Jack and Jill to fetch?
   (b) Calculate the expected utility for each of them.
      Suppose there is a small well at the foot of the hill. If they draw water from the small well, they will obtain 3 gallons of water with certainty (and will not have to hike up the hill).
   (c) Who prefers to draw water at the foot of the hill? Who prefers to hike up the hill to draw water?
   (d) Is Jack risk averse, risk neutral, or risk loving? How about Jill? Explain.

4. Adam, Michael, and Stella each have $24 to spend on beer at the pub. Their utility functions are $u_a = \sqrt[3]{b_a}$, $u_m = b_m$, and $u_s = b_s^3$, respectively, where b_i is the number of glasses of beer consumed by person i. The price of a glass of beer is $3. Suppose glasses of beer can be consumed in fractions – for instance, one can order half a glass. Assume there is a 50 percent chance that they will all get mugged on the way to the pub. If so, they all lose all their money.

(a) Calculate the expected beer consumption for each of them.

(b) Calculate expected utility for each of them.

   Suppose the neighborhood thug is selling protection for $6. An individual who pays for protection does not get mugged.

(c) Who will buy protection?

(d) If the neighborhood thug wants to sell protection to all three, and he can charge only one price, what price would he charge?

5. Ko is offered a lottery. There is a jar with six balls in it – one blue, two red, and three yellow. His outcome will be determined by the color of the ball he draws. If he draws a blue ball, he receives $10. If he draws a red ball, he loses $5. If he draws a yellow ball, he loses $1. Given Ko's utility function, $u_k(x) = x$, where x is the dollar amount won, does Ko accept the lottery?

6. Will buys a lottery ticket for $6. The ticket has equal probabilities of being type A, type B, or type C. A type A ticket pays $20 with a 30 percent probability and nothing with a 70 percent probability; a type B ticket pays $15 with a 40 percent probability and nothing with a 60 percent probability; and a type C ticket pays $10 with a 50 percent probability and nothing with a 50 percent probability. Calculate the expected value of Will's lottery ticket.

Chapter 20

Uncertainty and Asymmetric Information

20.1 Introduction

In the last chapter, we discussed von Neumann–Morgenstern utility functions, which are used to represent people's preferences in situations in which there is uncertainty – where information is imperfect or missing. We continue the analysis of decision making under uncertainty in this chapter. But now we focus on the problems that arise when information is distributed unequally, in the sense that some people in the market know more than other people.

More precisely, we are now considering markets for goods or services when there is uncertainty, and the uncertainty is more on one side of the market (e.g., the buyers' side) than on the the other side of the market (e.g., the sellers' side). These are called markets with *asymmetric information*; the information is "asymmetric" because people on one side know more than people on the other side. In a world of perfect certainty, there would be no asymmetric information, but in this chapter we allow uncertainty. It turns out that asymmetric information may create serious market failures – failures that may need remedies.

In particular, what happens when the sellers of some risky or uncertain good or service know more than the buyers? For example, what happens in the market for used cars, when the sellers often know much more about the condition of the cars they are selling than the buyers? We look at the used car market in Section 20.2. What happens in insurance markets if insurance companies cannot distinguish between low-risk clients and high-risk clients? In Section 20.3, we examine the problems created by asymmetric information in insurance markets.

Of course, the very existence of insurance may cause some people to take greater risks than they would take if they were not insured. This is called the *moral hazard* problem, and we examine it in Section 20.4.

Finally, in many economic situations the people in charge (called *principals*) cannot directly observe the effort of the people who work for them (called *agents*).

359

What problems are caused by the information asymmetry between principals and agents? We look at this problem in Section 20.5. In Section 20.6, we conclude this chapter with a brief discussion of what might be done to fix market failures caused by asymmetric information.

20.2 When Sellers Know More Than Buyers: The Market for "Lemons"

This story is based on a paper that was published in 1970 by the American economist George Akerloff (1940–). (George Akerloff, Michael Spence (1943–), and Joseph Stiglitz (1943–) won the 2001 Nobel Prize in Economics for their work on markets with asymmetric information.)

Consider the market for used cars. Considerable uncertainty is attached to any used car. It may break down and require a new engine or transmission tomorrow, or it may run perfectly, needing only occasional routine maintenance, for the next ten years. When people are buying and selling used cars, the sellers usually have better information about the cars' reliability than the buyers. The sellers know much more about the probabilities of nasty and costly mechanical failures that may happen next month or next year.

We assume there are two kinds of used cars: "quality cars" and "lemons." We assume they look exactly alike, and even a mechanic cannot tell the difference. However, a person who has owned a car for a reasonable period of time knows whether her car is a quality car or a lemon. The owner of a car knows its history of past repairs, and she therefore knows the probabilities of future repairs. A person who has not owned that car does not know those probabilities.

For simplicity, we assume all people in the car market, both buyers and sellers, are risk neutral. We will also assume that quality cars and lemons deliver the same utility to any owner; they differ only in expected repair costs.

Given her knowledge of the expected costs of future repairs, the owner of a lemon has a *reservation price* for her car. This is the minimum she would take for it, and it reflects both how much she likes it as a car, and the expected repair costs she will have to incur if she holds on to it. We assume that the reservation price for the lemon owner is $1,000. Similarly, the owner of a quality car has a reservation price, which reflects her knowledge of expected repair costs for the quality car. We assume that the reservation price for the quality car owner is $2,000. Remember, the owner of a car knows which type of car it is.

We assume that any potential car buyer has a willingness to pay for either type of car, contingent on the type. We assume that buyers would be willing to pay $1,200 for a lemon, and $2,400 for a quality car. When a potential buyer looks at a car, however, she does not know the type.

What would happen if potential buyers could distinguish between quality cars and lemons? A market price for lemons, somewhere between $1,000 and $1,200, would be established, and a market price for quality cars, somewhere between

$2,000 and $2,400, would be established. The markets would clear, and the result would be efficient or Pareto optimal. But buyers cannot distinguish between quality cars and lemons. What then happens in this market?

Let us assume, for simplicity, that there are roughly equal numbers of quality cars and lemons. If this is the case, buyers will think that buying a car is a lottery L, with a possible outcome of a lemon with probability 0.5, and a possible outcome of a quality car also with probability 0.5. Given that we have assumed risk neutrality, what potential buyers think about L simply depends on the dollar expectation of the lottery. This is

$$E(L) = 0.5 \times \$1,200 + 0.5 \times \$2,400 = \$1,800.$$

It follows that buyers are willing to pay up to $1,800 for a used car.

Soon sellers realize that buyers are willing to pay only $1,800 for used cars, so sellers with quality cars disappear. As sellers of quality cars disappear, buyers become less and less willing to pay as much as $1,800.

In equilibrium, no quality cars are being bought or sold; the market for quality cars disappears. The market price for used cars ends up somewhere between $1,000 and $1,200, but only lemons trade. This outcome is clearly inefficient because potential buyers and sellers of quality cars are unable to trade.

This is a market failure due to asymmetric information.

20.3 When Buyers Know More Than Sellers: A Market for Health Insurance

Often, buyers of insurance know more about the risks they face than the insurance companies that insure them. This is true for auto insurance, as drivers know more about how carefully they drive and how much they drive than the insurance companies know; similarly, property owners know more about how careful or careless they are with fires than their insurance companies know; and consumers often know more about the state of their health than their health insurers know. The following example illustrates what might happen in health insurance markets as a result of this kind of asymmetric information.

Health insurance/adverse selection example. Suppose there are two groups of health care consumers. In both groups there is a risk of some serious but nonfatal illness, which costs $100,000 to treat.

Group 1 consumers have a low risk of the illness. Their probability of having it is 0.01, or 1 percent. A consumer in this group is willing to pay up to $1,200 for an insurance policy that would provide her with free treatment if she gets the illness. If she were to pay for treatment herself, her expected treatment cost would be $0.01 \times \$100,000 = \$1,000$. The fact that she is willing to pay up to $1,200 for the insurance policy indicates that she is risk averse. If an insurance company (which is risk neutral) can tell that a consumer is in group 1, it is clearly advantageous for

Table 20.1. *A market for health insurance*

	Number of People	Expected Cost per Person	Willingness to Pay
Group 1	9,000	$1,000	$1,200
Group 2	1,000	$5,000	$6,000
Total Population	10,000	$1,400	

it to arrange a policy with that consumer at a price somewhere between $1,000 and $1,200.

Group 2 consumers have a high risk of the same illness. Their probability of having it is 0.05, or 5 percent. The treatment cost is the same as for the consumers in group 1. A consumer in this group is willing to pay up to $6,000 for an insurance policy that would pay for treatment. If she were to pay for treatment herself, her expected treatment cost would be $0.05 \times \$100,000 = \$5,000$. She is willing to pay up to $6,000 to insure against this risk because she is risk averse. If an insurance company can tell that a consumer is in group 2, it is clearly advantageous for it to arrange a policy with that consumer at a price somewhere between $5,000 and $6,000.

Under the condition of *complete information*, that is, if insurance companies know who belongs to which group, members of the two groups can be offered insurance policies with different prices. In a competitive market for insurance contracts, profits would be competed away in equilibrium. It follows that there would be two kinds of insurance contracts in a competitive equilibrium: insurance policies would be sold to consumers in group 1 at a price of $1,000 and to consumers in group 2 at a price of $5,000. By the first fundamental theorem of welfare economics, this outcome would be efficient, and all the consumers, who are all risk averse, would be insured.

We now assume that there are 9,000 people in group 1, and 1,000 people in group 2. The total population is 10,000. Over the total population, the probability of the illness is the total expected number of people who will get it, divided by 10,000. The total expected number of people who will get the illness is $0.01 \times 9,000 + 0.05 \times 1,000 = 140$. The probability of the illness over the entire population is therefore 0.014. If all cases are treated, the expected treatment cost, averaged over the entire population, is $0.014 \times \$100,000 = \$1,400$.

All these assumptions are summarized in Table 20.1.

Now, let us see what happens in this market when there is *asymmetric information*. The asymmetry is this: the potential insurance buyers, members of groups 1 and 2, know which group they are in, but the insurance companies do not. Because the insurance companies cannot distinguish between group 1 members and group 2 members, they must offer policies to everybody at the same price. We let P represent the insurance policy price.

In a competitive equilibrium, insurance companies are making zero expected profits. Therefore, P must be equal to the expected cost of treatment for the insured population. As calculated previously, the expected cost of treating the illness over the entire population is $1,400. However, $P = \$1,400$ will not work. The entire population cannot be insured at this price.

The reason is simple. At a price of $1,400, consumers in group 1 will not buy the insurance. They will drop out of the market. The only consumers who will buy the insurance are members of group 2, for whom the expected cost of treatment is $5,000. If only members of group 2 are buying insurance, however the insurance companies will need a price of at least $5,000. It follows that the competitive equilibrium is at a price of $5,000; group 2 members are insured, but group 1 members are uninsured. This market outcome is inefficient: Group 1 members cannot buy a product at a price that would be advantageous to them and to the insurance companies that would sell it to them. They are excluded from this market, in which there is a single price for the two very different groups of consumers.

This is an example of *adverse selection* in insurance, an outcome in which insurance companies, unable to distinguish between groups with very different risks and therefore charging everyone the same price, cannot insure an entire population of risk-averse consumers. All the consumers would like to purchase insurance at actuarially fair prices, and even prices that are above actuarially fair. However, there are so many high-risk consumers that the single market price is too high for the low-risk consumers. The low-risk consumers are, in effect, pushed out of the market.

This is another market failure due to asymmetric information.

20.4 When Insurance Encourages Risk Taking: Moral Hazard

In the example in the last section, we assumed that two groups of people had different probabilities of illness, and the insurance companies could not distinguish between group 1 members and group 2 members. The inability to distinguish between the two types led to a market failure. Another important insurance-based market failure occurs when insurance buyers change their behavior, and increase their probabilities of losses, because they have insurance. This leads to a market failure if the insurance companies fail to observe the changes in behavior and to charge premiums reflecting those changes.

When insurance buyers take more risks because they have insurance, we say that the insurance creates *moral hazard*. The very existence of insurance coverage causes increased losses and increased social costs.

The term "moral hazard" is now commonly used by economists (and by others who want to sound impressive) to describe bad behavior encouraged by the existence of compensation for losses. Economists (and many others) believe in incentives: positive incentives to encourage good behavior and negative incentives to discourage bad behavior. This is the idea of *the carrot and the stick.* Moral hazard is what results when you take away the stick, the negative incentives for bad behavior. For example, according to some analysts, government programs that rescued Wall Street firms after the crash of 2008 created moral hazard. Losses to big Wall Street firms were mitigated, some firms were saved from bankruptcy, and the negative consequences of risky financial decisions were reduced or eliminated. As a consequence, in the future Wall Street firms may not be as careful as they would have been, absent the rescue.

Other, more obvious, examples include the following:

1. *Liability and collision insurance for motor vehicle operators.* If motorists had to bear the full costs of the accidents they cause, they would likely drive more carefully. Of course, insurance companies try hard to discover which of their insured drivers are taking risks, by monitoring accident histories, speeding tickets, drunk driving arrests, and so on, but they cannot be completely successful.
2. *Fire and theft insurance for homeowners.* If homeowners had no insurance, they would probably be more careful with fires in barbecue grills, fireplaces, and woodstoves; and they would be more careful about defective wiring, locking doors at night, and so on.
3. *Flood insurance for homeowners.* Flood insurance compensates the homeowner for flood losses. Flood losses occur mainly in floodplains, next to rivers, and in low-lying coastal areas. In the United States, the federal government actually subsidizes flood insurance, which encourages people to build in flood-prone areas, exacerbating the moral hazard problem.

Driving while on cell phone/moral hazard example. Let us now turn to a numerical example. Assume there are 1,000 identical people, who like to drive while talking on their cell phones. Assume each driver has a 0.04 probability of one accident (per year), if she does not use her cell phone, and a 0.08 probability of one accident (per year), if she does. Any accident would result in $10,000 in damages to the driver's own car. (If accidents harm other drivers or their cars, the analysis is more complicated.) Expected losses are $400 per year if the driver is not a cell phone user, and $800 per year if she is a cell phone user. We assume that the insurance market is competitive, and the insurance companies end up charging premiums just sufficient to cover expected losses. If nobody uses a cell phone, the insurance premium will be around $400 per year; if everybody uses a cell phone, the insurance premium will be around $800 per year; and if it is a mix, the insurance premium will be somewhere between those extremes. The drivers like their cell phones, but not enough to pay the extra $400 in expected losses created by their use. We assume that using the cell phone while driving gives each driver $300 worth of convenience and pleasure per year.

We also assume that the drivers are risk averse; each driver would be willing to pay $600 per year to insure against a 0.04 probability of a $10,000 accident, and

Table 20.2. *Drivers and cell phones*

	Benefit to Driver	Benefit of Cell	Willing to Pay	Insurance Premium	Net Benefit
Insured, use cell	D	$300	$1,200	$800	D − $500
Insured, no cell	D	–	$1,200	$800	D − $800
Not insured, use cell	D	$300	$1,200	–	D − $900
Not insured, no cell	D	–	$600	–	D − $600

would be willing to pay $1,200 per year to insure against a 0.08 probability of a $10,000 accident.

Finally, we assume that the insurance companies cannot tell whether or not a customer uses her cell phone while driving.

What is the equilibrium in this example? Because insurance companies cannot tell whether a driver is talking on her cell phone while driving, if a driver is insured, she will use her cell phone. This results in the 0.08 probability of one accident (per year), with expected losses of $800 per year. Drivers are willing to pay up to $1,200 per year to insure against this risk. However, because the insurance market is competitive, with profits at or close to zero, the insurance premium is $800 per year. Therefore, everybody will buy insurance, and everybody will talk on cell phones while driving. The net benefit to each driver will equal the benefit of driving, say D, minus the $800 cost of insurance, plus the $300 value of being able to talk on the cell phone while driving, or $D − \$800 + \$300 = D − \$500$. If a driver did not buy insurance and continued to talk on her cell phone, her expected utility from this lottery would equal the utility of the certainty equivalent net benefit, which would be $D − \$1,200 + \$300 = D − \$900$, which is much worse than driving with insurance. If a driver did not buy insurance and stopped talking on her cell phone, her net benefit would be $D − \$600$, which is still worse than driving with insurance and talking on the cell phone.

All these assumptions are summarized in Table 20.2.

It follows that the equilibrium in this example is one in which everyone buys insurance, at a price of $800 per year, and they all use their cell phones while driving. However, this is an inefficient equilibrium. It is inefficient because if everyone stopped talking on their cell phones, they could buy insurance for $400 per year instead of $800 per year, and the net benefit for each driver would be $D − \$400 > D − \$500$. Finally, the availability of insurance creates moral hazard, because the insurance protection causes all the drivers to take an extra risk. The cost to society of that extra risk is $400 (the increase in expected accident losses per driver per year), whereas the benefit to the driver is only $300. In short, this is an example of a market failure created by moral hazard.

20.5 The Principal–Agent Problem

In the example in the previous section, all the drivers were identical, but there was an information asymmetry between the insurance companies and the drivers. The insurance companies could not see whether the drivers were talking on their cell phones while driving. The availability of insurance created a moral hazard; it encouraged drivers to misbehave, and that misbehavior resulted in a market failure, an inefficient equilibrium.

We now turn to another information asymmetry that may lead to market failure. In many economic contexts, two (or more) people are working on some project, more or less together, but with somewhat different goals. One is in charge; he is called the *principal*. The other is working for the principal; he is called the *agent*. Examples include an employer and an employee in an office or a factory; a general contractor and a subcontractor on a construction project; a patient and a doctor; a property owner who wants to sell his house and his real estate agent; a plaintiff in a lawsuit and his lawyer; a farmer and his farm laborer; and a legislature and the bureaucrats who write regulations and implement the law.

Generally, a principal can observe some of what the agent does, but not all of it, and the principal's observation of the agent's effectiveness is confounded by random events. For instance, the patient gets sicker after the surgery, but he does not know whether this is because the surgeon did not prepare for the operation well enough, or because his cancer was intractable. The property owner does not manage to sell his house, but he does not know whether this was because his real estate agent did not schedule enough showings, or because his only potential buyer was just laid off. In short, there is an information asymmetry between the principal and the agent, compounded by random noise.

The principal has a goal. The agent is on the principal's side but may not have the same goal. The principal can observe the outcome, but cannot observe all that the agent does or fails to do. The *principal–agent problem* is the (principal's) problem of maximizing his expected payoff, given the information asymmetry, and given the randomness inherent in the process leading from effort to outcome.

Principal–Agent Example, Introduced

We now set up an example. We assume that there is a farmer, who is the principal. He employs a farmworker, who is the agent. The farmer grows corn; for simplicity we assume that there are only two possible crop yields: 5 tons and 10 tons. Also for simplicity, we assume that both revenue and costs for the farmer, as well as wages for the farmworker, are measured in tons of corn. Therefore, the number of tons grown also equals the farmer's revenue. The output from the farm depends on the effort of the farmworker and on random events. The farmworker can exert high effort or low effort. (Of course, he prefers low effort, all else being equal.) The farmer can observe the output, but he cannot observe the worker's effort. Moreover, because of random noise, the farmer cannot conclude that the worker must have put in high effort if the output is 10 tons, or that the worker must have put in low effort if the output is 5 tons.

We let e represent the farmworker's effort level, and we assume that the two effort levels are $e = 1$ (low effort) and $e = 2$ (high effort). High effort, of course, causes the worker more disutility than low effort. In particular, we assume disutility levels equal to the effort levels; low effort causes disutility of 1, and high effort causes disutility of 2. To get the worker to work requires compensation that provides enough utility to offset the disutility of the work. The worker requires compensation that gives him at least 1 unit of utility for low effort, and at least 2 units of utility for high effort.

The connection between effort of the worker and output from the farm is as follows: We let $p(e)$ represent the probability of the high (10-ton) crop yield, a function of effort e, and we let $1 - p(e)$ represent the probability of the low (5-ton) crop yield. (As in other parts of this chapter, p stands for probability, not price.) We assume that if effort is low, then $p(e) = p(1) = 0.1$. That is, low effort implies a 10 percent chance of high output, and a 90 percent chance of low output. We further assume that if effort is high, then $p(e) = p(2) = 0.9$. That is, high effort implies a 90 percent chance of high output, and a 10 percent chance of low output.

We assume that our farmer, the principal, is risk neutral, and we assume that our farmworker, the agent, is risk averse. The principal offers the agent a contract, which specifies a wage to be paid contingent on the output level, high (10 tons) or low (5 tons). The wages depend only on output, which is observable, and not on effort, which is unobservable. We let w_h be the (contingent) wage if the output is high, and w_l be the (contingent) wage if the output is low; both are measured in tons. If output is high (10 tons), the farmer's profit (measured in tons) is $10 - w_h$. If output is low (5 tons), the farmer's profit is $5 - w_l$. Because the principal is risk neutral, he simply wants to maximize expected profit. Expected profit is

$$E(\pi) = p(e)(10 - w_h) + (1 - p(e))(5 - w_l).$$

It depends on the agent's effort e, and on the contingent wages w_h and w_l.

We assume that the agent, who is risk averse, has a square-root utility function. That is, for a given w, his utility is $u = \sqrt{w}$, and as a function of his effort e, his expected utility is

$$E(u|e) = p(e)\sqrt{w_h} + (1 - p(e))\sqrt{w_l}.$$

(A note about notation: $E(u|e)$ means "Expected utility, contingent on the effort level e.")

This gives

$$E(u|e = 1) = 0.1\sqrt{w_h} + 0.9\sqrt{w_l} \qquad \text{and} \qquad E(u|e = 2) = 0.9\sqrt{w_h} + 0.1\sqrt{w_l},$$

Table 20.3. *Assumptions, notation, wages needed to get the agent to work at given effort levels, and the principal's expected profits*

	Low Effort by Agent	High Effort by Agent
Crop yield probabilities (high, low)	$(0.1, 0.9)$	$(0.9, 0.1)$
Agent's wages if low yield	w_l	w_l
Agent's wages if high yield	w_h	w_h
Wages needed to get agent to work	$0.1\sqrt{w_h} + 0.9\sqrt{w_l} = 1$	$0.9\sqrt{w_h} + 0.1\sqrt{w_l} = 2$
Principal's expected profit	$0.1(10 - w_h) + 0.9(5 - w_l)$	$0.9(10 - w_h) + 0.1(5 - w_l)$

for low effort and high effort, respectively. If the wages contingent on output are set at the point at which the worker is just (barely) willing to work, expected utility based on the wages has to just offset the disutility of working. This gives

$$0.1\sqrt{w_h} + 0.9\sqrt{w_l} = 1 \quad \text{and} \quad 0.9\sqrt{w_h} + 0.1\sqrt{w_l} = 2,$$

for low effort and high effort, respectively. We lay out some of our example's assumptions, notation, and preliminary conclusions in Table 20.3.

The Principal's First-Best Outcome

Now we calculate the *first-best outcome* for the principal. This is the maximum expected profit the principal could achieve if he paid the worker just enough to get him to work, and contrary to our basic assumption about the principal–agent model, if the principal could actually observe and choose the worker's effort level. The principal has to offer the worker contingent wages, as shown earlier, to get him to work at the indicated effort levels. (The wages are still contingent on output.) We use the two necessary contingent wage equations to calculate the principal's maximum profits based on low effort and high effort. Then we select the effort level that results in a higher profit level for the principal.

Assuming low effort, the principal's objective function is

$$E(\pi) = 0.1(10 - w_h) + 0.9(5 - w_l) = 5.5 - 0.1w_h - 0.9w_l.$$

We use the agent's low-effort constraint $0.1\sqrt{w_h} + 0.9\sqrt{w_l} = 1$, which modifies to $w_h = 100 - 180\sqrt{w_l} + 81w_l$. Substituting the constraint into the principal's objective function, we get

$$E(\pi) = -4.5 + 18\sqrt{w_l} - 9w_l.$$

Maximizing $E(\pi)$ is now straightforward; it is equivalent to maximizing $2\sqrt{w_l} - w_l$. The objective function is maximized at $w_l = 1$; substituting back in the constraint equation gives $w_h = 1$, and substituting the contingent wage values back

Table 20.4. *Payoffs to principal and agent, assuming the principal* can observe and choose *the agent's effort, to maximize the principal's expected profit*

	Low Effort by Agent	High Effort by Agent
Crop yield probabilities (high, low)	(0.1, 0.9)	(0.9, 0.1)
Agent's wages if low yield	1	4
Agent's wages if high yield	1	4
Principal's expected profit	4.5	5.5

into the expected profit function gives

$$E(\pi) = 0.1(10 - 1) + 0.9(5 - 1) = 4.5.$$

This is the highest expected profit the principal can get if he chooses low effort by the agent.

Now, let us analyze high effort. Assuming that the principal chooses high effort by the agent, and pays him just enough to get him to do the work, the objective function is

$$E(\pi) = 0.9(10 - w_h) + 0.1(5 - w_l) = 9.5 - 0.9w_h - 0.1w_l.$$

We use the agent's high-effort constraint $0.9\sqrt{w_h} + 0.1\sqrt{w_l} = 2$, which modifies to $w_l = 400 - 360\sqrt{w_h} + 81w_h$. (It is a little easier to use the constraint to solve for w_l as a function of w_h in this case, rather than the reverse.) Substituting the constraint into the principal's objective function, we get

$$E(\pi) = -30.5 + 36\sqrt{w_h} - 9w_h.$$

Maximizing $E(\pi)$ is now straightforward; it is equivalent to maximizing $4\sqrt{w_h} - w_h$. The objective function is maximized at $w_h = 4$; substituting back in the constraint equation gives $w_l = 4$, and substituting the contingent wage values back into the expected profit function gives

$$E(\pi) = 0.9(10 - 4) + 0.1(5 - 4) = 5.5.$$

This is the highest expected profit the principal can get if he chooses high effort by the agent. The results of all these calculations are shown in Table 20.4.

The principal notes these results. He wants to maximize his expected profit. Therefore, the first-best outcome for the principal, the outcome he opts for if he can observe and choose the agent's effort, is the following: high effort by the agent, contingent wages of $w_l = 4$ and $w_h = 4$, and expected profit for himself of $E(\pi) = 5.5$.

The preceding calculations are hypothetical, and depend on the principal's ability to choose the effort level of the agent. However, the essential difficulty of the principal–agent problem is that the principal cannot see the agent's effort level. Let us now consider how this affects the analysis.

When the Principal Cannot Observe the Agent's Efforts

The first thing to note is that if the agent chooses low effort, the best possible outcome for the principal is $E(\pi) = 4.5$, as we figured earlier. If the contingent wages are equal, or close to equal, the agent is probably going to choose low effort. On the other hand, if there is a big enough difference between w_h and w_l, the agent will put in the extra effort, whether or not the principal can observe that effort. The next thing we do is to calculate the wage difference needed to "incentivize" the agent; that is, to induce him to work hard. The required wage difference is called an *incentive compatibility constraint.*

We derive the incentive compatibility constraint as follows. The agent's utility, net of his disutility from effort, is $0.9\sqrt{w_h} + 0.1\sqrt{w_l} - 2$ for high effort, and $0.1\sqrt{w_h} + 0.9\sqrt{w_l} - 1$ for low effort. The necessary condition for getting the agent to choose high effort, when he cannot be observed, is that the former be greater than or equal to the latter. This gives

$$0.9\sqrt{w_h} + 0.1\sqrt{w_l} - 2 \geq 0.1\sqrt{w_h} + 0.9\sqrt{w_l} - 1,$$

which, with minor rearranging, gives

$$\sqrt{w_h} - \sqrt{w_l} \geq 1.25.$$

The strong inequality would imply that the agent would surely choose high effort; the equality would imply the agent is indifferent between low effort and high effort. (The best possible outcome for the principal would have the agent indifferent, but still choosing high effort.)

The best conceivable outcome for the principal, based on the agent's choosing high effort, now requires two equations. The first (the incentive compatibility constraint) is needed for the agent to choose high effort instead of low effort:

$$\sqrt{w_h} - \sqrt{w_l} = 1.25,$$

and the second is needed for the agent to choose work instead of no work:

$$0.9\sqrt{w_h} + 0.1\sqrt{w_l} = 2.$$

Solving these two equations simultaneously gives $\sqrt{w_l} = 7/8$ and $\sqrt{w_h} = 17/8$. Squaring the terms yields $w_l = 0.7656$ and $w_h = 4.5156$. Finally, we can substitute w_l and w_h into the principal's expected profit equation. This gives

$$E(\pi) = 0.9(10 - w_h) + 0.1(5 - w_l) = 0.9(10 - 4.5156) + 0.1(5 - 0.7656)$$

$$= 5.36.$$

The results of all these calculations are shown in Table 20.5.

Table 20.5. *Payoffs to principal and agent, assuming the principal* cannot observe *the agent's effort, to maximize the principal's expected profit*

	Low Effort by Agent	High Effort by Agent
Crop yield probabilities (high, low)	(0.1, 0.9)	(0.9, 0.1)
Agent's wages if low yield	0.7656	0.7656
Agent's wages if high yield	4.5156	4.5156
Principal's expected profit	5.36	5.36

We conclude as follows. If our farmer, the principal in this story, could choose the effort level of our farmworker, the agent, the best possible outcome for the farmer would be an expected profit level of 5.5. In that case, the risk-neutral principal would be able to fully insure the risk-averse agent by offering him a constant wage, independent of output, as in Table 20.4. However, given that the principal cannot choose the worker's effort level, or even observe it, he needs to incentivize the agent by offering a nonconstant wage, dependent on output, as in Table 20.5 and the best possible outcome for the farmer is 5.36. The principal cannot see the agent's effort, nor infer it from the ultimate outcome, because of random noise. Since the agent's wage is dependent on output, the agent must bear the risk of variable crop yields and the principal must end up paying the agent enough to compensate for that risk in order to ensure high effort. Therefore, the absence of information creates an efficiency loss equal to the difference between 5.5 and 5.36. In short, the principal–agent relationship creates another market failure due to information asymmetry.

20.6 What Should Be Done about Market Failures Caused by Asymmetric Information

In the preceding sections, we have seen that imperfect information, and in particular asymmetrically distributed imperfect information, will lead to inefficiency or market failure. What should be done? The answer to this question, in a nutshell, is to devise some way to make the information flow from those who have it to those who do not, or to develop schemes that give the correct incentives to people. Remedies include the following:

1. *Signaling devices*. These are rules or mechanisms that cause the side with information to reveal that information. In the used car market, for instance, there are various possible signaling devices, including inspection stickers and dealer used car certifications. Car sellers might be required to provide repair histories. In the health insurance market, buyers of insurance policies might be required to undergo physical examinations, or to answer a series of questions about their health status on an application form. In real estate markets, where there are "lemon" houses, many states and cities require disclosure

statements in which a seller answers a long list of questions about plumbing, wiring, heating costs, susceptibility to flooding, and so on. Firms hiring employees often require proof of certification to establish a job candidate's ability to be an electrician, a welder, or a phlebotomist, proof of licensure to be a doctor or lawyer, or proof of a college degree to be a teacher or a stock analyst.

2. *Screening contracts.* With screening contracts, as opposed to signaling devices, the side of the market with poor information tries to get private information from the other side by drafting contracts that create incentives for the privately informed agents to self-select into groups with different risk characteristics. By choosing the contracts that they prefer, the buyers in effect reveal their information. For example, in the health sector, in which the actual health status of a person may be private information, health insurance contracts with different levels of premiums, copays, and deductibles might be designed by insurance companies to separate the buyers. Under certain conditions, it is possible to offer the buyers contracts that will successfully separate the different risk types. Each type will have incentives to choose a different coverage–copay combination, and insurance companies will be able to infer a buyer's risk characteristics by observing which contract she chooses. In the principal–agent relationship, it might be possible to design contracts or compensation schemes that better align the goals of the parties.

3. *Monitoring.* The moral hazard problems created by insuring drivers or homeowners can be reduced by requiring periodic updates of information on speeding violations, drunk driving arrests, and so on for drivers, and on building condition, repairs, additions, local real estate prices, and so on for homeowners. Agents who might exert low effort when their principals expect high effort can be subjected to monitoring. For example, we have had time punch clocks since the nineteenth century, and now we have GPS systems and numerous other exotic devices that allow employers to watch their employees, literally and figuratively.

4. *The legal system.* Legal contracts (and the common law) often provide incentives for sellers (or buyers) to inform buyers (or sellers). Many car sellers bundle warranties with the used cars they sell. If the car needs a repair within the next X months, for example, the dealer will provide it free. Insurance companies may be able to cancel a health insurance contract if the person who buys it misrepresents her health history. An auto liability insurance policy may be canceled if the driver misrepresents her driving record. Many goods (other than cars) are sold with guarantees or warranties attached. These are legal contracts that commit the seller to repair or replace the product in case of a defect. Legal rules of implied warranty may find that the seller of a defective product has obligations to the buyer, even if such obligations were never written or spoken. Legal liability rules often place costs on the seller of a defective product if that product results in an accident or an injury. Liability rules might also bear on moral hazard problems, and a principal, in some circumstances, might be able to sue an agent for low effort.

In fact, there is a whole world of guarantees and warranties, explicit and implicit; legal remedies when explicit or implicit promises are broken; litigation in which the party who was misled or not informed attempts to recover from the party who misled and hid the truth; and litigation in which the party which expected great effort sues the party that did not work hard enough.

20.7 A Solved Problem

The Problem
Consider the market for health insurance with two populations with different probabilities of illness, as described in Section 20.3. Follow all the assumptions about probabilities of illness, treatment costs, and so on as shown in Table 20.1, except for the assumption about the willingness to pay of group 2 members. Assume now that members of group 2 are only willing to pay $4,000 for an insurance policy. This willingness to pay is less than the expected treatment cost of $5,000, perhaps because group 2 members are risk lovers, or perhaps because they would simply prefer to live with the illness than to treat it at the high cost we are assuming. The reader should note that since group 2 members are only willing to pay $4,000 for a product that costs society $5,000 to provide, it would be inefficient for them to be insured.

(a) Suppose the insurance companies cannot tell the difference between group 1 consumers and group 2 consumers. Describe the equilibrium.
(b) What will happen if the insurance companies devise a test that allows them to tell the difference between a group 1 consumer and a group 2 consumer?
(c) If the government steps in and says the insurance companies are not allowed to discriminate between group 1 consumers and group 2 consumers, what happens?

The Solution
We are assuming that group 1 consumers face a 0.01 probability of illness and group 2 consumers face a 0.05 probability of illness. An illness in either group costs $100,000 to treat. The willingness to pay for an insurance policy is $1,200 in group 1 and $4,000 in group 2. The total population is 10,000.

Over the entire population, the expected number of people who will get sick is $0.01 \times 9000 + 0.05 \times 1000 = 90 + 50 = 140$. Therefore, the probability of illness, over the entire population, is $140/10,000 = 0.014$. It costs $100,000 to treat the illness. If all cases were treated, the expected treatment cost over the entire population would be $0.014 \times \$100,000 = \$1,400$.

(a) If insurance companies cannot tell the difference between group 1 consumers and group 2 consumers, they must charge everybody the same price. Assume the insurance companies try to charge a price P. (1) If $P \leq \$1,200$, everybody is willing to buy the policy, but the insurance companies lose money because the expected treatment cost over the entire population is $1,400. As a result, the insurance companies must raise their rates. (2) If $\$1,200 < P \leq \$4,000$, group 1 consumers all drop the insurance, leaving only high-risk group 2 consumers. But the expected payout for group 2 consumers is $0.05 \times \$100,000 = \$5,000$. The result is collapse. (3) If $\$4,000 < P$, nobody buys insurance.
(b) If the insurance companies devise a test to discriminate between consumers in different groups, they will want to charge different prices, say P_1 for group 1 consumers and

P_2 for group 2 consumers. Assuming that competition drives profits to zero in the insurance markets, the possible equilibrium prices are $P_1 = \$1,200$ and $P_2 = \$5,000$. All group 1 consumers would end up with insurance, and all group 2 consumers would end up without insurance since they prefer to remain uninsured rather than pay $5,000. This is the efficient outcome.

(c) If insurance companies are told that they are not allowed to discriminate between the two groups, one of two things happens:

  (i) The market collapses and no one gets insurance.

  (ii) The government subsidizes the insurance company losses for group 2 consumers. (Various rules incorporated in the 2010 Patient Protection and Affordable Care Act in the United States, called "ObamaCare" by its opponents, have this effect.) For example, if insurance companies charged a single price to all consumers of $P = \$1,200$, everybody would buy insurance. Insurance companies would break even on group 1 members, and those consumers would have no gains from the arrangement, as they are paying their maximum willingness to pay. On average, insurance companies would lose $\$5,000 - \$1,200 = \$3,800$ for each group 2 consumer. The government would have to subsidize the companies with $3,800 for each group 2 consumer. Each one of those consumers would gain $\$4,000 - \$1,200 = \$2,800$. The net loss to society, for each group 2 consumer, would equal the government's subsidy less the consumer's gain, or $\$3,800 - \$2,800 = \$1,000$.

Exercises

1. Harry has decided to start a used car dealership. There are three types of used cars – type A cars, which he values at $3,000; type B cars, which he values at $2,000; and type C cars, which he values at $1,000. The true type of the car is known to the owners but not to Harry. Type A, type B, and type C cars are worth $2,400, $1,600, and $800, respectively, to their owners.

    (a) Suppose Harry believes that the three types exist with equal probabilities. How much is he willing to pay for a used car? What types of cars does he buy in equilibrium?

    (b) After a month in business, Harry realizes that he is overpaying for the types of cars he is getting. He revises his prior beliefs and now thinks that he has zero probability of getting a type A car, and equal probability of getting a type B car and a type C car. How much is he now willing to pay for a used car? What types of cars does he buy in equilibrium?

2. There are 1,000 individuals in the city of Lincoln wishing to sell their used cars. The value of a car, V, ranges between $0 and $3,000. The distribution of values is such that the number of used cars worth less than $\$V$ is $V/3$. The true value of the car is known only to the owner. Potential buyers are risk neutral and value a car at its expected value. An owner may choose to have his car inspected for a fee of $300, and will then be able to sell his car for the true value.

    (a) Suppose nobody has his car inspected. What would the market price for used cars be?

(**b**) Now suppose every car worth more than $X gets inspected, whereas every car worth less than $X does not get inspected. What would the market price of uninspected used cars be, as a function of X?

(**c**) In equilibrium, the owner of a car worth $X is indifferent between getting an inspection and not getting an inspection. What is the equilibrium value of X?

(**d**) How many cars will not get inspected? How much will each car sell for?

3. Placido, José, and Luciano are singers. Their probabilities of laryngitis, known to each of them, are $p_p = 0.6$, $p_j = 0.2$, and $p_l = 0.1$, respectively. An individual who has laryngitis forgoes income of $1 million from a big concert.

(**a**) Calculate each singer's expected loss from laryngitis.

They are contemplating buying insurance, which will provide a payment of $1 million in the event of laryngitis. Each singer's willingness to pay for insurance is as follows: $WTP_p = $500,000$, $WTP_j = $175,000$, and $WTP_l = $125,000$. The insurance company knows that the probabilities of laryngitis are 0.6, 0.2, and 0.1, but does not know which tenor has which probability.

(**b**) Is Placido risk averse, risk neutral, or risk loving? How about José and Luciano? How can you tell?

(**c**) Calculate the expected value of the insurance company's total payout, assuming that the insurance company insures all three.

(**d**) Suppose the insurance company sets the price to equal the expected payout given earlier. Who will buy insurance? Will the insurance company make a profit or a loss?

4. There are 1,000 identical homeowners living in a small town. Let the benefit of home ownership be H. One of them, Kevin, is debating whether to get homeowners' insurance. If he locks the door 100 percent of the time, there is a 2 percent probability that his house will be burgled. If he locks the door 80 percent of the time, the probability of burglary rises to 6 percent. However, locking the door 80 percent of the time is more convenient, and gives him a utility equivalent to $100. If his house is burgled, Kevin loses $5,000. Kevin is willing to pay $250 to insure against a 2 percent probability of a $5,000 loss, and $750 to insure against a 6 percent probability of a $5,000 loss. Suppose the insurance market is competitive, and charges premiums sufficient to cover expected losses. Assume that insurance companies are unable to monitor how often a homeowner locks his door.

(**a**) If Kevin does not buy insurance, how often will he lock his door?

(**b**) If everybody locks his door 100 percent of the time, how much will an insurance policy cost?

(**c**) If everybody locks his door 80 percent of the time, how much will an insurance policy cost?

(**d**) How much will insurance policies cost in equilibrium? How often will Kevin lock his door? What is his net benefit?

(**e**) Explain why the outcome in part (d) is not socially optimal.

5. In the principal–agent model discussed in Section 20.5, we assumed that the agent was paid w_h if the farm output was high (10 tons), and was paid w_l if the farm output was low (5 tons). Suppose that instead of assuming contingent payments of w_h tons and w_l tons in the high-output and low-output cases, respectively, we simply assumed the

agent was paid a fixed fraction c of the output. (The symbol c stands for "commission.") That is, if the output is 10, the agent gets $10c$, and if the output is 5, the agent gets $5c$. (There are many principal–agent relationships such as this; for instance, a real estate agent selling a property may be paid 5 percent of the sales price, so $c = 0.05$ for such an agent.)

(a) Solve for the c that would make the agent indifferent between working at low effort and not working at all. Find the expected profit for the principal if the agent did low-effort work and was paid based on that c.

(b) Solve for the c that would make the agent indifferent between working at high effort and not working at all. Find the expected profit for the principal if the agent did high-effort work and was paid based on that c.

(c) If the agent is free to work at low effort or at high effort, how high would c have to be to guarantee that he works at high effort? (This is the incentive compatibility part of this exercise.) Comment on the c you have calculated.

6. There are two types of workers in Nephilim. Low-productivity workers produce $900 worth of output a month and high-productivity workers produce $3,000 worth of output a month. There are twice as many low-productivity workers as there are high-productivity workers. Both low- and high-productivity workers have utility function $u(w) = 2\sqrt{w}$, where w is the monthly wage.

(a) Suppose there is no way of distinguishing between the two types of workers, so everyone is paid the same wage. Assuming a competitive labor market, what is this wage?

Firm A has hired a consultant to solve this information asymmetry. The consultant suggests offering an elective training course. Workers who take the course will earn an extra $600 a month. The training course has no effect on productivity, but is extremely boring. Taking the course is equivalent to a X dollar monthly wage cut for low-productivity workers, and a Y dollar monthly wage cut for high-productivity workers.

(b) Suppose both high- and low-productivity workers choose to take the course. What can you say about X and Y?

(c) The consultant revises the $600 incentive down to $400. Now only high-productivity workers choose to take the course. What can you say about X and Y?

Index